P9-DFU-701

To the late Craig Claiborne:
restaurant critic, cookbook author,
mentor and friend to chefs everywhere.

85

Inspirational Chefs

RECIPES FROM NORTH AMERICA, MEXICO AND THE CARIBBEAN

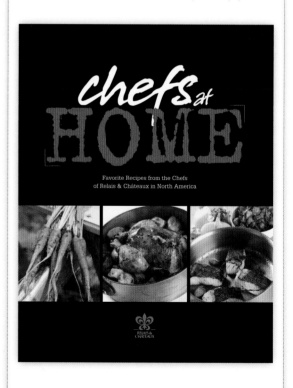

First published in 2010 by Network Book Publishing Ltd.
Network House, 28 Ballmoor, Celtic Court, Buckingham
MK18 1RQ, UK
www.networkpublishingltd.com

ISBN No: 978-0-9562661-3-2

Printed in China by CT Printing Ltd.

Publisher: Peter Marshall
Managing Editor and Art Director: Shirley Marshall
Editors: Sue Christelow, Katy Morris
Assistant Editor: Hilary Mayes
Design Director: Philip Donnelly
Designer: Duncan Boddy
Photographer: Myburgh du Plessis

The chefs in this book have much in common. They share a dedication to their craft, unparalleled creativity and an unerring palate. But in addition they belong to an elite fraternity. They are all members of Relais & Châteaux, the world's most discriminating collection of intimate hotels and fine restaurants throughout the world.

These chefs share a passion for hospitality and offer their guests a unique sense of place through their cuisine. Now for the first time they have collaborated in sharing some of their most exquisite creations.

From sea to shining sea, the entire continent of North America is celebrated in these intriguing recipes. Through the chef's profiles and glorious photos of their properties you can take an armchair tour of some of the most memorable dining destinations on this continent.

Come with us on an exciting gastronomic journey and meet some of the most talented chefs in North America.

Welcome to the world of Relais & Châteaux and to the inspirational work of 85 chefs who are united by what makes them different.

Patrick O'Connell

Patrick O'Connell

President of North American Relais & Châteaux delegations
Chef/Proprietor of The Inn at Little Washington

A balance between classic and modern
RELAIS & CHATEAUX
A signature dish
Always using what is seasonal and fresh

Perfect for entertaining your palate and your friends
RELAIS & CHATEAUX
A customer favorite
Luxurious textures and sophisticated alchemy

CONTENTS

■ RELAIS & CHATEAUX PROPERTIES IN NORTH AMERICA ■ GRANDS CHEFS RELAIS & CHATEAUX

Locations

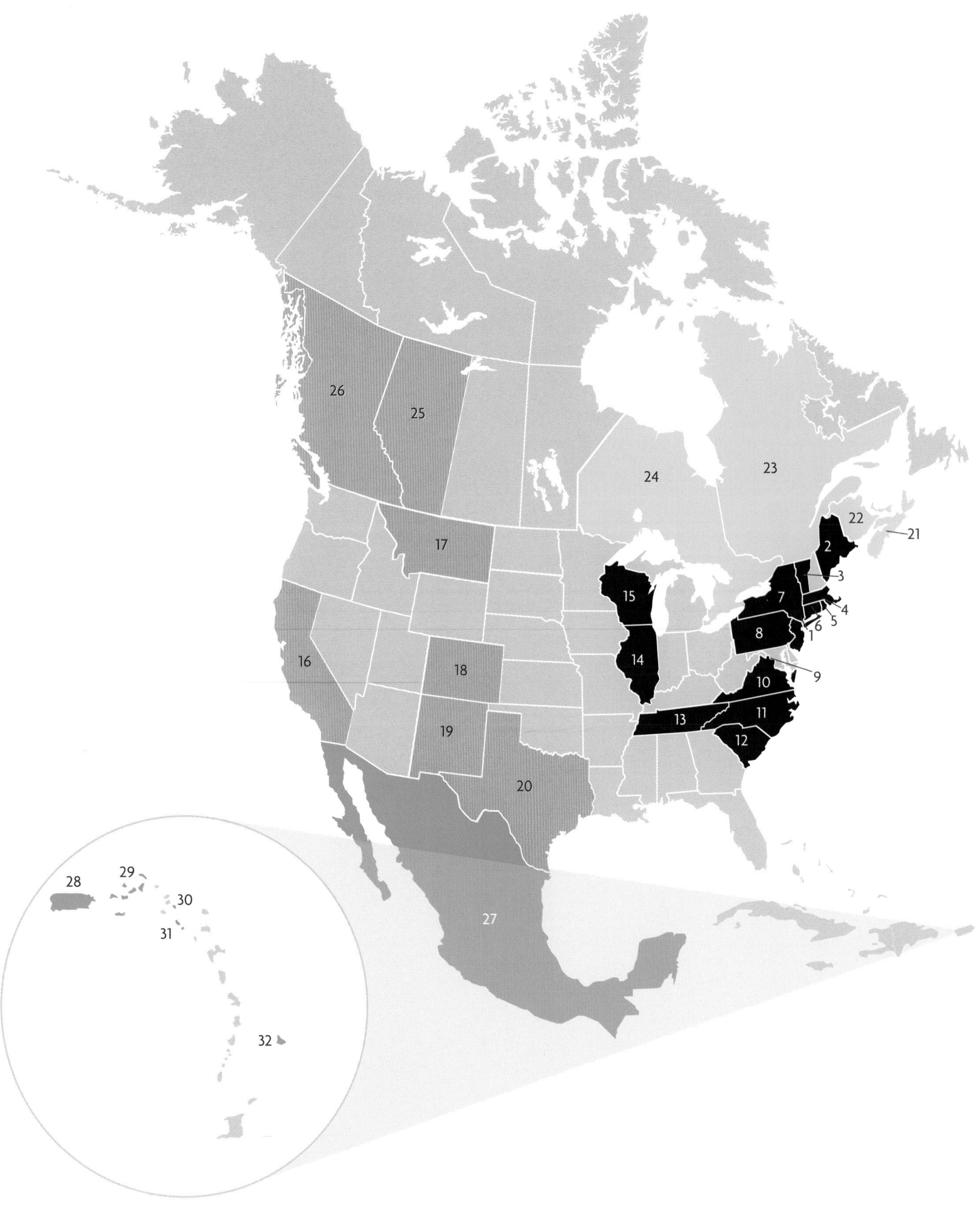
1
2
3
4
5
6
7
8
9
10
11
12
13
14
15
16
17
18
19
20
21
22
23
24
25
26
27
28
29
30
31
32

LOCATIONS

■ RELAIS & CHATEAUX PROPERTIES IN NORTH AMERICA ■ GRANDS CHEFS RELAIS & CHATEAUX

USA EAST

1 **New York City**
Daniel
Eleven Madison Park
Jean-Georges
Per Se

2 **Maine**
The White Barn Inn & Spa

3 **Vermont**
The Pitcher Inn
Windham Hill Inn

4 **Massachusetts**
Blantyre
The Charlotte Inn
The Wauwinet

5 **Rhode Island**
Castle Hill Inn & Resort

6 **Connecticut**
Thomas Henkelmann – Homestead Inn
The Mayflower Inn & Spa
Winvian

7 **New York State**
Lake Placid Lodge
The Point

8 **Pennsylvannia**
Glendorn
Hotel Fauchère

9 **Washington D.C.**
The Jefferson

10 **Virginia**
The Inn at Little Washington
Clifton

11 **North Carolina**
The Fearrington House Country Inn & Restaurant

12 **South Carolina**
Planters Inn

13 **Tennessee**
Blackberry Farm

14 **Illinois**
Everest

15 **Wisconsin**
Canoe Bay

USA WEST

16 **California**
Château du Sureau
The French Laundry
Gary Danko
Patina
L'Auberge Carmel
Auberge du Soleil
Meadowood Napa Valley
Rancho Valencia

17 **Montana**
Triple Creek Ranch

18 **Colorado**
The Home Ranch

19 **New Mexico**
The Inn of the Five Graces

20 **Texas**
The Inn at Dos Brisas
Hôtel St Germain

CANADA EAST

21 **Nova Scotia**
Trout Point Lodge of Nova Scotia

22 **New Brunswick**
Kingsbrae Arms

23 **Québec**
L'Eau à la Bouche Hôtel-Spa-Restaurant
Restaurant Initiale Inc.
Restaurant Toqué!
Auberge Saint-Antoine
Manoir Hovey
La Pinsonnière

24 **Ontario**
Langdon Hall Country House Hotel & Spa

CANADA WEST

25 **Alberta**
Post Hotel & Spa

26 **British Columbia**
Lumière
Sonora Resort Canada
Wedgewood Hotel & Spa
Wickaninnish Inn

MEXICO & THE CARIBBEAN

27 **Mexico**
Esperanza Resort
Las Mañanitas

28 **Puerto Rico**
Horned Dorset Primavera

29 **Virgin Islands**
Biras Creek Resort

30 **Saint-Barthélemy**
Hôtel Le Toiny
Eden Rock – St Barths

31 **St Kitts & Nevis**
Montpelier Plantation

32 **Barbados**
Cobblers Cove

A CULINARY JOURNEY

This epic culinary journey began at Trout Point Lodge of Nova Scotia and finished at Esperanza Resort in Mexico. 61 Relais & Châteaux properties in the USA, Canada, Mexico and the Caribbean have been visited to photograph their recipes for this cookbook, to capture these top chefs in their professional environments and to convey the beauty of the places and properties that are a part of the unique universe that is Relais & Châteaux. Join us as we recap this culinary journey so that you too can experience the Relais & Châteaux 'Route du Bonheur' of cooking.

In New York there are no less than four Grands Chefs; this cookbook features recipes from 20 Grands Chefs in all, masters of their craft who elevate fine dining to an art and turn each dish into a jewel.

A shared heritage bonds the states in the U.S. Northeast, marking them culturally and historically unique. Many of the dishes here feature the abundance of local seafood, with a choice of scallops from Cape Cod, Nantucket Bay and Maine, along with Atlantic lobster. Local sustainability is at the fore with native brook trout from Pennsylvania, Vermont venison, New England pheasant and Colorado lamb. Many chefs are committed to supporting their local farmers and suppliers, to using produce from their own gardens and working with the seasons. The result is delicious recipes using regional elk, venison, lamb, beef and sweetbreads and the most mouthwatering desserts using the fruits of the season – strawberries, blueberries and cranberries and even apples from New York state. Other chefs draw on historical dishes, adapting them to the modern world with today's ingredients and methods of preparation.

On to Wisconsin, known for its abundant walleye population in many of the state's lakes. Here this classic Midwestern catch is lightly battered to allow the firm white flesh to predominate and is served with simple accompaniments. As Wisconsin is also known as the 'dairy state', this is the perfect place for a buttermilk vinaigrette recipe and there just had to be an ice cream for dessert!

In Illinois, yet another Grand Chef has included three recipes from his gourmet restaurant using wild sturgeon from the Columbia River, a dessert including heirloom apples from Michigan and a lobster dish that has been on the restaurant's menu for 20 years – a true classic!

The state of Viriginia offers refined American cuisine courtesy of another Grand Chef. A must-try are the recipes incorporating striped bass from Chesapeake Bay and duck from Shenandoah Valley, both showcasing two of the best local ingredients.

Share with the diners of Washington D.C. the sophisticated seasonal cuisine and popular dishes from a chef who "loves taking dishes with a classic heritage and turning them into something pleasing to today's more enlightened palates".

You are ensured a taste of East Tennessee in all three recipes from the Grand Chef of that region. He works directly with his team of artisans to create dishes using seasonal produce and herbs from their own garden, the working farm, and the surrounding fields and forests.

North and South Carolina also sees an emphasis on farm-to-table cuisine. Here is an abundance of southern classics, including a twist on the local pulled pork BBQ that is famous in North Carolina, Low Country oyster stew, grits, gumbo, hushpuppies – they are all here in these recipes. Also a chocolate soufflé that has been on the menu for 30 years – one to not miss!

Four more Grands Chefs grace the Relais & Châteaux properties in California. Along with the other chefs of this region they use the freshest of seasonal produce, particularly the local citrus fruits and abundant local variety of vegetables, highlighted by sophisticated presentation. Of special note are the Monterey Bay spot prawns, the star shellfish of the bay of Carmel and the Californian white sturgeon. Unsurprisingly, Mexican influence creeps in with chefs nearer to the border.

The single Relais & Châteaux property in Montana has a chef who believes that "the most flavorful cuisine is made simply with the best high quality products". His selection of recipes includes a starter using pork belly from the Bitterroot Valley in the Rockies.

Unique in Colorado – here the chef takes the typical dude ranch meal and makes it exquisite. Of course you will find ribs, often from the animals raised on the ranch, but also some of the best trout and the sweetest of peaches, the Palisade variety, which grow at high altitude in the intense Summer sun.

New Mexico offers a fusion of Cajun Creole and authentic Native American cuisine. Included here is a signature dish that has been on the menu for 20 years – everybody loves it!

Renowned for its beef, the king of the meat – Wagyu – is used in a short rib carpaccio from Texas. An entrée also includes the area's famed fruit – ruby red grapefruit, teamed here with lobster, a delicious combination.

Eastern Canada offers a taste of the sea with its Newfoundland lobster, oysters from New Brunswick and Canadian diver scallops. As would be expected, maple syrup is a frequent ingredient not only in desserts but in a starter too, where it is used to make a foam with bacon to complement scallops, described by the chef as a "perfect match in Quèbec". Western Canada has a diverse range of dishes using seafood, with British Columbia spot prawns, halibut and Alaskan black cod. Once again local ingredients are to the fore with the exquisite Northwest Territories caribou, Mount Lehman rabbit and Quèbec foie gras. Through the centuries Canada's culture has been shaped by a succession of diverse peoples – native North Americans, French, British and American settlers and, in more recent times, waves of immigrants from every corner of the world – and this is apparent in its cuisine, and the recipes in this cookbook too.

The uniqueness of Mexico is apparent in recipes such as buñuelos – sugar dusted doughnut holes, an essential dish in Mexican culture and one that will have you begging for more! The Red Maguey Worms with Garlic and Chile are perhaps for the more adventurous, but an interesting dish from pre-hispanic gastronomy.

Finishing on a sunny note, the recipes from the Caribbean take the islands' natural flavors and combine them in every way possible with a myriad of ingredients. Mango, coconut, pineapple, papaya and rum – they are all here, whether paired with the freshest local tuna or playfully transformed from a classic cocktail into a pina colada verrine.

184 recipes from 85 chefs to give you a taste of Relais & Châteaux North America – have a nice day cooking!

SQUARE

New York City

The official Empire State – and of course home to the famous New York City, as well as Lake Ontario, Hudson Valley and the cities of Albany and Buffalo.

The state as a whole ranks as a major player in agriculture, offering orchids and fields galore – with a perfect climate for apples, cherries and plums. And New York City? This multicultural food capital boasts that there is nothing that can't be done or eaten in this city. Whether it's a bite of the classic American dish, making a stop in Chinatown or a taste of Little Italy – New York is simply 'The Big Apple' when it comes to food.

Daniel Boulud
Grand Chef Relais & Châteaux

Daniel Boulud is Chef-Owner of several award-winning restaurants as well as the Feast & Fêtes catering company. While he hails from Lyon, France, it is New York's dining scene that he has truly mastered and is today considered one of America's leading culinary authorities. Raised on his family's farm in the village of St. Pierre de Chandieu in France's Rhône Valley, Boulud remains inspired by the rhythm of the seasons and his cooking style driven by the quality of his ingredients. Since arriving in the U.S. in 1982, Boulud has become renowned for the contemporary appeal he adds to soulful cooking rooted in French tradition. His New York City restaurant Daniel is a three-Michelin-star Relais & Châteaux member. The chef has also extended his culinary reach internationally, to Beijing, Vancouver and London and soon also venture to Singapore.

Boulud's culinary accolades include James Beard Foundation awards for 'Outstanding Restaurateur', 'Best Chef of New York City' and 'Outstanding Chef of the Year'. The Chef's culinary style is reflected in his six cookbooks and his television series 'After Hours with Daniel'.

Daniel

"Preparing the finest American ingredients according to French culinary tradition," is Daniel's mantra.

In Manhattan, Daniel Boulud's first name alone suffices for this Lyon native who is today one of America's most celebrated Chef-Restaurateurs. His reputation may be international, but his warm and welcoming style remains very personal. Chef Daniel Boulud magically combines humble and noble ingredients elevating rustic and heart warming dishes to new levels of refinement, sophistication and pleasure. This is home to French cuisine brought to life with a celebration of American regional ingredients like Montana beef, Oregon morels and Nantucket Bay scallops. Using his French technique, the unique flavors of these finest products become the spot light of Boulud's dishes.

Serves 4
Preparation time: 1 hour 30 minutes
Cooking time: 10 minutes

Special equipment:
Parchment paper, 2" diameter ring mold, 5" diameter ring mold, cheesecloth, butcher's twine, slicing mandoline

MAINE SEA SCALLOP 'ROSETTE', FENNEL MARMALADE, ORANGE, SAFFRON VELOUTE

BY EDDY LEROUX

Layering the thin slices into a 'rosette' gives an unexpected look to these beautiful sea scallops, one of the finest examples we have of the wonderful seafood available from the coast of Northern Maine. The classic fennel and orange combination adds a refreshing note, and the saffron, a delicate earthiness.

INGREDIENTS

sea scallops:

8 large sea scallops
olive oil
salt & ground white pepper

fennel marmalade:

1 tbsp olive oil
2 heads fennel, stalks removed, chopped
1 tbsp garlic, minced
6 basil leaves
1 sachet (1 teaspoon each coriander, fennel seed, chili flake and 1 piece star anise wrapped in cheesecloth and tied with butcher's twine)
2 tbsp Pernod
1 tbsp vermouth
½ cup chicken stock or low-sodium chicken broth
salt & pepper

saffron velouté:

1 tbsp olive oil
reserved scallop muscles and trim
1 head fennel, chopped
1 shallot, sliced
2 sprigs fresh thyme
1 bay leaf
1 small pinch saffron
¼ cup orange juice
¼ cup chicken stock or low-sodium chicken broth
¼ cup heavy cream
salt & pepper

garnish:

1 navel orange
3 pieces baby fennel
glass noodles
frying oil, as needed
salt
2 oz micro limon cress (or chopped chives)

METHOD

sea scallops:

Remove the muscle from the scallops and reserve. Using a 2" diameter ring mold, cut each scallop into a perfect round; reserve the trim. Slice them very thin (about ⅛" thick). Place a 5" ring mold over a 6" square of lightly oiled parchment paper. For each portion, layer slices from two scallops inside the ring mold in a slightly overlapping circular pattern. Remove the mold and top the scallops with another piece of oiled parchment, oiled side down. Repeat to make four 'rosettes' and refrigerate. When ready to serve, heat the oven to 400°F, remove the top parchment, sprinkle the scallops with salt and pepper, and re-cover. Bake for 2-4 minutes, or until just cooked through.

fennel marmalade:

Heat the olive oil in a medium saucepan over a medium heat. Add the fennel, garlic, basil, spice sachet and cook, stirring until soft, for about 10 minutes. Add the Pernod and flambé. Add the vermouth and simmer until almost dry. Add the chicken stock, and return to a simmer until reduced by two-thirds. Season to taste with salt and pepper. Chill and then transfer to a cutting board; chop roughly. Re-heat when ready to serve.

saffron velouté:

Heat the olive oil in a medium saucepot over a medium heat. Add the scallop scraps and cook, stirring, for 3 minutes. Add the fennel, shallot, thyme, bay leaf and saffron. Cook, stirring until soft, for about 5 minutes. Add the orange juice, stir, and simmer until almost dry. Add the chicken stock and cream, and simmer for 5 minutes. Season to taste with salt and pepper, then transfer to a blender and purée until smooth. Pass through a fine meshed sieve and reserve hot.

garnish:

Cut the orange into supremes, then dice into small pieces and set aside. Using a mandoline, thinly slice the baby fennel and reserve in ice water. Fill a large saucepot one-third full with frying oil. Heat the oil to 375°F. Fry the glass noodles a handful at a time until puffed and crispy; transfer to a paper-towel lined tray and sprinkle with salt.

to serve:

Warm four 10" round dinner plates. For each plate, place a 5" ring mold in the center and spoon in a thin layer of fennel marmalade. Remove the ring from the plate. Remove the top layer of parchment from the rosette of cooked, sliced scallops. Flip the rosette onto the fennel marmalade and remove the remaining parchment. Glaze with saffron velouté and sprinkle with diced orange. Top with fried glass noodles, and garnish with shaved fennel and micro limon cress.

DUO OF FLORIDA FROG LEGS FRICASSEE WITH KAMUT BERRIES & BLACK GARLIC

LOLLIPOP WITH SPINACH, MUSHROOMS, CRISPY SHALLOTS

BY EDDY LEROUX

My earliest memory of cooking frog legs comes from the years I spent at Georges Blanc in Vonnas, an outpost of of Burgundy. The best frog legs I've found here in the U.S. comes from Florida's Southern Everglades. I prepare them in different ways according to the season, adding plenty of aromatics such as garlic, shallots and parsley to boost their mild flavor. I always serve them crispy on the outside so you get that nice contrast with the tender delicate meat on the inside.

Serves 4
Preparation time: 4 hours
Cooking time: 1 hour

Special equipment:
Cheesecloth, butcher's twine, deep fat thermometer, squeeze bottles

Planning ahead:
Soak the kumut berry mixture overnight in advance.

INGREDIENTS

frog leg lollipops and fricassee:

18 fresh frog hindquarters, skinned and cleaned
3 eggs, beaten with 1 tbsp milk, seasoned
⅓ cup all purpose flour, seasoned
⅓ cup fine white breadcrumbs, seasoned
grapeseed oil, as needed
all purpose flour, as needed
4 tbsp olive oil, divided
12 white button mushrooms, trimmed and quartered
2 sprigs of thyme
1 clove garlic, crushed
1 tbsp butter
1 cup baby spinach leaves
4 pieces of shallot confit, roughly chopped
2 tsp cracked black pepper
2 tbsp sherry vinegar
¼ cup chicken jus
½ bunch of parsley, leaves chopped
salt & white pepper

spinach purée:

2 cups spinach leaves, packed
3 tbsp brown butter
salt & pepper

garlic cream:

12 cloves garlic, peeled
½ cup heavy cream
½ cup milk
salt & ground white pepper

kamut berries:

½ cup kamut berries
2 cups chicken stock
1 sachet (2 sprigs of thyme, 1 tsp black peppercorn, 1 clove garlic, 1 bay leaf wrapped in cheesecloth and tied with butcher's twine)
½ cup heavy cream
⅓ cup garlic cream (see recipe above)
salt, as needed

fried shallot rings:

4 large shallots
milk, as needed
2 tbsp icing sugar
½ cup all purpose flour
frying oil, as needed

garnish:

4 cloves black garlic, sliced
baby spinach leaves

METHOD

frog leg lollipops:

Using a sharp knife, separate the legs of the hindquarters and then separate the legs from the thighs. With a paring knife, scrape the meat down twelve of the legs, starting from the joint end of the bone, forming a ball of meat at the foot end to resemble 'lollipops'. Reserve the remaining legs and thighs for the fricassee. Place the seasoned beaten eggs, ⅓ cup of all purpose flour, and white breadcrumbs into separate shallow dishes. Dip the frog leg lollipops one by one into the flour, egg and then breadcrumbs to coat the meat. When ready to serve, fill a sauce pot one-third full with grapeseed oil and heat to 350°F using a deep fat thermometer. Fry the frog legs until golden brown and cooked through; strain on a paper-towel lined plate, sprinkle with salt and serve immediately.

fricassee:

Trim the meat away from the bone on the remaining legs and thighs into small morsels. In a large sauté pan, heat 1 tablespoon of the olive oil over a medium-high heat. Add the mushrooms and sauté until browned, season with salt and pepper and then transfer to a paper-towel lined plate. When ready to serve, dredge the frog morsels in flour, and pat away any excess flour. In the same pan, heat the remaining olive oil over a high heat. Add the frog in a single layer, and brown on all sides, adding thyme and garlic halfway through cooking. Strain onto a paper-towel lined plate; discard the garlic and thyme. Add the butter to the same pan and reduce the heat to medium-high. Add the spinach and sauté until wilted. Add the shallot confit, and return the mushrooms and frog legs to the pan along with the 2 tablespoons of cracked black pepper. Toss to combine and then de-glaze with the sherry vinegar. Stir in the chicken jus and chopped parsley; check the seasoning. Serve hot.

spinach purée:

Bring a large pot of salted water to the boil and place a bowl of ice water on the side. Boil the

spinach until very tender, and then chill in the ice water. Strain well and transfer to a blender. Pureé with enough ice water to make a thick purée, and then blend in the brown butter. Season to taste. Re-heat and transfer to a squeeze bottle when ready to serve.

garlic cream:

In a medium saucepot, cover the garlic cloves with cold water and bring to a boil. Strain and repeat the process three more times. Fill a small bowl with ice water, and chill the garlic cloves. Return the garlic to the pot and cover with cream and milk. Bring to a simmer and cook until the garlic is very tender and the liquid begins to reduce, about 10 minutes. Transfer to a blender and purée until smooth; season to taste. Reserve in the refrigerator until ready to use.

kamut berries:

Rinse the kamut berries until the water runs clear. Combine the berries with the chicken stock and sachet, and soak overnight. The next day, transfer to a large saucepot and bring to a simmer – season the liquid with salt to taste. Simmer slowly for approximately 3 hours, or until very tender. Remove the sachet and strain the liquid. When ready to serve, add the cream and garlic cream and simmer until thickened; check the seasoning and serve hot.

fried shallot rings:

Slice the shallots into thin rings; separate the rings and then transfer them to a bowl. Cover with milk and soak for 1 hour. Strain and dry on a paper-towel lined plate. Fill a saucepot one-third full with frying oil and heat to 350°F using a frying thermometer. Combine the icing sugar and flour in a large bowl and toss in the shallot rings to coat. Shake away any excess flour and fry the rings until golden brown and crispy (you may need to do this in batches). Strain on a paper-towel lined plate and rest in a dry area until ready to serve.

to serve:

Pipe two diagonal lines of spinach purée about 4" apart on each warm dinner plate. Spoon the fricassee in the center and place three fried lollipops around the perimeter. Garnish with crispy shallot rings, sliced black garlic, and a few baby spinach leaves. Serve the kamut berries in a small pot on the side or spoon onto the plate. Serve hot.

CHOCOLATE & PEANUT BUTTER GANACHE, PRALINE FEUILLETINE, SALTED CARAMEL ICE CREAM

BY DOMINIQUE ANSEL

A dessert with peanut butter brings out the kid in all of us. But this one's actually pretty sophisticated. Crispy feuilletine and praline layers alternate with smooth, creamy peanut butter ganache and then a white chocolate and peanut butter cream, not to mention the salted caramel ice cream and caramelized peanuts. It's best to begin preparing the day before so as to refrigerate the bottom layer overnight, but you can cheat and speed things up in the freezer. We admit there are a lot of components here, but they're worth it, and you may even find additional uses for many of them.

Serves 9
Preparation time: 1 day
Cooking time: 45 minutes

Special equipment:
Candy thermometer, ice cream machine

INGREDIENTS

peanut butter feuilletine:

1½ tbsp peanut butter
½ cup almond praline paste (Valrhona)
2 oz Jivara chocolate (Valrhona), chopped
1 tbsp butter
½ -⅓ cup feuilletine (Barry Callebaut)

peanut butter ganache:

¼ cup milk
⅓ cup cream
2 tbsp caster sugar
2 egg yolks
3 oz Jivara chocolate (Valrhona), chopped
2½ tbsp peanut butter

peanut butter cream:

1 oz white chocolate, chopped
2 tsp peanut butter
1 cup heavy cream

caramelized peanuts: (makes extra)

1 cup raw peanuts
½ cup sugar
3 tbsp water
1 pinch of kosher salt
1 pinch of cinnamon
¼ tsp vanilla extract

salted caramel ice cream:

½ cup sugar
½ cup cream
1¼ cups milk
1 egg yolk
4 tbsp milk powder
½ tsp fleur de sel

garnish:

chocolate décor pockets, ¼" taller and wider than feuilletine/peanut butter ganache squares (or substitute chocolate glaze)
peanut butter powder
triangular chocolate tuile, optional
cocoa powder

METHOD

peanut butter feuilletine:

Line the bottom and sides of a 9" x 9" baking pan with greased parchment paper. In a small bowl with a rubber spatula, combine the peanut butter and praline paste. In a small saucepot, melt the chocolate and butter, whisking to emulsify. Place the feuilletine in a separate medium-sized bowl, and stir in the warm chocolate mixture to combine. Add the peanut butter/praline mix and stir to combine. Transfer the feuilletine mixture to the prepared pan. Spread into an even layer with a mini offset spatula and chill.

peanut butter ganache:

In a medium saucepot, combine the milk, cream, and half of the sugar; simmer until the sugar is dissolved. In a medium mixing bowl, whisk the remaining sugar with the egg yolks. Stream one-third of the hot cream mixture into the yolk mixture, whisking to combine, then return to the saucepot and cook, stirring, to reach 185°F. Place the chocolate and peanut butter in a separate medium heat-proof bowl. Slowly stream in the warm cream mixture, whisking to combine. Rest, stirring occasionally with a spatula to cool to room temperature. Scrape the ganache onto the chilled feuilletine mixture and spread an even layer with a mini offset spatula; chill.

peanut butter cream:

Combine the chocolate and peanut butter in a heat-proof bowl. In a small saucepot, bring the cream to a simmer, pour over the chocolate/peanut butter, stir to melt and thoroughly combine; cover and chill. When ready to serve, whisk the mixture until light and airy, and transfer to a piping bag fitted with a ¼" round tip.

caramelized peanuts:

Line a baking sheet with aluminum foil and set aside. In a large, heavy skillet over a medium heat, combine the water, sugar and peanuts. Stir until the sugar is dissolved. Continue to cook,

stirring frequently, while the liquid reduces and becomes syrupy. After about 10 minutes, the mixture will turn grainy and the peanuts will look sandy. Continue to cook and stir the mixture. The peanuts will get darker, and over time the grainy sugar will melt in spots and turn into syrup. Continue to stir frequently so that the peanuts do not burn and the sugar syrup gets evenly distributed. Once the peanuts are evenly browned, add the salt and cinnamon, stir several times, remove from the heat and stir in the vanilla extract. Scrape the peanuts onto the prepared baking sheet and spread in a thin layer. Cool, and then break into individual pieces.

salted caramel ice cream:

In a medium heavy-bottomed saucepot, combine half of the sugar, cream and milk and heat to 95°F on a candy thermometer. Whisk in the milk powder – in a heat-proof bowl, combine the egg yolk with the remaining sugar. Bring the milk mixture to a simmer, and slowly stream one-third into the yolk mixture, while whisking. Return the yolk mixture to the saucepot containing the remaining milk mixture, and while whisking, cook until it reaches 185°F. Remove from the heat and strain through a fine meshed sieve. Add the fleur de sel. Chill overnight, covered. Spin in an ice cream machine according to manufacturer's instructions.

to serve:

Remove the chilled feuilletine and ganache layers from the pan by turning onto a cutting board. Cut into nine 3" x 3" squares and transfer to a baking sheet, ganache side up. Using an offset spatula, place squares inside the chocolate décor pockets. If you don't have chocolate décor, spread chocolate glaze on top and chill.

To serve, transfer one square to a chilled dessert plate and, if using, place a triangular-shaped chocolate tuile on top, slightly offset from the center. Pipe peanut butter cream into 'Hershey-Kiss' shapes on top, covering the square halfway diagonally. Garnish with a sprinkling of cocoa and peanut butter powders, add a few caramelized peanuts, and serve with a scoop of ice cream.

Daniel Humm
Grand Chef Relais & Châteaux

Daniel Humm creates modern, sophisticated French cuisine that emphasizes purity, simplicity, seasonal flavors and ingredients. A classicist who embraces contemporary gastronomy, Daniel's delicate and precise cooking style is experienced through a constantly evolving menu. The restaurant's dramatically high ceilings and magnificent art deco dining room is the ideal backdrop for Daniel's delicious, artful cuisine.

A native of Switzerland, Daniel has worked at many of Switzerland's finest hotels and restaurants. At Gasthaus zum Gupf he earned a Michelin Star and was named "Culinary Discovery in Switzerland 2002" by Gault Millau.

In 2003 Daniel moved to the United States to become Executive Chef at Campton Place in San Francisco. In 2006, he became Executive Chef of Eleven Madison Park, quickly transforming the restaurant into one of the city's top dining destinations. Under Daniel's leadership, in 2007 Eleven Madison Park received its first three star review from *The New York Times.* In 2008, the restaurant won a James Beard Award for 'Outstanding Wine Service', and in 2009, it was awarded Four Stars from *The New York Times.*

Eleven Madison Park

Executive Chef Daniel Humm's philosophy is to sublimely enhance seasonal products.

What else? A simply remarkable wine list! A blend of colors, a melting pot of civilizations, cosmopolitan influences: it's here, in the very heart of Manhattan. In a spectacular art deco building overlooking Madison Square Park, Executive Chef Daniel Humm draws his culinary inspiration and purely expresses 'the spirit of grand New York'. As master of ceremonies at Eleven Madison Park, Daniel Humm creates modern, sophisticated French cuisine, revisiting classical flavors with a magical pinch of 'je ne sais quoi'.

Serves 4
Preparation time: 20 minutes
Cooking time: 45 minutes

Planning ahead:
The prawn salad can be prepared in advance then chilled.

INGREDIENTS

court bouillon for cooking the prawn:

¾ cup	fennel, chopped
¾ cup	celery, chopped
½ cup	leeks, cleaned and chopped
3	garlic cloves, peeled
1 cup	white wine
1 cup	orange juice
1 tbsp	orange zest
1 tsp	fennel seeds
1 tsp	coriander seeds
1 tsp	ground black pepper
1	whole star anise
2 tsp	kosher salt
3 cups	water
1½ lb	large prawns (about 16)

prawn salad:

1½ tbsp	mayonnaise
1½ tbsp	Greek yogurt
2 tsp	fresh tarragon, chopped
2 tsp	lime juice

salt & pepper
cayenne pepper

avocado:

2½ lb	ripe avocados, chilled slightly
1 tbsp	lemon oil

fleur de sel

vinaigrette:

1 cup	prawn poaching liquid
3 tbsp	lemon oil
1 tbsp	white balsamic vinegar

piment d'espelette
salt

garnish:

sorrel leaves
borage blossoms or nasturtium flowers
tarragon
4 tsp Greek yogurt

HAWAIIAN PRAWN ROULADE WITH AVOCADO & GREEK YOGURT

BY DANIEL HUMM

We spend a lot of time at the restaurant talking about the balance between what is classic and what is modern. This dish really strikes that balance, combining classic flavors with modern presentation. Additionally, if you feel intimidated making the roulade, skip that step and just enjoy the prawn salad on its own.

METHOD

court bouillon:

To cook the prawns, first make a court bouillon in a saucepan with the chopped fennel, celery, leeks, garlic, white wine, orange juice, orange zest, fennel seeds, coriander seeds, black pepper, star anise, salt and water. Bring to a boil and simmer for 20 minutes. Remove from the heat and cool the liquid to 140° F.

Add the prawns to the warm liquid and poach for about 5 minutes, using the residual heat, until they start turning pink. Let cool in the liquid and then peel them, slice in half lengthwise, and remove the thin black intestinal track.

prawn salad:

Cut the prawn into fine dice (you will have about 2 cups). Combine them with the mayonnaise, yogurt, tarragon, and lime juice. Season with salt, pepper and just a pinch of cayenne.

avocado:

Quarter the avocados and peel each quarter just before using. Discard any bruised and/or dark sections. Slice the quarters as thinly as possible with a mandoline or a very sharp knife with a steady hand. You will not get perfect slices every time. Dice the avocado leftovers and add to the prawn salad. Lay the slices on parchment or plastic wrap in overlapping layers. Press down on the avocado slices with another sheet of parchment or plastic; the goal is to create a smooth layer of avocado. Spread the prawn salad down the center of the avocado slices and roll like a cigar. Brush the roulades with the lemon oil and sprinkle with fleur de sel.

vinaigrette:

Reduce the prawn poaching liquid to a syrup. Add the lemon oil and the balsamic vinegar. Season with piment d'espelette and salt.

to serve:

Spread 1 teaspoon of yogurt on each plate. Place a roulade on top and garnish with borage or nasturtium flowers, sorrel, and tarragon. Drizzle with the vinaigrette and serve.

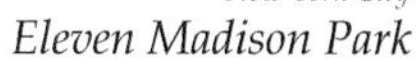

Serves 4
Preparation time: 1 hour 30 minutes
Cooking time: 1 hour

Special equipment:
Water bath

Planning ahead:
The fumet blanc can be made in advance, refrigerated, and then reheated. The truffle dice, both celery dice, and the tapioca pearls can also be prepared in advance.

INGREDIENTS

turbot:

4	portions of Chilean turbot, scaled and de-boned (ask your butcher to give you the bones for the sauce), 6 oz each

truffle coins (see method), 9 per portion
celery root coins (see method), 12 per portion
salt
truffle oil

turbot mousseline:

1 cup	turbot trimmings and scraps
1 cup	heavy cream, divided in two
1	egg white

salt
cayenne pepper
chopped truffle, as needed and as available

fumet blanc: (yields 1 qt)

2 tbsp	butter
¼ cup	shallots
⅛ cup	celery root, peeled
¼ cup	celery
⅛ cup	button mushrooms
¼ cup	Noilly Prat Vermouth
¼ cup	white wine
1 lb	turbot bones (cut into small pieces, rinsed in cold water, all meat and blood removed)
2 lb	ice cubes
1¼ cups	heavy cream
½ cup	crème fraîche

salt, cayenne pepper, lime juice, as needed

garnish for fumet blanc:

¼ cup	celery root, small dice
¼ cup	green celery, small dice, ribs removed
¼ cup	black truffle, small dice
½ cup	tapioca pearls, large

fleur de sel

ATLANTIC TURBOT 'SOUS VIDE' WITH CELERY & PERIGORD TRUFFLES

BY DANIEL HUMM

This is truly one of my favorite ingredients, I feel that truffles and celery provide a good backdrop to the purity of the turbot. The 'scales' as well as the use of the tapioca pearls add a certain playfulness to the dish.

METHOD

turbot:

Slice the truffles and celery root thinly on a mandoline. Using a small round cutter about the size of a nickel, punch out rounds.

Add the celery coins to cold water that has been seasoned liberally with salt. Bring to a simmer and cook for about 1 minute at a steady simmer. Strain and shock in ice water. Lay the turbot skin side down and make an incision with a sharp knife down the center of the fish, on the bone side, while being careful not to cut through to the other side. Then spread the incision with your fingers and slice an opening on the right and left sides to create an opening for the mousse (see recipe below). Pipe the mousse into the opening of the fish and be careful not to over fill. Flip the fish over, season with salt and arrange the celery and truffle coins in a mosaic style on top of the fish to create a 'scale' effect. Brush the 'scales' with truffle oil and vacuum seal the fish (each portion separately) in a sous vide bag and cook in a water bath at 58°C/136°F for about 7 minutes.

turbot mousseline:

Add the turbot trimmings and scraps to a food processor and start blending in the cream gradually. When the cream is fully emulsified into the fish, add the egg white followed by the seasonings (except the truffle), to taste. Pass this through a fine mesh sieve and then fold in the chopped truffle with a plastic spatula.

fumet blanc:

Cut all vegetables into small mirepoix. In a large high-sided rondeau or stock pot, melt the butter and sweat the shallots until translucent. Add the celery root and celery and continue to sweat over a low heat, allowing for no colorization. Add the turbot bones and sauté for a few minutes. Deglaze with white wine and cook until completely reduced. Deglaze a second time with the Noilly Prat and reduce by half. Cover the bones with ice cubes and bring to a boil over a medium high heat. While at a boil, skim off impurities, cover, and remove from the flame. Allow to sit for 30 minutes off flame. Strain through a chinois. Return to the heat and reduce by half. Add the heavy cream. Bring back to the boil, add the crème fraiche and season with salt, cayenne and lime juice.

garnish for fumet blanc:

Blanch the celery root and celery in salted boiling water until tender. Shock in ice water. Cook the tapioca pearls in salted boiling water until clear.

to serve:

When ready to serve, reheat the fumet blanc. Add the tapioca pearls, celery root dice, celery dice and truffle dice. Check for seasoning. Spoon about 1 cup of fumet blanc into each bowl. Remove the fish from the sous vide bags and season with fleur de sel. Place the fish in the center of a bowl, set in fumet blanc.

SUCKLING PIG CONFIT WITH PLUM CHUTNEY & FIVE SPICE JUS

BY DANIEL HUMM

This has become one of my signature dishes, although it originated in an effort to use all parts of the pig. While preparation does take some time I assure you it's worth the wait.

Serves 4
Preparation time: 30 minutes
Cooking time: 12 hours for the pork confit

Special equipment:
Large, high-sided baking dish, half sheet tray, mandoline

Planning ahead:
The confit should be prepared a day in advance. The chutney can also be made in advance.

INGREDIENTS

pork confit:

4 lb	pork shoulder, bone-in and with skin
½ cup	kosher salt
6	sprigs of thyme
2	shallots
1	carrot, medium-sized
1	celery root, small-sized
2	sprigs of thyme
1	bay leaf
8	black peppercorns
8 quarts	duck fat

salt & pepper

soubise:

2 cups	white onions
3 tbsp	butter
¼ cup	white wine
1 tbsp	salt
1	pinch xanthan gum
1 tbsp	cold butter
½ cup	water
5	white peppercorns, in a sachet

caramelized cipollini onions:

4	peeled cipollini onions
1 cup	white wine
1 tbsp	salt
4 tbsp	sugar
1 cup	chicken stock
1 tbsp	chicken jus

baby leeks:

8	baby leeks
4	sprigs of large chives
1 tbsp	butter

salt

five spice jus:

3 tbsp	sugar
3 tbsp	banjuls vinegar
4 tbsp	red wine
1 cup	chicken jus
1	five spice sachet (see below)

salt, to taste

five spice mix (add to a sachet):

½	cinnamon stick
3	cloves
2	star anise
½ tsp	fennel seeds
½ tsp	Szechuan pepper

plum chutney (yields 1 pt):

1 pt	port wine
¼ cup	sugar
1 cup	plums, pits removed, diced
1¼ cups	dried plums, small dice

METHOD

pork confit:

Rub the meat with salt and thyme and let it sit for about 4 hours. Wash the pork with cold water and dry with kitchen towel. Place in a large, high-sided baking dish and add the warm duck fat, vegetables and herbs. The entire piece of pork needs to be fully covered with the liquid duck fat. Cook in the oven at 300°F for about 12 hours, until the meat starts falling off the bone. Remove the skin carefully and lay on a half sheet tray with parchment paper – try to remove the skin in one whole piece and make sure there are no holes. Lay the skin with the underside facing up.

Separate the cooking juices from the duck fat, discard the fat. Reduce the cooking juices to a syrup consistency. Remove and shred all the meat from the bone and place into a bowl. Season the meat with the reduced cooking liquid, salt and pepper. The meat needs to be moist but not wet. Place a 1" thick layer of the meat into the half sheet tray, on top of the skin. Place another half sheet tray on top and weigh down to press. Chill for at least 12 hours (while being weighed down) before using, the longer the better.

When ready to serve, cut the meat into rectangles and sear skin side down in a sauté pan until crispy.

soubise:

Slice the white onions very thinly on a mandoline. Season with salt and set aside. Melt the butter in a large pot over a low heat. Add the onions and raise the heat to high. Sweat for 5 minutes. Add the white wine, a third of the water and the sachet, cover with a cartouche. Cook covered until the onions are tender, adding water a few drops at a time if the pan dries on the bottom. When the onions are cooked purée in a blender with the xanthan gum and cold butter. Strain the soubise and cool in an ice bath.

caramelized cipollini onions:

Combine the wine, onions and salt. Bring to a simmer and cook until half of the way done. Remove from the heat. With half of the sugar begin a caramel in a separate pan. Once melted add the rest of the sugar. Cook until a deep caramel, but not burnt. Remove from the heat and add stock to stop cooking. Once incorporated add jus for color and flavor. Simmer until evenly incorporated and reduced to a glaze. Add the onions and simmer on low until the onions are finished cooking. Be careful to not over cook!

baby leeks:

Clean the leeks and blanch whole in boiling salt water until tender. Chill in ice water. Also blanch the chives for a couple of seconds. Tie two leeks with chives together on both ends. Heat butter in a sauté pan to glaze the leeks. Season with salt.

five spice jus:

Caramelize the sugar, add the banjuls vinegar and reduce to a deep brown. Add the red wine and spice mix in a sachet. Reduce to a jam consistency. Add the chicken jus and reduce to a sauce consistency. Let steep for 20 minutes. Strain.

plum chutney:

Place the port, sugar and spice mix sachet into a large sauté pan and reduce until a slightly syrupy consistency. Add the fresh and dried plums to ¼ cup of this syrup and cook on a medium heat until soft.

to serve:

Place a quenelle of the rhubarb chutney on each plate. Place the confit next to it and garnish with the soubise, leeks, cipollini onions and finish with the five spice jus.

CHOCOLATE PEANUT BUTTER PALETTE WITH CARAMEL POPCORN & POPCORN ICE CREAM

BY DANIEL HUMM

Growing up, I would always dream about what my perfect candy bar would be ... this is it.

Serves 4
Preparation time: 30 minutes
Cooking time: 1 hour

Special equipment:
Quarter sheet trays

Planning ahead:
The entire recipe can be made in advance and refrigerated/frozen, even after being glazed. When ready to serve, allow to temper a bit.

INGREDIENTS

peanut butter shortbread:

3 tbsp + 1 tsp butter, softened
¼ cup peanut butter
½ cup powdered sugar
¾ cup all purpose flour
¾ cup almond flour
1 tbsp heavy cream

salted caramel:

2 tbsp granulated white sugar
¼ cup heavy cream
1 tbsp glucose
½ vanilla bean, split and seeds removed
1 tbsp butter, unsalted
¼ tsp salt

chocolate praline crisp:

1 tsp butter
2½ oz 40% Valrhona chocolate
½ oz 72% Valrhona chocolate
2 tbsp peanut butter
⅓ cup + 1 tbsp feuilletine

chocolate peanut butter mousse:

1 tbsp granulated white sugar
1 egg
½ oz 66% Valrhona chocolate
1 tbsp peanut butter
¼ cup heavy cream, whipped to soft peaks

chocolate glaze:

⅓ cup milk
⅓ cup cream
⅓ cup simple syrup
2 tbsp glucose
2½ oz 66% Valrhona chocolate
8 oz pate a glace
2 sheets gold gelatin sheets, bloomed (placed in cold water until softened; drain before use)

popcorn ice cream:

1 cup popcorn kernels
2 tbsp canola oil
4 cups whole milk
3 cups heavy cream
3 tbsp glucose
½ cup granulated white sugar

caramel popcorn:

2 tbsp popcorn kernels
2 tsp canola oil
½ cup peanuts, finely chopped
½ cup sugar
2 tbsp butter
1 tsp corn syrup
2 tbsp water
¼ tsp salt

cocoa nib syrup:

½ cup water
2 tbsp cocoa nibs
2 tbsp glucose

to serve:

½ cup peanut butter
½ cup peanuts, chopped
Gold leaf

METHOD

peanut butter shortbread:

Mix the butter and peanut butter with a rubber spatula or wooden spoon until creamy. Add the powdered sugar and almond flour. Incorporate the AP flour. Drizzle in the heavy cream and mix until just combined. Roll between two sheets of parchment to ¼" thickness and freeze. Spray a quarter sheet tray with cooking spray and line with parchment. Line the tray with the dough and prick with a fork. Chill for 10 minutes in a refrigerator. Bake at 350°F until a light golden brown. Cool.

salted caramel:

Warm the cream and glucose in a small pan and reserve. Bring the sugar to a dark caramel. Deglaze with the cream and glucose. Cook to 220°F then let it cool to 176°F and add the chocolate and salt. Let it cool further to 95°F and mix in the butter and vanilla bean with an immersion blender. Strain through a chinois.

chocolate praline crisp:

Gently melt both chocolates and butter together in a large mixing bowl. Add the peanut butter. Gently fold in the feuilletine.

chocolate peanut butter mousse:

Melt the chocolate and peanut butter over a double boiler. Combine the egg and sugar. Whisk constantly over the double boiler until very warm. Whip until lightened and forming ribbons. Fold the egg mixture into the chocolate mixture. Finish by folding in the whipped cream.

chocolate glaze:

Bring the milk, cream, syrup and glucose to just under a boil, then add the gelatin. Pour slowly over chopped chocolate and pate a glace. Let it rest for a minute. Combine with a whisk. Strain and cool.

popcorn ice cream:

Place popcorn kernels and the oil in a deep pot, cover and heat over a medium high flame. Periodically shake the pot to rotate the kernels. When the popping slows, remove the pot from the heat and allow the popping to finish. Be careful not to burn the popcorn. Reserve. Bring the milk, cream, sugar and glucose to just under a boil and pour over the popcorn. Cover with plastic wrap and steep for 1 hour. Blend half the base in a blender until relatively smooth. Pour back into the remaining base, whisk well and strain through a chinois. Blend again until totally smooth and strain once more. Add salt. Spin in an ice cream machine. Freeze.

caramel popcorn:

Preheat the oven to 325°F. Pop the corn kernels the same as directed in the ice cream recipe. In a small pot bring the sugar, butter, corn syrup and water to a boil and cook until a medium caramel color is reached. Pour the caramel onto the popcorn and sprinkle with peanuts and salt. Stir the caramel into the popcorn until it begins to stiffen. Place into the oven for 3-5 minutes or just until the caramel softens again. Stir. Repeat this process until the corn is completely covered. Spread out onto a silpat and let cool. Place in a sealed dry container to avoid humidity.

cocoa nib syrup:

Bring the water to the boil then add the nibs. Cover and steep for 20 minutes. Strain through a chinois and then through cheesecloth. Add the glucose and reduce to about two-thirds of the original volume. Chill.

to serve:

Per quarter sheet tray:

Spread the baked cookie dough evenly with ½ cup peanut butter, then freeze. Spread evenly with chocolate praline crisp and freeze again. Spread evenly with salted caramel and press ½ cup chopped peanuts into the caramel and freeze for a third time. Spread the mousse evenly over the peanuts/caramel. Freeze until completely solid. Remove from the sheet tray and cut into four 1½" pieces. Place on a glazing rack and refreeze.

Heat the glaze until warm to the touch. Strain. Pour the glaze over the bars, making sure that all the sides are covered. Refrigerate. Apply a small piece of gold leaf to the upper left corner.

Serve with the ice cream, caramel popcorn and garnish with the cocoa nib syrup.

Jean-Georges Vongerichten
Grand Chef Relais & Châteaux

Chef Jean-Georges Vongerichten's unique culinary style is a combination of his classical French training and his love for Asian techniques and flavors. He began his career at L'Auberge de L'Ill with Paul Haeberlin, and then worked under Paul Bocuse and Louis Outhier. With his three Michelin star training, Jean-Georges trekked across the globe to Bangkok, Shanghai, and Hong Kong where he developed his love for Asian flavors and techniques. After traveling throughout Asia, Jean-Georges moved to New York to helm the kitchen at the Lafayette. There, he shocked the culinary world by breaking with French tradition, incorporating light, spicy Asian flavors and techniques into his cuisine. Today, Jean-Georges has an empire of 26 restaurants that span the globe, including his flagship three-Michelin-star Jean Georges in New York City. He has been the recipient of several prestigious awards, including Best New Restaurant; Outstanding Chef; and Who's Who of Food and Beverage awards from the James Beard Foundation. He is also the author of four cookbooks.

Jean-Georges

The Jean-Georges restaurant has become an absolute must i[illegible] Manhattan. 'Genius' for some and 'great master of gastronom[illegible] others, Jean-Georges Vongerichten is a chef who generates superla[illegible]

The interior design is Zen, revealing the artist's love of streamlined elegance and Asia. In this Frenchman is famous for his 'Thai-French cuisine'. A fusion of two great culinary trac[illegible] that produces breathtaking results: red and white tuna marinated in olive oil and lemon foie gras brûlée in a cherry sauce with a white port jelly, black bass and radish bulb salac[illegible] candied fruits accompanied by homemade orange zest and kiwi sorbets ... It is impossibl[illegible] you anything more about the menu: Jean-Georges reinvents it every three months.

Serves 4
Preparation time: 30 minutes
Cooking time: 30 minutes

INGREDIENTS

chili oil:

1	dried ancho chile, stemmed and seeded
1½	dried chipotle peppers, stemmed and seeded
1	whole allspice berry
1	whole clove
¾ tsp	fennel seeds
1	small piece of mace or nutmeg, cracked
1	whole star anise
½	cinnamon stick
½ tsp	salt
½ cup	grapeseed, corn, or other neutral oil

ginger marinade:

¼ cup	sugar
¼ oz	kaffir lime leaves, roughly chopped
¼ cup	fresh lime juice
1 cup	peeled chopped fresh ginger
⅓ cup	extra virgin olive oil
½ cup	Champagne or other wine vinegar
½ cup	soy sauce

tuna and avocado:

1	4" square, 1" thick piece of sushi-grade tuna
salt	
1	fresh red Thai chili, seeded and minced
2	shallots, minced
2 tbsp	extra virgin olive oil
1	ripe avocado, seeded, peeled and diced
1 tsp	fresh lime juice
4	small bunches red radishes, stemmed, scrubbed, and cut into ¼" slices
½	small daikon radish, stemmed peeled, and cut into ½" slices
½	small icicle radish, stemmed peeled, and cut into ¼" slices

RIBBONS OF TUNA WITH GINGER MARINADE

BY JEAN-GEORGES VONGERICHTEN

Here, the taste and texture of tuna cut into linguine-like strands is sauced by a refreshing ginger marinade. The natural spiciness of radishes is heightened by the addition of homemade chili oil and tempered by cool avocado.

METHOD

chili oil:

Put the chilies, allspice, clove, fennel, mace, anise, and cinnamon in a large dry skillet and set over a medium heat. Cook, stirring occasionally, until fragrant and toasted, approximately 2 minutes. Transfer the toasted ingredients to a blender or spice grinder with the salt and blend until finely ground.

Transfer the mixture to a small saucepan and cover with the oil. Set over a medium-low heat until very warm, then remove from the heat and cool completely. Strain the oil through a fine mesh sieve and set aside at room temperature to use immediately, or cover and refrigerate until ready to use.

ginger marinade:

Put the sugar, lime leaves, and lime juice in a small saucepan. Set over a medium-high heat and bring to a boil, stirring occasionally. Remove from the heat and cool to room temperature, then strain the lime syrup through a fine-mesh sieve and set aside.

Put the ginger in the bowl of a blender and blend, adding the olive oil in a slow, steady stream through the feed tube, until the mixture becomes a smooth purée. Transfer to a medium mixing bowl and stir in the vinegar, soy sauce, and reserved lime syrup and set aside.

tuna and avocado:

Cut the tuna into thin strands lengthwise, ⅛" thick, so that the cut pieces resemble spaghetti. Season lightly with salt, then gently toss with the chili, shallots, and 1 tablespoon of the olive oil.

Season the avocado lightly with salt, then toss gently with the lime juice and the remaining 1 tablespoon of olive oil. Season the radishes lightly with salt, then toss gently with half the reserved chili oil.

to serve:

Divide the avocado among four serving bowls and decoratively arrange half the radish slices, then half the tuna strands on top. Stack the remaining radishes and tuna on top, spoon the ginger marinade around the dish, and drizzle the remaining chili oil all around. Serve immediately.

Serves 4
Preparation time: 15 minutes
Cooking time: 30 minutes

INGREDIENTS

sauce:

½ cup	fresh orange juice
2 tbsp	soy sauce
¼ cup	rice vinegar + 2 tbsp
1 tbsp	Shaoxing wine
1	whole star anise
2 tbsp	fresh ginger, peeled and roughly chopped
¼ cup	sugar
1 tbsp	black tea leaves, preferably Oolong
salt	

squab:

4	semi-boneless squabs
1 tbsp	unsalted butter + more as needed
salt & freshly ground black pepper	
1 tsp	ground star anise

garnish:

12	¼" pieces crystallized tamarind candy
1	Asian pear, peeled, cored, and small cubed
1 tsp	coarse salt

SQUAB A L'ORANGE WITH CRYSTALLIZED TAMARIND

BY JEAN-GEORGES VONGERICHTEN

This new version of a French classic is much easier than the original. Squab is more satisfying here than duck, but duck also works well. The crystallized tamarind is a nice touch, but you can leave it out if you have trouble finding it (but it is available in most Asian markets).

METHOD

sauce:

Preheat a broiler. Put the first six ingredients into the bowl of a blender and purée. Transfer the mixture to a saucepan and stir in the sugar and tea over a medium heat. Bring to a boil, stirring occasionally, then remove from the heat, cover, and steep for 5 minutes. Cool the mixture completely, then strain through a fine mesh sieve and season to taste with salt. Set aside.

squab:

Rub the squab with butter, then season with salt, pepper and anise. Put on a buttered baking sheet, skin side up. Broil for 5 minutes, or until medium-rare.

to serve:

Spoon the sauce onto the serving plates, and put the broiled squab on top. Garnish with the tamarind candy, Asian pear, and salt, then serve.

Chef's tip:

To semi-bone the squabs, just take a sharp boning knife and cut straight down along either side of the breast; you will end up with a boneless breast attached to the bone-in leg and wing.

Serves 4
Preparation time: 25 minutes
Cooking time: 7 minutes

Special equipment:
Four 4 oz molds, custard cups or ramekins

INGREDIENTS

½ cup	butter + some for buttering the molds
4 oz	bittersweet chocolate (preferably Valrhona)
2	eggs
2	egg yolks
¼ cup	sugar
2 tsp	flour + more for dusting

JEAN-GEORGES' CHOCOLATE CAKE

BY JEAN-GEORGES VONGERICHTEN

This recipe was the result of what I thought was a catering disaster. I was serving warm chocolate cake to guests at a party, but when I saw them taking their first bites, I realized that all the cakes had been undercooked. It was the best mistake I ever made. Today, I could never imagine taking this cake off the menu, it's a customer favorite.

METHOD

In the top of a double boiler set over simmering water, heat the butter and chocolate together until the chocolate is almost completely melted. While that's heating, beat together the eggs, yolks, and sugar with a whisk or electric beater until light and thick.

Beat together the melted chocolate and butter; it should be quite warm. Pour in the egg mixture, then quickly beat in the flour, just until combined.

Butter and lightly flour the molds, custard cups, or ramekins. Tap out the excess flour, then butter and flour them again. Divide the batter among the molds. (At this point, you can refrigerate the desserts until you are ready to eat, for up to several hours; bring them back to room temperature before baking.)

Preheat the oven to 450°F. Bake the molds on a tray for 6 -7 minutes. The center will still be quite soft, but the sides will be set. Invert each mold on to a plate and let them sit for about 10 seconds. Unmold by lifting up one corner of the mold; the cake will fall out onto the plate.

to serve:

Serve immediately with a smear of chocolate sauce, chocolate crumbs and vanilla-bean ice cream.

Eli Kaimeh

As the next Chef de Cuisine, Eli Kaimeh will lead a kitchen renowned for both its cuisine and its dedication to excellence. Kaimeh has been a member of the Per Se team since the beginning, starting as a Chef de Partie when the restaurant opened in 2004. His desire and ability, along with a deep understanding of Chef Thomas Keller's culinary philosophy has prepared him to contribute to its continued evolution. Kaimeh's commitment was apparent from the outset to departing Chef Jonathan Benno, which led to a focused mentor program that continues to this day. During his tenure, Per Se has garnered many outstanding accolades including a 4-star rating from the *New York Times*, a 3-star rating from the French-based *Michelin Guide* and recognition as the #1 restaurant in the Americas from the UK-based *Restaurant* Magazine.

Prior to his time at Per Se, Kaimeh honed his culinary skills in some of New York's most highly regarded restaurants including Gramercy Tavern, Tocqueville Restaurant and Restaurant Daniel. He holds an Associate's degree in Occupational Studies from The Culinary Institute of America. Growing up in Brooklyn, NY, food was always the focal point at the Kaimeh home. Cooking reminds him of watching his grandmother pass down family traditions and values to his mother and to himself.

Per Se

Per Se offers a festival of culinary delights that will convince you perfection does indeed exist.

Following the success of his California restaurant, The French Laundry, Thomas Keller brought his distinctive hands-on approach from the Napa Valley to New York City, reflecting an intense focus on detail, extending not only to cuisine, but also to presentation, mood and surroundings. Chef de Cuisine Eli Kaimeh interprets modern American recipes with a touch of French influence in the elegant dining room with a view of Central Park. Representative dishes include 'Oysters and Pearls', a sabayon of pearl tapioca with poached oysters and caviar and 'Calotte de Boeuf Grillée' with crispy bone marrow, russet potato mille-feuille and forest mushrooms with sauce bordelaise ... "A good meal is not only about good food and good wine. Above it all should be an emotional experience," asserts Thomas Keller.

MASCARPONE ENRICHED GREEN GARLIC 'AGNOLOTTI'

BY ELI KAIMEH

Agnolotti, a version of ravioli from Piedmont, are the perfect stuffed pasta because when they are cut they always seal without air pockets. Their pillow shape also lends to catching sauces well.

Serves 6
Preparation time: 8 hours
Cooking time: 10 minutes

Special equipment:
Pasta machine, pastry scraper, pastry crimping wheel, chinois, pastry bag, pastry tip (No. 5), slow cooker

Planning ahead:
The filled pasta and beans can be cooked ahead.

INGREDIENTS

pasta dough:

6	egg yolks
1	large egg
8 oz	'00' flour
1½ tbsp	olive oil
1 tbsp	milk

green garlic filling:

⅓ lb	butter
6 cups	green garlic tops
¾ cup	vegetable stock
1 ⅓ cup	heavy cream
2 cups	Swiss chard leaves
2	heads of garlic, roasted and cloves puréed
⅓ cup	semolina
⅓ cup	mascarpone
¼ cup	parmesan

cassoulet of pole beans:

½ lb	dried heirloom pole beans
4 cups	water
4 cups	vegetable stock
¼	onion
½	medium carrot
½	leek

bouquet garni of thyme, peppercorns and parsley stems
kosher salt

whole grain mustard emulsion:

2 cups	vegetable stock
3	shallots, sliced
3	sprigs of thyme
2 tbsp	heavy cream
1 lb	butter
1 tbsp	roasted garlic purée
2 tbsp	whole grain mustard

garnish:

parsley melba
thyme leaves

METHOD

Pasta dough:
Mound the flour on the board and create a well in the center. Push the flour to all the sides in a circular motion to create a wall that is 1" wide. The well should be wide enough to hold all the eggs without spilling. Add the wet ingredients into the well and use your fingers to break up the eggs. Begin incorporating some of the flour into the eggs by moving your fingers in a circular motion. This will slowly pull flour into the wet mixture. An even slow pace is key to avoiding lumps. Use a pastry scraper to occasionally push flour into the eggs. Eventually the mixture will become too thick to turn with your fingers. At this point begin incorporating the remaining flour with the pastry scraper. Lift the flour up over the dough and cut into it using the scraper. The dough will appear rough. You now begin to knead the dough by pressing it in a forward motion using the heels of your hands. As you do this, occasionally reform the dough into a ball and begin again. This process will take at least 15 minutes and is finished when the dough develops elasticity. Double wrap the dough in plastic wrap and allow to rest for 30-60 minutes. Using the pasta machine, begin to sheet your dough in 5 oz portions on the widest possible setting. Always keep your unused pasta wrapped tightly. Fold the sheet in half, turn a quarter turn and run it through the machine a second time; repeat two more times, but fold the piece of pasta lengthwise at the last pass to ensure a narrower product. Now set the rollers down a degree and pass your pasta sheet. Continue setting the rollers down a degree until the pasta sheets are at least 5" wide and thin enough to see your hand through.

green garlic filling:
Sweat the garlic in butter. Add the stock and glaze. Add the cream, chard and purée and cook for 3 minutes – work quickly to preserve the color. Purée in a high speed blender and quickly strain into a clean saucepot. Add the semolina and cook for an additional 2 minutes. Add the mascarpone and parmesan then cool rapidly over an ice bath.

agnolotti formation:
Place your filling in a pastry bag with a No.5 tip. Pipe a tube of filling across the bottom of a pasta sheet. Leave a ¾" border around the filling. Pull the bottom edge of the pasta over the filling. Seal the edge by lightly pressing on it with your index finger. You should have ½" of excess dough in front of your filling. Remove any air pockets with your finger. Seal the ends of the dough and begin to portion by pinching the filling with your thumb and forefingers. Each indentation should be 1 apart and ¾" wide. With a crimping wheel, separate the portioned pasta from the remaining pasta sheet. Individually cut the agnolotti by cutting through the pinched portion with the crimping wheel. Place the finished product carefully on a tray dusted with corn meal.

cassoulet of pole beans:
Soak the dried beans in cold water for 2 days. Combine all the ingredients and allow to cook in a slow cooker for 5-6 hours, or until the beans are tender. Let the beans cool in the cooking liquid then season.

whole grain mustard emulsion:
In a small saucepan, combine the stock, shallots and thyme and cook until there is only about 1-2 tbsp of liquid remaining. Add the cream and reduce slightly. Whisk in the butter in small pieces until fully emulsified. Strain into a clean saucepan then stir in the purée and mustard. Adjust the seasoning and keep warm until ready to serve.

to serve:
Arrange all elements on a plate as pictured.

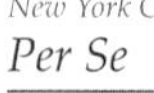

SNAKE RIVER FARM'S 'CALOTTE DE BŒUF'

BY ELI KAIMEH

Calotte, or the cap of the rib-eye of beef, is a particularly special cut that is used at Per Se because of its tenderness, flavor and marbling.

Serves 4
Preparation time: 45 minutes
Cooking time: 20 minutes

Special equipment:
Grill pan, kitchen twine

Planning ahead:
The asparagus can be prepared up to a day ahead. The sauce can be refrigerated for 2-3 days.

INGREDIENTS

calotte de bœuf:

2-2½ lb cap of beef rib-eye (or rib-eye of beef), trimmed of excess fat and gristle, at room temperature
canola oil
kosher salt
freshly cracked Tellicherry peppercorns

risolée of new crop potatoes:

2 lb marble or small new crop potatoes or about 12 each
1 tsp unsalted butter, at room temperature
canola oil
kosher salt

asparagus:

2 lb medium green asparagus or about 12 pieces
kosher salt

morel mushrooms:

1 tbsp unsalted butter
1 cup morel mushrooms, washed, stems peeled and cut into 1" pieces
kosher salt
freshly cracked Tellicherry peppercorns

sauce Bordelaise:

1 cup red wine, such as Cabernet Sauvignon
⅓ cup shallots, sliced
½ cup carrots, sliced
¼ cup mushrooms, sliced
10 sprigs of Italian parsley
2 sprigs of thyme
1 bay leaf
2 tbsp garlic, sliced
6 Tellicherry peppercorns
1 cup veal stock

METHOD

calotte de bœuf:

Pat the meat dry so it will sear well, lightly coat with canola oil and season generously. On a hot grill pan, cook the steak as desired. Allow to rest for at least 5 minutes before portioning. Finish with the peppercorns.

risolée of new crop potatoes:

Add the potatoes to a pot of cold water and bring to a boil. Lightly blanch until the center of the potato is cooked through. Strain and allow them to cool at room temperature. Peel and when ready to serve, sauté the potatoes in canola oil until lightly crisped. Finish with butter to achieve a golden color and season.

asparagus:

Remove the tough ends of the asparagus by holding the center of each stalk with one hand and bending the bottom end of the stalk until it snaps off naturally. Line up the asparagus spears, tips facing the same direction, on a cutting board and trim the ends so that the spears are of equal length. Peel the asparagus spears, beginning about 1" below the base of the tip. Bring a large pot of generously salted water to a boil and prepare an ice bath. Divide the asparagus spears into four piles, again with the tops facing the same way. Cut four pieces of kitchen twine about 2' long and tie the spears into bundles; leaving a 3" end of the twine free, start by wrapping the twine securely around the top of the bundle (just below the tips), then wrap the remaining twine down and around the bottom and tie the ends of the twine together. When the water is boiling, add the asparagus and blanch for 4-6 minutes, or until just tender. Transfer to the ice bath (leave the water boiling). When the asparagus bundles are cold, transfer to paper towels, remove the twine, and let drain; then refrigerate for at least 15 minutes.

morel mushrooms:

Completely remove any dirt by trimming, brushing and rinsing as needed. Some wild mushrooms may have more dirt than can be rinsed away; soak them in warm water as a last resort. Heat the butter in a skillet over a medium heat. Add the mushrooms, season and cook for about 5 minutes, or until the mushrooms are tender and slightly 'toasty' around the edges, and any liquid has evaporated.

sauce Bordelaise:

In a medium saucepan, bring the wine, vegetables and herbs to a simmer, and simmer until almost all the liquid has evaporated. Add the peppercorns and veal stock and simmer for another 10-15 minutes, or until the stock is reduced to a sauce consistency (about ½ cup). Strain the sauce through a fine-mesh strainer into a small saucepan.

to serve:

Re-warm the sauce over a low heat. Slice the meat against the grain into 1" slices, and into four even portions. Spoon the sauce on to the plate and place the meat on the sauce. Arrange the asparagus, mushrooms and potatoes on the plate.

'SWISS ROLL'
BY ELWYN BOYLES

Our Swiss roll is a refined and elegantly plated interpretation of the classic dessert we all enjoyed as young children.

Serves 30
Preparation time: 8 hours
Cooking time: 4 hours

Special equipment:
Two standing mixers with paddle and whisk attachments, ice cream machine, siphon loaded with 3 CO_2 chargers

INGREDIENTS

chocolate roulade: (yields 2 half-sheet pans)

¾ cup sugar
6 eggs
2 egg yolks
2 cups all purpose flour
2 tbsp corn starch
¼ cup cocoa powder

Swiss roll mousse:

6 oz chocolate, manjari 64%
1 cup heavy cream
¾ lb butter
½ cup sugar
2 egg whites

spiced Anglaise cremeux:

2 cups heavy cream
2 cups milk
2 tbsp corn syrup
2 fresh bay leaves
2 star anise
1 used vanilla bean pod
1 cup sugar
4 egg yolks
11 oz chocolate, manjari

yogurt sherbet: (yields approximately 1 qt)

4 cups milk
2 bananas, coarsely chopped
½ cup glucose powder
¼ tsp sorbet stabilizer
¼ tsp ice cream stabilizer
1¼ cups sugar
2 cups Greek yogurt
½ lemon, juice

banana-passionfruit cream:

4 cups banana purée
2 cups passionfruit purée
½ cup sugar
4 ½ gelatin sheets, bloomed
1 lemon, juice

chocolate covered banana jelly:

4 cups banana purée
½ cup sugar
8 gelatin sheets, bloomed
1 tsp agar agar
1 lemon, juice
cocoa powder
chopped peanuts
tempered chocolate, 70%

banana tuile:

½ cup sugar
½ cup all purpose flour
2 bananas
1 lemon, juice
½ tsp citric acid

chocolate sauce:

⅓ cup water
½ cup sugar
2 tbsp cocoa powder
1 oz chocolate, manjari, 64%

chocolate décor:

tempered chocolate, 70%
acetate sheets

METHOD

chocolate roulade:

Preheat the oven to 400°F. In the mixer with the whisk attachment, whip the sugar, eggs and egg yolks on medium speed until the mixture has a ribbon-like texture. Fold in the dry ingredients. Pour the mixture evenly into two half sheet pans. Bake for 5 minutes or until the top springs back to the touch.

Swiss roll mousse:

Bring the cream to a boil and immediately pour into a large bowl filled with the chocolate to make a ganache. In the mixer fitted with the paddle attachment, cream the butter and combine with the mousse mixture. In a standing mixer fitted with the whisk attachment, whip the egg whites to soft peaks. Meanwhile, in a clean saucepan, cook the sugar to 244°F. It is important that the egg whites form soft peaks and the sugar reaches 244°F at the same time. Slowly pour the cooked sugar into the whisking egg whites to form an Italian meringue. Once the meringue has cooled, fold into the ganache.

spiced Anglaise cremeux:

In a saucepan, combine the milk, cream, corn syrup, bay leaves, star anise and vanilla bean pod and bring to just before the boil. In a mixing bowl, whisk the egg yolks and sugar until the mixture turns a pale yellow. Temper the hot liquid into the sugar and yolk mixture. Return the mixture to the heat and allow to cook until it thickens slightly. cool over an ice bath, then strain. Rewarm the anglaise to just under a simmer. Pour the warm mixture over the chocolate and mix until the chocolate is fully melted and incorporated into the cremeux. Using a high speed blender, incorporate air into the cremeux. Pour the cremeux into a container and allow to cool and set.

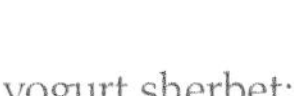

yogurt sherbet:

In a saucepan, combine the milk and bananas and bring to just before the boil. Remove from the heat and allow to infuse until it has completely cooled to room temperature. Strain the milk into a clean saucepan and combine the remaining ingredients, except the yogurt. Heat gently until the sugar has completely dissolved. Mix in the yogurt until it has been fully incorporated and finish with the lemon juice. Cool completely, then place in an ice cream machine.

banana-passionfruit cream:

In a saucepan, combine the purées with the sugar until the sugar dissolves. Add the gelatin

and combine until fully incorporated. Finish with the lemon juice. To serve, place the cream into a siphon loaded with 3 CO_2 chargers.

chocolate covered banana jelly:

In a saucepan, combine the banana purée, sugar and agar agar and bring to the boil. Add the gelatin and combine until fully incorporated. Add the lemon juice into the mixture. Pour into a parchment paper lined quarter sheet pan and allow to set. Once set, cut into ¼" cubes and dust with the cocoa powder. Dip the cubes into tempered chocolate and roll in the peanuts. Allow to set.

banana tuile:

Preheat the oven to 200°F. Combine all the ingredients in a high speed blender. Once fully incorporated, place in a plastic pastry bag and snip the tip of the bag. Line a sheet pan with parchment paper, then pipe strips of tuile. Place in an oven and allow to dry until set.

chocolate sauce:

In a small saucepan, heat the water and sugar until the sugar has completely dissolved. Vigorously whisk in the cocoa powder. Continue to whisk while adding the chocolate so as to maintain the emulsion. Bring back to a boil, then remove and cool over an ice bath.

chocolate décor:

Cut acetate sheets into 9" x ¾" strips. Spread the tempered chocolate on to the acetate strips and form into a ring. Allow to set before removing the acetate.

to serve:

Arrange all the elements on a plate as pictured.

USA Northeast

Incorporating Maine, Massachusetts, Connecticut, Pennsylvania, Vermont and Rhode Island among others, the U.S. Northeast is renowned for being one of the most scenic parts of North America.

Whether it is Vermont's Green Mountains with their maple syrup, the shellfish of rocky Maine or Pennsylvanian mushrooms, each state has a specialty. Colonial charm is key in the Northeast and nothing says colonial more than Boston's stately architecture or the gingerbread cottages of Martha's Vineyard. So settle back, enjoy the clam chowder that these states are so famous for and take in the freshness of the American Northeast.

Christopher Brooks
Grand Chef Relais & Châteaux

English-born, Christopher Brooks' background incorporates a blend of classical French training, and experience in English country inns and Relais & Châteaux establishments in England and the USA. Brooks returned to Blantyre in March, 2000 as Chef de Cuisine after his time at Relais & Châteaux properties on the East Coast and a previous stint as Sous Chef of Blantyre.

Brooks and his team have received recognition from *Zagat, Condé Nast Traveler Gold List, Travel & Leisure* to name a few. An important part of the team is Chef de Cuisine, Arnaud Cotar, who is from a family of French chefs. He trained at Relais & Châteaux properties in Europe and is a partner in the creation of Blantyre's award-winning dishes.

Brooks enjoys discovering effective combinations. "Food should be fun, though delivered with a proper respect for performance and presentation. As far as I'm concerned, my staff and I are on stage whenever someone enters the restaurant. There is the same demand for a combination of show and substance that the audience demands of great theater."

Blantyre

Located halfway between Boston and New York City this beautiful country house hotel is nestled amid 115 acres of lawn and woodlands.

Blantyre boasts a renowned cuisine and exceptional wine cellar and The Main House, Carriage House and four cottages are reminiscent of a gentler time of elegance and romance. This stately Tudor house was built in 1902 and is resplendent with luxurious guest rooms. The intimate, full treatment spa is connected to the Carriage House, a few minutes walk from the Tudor style Main House. This enchanting resort has activities galore, including tennis and croquet in the Summer. In the Winter, the property offers a Winter wonderland with ice skating, snowshoeing, sleigh riding and a Christmas tree 100 feet high.

CAPE DIVER SCALLOPS WITH CRUSHED AVOCADO & CITRUS SALAD

BY CHRISTOPHER BROOKS

A crisp Summer dish. A citrusy base enhanced by the addition of another layer of flavor – vanilla, then sweet scallops – all topped with peppery watercress.

Serves 4-6
Preparation time: 30 minutes
Cooking time: 6 hours to infuse and 6 minutes to cook

INGREDIENTS

citrus salad:

1 pink grapefruit
2 oranges
1 lemon
1 lime
½ tsp sugar
¼ vanilla bean

crushed avocado:

1 large ripe avocado, peeled and pitted
salt & pepper, to taste

scallops:

2 tsp olive oil
12 large diver scallops, dry

to serve:

1 bunch of watercress, washed and picked over

METHOD

citrus salad:

Over a bowl to catch the juice, peel the grapefruit, oranges, lemon and lime. Cut the citrus fruits into segments, making sure no pith or coarse membrane remains. Take 2-3 tablespoons of the collected juice from the bowl and combine with the sugar in a small saucepan. Reserve the remaining juice for the avocados. Scrape out the vanilla seeds from the bean and add them to the mixture. Cook over a moderate heat to make a syrup. Pour this over the citrus segments and allow to cool in the fridge for 6 hours so the vanilla infuses the fruit.

crushed avocado:

Just before serving, crush the avocado with 2 tablespoons of the reserved citrus salad juice and season to taste with salt and pepper.

scallops:

Heat the olive oil in a large frying pan over a high heat. When it shimmers, add the scallops. Let them sear without moving them for 2-3 minutes or until a deep, golden brown. Turn and sear the other side for 2-3 minutes until golden.

to serve:

While the scallops are cooking, assemble the salad by placing some crushed avocado in the center of four to six plates. Top with the citrus salad and then the watercress. Finally add the scallops. Serve immediately.

Chef's tip:

This dish is also very good prepared with grilled chicken breast. Save the orange and grapefruit peels to make confit at a later time.

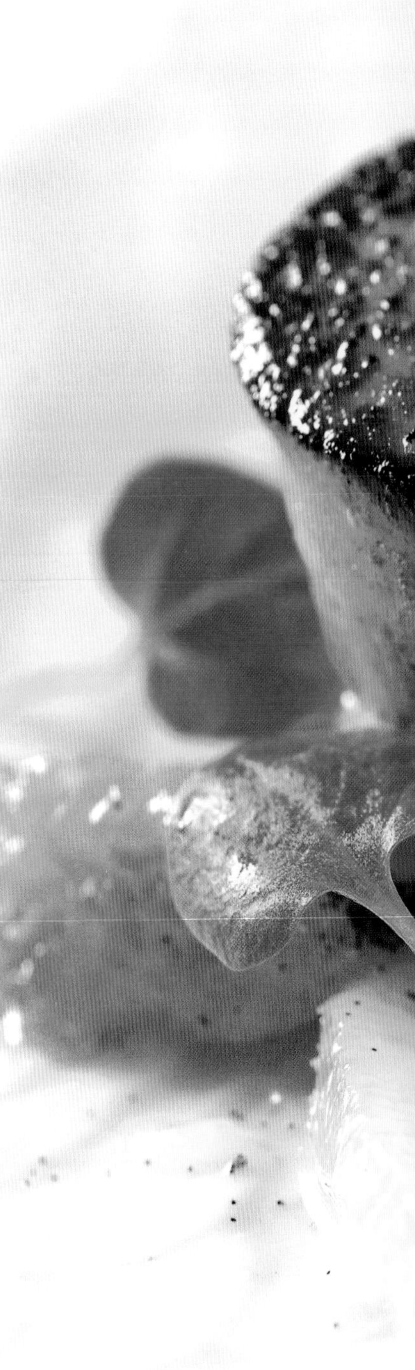

RACK OF LAMB WITH MORELS, PEAS & CHICKPEA PANISSES

BY CHRISTOPHER BROOKS

Serves 4 to 6

Preparation time:	1 hour 30 minutes + 1 hour lamb resting time
Cooking time:	45 minutes

Special equipment:
Four to six 4 oz ramekins

Planning ahead:
The chickpea panisse batter can be cooked a day in advance. The lamb rack should be prepared 1 hour in advance of cooking

INGREDIENTS

mint hollandaise:

2	egg yolks
1 tbsp	lemon juice
1 tsp	water
5 oz	unsalted butter, cut into 20 pieces
salt & white pepper to taste	
2 tsp	finely chopped young mint leaves (or more to taste)

chickpea panisses:

1¼ cups	chickpea (besan) flour
2 cups	water
1 tbsp	olive oil
1 tbsp	lemon thyme, chopped
¼	clove garlic, crushed
salt & pepper to taste	
10	black olives, pitted and coarsely chopped
¼ cup	cornmeal

rack of lamb

2	French-trimmed lamb racks
salt & pepper, to taste	
2	small garlic cloves, sliced into thin strips
¼ tsp	rosemary leaves
3 tbsp	olive oil
1 tbsp	unsalted butter
4 oz	morels or baby bella mushrooms, cleaned
1 cup	blanched peas

A dish of contrasts – the distinct flavor of the lamb blends with the earthiness of the morels and the slight crispiness of the creamy-centered panisses, finished with refreshing mint.

METHOD

mint hollandaise:

Fill the bottom of a double boiler with a couple of inches of water. Set it over a low heat and assemble the pot. Add the egg yolks, lemon juice and water and whisk until the yolks thicken. Take care not to splash the yolks too much up the side of the bowl where the heat could make them crusty and useless. When the mixture is hot and thick enough to coat the back of a spoon, add in 1 piece of butter over a very low heat, (be sure to do this before the eggs get too hot and begin to scramble. Should they seem to be coagulating, quickly remove them from the heat and whisk in a tablespoon of cold water until the mixture reconstitutes). When the first piece of butter has been absorbed, add another. Continue in this way, keeping the heat low and stirring in the butter pieces one at a time until they are used up and you have a thick sauce. Season the mixture with salt and white pepper. Taste and add more salt and pepper if needed, plus a few more drops of lemon juice if you want a tarter tang. Remove from the heat and stir in the finely chopped mint.

chickpea panisses:

Oil the base and sides of four to six ramekins with olive oil. Sift the flour to remove any little lumps and set aside.

In a medium saucepan, bring the water to the boil. When it is bubbling, add the olive oil, thyme, garlic, salt and pepper to taste. As soon as the water returns to the boil, add the chickpea flour, whisking continuously so the mixture thickens into a smooth batter. This takes only a minute. If by mischance the batter is lumpy, whiz it in a food processor to smooth it out. Stir in the olives.

Divide the mixture between the ramekins, patting the batter into the bottom and smoothing the tops. Let it cool. (You can proceed to this point ahead of time and complete the cooking of the panisses when the lamb racks are in the oven.)

To finish the panisses, preheat the oven to 350°F and line a baking sheet with parchment paper. Sprinkle the cornmeal on a plate. Unmold the panisses from the ramekins and press each side into the cornmeal to lightly coat it. Sear them for a couple of minutes on each side in a lightly oiled nonstick pan. Remove to the baking sheet and bake for 5 minutes.

rack of lamb:

Rub the fat of the lamb racks with salt and season lightly with pepper. Using the point of a sharp knife, make incisions in the fat and into the meat; then insert a sliver of garlic and rosemary leaves into each slit. Cover and leave to rest for 1 hour.

Preheat the oven to 400°F. Grease a roasting pan with olive oil. Trickle a little olive oil over the lamb and place in a roasting pan. Bake for 25 minutes, then remove from the oven and leave to rest in a warm spot near the stove, covered with a cloth.

Heat the butter with a teaspoon of olive oil in a frying pan. Toss in the mushrooms, season them lightly with salt and sauté for 4-5 minutes or until any liquid has evaporated and the mushrooms are browned and tender. During the last minute or so, toss in the peas. Season with salt and pepper to taste.

to serve:

Divide the rack of lamb into chops and place a panisse, some olives and mushroom-pea mixture with each chop. Serve the mint hollandaise on the side.

Chef's tip:

Look for besan in specialty grocery stores selling Indian or Mediterranean products.

Serves 8
Preparation time: 40 minutes
Cooking time: 45 to 55 minutes

Planning ahead:
The dates will take up to 2 hours to cool down.

INGREDIENTS

cake:

3 cups all purpose flour
2 tsp baking powder
8 oz chopped dates
1½ cups boiling water
2 tsp baking soda
½ lb/2 sticks unsalted butter
1½ cups sugar
4 eggs

toffee sauce:

2 cups dark brown sugar
2 cups whipping cream
2 oz/½ stick unsalted butter

STICKY TOFFEE PUDDING

BY CHRISTOPHER BROOKS

Serve only on very special occasions. "A minute on the lips; forever on the hips."

METHOD

cake:

Preheat the oven to 350°F. Grease a 9" square baking pan and line the bottom with parchment paper. In a small bowl, mix the flour and baking powder.

Put the dates into a small saucepan and pour on the boiling water. Simmer for 5-8 minutes or until completely soft. Stir in the baking soda and leave to cool to room temperature.

In a large bowl, or the bowl of an electric mixer, cream the butter and sugar until pale and fluffy. Mix in one of the eggs. When thoroughly blended, mix in a second egg with a tablespoon of the flour mixture. Add the remaining 2 eggs, one at a time, adding 1 tablespoon of flour with each and mixing well after each one. Thoroughly blend in the remaining flour mixture and then gently mix in the dates and their liquid. Pour into the prepared pan. Bake in the center of the oven for 45-55 minutes. Test for readiness by inserting a toothpick or skewer into the center. If it comes out clean, remove the cake from the oven.

toffee sauce:

Put the sugar, cream and butter into a saucepan and stir over a gentle heat until the butter has melted and the sugar is dissolved. Increase the heat and simmer for a couple of minutes.

to serve:

Turn on the broiler. With a skewer, make some holes in the warm cake and pour over enough sauce to cover the top and run into the holes. Place the cake under the broiler just until it sizzles. Cut into squares and dish up immediately. Pour on more sauce, reheated if necessary. Offer the remaining sauce at the table. Serve with ice cream or whipped cream.

Chef's tip:

When the cake with the sauce on top is under the broiler, watch it very carefully to make sure it doesn't scorch; let it just sizzle.

Thomas Henkelmann
Grand Chef Relais & Châteaux

"Like a painter interprets a landscape, I cook my interpretation of French food. It is my passion and my life." Critically acclaimed for his 'flawless French food', Thomas Henkelmann's contemporary French cuisine is inspired by the distinct line drawn through the Black Forest in Germany, Alsace and Paris in France, to New York and Connecticut in America. Classical French training with the renowned Auberge de L'Ill in Alsace and Aubergine in Munich, his German background and time spent in New York City as Executive Chef of Maurice restaurant at Le Parker Meridien, and his individual journey, resulted in a very personal vision. Chefs Paul and Marc Haeberlin of Auberge de L'Ill marked his food and his life. They imbued their respect for preserving purity and subtlety on the plate. The esteem in which he holds his profession is a direct result of their passionate regard for professionalism and refinement.

His eponymous restaurant Thomas Henkelmann opened in 1997. He is now a Relais & Châteaux Grand Chef, and is lauded as 'Extraordinary' by the *New York Times*.

Thomas Henkelmann
- Homestead Inn

The Homestead Inn is a beautiful 18th century Victorian manor house situated near the waters of Long Island and Thomas Henkelmann is the most French of German chefs.

Born in the Black Forest, this devotee of French gastronomy learned his trade in Alsace before moving his pots and pans to Connecticut. Inspired by his travels, each of his recipes makes a veiled reference to his origins. Thomas Henkelmann likes to break down boundaries between products and to create surprising combinations, such as his champagne sauerkraut accompanied by a seafood mousseline. His partner Theresa – an interior designer – has turned this hotel into a setting worthy of his cooking by creating a European atmosphere inspired by Balinese and Chinese styles. This must be Greenwich's most tasteful address.

NAPOLEON OF ATLANTIC HALIBUT WITH SALMON TARTARE & ONION COMPOTE

BY THOMAS HENKELMANN

A festive, elegant and eye pleasing dish, perfect for entertaining your palate and your friends.

Serves 10
Preparation time: 45 minutes
Cooking time: 1 hour

INGREDIENTS

2½ lb halibut fillet, cut into rectangles 3" x 5" and ⅕" thick (30 slices)
1 lb salmon fillet cut into small cubes
½ lemon
salt & pepper

marinade:

1½ oz shallots, finely diced
1½ oz small non-pareil capers
½ oz extra virgin olive oil
½ oz basil leaves, julienne
salt, freshly ground white pepper and freshly ground coriander

onion compote:

¾ lb sweet local onions, sliced
2 oz sweet cream butter
1½ oz Champagne vinegar
½ oz blossom honey
salt & pepper, to taste
½ qt water

creamed spinach:

1 lb fresh spinach, cleaned, finely chopped and blanched
2 oz sweet cream butter
2 oz shallots, peeled and finely diced
4 pieces of salted anchovy fillet, very finely diced
4 oz heavy cream
salt & pepper, to taste

sauce mousseline reduction: (makes extra)

1 cup Champagne vinegar
1 cup dry white wine
1 cup water
2 oz shallots, peeled and sliced
⅓ oz black peppercorns
1 oz fresh tarragon

sauce mousseline:

2 egg yolks
3 oz mousseline reduction
2 oz clarified butter, warm
1½ oz heavy cream, whipped
salt, pepper and cayenne, to taste

tomato fondue:

8 beefsteak red or yellow tomatoes
2 shallots, brunoise
extra virgin olive oil
bouquet garni of basil stems, garlic clove and pepper corns wrapped in cheesecloth
butter or olive oil
salt & finely ground pepper

garnish:

yellow heirloom tomato fondue
basil flowers

METHOD

marinade:

Combine all the ingredients and marinate the salmon for 10 minutes to make a tartare.

onion compote:

Bring the water, Champagne vinegar and butter to a boil. Add the sliced onions and simmer on a low heat for approximately 1 hour. Once the liquid is almost syrupy add the honey, and salt and pepper to taste. Remove from the heat and refrigerate.

assembling the Napoleon:

Place the first layer of the cut halibut fillet on a small piece of parchment paper brushed with olive oil. Touch it with half a lemon, salt and pepper. Evenly spread out the onion compote and top with the second layer of halibut fillet. Now evenly spread the marinated salmon tartare on top of the second fillet. Place a third halibut fillet on top. Refrigerate.

creamed spinach:

Warm the butter, then add the shallots and anchovies. Sweat without giving any color. Add the cream and reduce to half. Finally, add the spinach and season to taste.

sauce mousseline reduction:

Combine all the ingredients and bring to a boil. Simmer at low heat for 20 minutes. Strain and store in the refrigerator.

sauce mousseline:

Mix the egg yolks with the reduction and whisk over a hot water bath until it reaches a sabayon-like consistency. Add the warm clarified butter and the whipped cream. Strain and season to taste. Keep in a warm place.

tomato fondue:

Blanch, peel and seed the tomatoes. Place the seeds and pulp in a chinois set over a bowl to catch the tomato water. Sweat the shallots in a little oil until translucent. Add the bouquet garni. Dice the tomatoes into ½" cubes and add to the shallots. Cook slowly over a low heat until most of the liquid has evaporated. Reduce the tomato water to a quarter and add it to the tomatoes at the end of the cooking time. Finish with a little butter or olive oil. Season with salt and pepper.

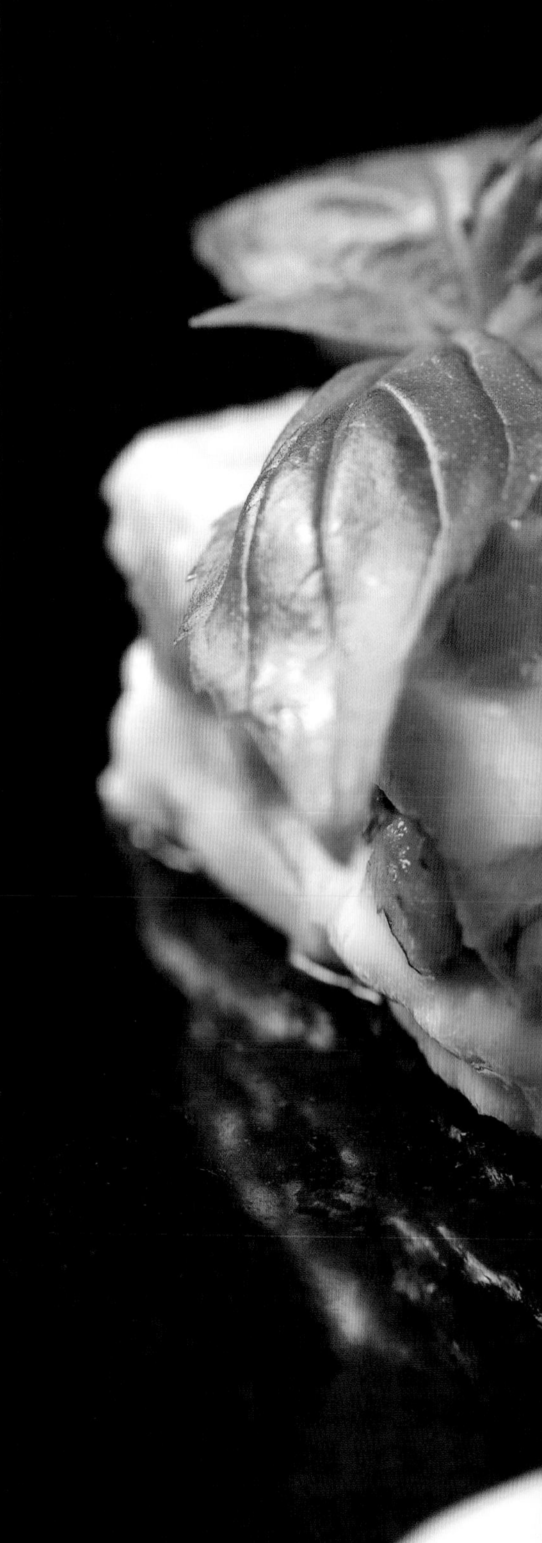

to serve:

When ready to cook preheat the oven to 400°F. On a baking pan place a sheet of parchment paper and sprinkle it with about 1 tablespoon of water. Carefully place the Napoleon of halibut on the parchment and place in the oven to bake for 8-11 minutes.

Using a 4" ring place the creamed spinach in the center of the plate to about ½" height in the ring. Remove the ring from the creamed spinach and place the Napoleon of halibut in the center. Top with the tomato fondue and surround the halibut and creamed spinach with sauce mousseline. Garnish the tomato fondue with a basil flower.

OVEN BAKED LOIN OF RABBIT WITH FOIE GRAS

BY THOMAS HENKELMANN

Luxurious textures and a sophisticated alchemy of flavors blend to entice each sense of the palate.

Serves 4
Preparation time: 30 minutes
Cooking time: 15 minutes

Special equipment:
Mandoline

Planning ahead:
Have your butcher prepare the rabbit with the loins attached to the tenderloin.

INGREDIENTS

loin of rabbit:

1 lb rabbit saddle
2½ oz Hudson Valley duck foie gras
salt & freshly ground pepper
¼ oz extra virgin olive oil

artichoke purée:

2 medium-sized artichoke hearts (reserve the bottoms for the chips)
1 shallot, sliced
1 oz dry white wine
¼ oz unsalted butter
bouquet garni
salt & freshly ground pepper
¼ oz extra virgin olive oil

artichoke chips:

4 artichoke bottoms
vegetable oil
salt

vinaigrette:

½ oz dried raisins
½ oz pine nuts
¼ oz capers
½ oz extra virgin olive oil
¼ oz balsamic vinegar
salt & pepper

to serve:

baby bok choy

METHOD

loin of rabbit:

Preheat the oven to 400°F. Remove the two loins and two tenderloins from the rabbit saddle with the flanks attached. Trim the flanks to approximately 2½" in length. Cut the foie gras in two strips matching the loin of rabbit. Season the foie gras with salt and pepper, and sear it in a very hot frying pan for 3-4 seconds. Set in a cool place. Spread out the loins of rabbits with the flanks attached. Set the tenderloins of rabbit on top of the smaller part of the rabbit loin and the seared, cooled foie gras slightly next to the loin. Wrap the flank around the loin and secure with butcher's string. Heat a frying pan with the olive oil and sear quickly on three sides and turn on to the unseared side. Place the frying pan into the oven and cook for 8-10 minutes.

artichoke purée:

Using a small pot sweat the shallot in the olive oil until tender (not colored). Add the artichoke hearts and the dry white wine. Cover the pot and steam the artichoke with only the white wine for 3-4 minutes, add water just to cover the artichokes and add the bouquet garni. Season with a little salt and pepper and cook until tender. Remove from the liquid and steam dry the artichokes in a warm place for a few minutes. Purée the artichoke hearts with butter until smooth, and then push through a sieve.

artichoke chips:

Thinly slice the artichoke bottoms using a mandoline, then fry in vegetable oil until crisp and drain on a paper towel. Salt lightly.

vinaigrette:

Toast the pine nuts in a dry sauté pan then deglaze and lightly reduce with the balsamic vinegar. Whisk the olive oil into the balsamic vinegar reduction to emulsify. Season to taste with salt and pepper and add the raisins and capers. Keep warm.

to serve:

Form a small circle with the bok choy. Slice the rabbit roulade into three same-sized pieces and arrange them evenly around the bok choy. Create three teaspoon-size quenelles of artichoke purée and arrange them between the rabbit slices. Place one artichoke chip on each quenelle like a sail. Spoon a small amount of the vinaigrette around the outer edge of the rabbit and artichoke.

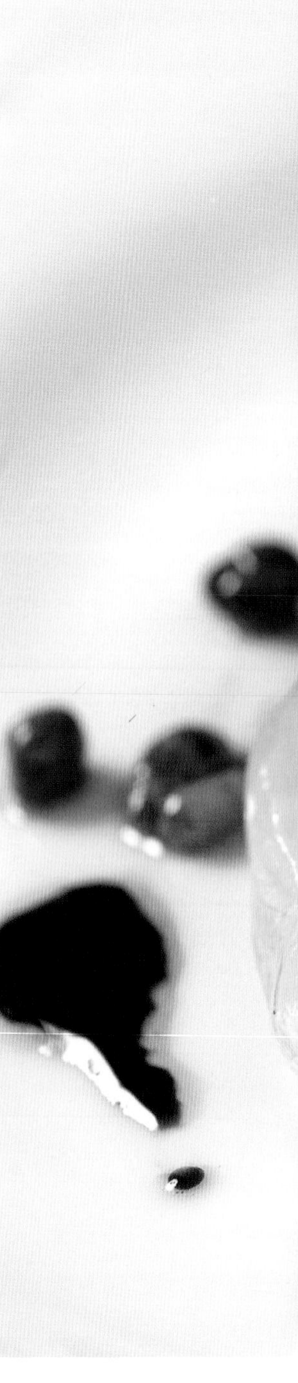

SEMOLINA SOUFFLE WITH CHOCOLATE SORBET, ORANGE SEGMENTS & ORANGE GRAND MARNIER SAUCE

BY THOMAS HENKELMANN

Goldilocks would proclaim this mouthwatering dessert "just right" for a perfect ending to a perfect meal.

Serves 4-6
Preparation time: 20 minutes
Cooking time: 10-12 minutes

Special equipment:
Ice cream maker

INGREDIENTS

soufflé:

8 oz	milk
1½ oz	butter
2 oz	semolina
3	egg yolks
3	egg whites
1 oz	granulated sugar
1	pinch of lemon zest
1	pinch of freshly grated ginger

orange segments and Grand Marnier sauce:

2	Navel oranges, peeled and segmented
2 oz	freshly squeezed orange juice
1 oz	Grand Marnier
½ oz	granulated sugar

chocolate sorbet:

20 oz	water
4 oz	dark chocolate (70% cocoa content)
4 oz	granulated sugar
1½ oz	cocoa powder
½	Bourbon Vanilla bean cut in half and scraped out
3½ oz	trimoline or inverted sugar

to serve:

powdered sugar

METHOD

soufflé:

Preheat the oven to 430°F. Butter and sugar coat four to six individual soufflé forms. Bring the milk and butter to a boil and add the semolina while stirring with a wooden spatula until it reaches a firm consistency. Place the base into a mixing bowl and add the egg yolks, lemon zest and ginger, mixing well. Whisk the egg whites with the sugar until firm. Fold into the semolina base. Fill each soufflé form to three-quarters full. Place the filled forms in a hot water bath and place in the oven for approximately 10-12 minutes.

orange segments and Grand Marnier sauce:

Squeeze the pulp from the segmented oranges into a saucepan holding the fresh orange juice. Add the sugar and reduce to half over a medium-high heat. Add the Grand Marnier. Set aside.

chocolate sorbet:

Bring the water with the scraped vanilla bean, the sugar and trimoline/inverted sugar to a boil. Remove from the heat and mix in the chocolate and the cocoa powder. Strain and freeze the sorbet mix in an ice cream maker.

to serve:

Place the orange segments in the center of a dessert plate, spoon some Grand Marnier sauce over the segments. Place a scoop of the sorbet next to the orange segments and finish by placing the unmolded soufflé on top of the segments in the center of the plate. Sprinkle with powdered sugar and serve immediately.

onathan Cartwright

Grand Chef Relais & Châteaux

Originally from Yorkshire, England, Jonathan Cartwright brings to New England an nternational sensibility and mastery of cuisine gained while serving some of the world's finest Relais & Châteaux properties, ncluding Blantyre, the Horned Dorset Primavera, and the Hotel Bareiss. "My menu creations are influenced by a love of European-style cooking acquired from my experiences. This is fused with the many culinary and cultural inspirations of my home for the last 15 years, coastal Maine."

The cuisine of The White Barn Inn & Spa is the finest contemporary New England cuisine with a European flair. Chef Cartwright uses as many local ingredients as possible, highlighting seafood from Kennebunkport waters as well as native game and poultry. He adapts traditional recipes and presents them using classical European techniques and style. "The team is the most important ingredient in the restaurant business; as a child I dreamt of winning the Tour de France and now I see similarities between running a high class kitchen/restaurant and leading a team in the Tour de France, with its many challenges each day."

The White Barn
Inn & Spa

Jonathan Cartwright is a respected and dedicated chef, who has turned the White Barn Inn into a great place to eat as well as a peaceful, elegant place to stay and a unique center of relaxation.

As a young boy he wanted to be a cyclist and win the 'Tour de France'. But, at the age of 15, he discovered cooking and became more interested in wearing a white apron than the yellow jersey. "Cooking requires the same determination as cycling, the same effort and the same team spirit," says this passionate perfectionist. Above all, Jonathan values the quality of his products and he can tell you the life story of the fresh Kennebunkport lobster, star of his menu, from its birth to the moment it arrives in his kitchen. To be savored as it is or in a bisque or a cognac sauce, among the other creations inspired by local produce.

PAN-SEARED MAINE DAY BOAT SCALLOPS ON CELERIAC PUREE, CELERIAC LOBSTER RAGOUT & COGNAC-CORAL-BUTTER SAUCE

BY JONATHAN CARTWRIGHT

Many of our popular dishes feature the abundance of local seafood and the famed Maine lobster. This dish was created to highlight the sweet local scallops and succulent lobster paired with the earthiness of the celeriac.

Serves 4
Preparation time: 1 hour 30 minutes
Cooking time: 8 minutes

INGREDIENTS

scallops:

4 10 scallops, day boat or diver harvested
2 tbsp 10% blended oil

celeriac lobster ragout:

1 tbsp olive oil
½ shallot, finely diced
½ lb celeriac, diced
2 tbsp butter
½ cup heavy cream
2 oz cooked lobster meat, cubed
1 pinch of chopped mixed herbs - chives, tarragon, and parsley
salt & pepper

cognac-coral-butter sauce:

½ cup heavy cream
¼ cup cognac
½ cup Muscat, Essencia or a similar sweet white wine
½ cup lobster stock
½ lb unsalted butter, cold and diced
1 tbsp lobster coral
½ lemon, juice
salt, pepper & cayenne pepper

celeriac purée: (yields ½ cup)

1 lb celeriac, peeled
½ cup milk
water
1 tbsp butter
salt & pepper

garnish:

micro greens
4 fried celeriac chips

METHOD

celeriac lobster ragout:

Sweat the shallot in the olive oil for 2 minutes over a medium heat, add the celeriac, then the butter and reduce the heat to slowly cook the celeriac for 3 more minutes. Add the cream and gently cook for 2 minutes more, season to taste, add the herbs and the diced lobster.

cognac-coral-butter sauce:

In a thick bottomed pan reduce the cream, cognac, Muscat and lobster stock by three-quarters, to a total of ¼ cup. Whisk in the butter and lobster coral and season to taste with salt, pepper, cayenne, and lemon juice, strain and keep in a warm place.

celeriac purée:

Cut the celeriac into 1" cubes. In a pan use half of the milk and enough water to cover the celeriac. Add a pinch of salt and boil until tender. Strain the celeriac and purée in a food processor. Boil the remaining milk and the butter together, add the purée of celeriac, mix to a smooth paste and season to taste.

to serve:

Season the scallops and sear in hot oil for 2 minutes on each side. When they are cooked, drain on kitchen towel. In a bowl make a swirl of the celeriac purée; place a mound of the lobster ragout next to the thick part of the swirl. Add a swirl of the cognac-coral-butter sauce, going in the opposite direction, on the other side of the bowl, forming a yin-yang effect with the celeriac lobster ragout in the middle. Place a seared scallop on top of the ragout, a fried celeriac chip on top and sprinkle some micro greens around the bowl for garnish.

PAN ROAST NEW ENGLAND PHEASANT BREAST WITH MUSHROOM & CRANBERRY PUREES, BRAISED RED CABBAGE & MADEIRA SAUCE

BY JONATHAN CARTWRIGHT

Game bird is used often on menus in and throughout Europe. This is an example of how the White Barn Inn uses a local farmed pheasant and presents it with European flair. The dish consists of tart New England cranberries balanced with the creaminess of the mushroom purée, and the red cabbage gives the dish a richness of color and texture.

Serves 4

Preparation time: 3 hours

Cooking time: 15 minutes

Planning ahead:

Both the braised cabbage and the Madeira sauce can be made a day in advance.

INGREDIENTS

pheasant:

4 pheasant breasts
1 tbsp blended oil
Maine sea salt & fresh white pepper
1 tbsp butter

braised red cabbage: (makes 6 portions)

1 head of red cabbage, thinly sliced
1 onion, sliced
½ cup sherry vinegar
1 cup red wine
3 tbsp honey
1 sprig of thyme, chopped
Maine sea salt & fresh white pepper
2 tbsp butter

mushroom and cranberry purées:

6 shallots
2 tbsp butter
1 cup mixed mushrooms (eg. button, oyster, cepes, chanterelles), chopped
½ cup heavy cream
½ cup cranberries
Maine sea salt & fresh white pepper

Madeira sauce:

½ cup vegetables (eg. onion, celery, carrot, leek), diced
1 clove garlic
2 tbsp butter
1 sprig of thyme, chopped
6 black peppercorns
1 cup veal jus
½ cup port wine
¼ cup Madeira

garnish:

Brussels sprout leaves, blanched
crispy sweet potato chips

METHOD

braised red cabbage:

Pour the vinegar, red wine and honey over the cabbage. Season with salt and pepper and add the chopped thyme. Leave to marinate for at least 12 hours.

Melt the butter in a pan, add the onion and sweat for 5 minutes on a low heat until transparent. Add the marinated cabbage and bring to a boil. Once the cabbage boils, cover with a lid and braise in a 300°F oven for 3 hours.

Check for taste and adjust the seasoning if needed.

mushroom and cranberry purées:

Dice 1 shallot and sweat it in 1 tablespoon of butter for 3 minutes over a medium heat. Add the mushrooms and continue to sweat for 2 minutes then season, cover the pan with a lid and continue cooking until the mushrooms are soft. Purée in a blender until smooth, add a ¼ cup of cream, season to taste and pass through a fine sieve.

Slice the remaining shallots and, in 1 tablespoon of butter, sweat them until tender. Add the cranberries and cook for 5 minutes. Purée in a blender until smooth, add a ¼ cup of cream, season with salt and pass through a fine sieve.

Madeira sauce:

Sweat the vegetables and garlic in the butter on a medium heat, cook for 3-4 minutes. Add the thyme, peppercorns, port wine and Madeira, increase the heat and reduce by half. Add the veal jus, then simmer and reduce enough to coat the back of a spoon, season to taste and strain.

pheasant:

Heat a frying pan and add the blended oil, season the pheasant breasts and sear them skin side down until golden brown. Turn the breasts, reduce the heat to medium and add the butter, then cook the breast until pink in the center, 5 minutes a side.

to serve:

Warm the braised cabbage, and the cranberry and mushroom purées. Place the cabbage in the center of a plate, drag the purées on each side and place the pheasant breast on top of the cabbage. Spoon some of the Madeira sauce around the pheasant. Garnish with blanched Brussels sprout leaves and crispy sweet potato chips.

Serves 4
Preparation time: 2 hours
Cooking time: 50 minutes

Special equipment:
Propane torch, ice cream machine

INGREDIENTS

chocolate crème brûlée:

2 cups heavy cream
½ cup sugar
10 egg yolks
1½ cups milk chocolate, melted

sauce Anglais:

3 oranges, juice and zest
2 cups cream
10 egg yolks
½ cup sugar

orange sherbet:

2 cups whole milk
¾ cup sugar
3 oranges, juice and zest

tuile:

1¼ cups sugar
2 cups all purpose flour
1¼ cups melted butter
¾ cup egg whites, warmed

to serve:

sugar
chocolate pieces
segments of orange

MILK CHOCOLATE CREME BRULEE WITH ORANGE SHERBET

BY JONATHAN CARTWRIGHT

With the collaboration of my Sous Chef and Executive Pastry Chef Derek Bissonnette, we created this presentation of crème brûlée. More often classical crème brûlée is cooked and served in individual ramekins. Our version is cooked in a larger pan, and cut out into portions. This provides more opportunity for different presentations. This recipe, however, can be applied to a classical presentation and prepared in individual ramekins.

The sherbet in this recipe and the garnish of orange segments are meant to cut through the richness of the crème brûlée. The light tuile is designed to give crispy texture. Eating all of these together should give a nice balance of sweet, tart and crunch.

METHOD

chocolate crème brûlée:

Boil the cream and sugar together. Once it boils, slowly add one-third of the mix to the beaten egg yolks and then slowly add the remainder of the mix, whisking constantly (tempering). Once the yolks are tempered, return them to a clean pan and cook until the mixture coats the back of a wooden spoon. Do not boil this custard mixture or the eggs will scramble.

While the egg custard is still hot, add the chocolate and stir until melted. Pour this mix into a baking pan and cook in a water bath in a 210°F oven for 45-50 minutes, checking that it is set evenly through the tray.

sauce Anglais:

Boil the orange juice and continue to reduce until it becomes a paste. Add the cream, sugar and the zest, bring to a boil, remove from the heat and infuse the flavor for 10 minutes. Strain and return to the boil. Once boiling, slowly add one-third of the mix to the beaten egg yolks and then slowly add the remainder, whisking constantly (tempering). Once the yolks are tempered return them to a clean pan and cook the mixture, stirring continuously until it coats the back of a wooden spoon. Do not boil this custard mixture or the eggs will scramble.

orange sherbet:

Boil the milk with the zest and sugar, then cool, and add the juice (it is important to cool the milk or the acidity in the juice will curdle it). Spin in an ice cream machine, until it is hard enough to scoop. Follow the directions on your individual ice cream machine.

tuile:

Mix the melted butter and egg whites together, add the sugar and then the flour. This can be done by hand, with a whisk and a wooden spoon, or in a mixer with the paddle attachment. Spread out on a silpat mat and cut into eight circles using a spatula and a plastic disk (a disk can be cut from an old plastic container lid – it should be ½" bigger than the cutter used for the brûlée) then in half while still uncooked. Cook at 225°F, until set. Allow to cool before lifting the half disks from the silpat mat with a pallet knife.

to serve:

Cut three rounds of the crème brûlée out of the pan, with a cutter. Cut down the center in half, stand on the flat side and cut in half to form half disks (see photograph). Sprinkle the curved side of the half disks with sugar and caramelize the tops of the crème brûlée using a propane torch. Place a tuile on each side of the brûlée half disks, slide another crème brûlée half disk next to the tuile, add another tuile and then a third piece of crème brûlée finishing with a tuile. Garnish with chocolate pieces and segments of orange. Finish with the orange sauce Anglais and a scoop of sherbet.

onathan Cambra

n his early 30s, Executive Chef Jonathan ̄ambra has already achieved much success n his culinary career – the culmination of vhich is his current position as Executive Chef at Castle Hill Inn & Resort. However, it is not ıge that sets Jon apart in his field; rather it s his continuous passion for excellence and reativity that defines this young talent.

Garnering much of his inspiration and passion for the industry through his time spent at the renowned New England Culinary nstitute, Jon hit the ground running upon graduation, embarking on his professional career by cooking in some of the best local and regional restaurants where he rapidly rose through the ranks in the kitchen.

Today, Chef Cambra is regularly invited with his team to participate at such prestigious culinary arenas as the James Beard House in New York. Under his leadership, the property has received numerous accolades and attention from local, regional and national culinary media.

Jon leads Castle Hill's talented culinary n forward with his vision of sustainable agriculture, locally-purchased ingredients, and organic first. Drawing on his Portuguese roots, on continues Castle Hill's tradition of subtle Mediterranean spices and influences in his dishes. In the Winter months, guests can look forward to enjoying heartier, rustic foods and in the Spring and Summer, Jon's menu will change to lighter, local dishes abundant with select meats, local produce, seafood and fish dishes.

Castle Hill
Inn & Resort

You will always have a panoramic view of the deep blue of the Atlantic when you are at this magnificent resort, whether you are in your suite, relaxing on the terrace or sitting at a table in the restaurant.

Set in 16 hectares of grounds bordering the ocean, this hotel is a romantic haven of well-being. For a long time, this extraordinarily beautiful stretch of the ocean was the theater for America's Cup regattas. Local and regional cuisine plus exceptional wines are on the menu. Guests can also discover Newport, a magnet for music lovers from around the world, with its two festivals devoted to jazz and folk music.

AQUIDNECK FARMS' BEEF SHANK TERRINE, POACHED EGG, BRIOCHE TOAST, BLACK TRUFFLE, SHERRY-BANYULS REDUCTION

BY JONATHAN CAMBRA

Inspired by the local food movement, Castle Hill's Beef Terrine features beef from Aquidneck Farms in Middletown. The beef is 100% grass-fed, and the poached egg that accompanies this rich and succulent dish is also from a local farm.

Serves 6-8
Preparation time: 1 hour
Cooking time: 3-4 hours

Special equipment:
Large rondeau

Planning ahead:
The terrine should be made the day before and refrigerated overnight.

INGREDIENTS

beef shank terrine:

8 beef shanks
oil
kosher salt
cracked black pepper
1 onion, chopped
½ carrot, chopped
½ celery stick, chopped
5 garlic cloves
4 bay leaves
½ gal veal stock
½ gal chicken stock
½ bunch of thyme
2 tbsp black peppercorns
1 bottle red wine
2 cups port wine
salt & pepper

sherry-Banyuls reduction:

2 onions, chopped
4 garlic cloves
1 bottle sherry wine
¼ bunch of thyme
2 bay leaves
1 tbsp black peppercorns
1 bottle Banyuls vinegar
1 gal chicken stock
1 qt braising liquid from beef shank terrine
kosher salt

to serve:

brioche
clarified butter
salt & pepper
flour
1 egg per serving
black truffle

METHOD

beef shank terrine:

Heat a large rondeau, and add oil. Heavily season the beef shanks with kosher salt and cracked black pepper. Once the oil is at smoking point, add the beef shanks and sear until dark brown on all sides, then remove from the pan.

Add the celery, carrot, onion, and garlic cloves. Cook over a high heat until the vegetables are caramelized, stirring often. Add the beef shanks back to the pan. Deglaze with the red wine and port, and allow to reduce by half. Add only enough veal stock and chicken stock to barely cover the shanks. Add thyme, peppercorns, and bay leaves. Bring to a simmer, and place uncovered in a 350°F oven. Cook until the meat is tender, about 2 hours. Once cooked, remove the meat from the pot, strain out the braising liquid, return to the stove and reduce by half.

Line a terrine mold with plastic wrap, with enough plastic left over to wrap the top once it's filled.

Pull the shank meat apart in large chunks, and put into a terrine mold, pressing it down lightly until the mold is filled.

Once the braising liquid is reduced, pour into the terrine until it just covers the meat. Wrap the top with plastic wrap. Place another terrine mold on top, and use weights to press the terrine. Refrigerate overnight. The next day, remove the terrine from the mold, and slice into desired portions.

sherry-Banyuls reduction:

In a pot, caramelize the onions and garlic. Deglaze with the sherry wine, add the bay leaves, thyme and peppercorns, and reduce by three-quarters. Add three-quarters of the bottle of Banyuls vinegar and reduce again until it's almost a syrup consistency. Add the chicken stock and braising liquid, and season with kosher salt. Reduce to a sauce consistency. Add the remaining Banyuls vinegar and re-season. Bring back to a boil, and then turn off the heat and leave to cool.

to serve:

Cut brioche to the same size as the sliced terrine. Brush with clarified butter, salt and pepper, and toast until golden brown.

Dust sliced terrine lightly with flour, and lightly sear on both sides. Finish in the oven until warmed through. While the terrine is cooking, poach an egg in lightly acidulated water.

On a plate, place brioche toast in the center and top with a slice of the beef terrine. Drizzle the top of the terrine with the sauce and add more around the plate. Place the poached egg on top of the slice of terrine. Place a few slices of black truffle on top of the egg.

ELYSIAN FIELDS' LAMB RACK & LAMB LEG PIE, SWISS CHARD, RED WINE DEMI-GLACE

BY JONATHAN CAMBRA

Castle Hill's Rack of Lamb meat is from Elysian Fields in Pennsylvania, where the lamb is raised holistically and humanely. We feel that it's the finest domestic lamb available.

Serves 4
Preparation time: 2 hours
Cooking time: 3-4 hours for braised lamb meat; 20-30 minutes for final cooking if the lamb pies are made in advance.

Special equipment:
3" ring mold, large rondeau

Planning ahead:
The lamb rack needs to marinade for 3-4 hours. The lamb pies can be made a day in advance.

INGREDIENTS

braised lamb for the pie:

½ cup canola oil
kosher salt & cracked black pepper, to taste
1 Elysian Fields whole, bone-in, lamb leg
1 Spanish onion, ½" pieces
½ carrot, ½" pieces
½ stick of celery, ½" pieces
5 garlic cloves, peeled
4 bay leaves
¼ oz fresh thyme
2 tbsp black peppercorns
1 bottle red wine, Cabernet
2 cups port wine
½ gal veal stock
½ gal chicken stock

lamb pie:

pie dough
1 cipollini onion, peeled, blanched, and quartered
1 carrot, medium diced and blanched
1 parsnip, medium diced and blanched
1 Yukon gold potato, medium diced and blanched
2 tbsp thyme, chopped
reserved lamb braising liquid
kosher salt & black pepper

red wine demi-glace: (yields ½ qt)

¼ Spanish onion, ½" pieces
¼ carrot, ½" pieces
⅕ stick of celery, ½" pieces
2 garlic cloves, peeled, left whole
1 bottle red wine, Cabernet
2 bay leaves
2 sprigs of thyme
4 black peppercorns
½ gal veal stock

8-bone lamb rack:

1 Elysian Fields' 8-bone lamb rack, Frenched and fat cap removed
2 tbsp canola oil
2 tbsp finely chopped herbs e.g. thyme, rosemary
kosher salt & cracked black pepper

to serve:
Swiss chard, sautéed

METHOD

braised lamb for the pie:

Heat a large rondeau, and add the oil. Heavily season the lamb leg with kosher salt and cracked black pepper. Once the oil is at smoking point, add the leg, and sear until dark brown on all sides, then remove from the pan. Add the celery, carrot, onion, and garlic cloves. Cook over a high heat until the vegetables are caramelized, stirring often. Add the lamb leg back to the pan. Deglaze with the red wine and port, and allow to reduce by half. Add only enough veal stock and chicken stock to barely cover the leg. Add the thyme, peppercorns, and bay leaves. Bring to a simmer, and place uncovered in a 300°F oven. Cook until the meat is tender, for about 3 hours, then remove from the pot and cool. Strain the braising liquid and reduce by half, then cool. Pull the meat off in large chunks and reserve.

lamb pie:

Preheat the oven to 350°F. Toss the braised lamb with the onion, carrot, parsnip, potato, and chopped thyme. Add enough braising liquid until it's just barely a wet consistency. Season with kosher salt and pepper.

Roll out the pie dough, and cut into two different size circles, 5" and 3" You will need four of each size. Place the 5" circles into 3" ring molds – it should come up right to the top of the mold. Cut off any excess dough. Fill with the lamb-vegetable mixture. Add about 1 oz of the braising liquid on top of the meat. Top with the 3" circles of pie dough, and use a fork to secure the top of the pie to the sides. Bake in the oven until golden brown. Cool down and reserve until needed. Reheat when the lamb rack is ready to serve.

red wine demi-glace:

In a pot, caramelize the onion, carrot, celery, and garlic. Deglaze with the red wine, add the bay leaves, thyme, and peppercorns, and reduce by three-quarters. Add the veal stock and reduce to a sauce consistency. Season if needed.

8-bone lamb rack:

Marinate the lamb in the freshly chopped herbs for 3-4 hours, then set aside. Preheat the oven to 450°F. Preheat a sauté pan, add the oil, season the lamb and place in the pan, sear on all sides until golden brown. Place in the oven and cook until medium rare, about 15-20 minutes.

to serve:

Slice the lamb between the bones and fan two chops onto each plate, serve with the lamb pie, sautéed Swiss chard and the red wine demi-glace.

ORANGE BLOSSOM SCENTED CREME FRAICHE PANNA COTTA, SPARKLING STRAWBERRY CONSOMME, VANILLA GENOISE CAKE, STRAWBERRY CHIPS

BY JONATHAN CAMBRA

Serves 10
Preparation time: 20-30 minutes
Cooking time: 45 minutes

Special equipment:
3 oz rubber molds

Planning ahead:
The strawberry consommé should be started three days before required. The panna cotta should be prepared the day before to set overnight. The strawberry chips may need to be prepared overnight.

A fresh and delicate dessert that uses local strawberries from Sweet Berry Farm. It has a creamy and elegant finish that makes for a light and refreshing finish at the height of the strawberry season.

INGREDIENTS:

panna cotta:

- 8 oz granulated sugar
- 4 oz whole milk
- 8½ oz heavy cream
- 2 oz cup buttermilk
- 1½ cups crème fraîche
- 1¾ tbsp gelatin powder
- orange blossom water to taste (1-2 tbsp)

Génoise cake:

- 14 eggs
- 8 egg yolks
- 2½ cups sugar
- 3½ cups cake flour
- 1 cup almond flour
- 1 tsp vanilla
- ¼ tsp salt

strawberry consommé:

- 2 gal strawberries, washed, stemmed, and quartered
- 1 bottle sweet white wine (Reisling or other)
- 1 qt water
- 1 cup sugar (more if needed)
- 2 lemons, zest and juice
- 2 oranges, zest and juice
- powdered gelatin, as needed

strawberry chips:

- 12 large, ripe strawberries, sliced in ¼" slices
- 1 lemon, juice
- 1 cup sugar
- 1 cup water

to serve:

- Champagne

METHOD

panna cotta:

Combine and heat the sugar, milk, cream, and buttermilk, do not allow to simmer. Remove from the heat, and stir in the crème fraîche. Bloom the gelatin in cold water, then add a little of the warm cream mixture to dissolve the gelatin, combine and stir thoroughly. Add orange blossom water to taste. Pour into 3 oz rubber molds, and chill overnight in a refrigerator.

Génoise cake:

Combine the eggs, yolks, and sugar in a large bowl. In a double boiler over a medium heat, whisk vigorously until ribbon stage and when it has at least doubled in volume. Remove from the heat, and whip the batter with an electric mixer until cool. It should thicken even more, and become pale yellow in color. Sift in the cake and almond flours, vanilla and salt. Fold together very carefully, and do not over mix. Line a sheet pan with parchment paper and a cake frame. Bake at 350°F until golden brown and a toothpick comes out clean when inserted. Cool and reserve.

strawberry consommé:

Combine all the ingredients, except the gelatin, and simmer until the strawberries are tender (5-10 minutes). Purée in a blender until smooth, and then strain through a chinois. Adjust the sweetness if needed. Weigh the purée in ounces and multiply by 0.75 – this is the amount of gelatin that is needed. Bloom the gelatin in cold water, and then incorporate into the warm strawberry purée. Pour into a shallow hotel pan and freeze overnight.

The next day, line a 2" perforated hotel pan with cheesecloth, and place a 4" hotel pan underneath. Place the frozen purée on the cheesecloth, and allow to drip in the refrigerator for the next 2 days. Reserve the liquid that has dripped through and discard the rest of the purée.

strawberry chips:

Heat the water, sugar and lemon juice and bring to a boil. Turn off the heat, and allow to cool to room temperature. Dip the sliced strawberries in the simple syrup and place on a silpat-lined sheetpan. Place in a food warmer set to a low temperature (200°F) or in an oven on the lowest temperature. Dry for several hours, or overnight, until the sliced strawberries harden when left at room temperature for 1 minute.

to serve:

Cut the Génoise cake to the same size as the panna cotta. Unmold the panna cottas and place on a sheetpan. Place the cake in the bottom of a bowl, top with diced fresh strawberries that have been macerated with a little sugar and place the panna cotta on top. Take a small amount of the strawberry consommé, and mix with about half as much Champagne. Pour into the bowl around the cake and panna cotta. Garnish with the strawberry chips.

AJ Black

Chef/Restaurateur AJ Black was born in Sicily on August 12, 1967. He grew up in the restaurant business in Rome and trained at the Italian Culinary Institute, and completed his internship at the Grand Hotel. With his passionate character and strong ambition, he opened his first restaurant at the age of 19, in the Laterno District on the Via San Giovanni (Café Roma). He has always been inspired by his early childhood in Sicily, where cooking with his family was an event, an act of love, and a chance to create with gastronomic masters, transforming the freshest ingredients from the garden and the field. His intention has always been to draw from this foundation, skill, and the very best of Italian cooking, to create his own individual style that has been hailed as simpatico, classic, and chic. Chef AJ's elegant style in cuisine is always evolving, his passion for every intimate dish he creates is immeasurable.

The Charlotte Inn

This is a captain's house in pure traditional British style in the heart of Martha's Vineyard, erstwhile haunt of whale hunters.

Ulysses Simpson Grant, Jackie Kennedy and Bill Clinton all fell under its charm. Offering a window into another time, which envelops you in its romantic atmosphere, the Charlotte Inn was built in 1864 for Samuel Osborne, a famous merchant. The staff, alert to the smallest detail, cultivate a deliciously old-fashioned elegance and courtesy. Antique lamps and exquisite silk or linen fabrics decorate the suites. Between one iced tea and the next on the flower-filled patio, go off to discover the wild island surrounding you, from its lighthouse to its beaches, ideal for waterskiing and kayaking.

LOBSTER RAVIOLI IN A BROWN BUTTER SAGE LOBSTER SAUCE

BY AJ BLACK

Italian comfort food, ravioli 'pillows' of lobster meat and fresh sage with a brown butter sauce, a perfect decadence with the fresh lobster tail from the regional Atlantic coast.

Serves 2
Preparation time: 15 minutes + 3 hours for chilling
Cooking time: 15 minutes

INGREDIENTS

pasta: (makes enough for 6 people)

4 cups	all purpose flour
5	eggs
½ tsp	salt

lobster mousse:

1	lobster, body
1 tbsp	garlic oil
1 tsp	butter
1	sprig fresh italian parsley
Kosher salt & pepper to taste	
2	sage leaves
1 tbsp	cream

lobster and sauce:

6	fresh pasta lobster ravioli
¼ cup	butter
1 cup	cream
2	lobster claws (Maine lobster), shelled
3 oz	fresh lobster meat, chopped
6	fresh sage leaves
1 tbsp	fresh lemon zest
1	pinch sea salt
1	pinch white pepper

METHOD

pasta:

Sieve the flour onto a working surface and form into a little hill. Make a well in the center, then add the eggs and the salt. Work in the eggs with a fork, blending the white to the yolk, and start to work in the flour around the edge of the well with your hands to form it into a coarse dough. Knead for about 15 minutes until smooth. Wrap in foil and leave for an hour.

Dust a clean surface with fresh flour, placing the dough out from the foil wrap. Using a rolling pin, roll out the dough until it is even and thin. Cut the pasta to the desired shape, in this case ravioli shapes.

lobster mousse:

Boil the lobster and save the claws for the sauce. Chop the cooled body meat of the lobster. Sauté the garlic oil and butter, add the chopped lobster meat, chopped fresh italian parsley, and salt and pepper to taste. Cook for 3 minutes then leave to cool. When cool place the sautéed mixture into a food processor, add the fresh sage leaves and process until fine. Slowly add the cream while the mixture is blending to create a mousse texture. Add the salt and pepper to taste.

Spoon a tablespoon of the lobster mousse into the center of each fresh raviolo, place another piece of pasta on top and press to close the edges surrounding the perimeter of the pasta, keeping the lobster mixture inside the center. Use a knife or a ravioli cutter to seal the shape creating a 'pillow' effect. Finish by placing the fresh raviolis in the freezer for 2 hours to rest, then they will be ready for cooking.

lobster and sauce:

Sauté the butter, lemon zest, salt, and pepper, and bring them to a light brown color. Then add the lobster claws and lobster meat, follow with the cream then fresh sage, and allow to simmer and reduce the heat.

Boil the ravioli, add to the sauce and sauté.

to serve:

Place the individual raviolis onto the center of the plate, put a claw on top, and drizzle with the brown butter sage sauce to coat the ravioli.

Serves 6
Preparation time: 20 minutes
Cooking time: 3 hours 50 minutes

INGREDIENTS

lamb ratatouille:

2	carrots, thinly sliced on bias
6	shallots, whole
2	leeks, thinly sliced on bias
2	garlic whole heads with tops sliced off
5	cipollini onions
2	heirloom tomatoes, chopped thick
4	red potatoes, sliced thin on the bias
5	white button mushrooms
1	fresh lamb leg, 8 lb
1½	bottles good Italian red wine
⅛ cup	extra virgin olive oil
½ cup	fresh beef stock
2 tbsp	each of fresh herbs: cilantro, Italian parsley, sage, rosemary, Genova basil and thyme
1 tbsp	fresh lemon zest
1 tbsp	fresh cracked pepper
1 tbsp	sea salt

risotto rustica:

2½ cups	risotto rice
2 cups	fresh chicken stock
1 cup	Pinot Grigio
1 tbsp	butter
kosher salt	

LAMB RATATOUILLE WITH RISOTTO RUSTICA

BY AJ BLACK

One of my favorite flavors in meat is lamb. This recipe reminds me of home as a child, and the use of the regional lamb from the Farm Institute on Martha's Vineyard makes it really special for us.

METHOD

Prepare a large roasting pan on a high heat, and sear the lamb leg with its own natural fat for 5 minutes on each side until golden brown. Put in a hot 400°F oven for 20 minutes on each side. While the lamb is roasting in the oven, bring another pan to a high heat with the extra virgin olive oil, adding the vegetables and salt and pepper to taste, until golden brown.

Take the lamb out of the oven, and add the sautéed vegetables, all the fresh herbs, lemon zest, stock and wine. Put back in the oven (reduced to 300°F), and roast covered for 3 hours, turning the lamb every 40 minutes.

Partially cook the risotto with the listed ingredients to start. Complete the cooking of the risotto with ½ cup of the vegetable sauce from the lamb roast, then finish until fluffy and creamy.

to serve:

Plate the slices of lamb over a small bed of risotto, top with pan juice drizzle and a pinch of lemon zest.

Serves 2
Preparation time: 10 minutes
Cooking time: 23-35 minutes

INGREDIENTS

cake:

5	eggs
6 tbsp	sugar
3 oz	dark chocolate, melted
3 oz	semi-sweet chocolate, melted
2 tbsp	all purpose flour

butter (to grease pan)

1 tbsp	cocoa powder (to flour pan)

chocolate ganache coating:

1 cup	heavy cream
6 oz	dark chocolate, finely chopped
6 oz	semi-sweet chocolate, finely chopped

red glaze:

½	jar good seedless raspberry preserve
¾ tsp	lemon juice
2 tbsp	orange flavored liqueur

powdered sugar, to taste

to serve:

whipped cream
fresh berries

CHOCOLATE CAKE

BY AJ BLACK

Always a winner, I say just make it chocolate! Excellent decadence to be enjoyed with a fine Italian red vintage or a steamy shot of espresso.

METHOD

cake:

Preheat the oven to 350°F. Grease, and flour with cocoa powder, a 12" round pan.

Separate the eggs, and reserve the whites.

Mix the yolks and sugar with an electric mixer until they are light and fluffy (approximately 4 minutes). Whisk in the melted chocolate and flour until smooth.

Whisk the egg whites until they form medium peaks in a separate bowl. Gently fold the egg whites into the chocolate mixture, then fold in the flour and pour into the greased and floured pan.

Bake for 25-35 minutes or until done and allow to cool for 30 minutes.

chocolate ganache coating:

In a small saucepan, bring the cream to a light boil then remove from the heat. Place the chocolate in the food processor and, with the motor running, carefully pour in the hot cream in a steady stream until it is all processed and smooth. Pour the mixture into a bowl to cool.

red glaze:

Combine all the ingredients together on low heat in a small pan and melt them together for a few minutes, adding sugar to taste. Remove from the heat and allow to cool. The sauce can be refrigerated until ready to use.

to serve:

Apply the ganache to the cake decorate the top with red glaze. Decorate the plate with glaze and serve with cream and fruits as desired.

Joe Schafer

Joe Schafer received an Associates degree from New England Culinary Institute in Essex Junction Vermont. He has worked at several Relais & Châteaux properties including Lake Placid Lodge, Triple Creek Ranch, Restaurant Hélène Darroze and The White Barn Inn.

Joe's food is heavily influenced by classic French technique focusing on seasonal ingredients and local products. He strives to make food fitting for the surroundings at Glendorn which reflect rustic elegance and comfortable sophistication.

Joe is originally from upstate New York.

Glendorn

Built in the 1920s, this inn has kept all its original charm and authenticity and is situated in a gorgeously green and unspoilt part of Pennsylvania, halfway between Pittsburgh and Buffalo.

On the program are walks in the fresh air, fly fishing at Lake Bondieu (just a few minutes away), Pennsylvanian clay pigeon shooting, snooker ... and total rest. The main lodge and individual chalets are built with sequoia wood and blend perfectly into the breathtaking natural surroundings: a forest of hemlock spruces where it is not rare to spot foxes, deer or beavers, and you will be lulled by the soothing murmur of bubbling streams.

PENNSYLVANIA VENISON TENDERLOIN, BRAISED LEG, PARSNIP PUREE, FOIE GRAS & NATIVE SPRUCE NEEDLE SAUCE

BY JOE SCHAFER

Serves 4
Preparation time: 30 minutes
Cooking time: 2-3 hours

INGREDIENTS

stew:

1 lb venison leg meat
1 carrot
1 parsnip
1 celeriac
8 strips of bacon
9 oz oyster mushrooms
2 oz flour
1 oz grapeseed oil
handful of juniper berries
4 cloves garlic
2 bay leaves
1 pt cabernet sauvignon
2 pt venison or veal stock

tenderloin:

venison tenderloin
1 Swiss chard leaf
salt & pepper

parsnip purée:

5 parsnips
cream, as needed
1 pinch of salt

sauce:

1 qt venison stock, reduced to 2oz
10 fl oz port
10 fl oz Madeira
2 sprigs of spruce tree needles
9 oz foie gras, diced

garnish:

parsnips, roasted
cranberries
crispy julienne of parsnips

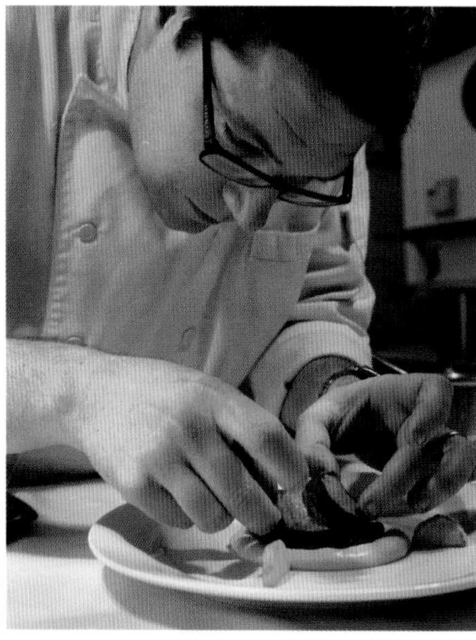

Venison is a local ingredient specific to our region of Pennsylvania. We offer a tasting menu that changes completely every day. This is just one example of the many preparations we use with this ingredient.

METHOD

stew:

Preheat the oven to 250°F. Start with an oven ready pan with a cover. Render the bacon with the grapeseed oil. Cut the venison leg meat into 1" pieces. Season with ample salt and pepper. Dredge the meat in flour, covering it completely. Brown the meat in the bacon fat in small batches, making sure every piece is caramelized. Remove the meat from the pan and deglaze with the wine. Add the remaining vegetables and aromatics. Reduce the wine until it has virtually gone. Add the meat back into the pan and cover with the stock. Bring to the boil and check the seasoning. Place the covered pan in the oven. Let cook for 4-6 hours.

tenderloin:

Trim the tenderloin, removing all the connective tissue and silver skin. Place a pot of salted water on the stove to boil. Quickly blanch the Swiss chard leaf for 5 seconds and place in ice water immediately. Pat dry with paper towel and remove the center rib. Place the tenderloin in the Swiss chard leaf and roll as tightly as possible. Wrap in plastic wrap and tie the ends of the cylinder with butcher's twine. Place a wide pot on the stove and gently bring the water up to 130°F. Drop the venison into the water and allow to stand for 10 minutes.

parsnip purée:

Peel the parsnips and cut into coins. Cover with cream and salt. Simmer until the cream has reduced by two-thirds. Place everything in a blender and pureé until smooth.

sauce:

In a pan add the port and Madeira and reduce by two-thirds. Add the venison stock and reduce until a sauce consistency. Add the sprigs of spruce tree needles for 1-2 minutes. Strain into a blender and mix with the foie gras.

to serve:

Pipe a circle of parsnip purée on to a plate, fill with the stew and top with slices of tenderloin. Add sauce, parsnips and cranberries decoratively. Top the tenderloin with the crispy parsnips.

NATIVE BROOK TROUT, PROSCIUTTO, BRAISED ARTICHOKE, BEURRE NOISETTE

BY JOE SCHAFER

Trout is a local ingredient specific to our region of Pennsylvania. A fresh catch is really important here at Glendorn and we are lucky to have these ingredients locally.

Serves 2
Preparation time: 1 hour 30 minutes
Cooking time: 1 hour 30 minutes

INGREDIENTS

1 8" fresh Brook trout, filleted
2 thin slices of prosciutto
4 fl oz heavy cream

filling:

3½ oz fresh spinach
1 lemon, zested
fresh nutmeg, grated
2 oz fromage blanc

artichokes:

4 small fresh artichokes
9 oz ventriche or pancetta
10 fl oz sauvignon blanc
10 fl oz chicken stock
1 carrot, diced
1 onion, diced
1 oz celery seeds
1 bay leaf
2 sprigs of thyme
1 head of garlic, halved
olive oil
salt & white pepper
splash of aged sherry vinegar
olive oil

beurre noisette:

8 oz unsalted butter
10 fl oz heavy cream
2 lemons, juiced
1 pinch of soy lecithin

to serve:

1 carrot
trout roe
micro greens

METHOD

artichokes:

Start by rendering the ventriche or pancetta in a generous amount of olive oil. Add the garlic, carrot and onions. Sweat these items over a low heat for several minutes. Add the white wine, sherry vinegar and chicken stock, then add the bay leaf, thyme, celery seeds, salt and white pepper.

Meanwhile, clean the artichokes by removing as many leaves as possible by hand. Cut the remainder of the leaves off at the base of the heart, and with a spoon remove the choke (fibrous hairs) from the base of the artichoke. Trim the remainder of the artichoke with a paring knife, and remove all the green from the stem and base. Quickly place into acidulated water to prevent oxidation. Once you have cleaned all the artichokes place them in the cooking liquid and simmer for 1½ hours. Once the artichokes are fully cooked, tender yet still holding their shape, reserve two for garnish and place the remainder in a blender. Add just enough of the cooking liquid to make a smooth purée.

filling:

Sauté the spinach in olive oil. Place on paper towels to soak up any excess liquid. Put in a bowl, add the lemon zest and nutmeg then fold in the fromage blanc.

beurre noisette:

Place the butter in a pan over a medium heat. Keep a watchful eye on the butter – you want to cook it until it turns slightly brown and smells of popcorn. Once you reach this stage quickly remove the pan from heat and add the lemon juice, cream and soy lecithin, and mix.

to serve:

Place a small amount of plastic wrap on a cutting board. Start with the thin slices of prosciutto ham placed side by side so that they overlap slightly. Then place the fish flesh side up on the ham. Spoon a small amount of filling into the center of the fish. Gently fold one fillet onto the other. Carefully tuck one side under the other so as to make a cylinder. Encapsulate the whole thing in prosciutto and then roll tightly with plastic wrap. Refrigerate until ready to serve, then remove the plastic wrap. Present on a plate, on top of the artichoke purée, with the carrot, trout roe and micro greens, and finish with the beurre noisette.

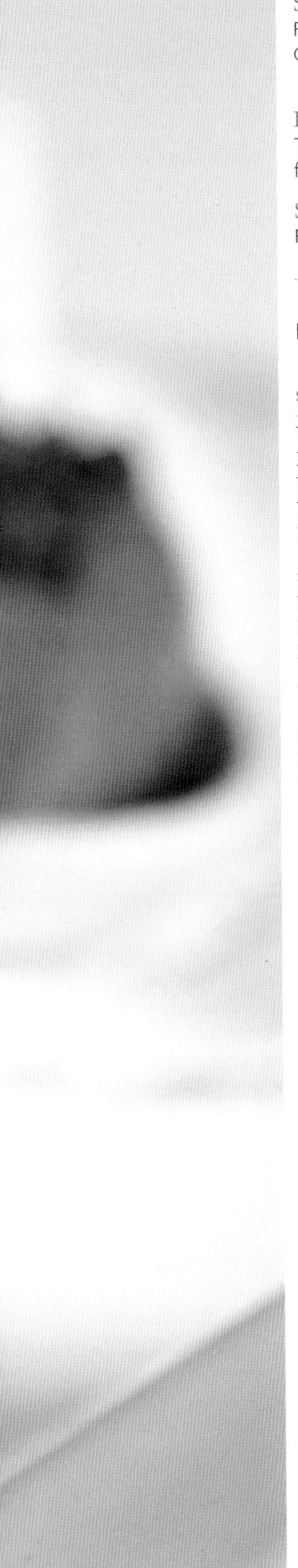

Serves 4

Preparation time:	14 minutes
Cooking time:	30 minutes + freezing time for sorbet

Planning ahead:
The sorbet must be made the day before and frozen for 24 hours.

Special equipment:
Pacojet

INGREDIENTS

sorbet:

1 lb	strawberry purée or fresh strawberries
3 oz	sugar
1½ oz	glucose
7 fl oz	water
½ fl oz	vodka

soufflé base:

2 lb 4 oz	mango purée
3½ oz	sugar
1	pinch of cornstarch

few drops of citric acid

soufflé:

3½ oz	soufflé base (see recipe above)
2½ oz	sugar + extra to coat the ramekins
3 oz	egg whites

butter

garnish:

coco nibs

MANGO SOUFFLE, COCO NIBS & STRAWBERRY SORBET

BY JOE SCHAFER

A timeless classic that people enjoy. We do innumerable combinations of soufflé and ice cream, usually what is seasonal and fresh.

METHOD

sorbet:

Bring the strawberry purée/strawberries, sugar, glucose and water to a boil. Let cool to room temperature and add the vodka. Place in a Pacojet beaker and freeze for 24 hours. Spin when needed.

soufflé base:

Add the citric acid to the pureé and reduce the purée by two-thirds. Wet the sugar and cook to a softball stage at 238°F. Add to the reduced purée and add the cornstarch. Bring to a boil and let the mixture fully thicken. Cool in a refrigerator.

soufflé:

Preheat the oven to 350°F. With a pastry brush and very soft butter brush the inside of four ramekins. Coat completely with sugar and refrigerate. Bring the egg whites to room temperature and whip in a mixer on a low speed. Slowly add the sugar and let whip for 10 minutes. Gently fold the egg whites into the soufflé base by hand with a rubber spatula. Overfill the ramekins with the mixture and level with the back of a knife. Bake in the oven for 14 minutes.

to serve:

Garnish the soufflé with coco nibs and serve with the sorbet.

Christopher P. Bates

Christopher P. Bates grew up in Arkport, NY, at the opposite end of the state from the hustle and bustle of New York City. He grew up literally in front of the stove, cooking side by side with his mother, where he learned the importance of cooking from the heart. Procuring local provisions is not a trend for Christopher; it is the reality of how he learned to prepare food, with produce from his family's and neighbor's home gardens.

Through this constant affair with cuisine the focus quickly grew from a passion for 'food' to a passion for 'all things consumable'. With this philosophy in mind Christopher has spent considerable time as a sommelier, server and bartender. Years of varied experiences have broadened his influences and enabled him to create cuisine that is complex, elegant and provides a platform for all the elements of an exquisite dining experience.

Christopher is the Hotel Fauchère's Executive Chef and shares the General Manager position along with his partner Isabel Bogadtke.

Hotel Fauchère

The Hotel Fauchère is a casually elegant destination with exquisite cuisine offering two restaurants, a pâtisserie, 16 superbly-restored guest rooms (marble baths, heated towel racks, Kiehl's amenities, Frette linens) and adjacent meeting facilities.

Founded in 1852 by Delmonico's Master Chef, Louis Fauchère, and run by his descendants until closing in 1976, the hotel's extraordinary culinary legacy was reclaimed in 2006 after a meticulous five-year restoration. The Delmonico Room offers a contemporary interpretation of the classics, while the sleek, minimalist Bar Louis – with a giant photograph of Andy Warhol and John Lennon above the bar – features bistro-style global cuisine, including Sushi Pizza, its signature dish. Within walking and hiking distance are historic attractions, shopping, important architecture and the north gate to a 70,000 acre national park with its spectacular waterfalls.

'FAUSCRAPPLE', BITTER GREENS, MUSTARD, WHITE SPRUCE

BY CHRISTOPHER P. BATES

This dish is one of our signature dishes, as we feel it is quite steeped in 'Pennsylvanianess'. The tradition of the pig harvest has been important in Pennsylvania for hundreds of years. Once most of the 'choice' meat had been removed the next step in processing would take place. This is when the famous Pennsylvania Scrapple would be made. The remnants of the carcass would be boiled, loosening the meat and creating a gelatinous broth. Once the bones were removed, any meat that remained would be picked off, blended with any other variety of meats (offal) and grains, and returned to the broth to be cooked down to a thick, syrupy consistency. The mixture was then spread into loaf pans, leveled and tapped as it settled. The tapping helped remove any air bubbles, and the settling allowed the abundant fat to rise to the top. Since the mixture was near a boil when it went into the pan, and the fat prevents oxygen from entering, the loaves were, in theory, preserved. This meant that in the days before refrigeration, this meat could last in a cool basement long after the 'harvest'. Scrapple was and still is a local delicacy in many parts, served sliced thin and crisped as a breakfast meat, alongside eggs, potatoes and toast. Our tête takes a very similar preparation, though uses only the head of the hog.

Serves 6
Preparation time: 3 hours
Cooking time: 1 hours

Planning ahead:
The tête de cochon must be prepared 2-3 days in advance. The vinaigrette can be made in advance. The jelly will take approximately 6 hours to set.

INGREDIENTS

tête de cochon:

- 1 pig's head meat, 70% meat to 30% fat/skin ratio (butcher will prepare), and the tongue, all cooked
- ½ cup parsley, julienne
- ½ cup mixed chopped herbs (chives, thyme, tarragon)
- ½ cup cornichons, small dice
- salt & pepper

olive oil croutons:

- ½ loaf of Ciabatta bread or other chewy white bread, crusts removed, sliced into 6 wafer thin slices, rest chopped to ¼" x ½" cubes
- 2 tbsp olive oil
- salt & pepper

bitter salad:

- 2 endives, julienne
- 1 frisée, torn into small pieces
- ¼ cup pickled beans
- ¼ cup olive oil croutons (see recipe above)
- 2 tbsp mustard vinaigrette (see recipe below)

mustard vinaigrette:

- ¼ cup whole grain mustard
- 1 lemon, juice
- 1 cup olive oil
- 2 egg yolks
- lemon juice, salt & sugar, to taste

fennel jelly:

- 2 cups fennel tops
- ½ cup parsley
- 1 sheet of gelatin, bloomed in water

to serve:

- olive oil croutons, crushed finely
- white spruce ice cream
- 6 white spruce branch tips (1" only with bottom needles removed)
- ¼ cup chives, finely sliced
- Maldon salt
- black lava salt

METHOD

tête de cochon:
Add the parsley, mixed herbs and cornichons to the meat mix and fold together. Season. Warm to just melt the natural gelatin in the meat, so heat it until it is loose and soupy. Spray a pan large enough to hold the meat mixture with pan spray or line with plastic wrap. Fill the mold half full of the mixture, lay the tongue down the middle and top with the remaining mixture. Place a pan that fits inside the mold into it and weigh it down with a 5 lb weight. Place in the refrigerator to cool. Allow 2-3 days for best flavor. Invert to unmold.

olive oil croutons:
Preheat the oven to 350°F. In a large bowl drizzle the oil over the cubes of bread, season and mix gently. Spread on a baking tray lined with parchment paper or foil. Bake for 3-4 minutes or until golden brown, rotating halfway through baking. To coat the slices, rub over the film of oil left in the bowl. Lay on a parchment lined tray and bake until crispy brown.

bitter salad:
In a small bowl, mix all the ingredients just before serving.

mustard vinaigrette:
Mix the lemon juice into the egg yolks. Drop by drop add the oil while constantly mixing. Do not add too quickly. Then add the mustard. Adjust the taste with lemon juice, salt and sugar. Adjust the consistency with water until pourable. Refrigerate in a squeeze bottle or jar.

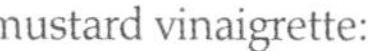

fennel jelly:

Fill a large container with ice and water. In a large pot of boiling water blanch the fennel and parsley for 20 seconds. Remove and plunge directly into the ice water for 1 minute. Remove and squeeze thoroughly to dry. Roughly chop then blend with 3 or 4 ice cubes in a blender for 30-40 seconds on high. Strain through a fine strainer. Measure 3 oz of the liquid and warm gently. Add the gelatin and stir until dissolved. In a shallow container, spray a film of pan spray and pour the fennel liquid to a depth of ⅓". Refrigerate for 6 hours or until firmly set. Cut into ⅓" cubes.

to serve:

Decorate each plate with a swirl of vinaigrette. Remove the tête de cochon from the mold gently. Trim the sides and ends to make a clean block and slice six even slices ½" thick. Sprinkle the top with chives. Place in the center of the plate on the vinaigrette line. To the right of the tête, place a tablespoon of crouton crumbs. To the left, place some salad. Spear one spruce tip into each jelly cube and place to the right of the croutons. Add a quenelle of ice cream on the crumbs. Sprinkle with the salts.

LOBSTER A LA WENBERG, HALO OF CONNECTING FLAVORS

BY CHRISTOPHER P. BATES

Lobster Newberg is a dish that has featured on the menu of the Hotel Fauchère nearly since its inception in 1852. Years of research have still left the truth of its origin up for question, with claims being made that the dish originated at the Hotel Fauchère and was created by the master himself, Louis Fauchère. This has since been disproved, and it appears that the dish was created at Delmonico's Restaurant. According to their history, Sea Captain Ben Wenberg arrived back from a journey and dined at Delmonico's one night. He offered to share a new technique in preparing lobster that he had learned. The Delmonico brothers were so impressed, they put the dish on the menu, naming it Lobster à la Wenberg. A later dispute between the brothers and Captain Wenberg caused them to remove his namesake dish. But the dish had become so popular that customers demanded it back. It was then returned to the menu with the letters rearranged as Lobster à la Newberg. The then head chef, Ranhofer, later printed the recipe in his book, but from it we can see he made some changes. The wine was changed from sherry to Madeira and eggs were added to thicken the sauce. No major crime, but changes nonetheless. We have decided to work with the original Wenberg recipe for the current version of the dish that we serve in The Delmonico Room. The single item that made this dish so exotic at the time is now commonplace: cayenne pepper.

Serves 4
Preparation time: 2 hours
Cooking time: 2 hours

Special equipment:
Microplane

Planning ahead:
The cayenne essence can be made in advance.

INGREDIENTS

lobster:

4 hard shell lobsters, 2 lb each: heads, tails, claws and knuckles separated: bodies, heads, shells and the best 4 claws reserved; tails on a skewer, reserved; meat removed from the knuckles and remaining claws

Wenberg sauce:

4 reserved lobster bodies/heads
reserved shells
¼ cup butter
2 tbsp best quality butter you can find
2 cups heavy cream
½ cup cognac or other high quality brandy
½ cup high quality Dry Fino sherry
1 tsp cayenne pepper

kabocha squash:

2 large kabocha squashes, ⅛" brunoise

cayenne essence:

1 tbsp cayenne pepper
½ cup olive oil

base for the halo of flavors:

reserved cooked kabocha dice
reserved lobster knuckles meat
reserved lobster claws meat
1 tbsp best quality extra virgin olive oil
salt & pepper

halo of flavors garnishes: (all optional – these are what we use currently but change seasonally)
12 candied Cara Cara orange peel
12 ⅙" x ⅙" cubes of chervil jelly
12 ⅙" x ⅙" cubes of cognac jelly
½ tsp Meyer lemon zest, microplaned
½ tsp ginger, microplaned
¼ tsp fresh nutmeg, microplaned
¼ tsp hard Italian licorice, microplaned
¼ tsp Piment d'Espelette
1 tsp soy meringue
1 tsp parsley froth

sautéed kabocha:

reserved raw kabocha dice
1 tbsp butter
10 Szechuan peppercorns, crushed

METHOD

Wenberg sauce:

Roughly chop the bodies. In a heavy bottomed saucepan, melt the ¼ cup of butter over a medium heat and add the shells, bodies and heads. Stirring, allow them to caramelize but not burn. Add the cream and reduce by half. Strain. Add the cognac and the sherry, whisk to mix and strain through a fine strainer into a clean heavy bottomed sauté pan. Over a medium heat, simmer for 5-10 minutes, stirring so it doesn't burn. Whisk in the cayenne, and add the quality butter, bit by bit, while stirring.

kabocha squash:

Divide in half and keep one lot raw and refrigerated and blanch the rest in boiling water until just soft. Shock in ice water and refrigerate.

cayenne essence:

Add the cayenne and oil to a heavy bottomed pan. Warm. Hold warm on a low heat until the cayenne begins to toast. Strain through a coffee filter into a spritz bottle or a glass jar.

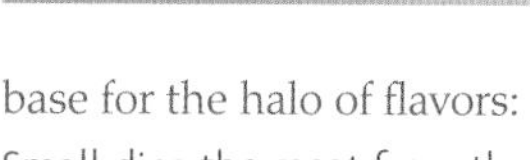

base for the halo of flavors:

Small dice the meat from the lobster claws and knuckles to match the size of the kabocha. In a bowl, mix everything together and season. Divide into ten bowls (or however many garnishes you will be using, if any).

halo of flavors garnishes:

To each of the ten bowls add one of the garnishes, essentially making ten different salads. One by one, spoon each of these into the serving bowls, forming a ring around the outside.

sautéed kabocha:

In a heavy sauté pan, heat the butter with the peppercorns. Toast for 10-15 seconds. Add the squash, sauté until tender, but still with considerable texture, 1 minute or so. Drain on a folded paper towel to remove the excess butter.

lobster:

In a heavy sauté pan, heat the Wenberg sauce and the 4 tails and 4 remaining claws. Heat gently over a medium heat, allowing no more than a slow simmer. Turn the lobster often and spoon the sauce over the top in order to heat evenly. Cook until warmed through, but with the center still translucent. If the lobster is overcooked it will become tough and 'squeaky' when you chew. The heating should only take about 5 minutes. The lobsters can be left in the warm sauce until you have finished the rest of the plate as they cool down extremely quickly. When everything else is ready remove the lobster tails and claws to a paper towel to dry, remove the skewer and slice the tails into four or five medallions each.

to serve:

Place a mound of the sautéed kabocha into the center of each plate, and add the tail medallions. Top with a claw. Spritz two or three times with cayenne essence or simply drizzle from the tip of a small spoon. Pour the remaining sauce into a pitcher for your guests to pour at the table.

Chef's tip:

The cayenne essence makes far more than you need, but it will keep indefinitely, and makes a great addition to any recipe that could use a bit more heat.

FAUCHERE FLORIDA-ALASKA

BY BENJAMIN YOUNGQUEST

Baked Alaska is a ubiquitous American dessert creation, and stories about its genesis are abundant and varied. One form of the Baked Alaska has its roots in the kitchen at the famed Delmonico's restaurant, whose chef was the celebrated Louis Fauchère – the original owner and namesake of our hotel. This version was created in honor of the purchase of Alaska (and some say Florida) and the subsequent enlargement of the United States. Toasted and sometimes set on fire, the dessert was a favorite of the 20th century.

In creating a modern nod toward this traditional dessert, I played with the idea of contrasting a local flavor from Alaska (salmonberry) with the citrus for which Florida has become so well known. Instead of ice cream encased in cake and Swiss meringue, I went with a more delicate layered parfait center, and omitted the cake altogether. The result is a more ethereal version of a classic stand-by.

Serves 8
Preparation time: 3 hours
Cooking time: 4-6 hours

Special equipment:
Mixer with whip attachment, acetate, 2" diameter PVC tubing cut into eight 3" segments. blow torch

Planning ahead:
Freeze the cylinders for 6-8 hours.

INGREDIENTS

citrus parfait:

1 Cara Cara orange, zest
1 Meyer lemon, zest
1 grapefruit, zest
1 pinch of kosher salt
7 oz heavy cream
2 oz sugar
3½ oz Greek (pressed) yogurt
1 gelatin sheet, bloomed
3½ oz egg whites
4½ oz sugar

salmonberry parfait:

7 oz salmonberry purée
2 oz sugar
1 pinch of kosher salt
3½ oz heavy cream
1 gelatin sheet, bloomed in water
3½ oz egg whites
4½ oz sugar

pomelo curd:

½ large pomelo, zest and juice
9 oz sugar
4 eggs
6 oz butter
2 gelatin sheets, bloomed in water

pomelo confit:

1 large pomelo, zest
18 oz sugar
3½ oz honey
18 oz water

blood orange gelée:

7 oz blood orange juice
5½ oz simple syrup
4½ gelatin sheets, bloomed in water

Meyer lemon gelée:

7 oz Meyer lemon juice
7 oz simple syrup
5 gelatin sheets

Swiss meringue:

7 oz egg whites
10½ oz sugar

additional garnish:

1 Cara cara orange supreme
1 blood orange supreme
1 red grapefruit supreme
salmonberry jam

METHOD

citrus and salmonberry parfaits:

Citrus: In a pot, bring the cream, zests, and 1¾ oz sugar to just off a boil. Remove from the heat, cover with a lid and steep for 30 minutes. Warm the yogurt in a saucepan and stir in the gelatin until dissolved, pass through a chinois into a bowl and cool. Strain and chill on an ice bath. Then whip until it forms medium peaks. Fold into the yogurt mixture.

Salmonberry: In a pot bring the purée, 1¾ oz sugar and salt to a boil. Remove from the heat and stir in the gelatin. Pass through a chinois into a bowl and cool at room temperature. Whip the cream to medium peaks. Gently fold the cream into the purée.

Both (separately): In a saucepan, mix the remaining sugar with just enough water to hydrate (achieving a 'wet sand' effect). Cook over a medium heat until the sugar reaches 350°F. Meanwhile put the egg whites in the mixer bowl with the whip attachment. When the sugar begins to boil, start whipping the whites on speed 1. When the sugar achieves the correct temperature, quickly pour it into the mixing bowl and increase to speed 3. When all the sugar is added, turn to full speed until medium peaks form. Next, using a rubber spatula, add a small amount of this meringue to the cream/yogurt mixture, mixing thoroughly until smooth. Gently fold in the rest of the meringue. Portion into a piping bag and pipe into prepared acetate-lined cylinder molds (see below).

pomelo curd:

Fill a saucepan halfway with water and bring to a boil. In a metal bowl place the juice and zest, sugar, and eggs. Mix with an immersion blender. Add the butter. Place the bowl atop the saucepan on a medium heat. Cook the curd until it reaches 180°F. Stir in the gelatin. Pass through a chinois. Ice down and reserve.

pomelo confit:

Cut long, straight strips of zest (with about an ⅛" of pith attached) from the pomelo. Do the following three times: place in a pot, cover with cold water, bring to a boil, strain. Put back in a pot and add the sugar, honey, and water. Bring to a boil, stirring occasionally, until the sugar dissolves. Turn down to a low heat and cook until the zest strips are translucent. Remove from the heat, transfer to a container, and cool. Cut into squares.

blood orange and Meyer lemon gelées: (same instructions for both)

In a saucepan, bring the juice and syrup just to a boil. Let cool slightly and add the gelatin. Stir to dissolve and pass through a chinois. Pour into a container lightly filmed with oil to ⅓" deep. Refrigerate for at least 2 hours to set. Cut into squares.

Swiss meringue:

Bring a pot of water to a boil. Put the egg whites and sugar into the bowl of a mixer but whisk by hand (while half submerging the bowl in the boiling water) until all the sugar is melted, the mixture has a white and glossy appearance and is hot to the touch (at least 130°F). Whip with a mixer on high speed until medium peaks form. Fill a piping bag with the meringue.

to assemble the cylinder:

Wrap a small square of plastic wrap tightly around one end of the PVC segments. Stand the wrapped end on a half sheet tray. Spread a thin layer of meringue on one side of eight acetate segments (7" x 3"), leaving a little uncovered on one tall side of the segment. Carefully line the PVC cylinders with the meringue-coated acetate, taking care not to let the meringue covered areas overlap on themselves, as this will make the cylinder harder to unmold later on. Now, pipe a ¼" layer of meringue into the bottom of each cylinder. Next, pipe each cylinder almost half full with the salmonberry parfait. Freeze for 1 hour, then pipe almost full with the citrus parfait. Freeze for 1 hour. Finally, pipe to the top with Swiss meringue, leaving a decorative swirl. Return to the freezer for 6-8 hours. Unmold carefully. Use a blow torch to brown lightly.

to serve:

On a long rectangular plate, paint a stripe of salmonberry jam in the top left corner, running along the top of the plate to the middle. Place the cylinder in the center of the plate. Pipe a quarter-sized round of curd at the bottom middle of the plate and pull it to the bottom right corner using a wet spoon. In the trench left by the spoon place in order from left to right, one blood orange geleé square, one Meyer lemon gelée square, one pomelo confit square, one blood orange supreme, one Cara Cara supreme, and one grapefruit supreme.

Brian Sutton

Brian Sutton graduated from the renowned Colchester Institute of Culinary Arts, England, putting in an extra year in the pastry department to round out his expertise. He was then recruited to work at Keswick Hall, in Charlottesville, Virginia, where he met and worked alongside former mentor, Kevin McCarthy, previously the Executive Chef at the highly regarded resorts, The Point and Lake Placid Lodge.

Sutton moved back to Europe for a stint, but he returned to The Point, becoming Sous Chef along the way. He moved on to The Willcox, eventually working under the direction of Guenter Seeger. Sutton was lured out to Las Vegas to work under Daniel Boulud at Wynn Las Vegas, again watching, learning, and absorbing the technique of a great chef. He returned to Seeger's, and is now back at Lake Placid Lodge again. He loves developing the seasonal menus for Lake Placid Lodge's dinners, as well as the meals at Maggie's Pub. He loves the small scale, the local ingredients, the interplay of ideas with his staff, and the perfectionism expected.

Lake Placid Lodge

Situated on the shores of Lake Placid, The Lake Placid Lodge is a beautifully handcrafted Lodge nestled in the Adirondack Mountains.

A remarkable arts and crafts style lodge, the Main Lodge offers the finest accommodation and dining in a comfortably rustic, yet refined setting. Pamper yourself in the Main Lodge, the private cabins or the remodelled Lakeside suites, offering gorgeous views of Lake Placid and Whiteface Mountain. The guest rooms, suites and cabins feature luxurious featherbeds, wood burning fireplaces, rustic furnishings, and deep soaking baths. The Dining Room offers a prix-fixe menu with dining available on the deck overlooking Lake Placid and Whiteface Mountain. For a relaxed setting try the 'Pub' which serves lunch, dinner and an all day menu, and also offers outside dining on the deck.

Serves 4
Preparation time: 35 minutes
Cooking time: 3 hours 40 minutes

Planning ahead:
The pork belly needs to be prepared at least 2 days in advance.

INGREDIENTS

parsnip and pear soup:

2	parsnips, peeled and chopped
1	medium onion, diced
2	pears, peeled, cored and diced
2	stalks of celery, chopped
4	sprigs of thyme
4 oz	unsalted butter

water, to cover
heavy cream
salt & pepper and rice vinegar, to taste

pork belly (makes extra):

1	uncured pork belly
8 oz	granulated sugar
8 oz	salt
1 gal	apple cider
½	bunch of thyme
2	cinnamon sticks

crisp sage:

2 cups	frying oil at 325°F
20	fresh sage leaves

salt
apple, julienne, to garnish

PARSNIP & PEAR SOUP WITH CIDER BRAISED PORK BELLY & CRISPED SAGE

BY BRIAN SUTTON

This is a warm, velvety soup that is slightly sweetened by the pear and braised pork belly. Crispy sage adds a little texture, perfect for the cool Adirondack Fall evenings.

METHOD

parsnip and pear soup:

In a large pot melt the butter over a medium heat, add the parsnips, celery, onion and thyme and sweat for 15 minutes, stirring regularly. Add the pears, cover with water and season with salt and pepper. Simmer for 40 minutes and remove from the heat. In a blender purée the soup until smooth and strain through a fine mesh sieve. Adjust to the desired consistency with the cream, then season with salt, pepper and rice vinegar. Set aside until needed.

pork belly:

Mix the sugar, salt, thyme, and cinnamon. Add enough apple cider to form a paste. Smother the pork with the paste and refrigerate for 24 hours. Wash off the paste and set aside. Preheat the oven to 300°F. Bring the remaining cider to a boil and pour over the pork, cover and place in the oven for 3 hours. Remove from the oven and let cool in the cider. When cool store in a refrigerator for 24 hours. When the pork is needed remove from the liquid, slice into 2" cubes and brown under a salamander.

crisp sage:

Fry the sage leaves in oil until they become crisp (about 30 seconds). Remove from the oil and place on a paper towel. Sprinkle with salt and set aside.

to serve:

Warm the soup and check the seasoning. Pour into a bowl, place a piece of the pork belly in the middle and sprinkle five crisp sage leaves on top. Garnish with julienne apple.

ROASTED ELK WITH CONFIT CABBAGE & SHIITAKE MUSHROOMS

BY BRIAN SUTTON

Being in the Adirondack Park, our customers expect to see some kind of game dish on our menu. Sometimes we use venison but elk is slightly more refined. We serve it with earthy cabbage and shiitake mushrooms.

Serves 4
Preparation time: 25 minutes
Cooking time: 45 minutes

INGREDIENTS

elk:

4	elk loin medallions, 5 oz each
8 oz	shiitake mushrooms, stemmed and julienned
6	sprigs of thyme
2 cups	veal glace

confit cabbage:

1	head of hearty white winter cabbage, core removed and julienned
2	medium onions, julienned
4	sprigs of thyme
6 oz	duck fat

to serve:

salt & pepper, to taste
vegetable oil, as needed
celery root, freshly grated, (optional)

METHOD

confit cabbage:

In a medium-sized pot warm the duck fat over a medium high heat. Once hot add the cabbage, onions, four sprigs of thyme and season with salt and pepper. Sweat the ingredients for 8-10 minutes, then reduce the heat to low and simmer for 45 minutes or until tender. Set aside in a warm place until needed.

elk:

Season the elk with salt, pepper and the remaining sprigs of thyme. In a heavy skillet over a high heat sear the elk in vegetable oil on all sides, reduce the heat to medium and cook until medium rare, making sure to constantly rotate the meat so that it cooks evenly on all sides. Remove from the pan and set in a warm place until needed. In the same pan sauté the shiitake mushrooms until they are wilted and then add the veal glace, and simmer for 5 minutes. Adjust the seasoning and set aside.

to serve:

Place the cabbage in the center of a large serving platter – be sure to remove any excess duck fat. Place the elk medallions on top and pour the sauce over. A nice garnish is freshly grated celery root.

MAPLE CREME WITH ROASTED APPLES

BY BRIAN SUTTON

Serves 4
Preparation time: 10 minutes
Cooking time: 15 minutes

Planning ahead:
The crème needs to be refrigerated overnight.

The Maple Crème is a simple dessert, smooth with a delicate note of maple syru, that we buy from a local farm, here in Lake Placid. It is all tied together with NY state apples and vanilla.

INGREDIENTS

crème:

1 pt	heavy cream
3½ oz	maple syrup
3	sheets of gelatin

roasted apples:

4	apples, peeled and sliced thinly
2 oz	unsalted butter
1	vanilla bean, cut in half
2 oz	maple syrup

METHOD

crème:

Place the gelatin sheets in cold water to soften. Bring the cream to a boil with the maple syrup, remove from the heat and add the gelatin. Pour the mixture evenly into four sprayed ramekins and refrigerate overnight.

roasted apples:

Over a medium heat sauté the apples in the butter with the vanilla bean until they begin to wilt. Remove from the heat, add the maple syrup and cover to let them steep for 15 minutes.

to serve:

Invert the crèmes into a bowl and place the warm apples around the outside. Be sure to get some of the liquid as well.

Justin Ermini

Mayflower Inn's Executive Chef, Justin Ermini, trained at the Culinary Institute of America. His career began at La Gauloise Bistro in Louisiana and has since included The Putney Inn, Vermont; Postrio in San Francisco; New York's James Beard House and Jean-Georges, a three Michelin star restaurant. This was followed by his first stint at The Mayflower Inn in Connecticut; California's Belly Italiano and Watergrill, which has a Michelin star, and the current return to The Mayflower. He has also spent some time in Florence, Italy, visiting restaurants and establishing relationships with wine makers and food distributors.

Justin enjoys the Litchfield county area for its wonderful ingredients such as fresh milk from Arethusa Farm, meat from Greyledge Farm, and Waldingfield Farm, where he can pick his own heirloom tomatoes. He loves working with local purveyors and being hands-on with the farmers.

The Mayflower Inn & Spa

This property is one of the most acclaimed destination spas in the U.S. and is nestled on 58 acres of lush grounds less than two hours from the Big Apple.

Enjoy an amazing array of treatments as well as classes in dream interpretation, dance, painting, writing, yoga and Tai Chi among others in the spa with its stunning decor, enhanced by a calming palette of blue and white. Workshops on topics such as marriage, sleep and stress are led by renowned experts in their respective fields. The culinary offering includes the healthy and delicious cuisine of the spa as well as the fine dining experience available at The Inn, and the guest rooms reflect the tranquil elegance evident throughout the property.

DUNGENESS CRAB 'LOUIE', HEIRLOOM TOMATO, AVOCADO MOUSSE, DEVILED QUAIL EGG, CUMIN TUILE, CAPER BERRIES

BY JUSTIN ERMINI

Perfect for those with a wandering eye, there is something to attract all in this pretty dish. The smooth avocado mousse and juicy crab make this dish an artistic classic.

Serves 4
Preparation time: 1 hour
Cooking time: 30 minutes

Special equipment:
Fine micro plane zester, ice cream machine

INGREDIENTS

crab:

½ cup Dungeness crab meat
1 heirloom tomato
16 pieces cumin tuile (see recipe below)
8 caper berries
¼ oz micro cilantro
lemon juice
extra virgin olive oil

avocado mousse: (yields ½ qt)

½ oz extra virgin olive oil
¼ oz shallots, diced
1½ cloves garlic
2 avocados (peeled and deseeded)
1½ tbsp cilantro
2 oz lime juice
4 dashes of Tabasco sauce
3 eggs, separated
¾ cup heavy cream
salt & cayenne pepper, to taste

deviled quail eggs: (yields 1 cup)

3 hard boiled quail eggs (yolk only)
¼ tsp Dijon mustard
¼ tbsp parsley, chopped
¼ tbsp tarragon, chopped
1 tsp extra virgin olive oil
1 tbsp mayonnaise
salt & pepper, to taste
4 quail eggs

cumin tuile: (yields ¼ qt)

¼ cup butter, melted
1 tsp honey
¼ cup powdered sugar
1¼ oz cake flour
1¼ oz bread flour
¼ cup egg whites
2 tbsp toasted cumin
fleur de sel
salt & pepper, to taste

METHOD

avocado mousse:

Sauté the shallot and garlic in the olive oil, let cool and place in a blender. Add the egg yolk, cilantro, lime juice, Tabasco, avocado and blend. Finish with the cream and season. In a bowl whip the egg whites to soft peaks. Fold all together and spin in an ice cream machine for 15 minutes or until the right consistency.

deviled quail eggs:

Grate the egg yolk on a fine micro plane zester. Fold in the rest of the ingredients, apart from the 4 quail eggs. Season to taste. Bring a pan of

water to a boil. Add the quail eggs and cook for 3 minutes 30 seconds and shock in an ice bath. Peel, split and de-yolk. Stuff with the deviled egg mixture.

cumin tuile:

Preheat the oven to 325°F. Sift both flours with the powdered sugar. Mix with the rest of the ingredients, except the fleur de sel, in a mixer. Spread the mixture onto a silpat mat evenly, and sprinkle with fleur de sel. Bake until golden brown, about 5-7 minutes.

to serve:

Lightly dress the crab and tomato with lemon juice and extra virgin olive oil. Cut the caper berries in half. Place on a plate along with two deviled egg halves, and top with a cumin tuile. Garnish with the micro cilantro and a quenelle of avocado mousse.

FOUR STORY HILL FARM'S SWEETBREADS, QUAIL EGG RAVIOLI, DELICATA SQUASH PUREE, PEARL ONIONS, SPECK

BY JUSTIN ERMINI

Delicately paired with soft, seasonal squash the sweetbreads really tempt the palate. The tasty quail egg ravioli and pearl onions are the perfect accompaniment.

Serves 4
Preparation time: 4 hours
Cooking time: 1 hour

Special equipment:
Mixer with dough hook, 4" circle cutter

INGREDIENTS

16	veal sweetbreads, 2 oz each
2 oz	speck (large dice)
1	lemon
3 oz	butter
2 oz	sage
salt & pepper	
2 oz	veal jus

pasta dough:

4	whole eggs
2	egg yolks
1¼ oz	'00' flour
½ tbsp	sea salt
1 tbsp	extra virgin olive oil

spinach and mascarpone filling: (yields 4 cups)

6 cups	baby spinach
½ cup	parmesan reggiano, grated
1 cup	mascarpone cheese
2 tbsp	sea salt
½	lemon, zest
¼ tsp	nutmeg, freshly grated
¼ tsp	white pepper

quail egg ravioli:

6 oz	spinach and mascarpone filling (see recipe above)
4	quail egg yolks
1	whole egg, beaten for egg wash

braised pearl onions:

20	pearl onions, peeled
6 tbsp	butter
2 cups	chicken stock
3 tbsp	water
3 tbsp	sugar
1 tsp	sherry vinegar
salt & pepper, to taste	

delicata squash purée:

1	delicata squash, halved and seeded
4 tbsp	butter, 2 tbsp chopped, other 2 tbsp reserved for later
1 tsp	brown sugar
¾ cup	water (reserve ¼ cup)
1 tbsp	salt

METHOD

pasta dough:

In a mixer on speed 1 with the dough hook add the flour, then slowly add the eggs and yolks. Mix for 5 minutes and finish with the salt and olive oil. Mix for 2 more minutes and let rest for 15 minutes, covered with a damp cloth.

spinach and mascarpone filling:

Blanch the spinach in salted boiling water for 3 minutes and shock in an ice bath. Press through cheese cloth until completely drained of all excess water. Chop the spinach very finely and fold in the mascarpone, parmesan, lemon zest and seasonings.

quail egg ravioli:

Roll out the pasta dough on #1 on a pasta machine to 1 ft long; repeat the process twice.

Place a 1½ oz dollop of spinach and mascarpone filling four times on the pasta sheet – space it out by 2" each time. Make a well in the center of each dollop of filling and fill with a quail egg yolk. Brush a circle of egg wash around each dollop. Carefully place the other pasta sheet on top pushing out all the air when sealing the ravioli. Cut with a 4" circle cutter and place on a flat service dusted with flour, so it won't stick.

braised pearl onions:

In a sauteuse, add the water and sugar and make a light caramel. Add the pearl onions and coat with the caramel. Add the chicken stock, butter, salt and pepper. Cook on a medium heat, until medium firmness, do not cook completely soft or the onions will be overcooked during the carry over cooking. Finish with sherry vinegar to taste and pour into a slotted pan to separate the liquid and onions. Reserve the liquid for reheating.

delicata squash purée:

Preheat the oven to 375°F low fan. Lay the squash, face up in a hotel pan. Sprinkle each squash half with the 2 tablespoons of chopped butter, sugar, and salt. Pour ½ cup of water in the pan and cover. Roast for 35 minutes. Scoop out the inside of the squash (no skin at all) and purée. While blending, add the remaining 2 tablespoons of cold butter, then add the remaining ¼ cup of water gradually while further blending until smooth. Add salt to taste.

to serve:

Dust the sweetbreads in flour and sear in a pan on a high heat. When browned on both sides, degrease the pan and add the butter, and speck. Add the pearl onion and when the butter is browned add the lemon and sage and season with salt and pepper. Add the quail egg ravioli to salted boiling water and cook for 3 minutes. Arrange on the plate as pictured.

ORANGE BLOSSOM HONEY PANNA COTTA

BY MAYRA VICTORIA

Summer in a dish, this Orange Blossom Honey Panna Cotta is a sure winner with all. The smooth silky panna cotta and the hazy orange blossom honey are beautifully set off with the chamomile foam – the ultimate finish for any dessert.

Serves 4

Preparation time: 4 hours 30 minutes
Cooking time: 40 minutes

Special equipment:
4 silicone molds with 4 oz cavities (if possible the half dome but any other shape will work – if you don't have silicone molds ramekins will do), mixer with a paddle attachment, immersion blender (or milk frother)

INGREDIENTS

panna cotta:

2½ oz	orange blossom honey or clove honey
1⅔ cups	heavy cream
½ cup	milk
3	gelatin leaves

pine nut streusel:

2 oz	butter (ice cold and cut into ½" cubes)
2 oz	all purpose flour
2 oz	ground pine nuts (grind in a spice grinder with 2 tbsp of all purpose flour)
2 oz	confectioner's sugar
⅛ tsp	salt

chamomile foam:

1 cup	whole milk
1¾ oz	granulated sugar
2	good quality chamomile tea bags
¾ tsp	soy lecithin granules

mint poached persimmons:

3	medium-sized Fuyu persimmons, peeled and small diced
4 oz	water
4 oz	sugar
2	mint sprig
¼ tsp	lime juice

garnish:

toasted pine nuts

METHOD

panna cotta:

In a medium-sized pot combine the milk, cream and honey and bring to a boil over a medium heat. Meanwhile, in a small bowl filled with water and a couple of ice cubes, place your gelatin leaves to 'bloom'. Once the cream mixture boils take the gelatin leaves, squeeze out any excess water, add to the pot, and whisk until dissolved. Quickly pour the mixture into a medium bowl sitting inside a larger bowl filled with water and ice (an ice bath). Constantly stir while the mixture cools down until it resembles a loose yogurt consistency. Carefully pour the mixture into the molds and place in a freezer for a minimum of 4 hours. Once frozen take out of the molds and place onto a parchment lined baking tray. Allow to thaw in the refrigerator.

pine nut streusel:

Preheat the oven to 325°F, place a rack on the middle shelf. In the bowl of a mixer fitted with the paddle attachment, place the dry ingredients. On a low to medium speed paddle the dry ingredients to evenly distribute them. Add all the cold butter at once and watch closely as you mix for 5-7 minutes. The mixture should resemble small pebbles. Remove from the mixer and spread over a parchment lined baking pan. Bake in the oven for about 8 minutes. Remove from the oven and, with a whisk, toss the crumble to distribute and break apart. Return to the oven and continue to bake for 5 more minutes. Repeat the process with the whisk and finish baking for 3 minutes or until golden brown.

chamomile foam:

In a small pot combine the milk and sugar, then bring to a boil over a medium heat. Remove from the heat, add the chamomile tea bags, and allow to infuse for 5 minutes. Strain or scoop out the tea bags. Bring the milk mixture back up to a boil and off the heat add the lecithin granules. Use the immersion blender to incorporate the lecithin. With the immersion blender carefully froth the milk mixture.

mint poached persimmons:

In a small pot bring the water and sugar to a boil. Off the heat add the mint sprigs and allow to infuse for 5 minutes. Strain out the mint and add the lime juice. Bring back to a low simmer and add the persimmons. Poach the persimmons for about 8 minutes. Pour the persimmons and syrup into a small bowl sitting in a larger bowl with water and ice in it to cool down immediately.

to serve:

Take four soup bowls and with a wide spatula gently lift one panna cotta from the baking tray and place in the center of the bowl. Repeat with the others. Using a spoon take some of the persimmons with none of the syrup and place around the base of the panna cotta in small clusters. Sprinkle some of the pine nut streusel and toasted pine nuts over the panna cotta and around the base. Froth the chamomile foam and, with a spoon, skim just the foam off the top (making sure not to take any of the milk as this will destroy your luscious foam), and dollop it over the top. Serve and enjoy.

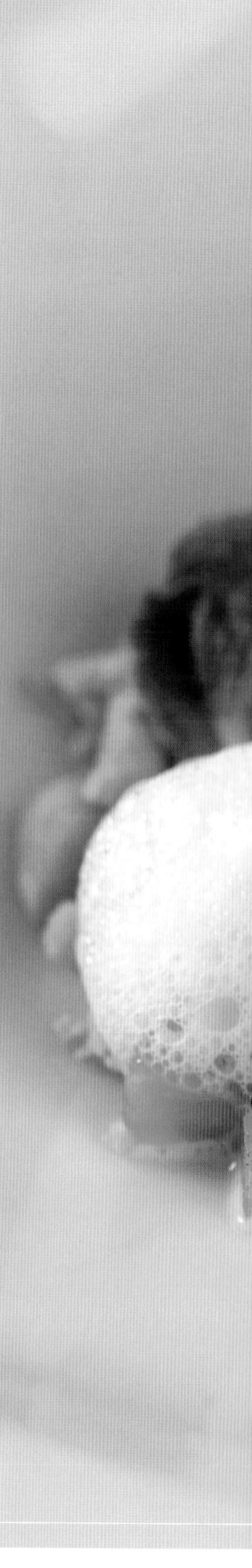

Sue Schickler

Sue Schickler's interest in cooking was, like many chefs, formed early in a family that appreciated good food and wine. As a child Sue spent time cooking with her father and mother and was introduced to the restaurant life by dear family friends who owned a restaurant in Cleveland, Ohio. Sue's style of cooking, which could be defined by a lightness of touch and an emphasis on respect for ingredients, was developed while working at restaurants in Annapolis, Maryland and Rehoboth Beach, Delaware.

Image courtesy of Jim Westphalen

The Pitcher Inn

Set among Vermont's Green Mountains, The Pitcher Inn is a delightfully distinctive and elegant hotel that celebrates intellectual curiosity, culinary excellence with a delicious menu influenced by French and Italian cooking, and sport due to its location at the foot of the Sugarbush ski and golf resort.

Above your bed is a blackboard covered in chalk-written algebraic formulae! Did Einstein once sleep here? In another suite, a chessboard painted on an old chest serving as a coffee table invites you to commence a strategic duel by the fireside. The Trout Room, eclectically decorated in a fishing theme, inspires all of its occupants to try their hand at fishing

SQUASH & TALEGGIO RAVIOLI WITH YOGURT, ALMONDS & BROWN BUTTER

BY SUE SCHICKLER

I love the combination of the warm, melted taleggio with the lemony, brown butter in this dish.

Serves 4-6
Preparation time: 50 minutes
Cooking time: 1 hour

INGREDIENTS

ravioli:

1	recipe pasta dough
1	butternut squash
1	buttercup squash
1 tbsp	extra virgin olive oil
5 oz	butter, cut in cubes
salt	
8 oz	taleggio, rind removed and cut into ½" cubes

brown butter:

4 oz	unsalted butter
1 tbsp	lemon juice
½	shallot, minced
salt	
4	sage leaves, thinly sliced

to serve:

½ cup	Greek yogurt, not reduced fat
¼ cup	Marcona almonds, roughly chopped

METHOD

ravioli:

Cut the squashes in half lengthwise and scoop out the seeds. Brush with olive oil and bake cut side down on a parchment-lined sheet pan at 350°F until soft, about 35-40 minutes. When cool enough to handle, scoop out the flesh and purée the squash in a food processor. Add the butter and season to taste with salt. Pass through a tamis sieve and fill a pastry bag with the squash. With a pasta machine, roll out the pasta into two sheets. Pipe small mounds of squash on one sheet, and press a cube of taleggio in each one. Lightly spray the pasta with water and cover with the second sheet of pasta. Press together around each mound and cut into ravioli with either a round or square cutter.

brown butter:

In a small pan, melt the butter. Cook over a medium heat, swirling the pan, until the butter has a nutty aroma and has browned. Remove from the heat and carefully add the lemon juice. Add the shallot and return to the heat for a minute to soften them. Season to taste with salt and add the sage.

to serve:

Bring a large pot of salted water to the boil. Add the ravioli and cook until the pasta is tender, about 5-6 minutes. Remove from the water and arrange the ravioli in pasta bowls. Place a spoonful of yogurt in the center of each bowl, spoon the brown butter over the ravioli and top with the almonds.

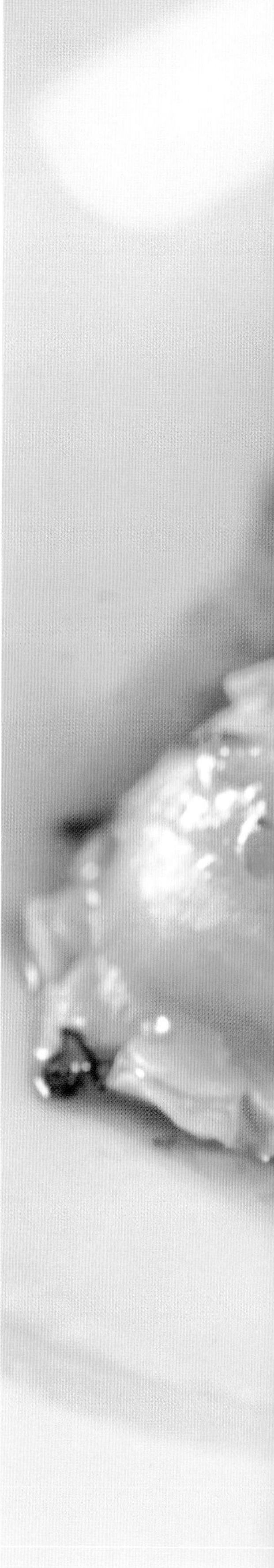

Serves 4
Preparation time: 1 hour
Cooking time: 2 hours

BRAISED RABBIT LEG WITH STUFFED LOIN, SPAETZLE, BRAISED ENDIVE & RIESLING

BY SUE SCHICKLER

The slightly bitter flavor of the endive is a nice complement to the richly flavored rabbit and sauce.

INGREDIENTS

rabbit legs:

4	rabbit hind legs
1	onion, minced
2	leeks, white and pale green parts only, cut into small dice
1	fennel bulb, cut into small dice
1	sprig of thyme
1 qt	brown rabbit stock, made from the carcasses and forelegs of the rabbits
2 cups	Riesling wine
salt	

rabbit loins:

4	rabbit loins with the flap attached
1 cup	fresh breadcrumbs
1	leek, cut into small dice
1	shallot, minced
½	celeriac, peeled and cut into small dice
2	parsnips, peeled and cut into small dice
2	sprigs of tarragon, leaves blanched and chopped
8-10	prunes, soaked overnight in ¼ cup Armagnac
2 tbsp	pistachios, roasted and rough chopped
2 tbsp	extra virgin olive oil
2 tbsp	butter
2 tbsp	clarified butter
salt	

spaetzle:

2 cups	all purpose flour
2	eggs
⅔ cup	water
salt and grated nutmeg, to taste	
3 tbsp	clarified butter
2 tbsp	onion, minced
1 tbsp	parsley, chopped
¼ cup	parmesan, grated

endive:

4	heads Belgian endive
2 tbsp	clarified butter
1	carrot, peeled and small diced
½	onion, small diced
1	stalk celery, small diced
½	bulb of fennel, small diced
2 cups	chicken stock

sauce:

braising liquid from the legs	
1 cup	heavy cream
2	egg yolks
¼ cup	crème fraîche
2 tbsp	tarragon, blanched and chopped
1 tbsp	chervil, chopped chervil
1 tbsp	lemon juice
1 tbsp	cold butter

METHOD

rabbit legs:

In a pan large enough to hold the legs in a single layer sweat the vegetables until tender. Add the wine, turn the heat up to medium, and let the wine reduce by half. Add the thyme sprig and place the legs on top of the vegetables. Bring the stock to a boil and add enough to not quite cover the legs. Season with salt, cover with parchment paper and set the heat to a gentle simmer. Cook until the legs are tender, about 45 minutes to an hour.

rabbit loins:

Prepare the filling by sweating the vegetables until tender in the olive oil and butter. Add the prunes, pistachios, tarragon and enough breadcrumbs to hold together as a filling. Season with salt. Lay the loins out on a work surface and place the filling on the flaps close to the loins. Use the flaps to wrap the filling and the loins. Tie each one with twine. Heat the clarified butter in a sauté pan and sear the loins on all sides. Finish cooking in a 350°F oven for about 6 minutes, until the loins are medium rare.

spaetzle:

Combine the flour, eggs, water and seasoning in a bowl. Set aside to rest for 20 minutes. Bring a large pot of salted water to a boil and push the dough through a spaetzle maker or a colander into the water. Cook the spaetzle for about 1 minute after it comes to the surface, then remove to an ice bath. To serve, sauté the onion in clarified butter. Add the spaetzle and sauté until lightly browned. Season with salt and add the parsley and parmesan cheese.

endive:

In a shallow braising pan heat the clarified butter. Cut the endives in quarters lengthwise and remove most of the core, leaving just enough to hold the endives together. Brown the endives on the cut sides and remove from the pan. Add the vegetables to the pan, lower the heat and cook until the vegetables are softened. Place the endives on top of the vegetables and add the stock. Season to taste, bring to a simmer, cover with parchment paper and cook in the oven until tender, about 25 minutes.

sauce:

Remove the legs from the liquid and strain the broth into a saucepan, pressing on the vegetables. Add the heavy cream and gently simmer until the sauce is slightly thickened and flavorful. Lower the heat, combine the egg yolks and crème fraîche, and whisk into the sauce along with the tarragon and chervil. Gently heat until thickened, adjust the seasoning, adding a dash of lemon juice, and whisk in the butter.

to serve:

Place a small portion of spaetzle on each plate, with endive spears off to the side. Place the sliced loins and a leg on each plate. Nap the legs with the sauce (coat lightly all over in a thin layer) and spoon a little more sauce around the edge of the plate.

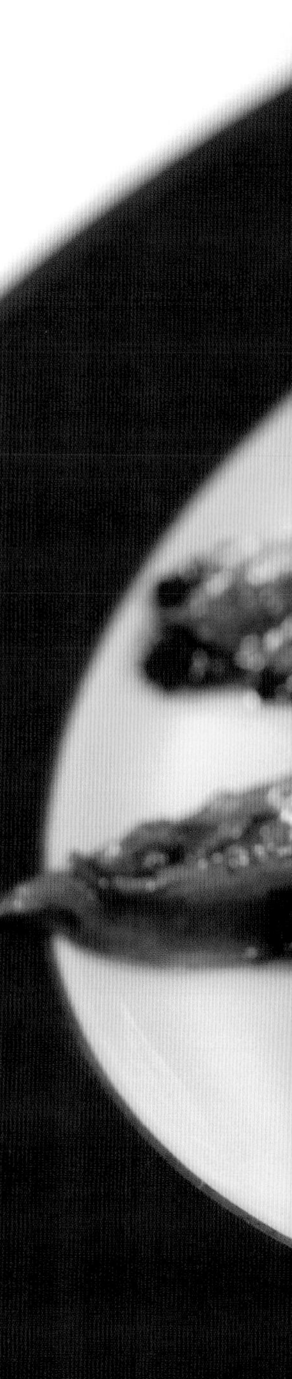

OLIVE OIL CAKE WITH BLUEBERRY COMPOTE, LEMON CURD & OLIVE OIL ICE CREAM

BY JIM GIOIA

The flavors of lemon and fruity olive oil make this a perfect Summer dessert, when blueberries are in season.

Serves 12
Preparation time: 45 minutes
Cooking time: 35-40 minutes

Special equipment:
Ice cream machine

Planning ahead:
The ice cream should be made in advance.

INGREDIENTS

cake:

5	eggs, separated
¾ cup	sugar
¾ cup	extra virgin olive oil
½	lemon, juice
1	lemon zest
1 cup	cake flour, sifted

blueberry compote:

2 pt	blueberries
½ cup	water
½ cup	sugar
3	strips of lemon zest

olive oil ice cream:

10	egg yolks
10 oz	sugar
2 cups	whole milk
2 cups	heavy cream
¾ cup	extra virgin olive oil

lemon curd:

6	eggs
2	egg yolks
2 cups	sugar
5	lemons, juice and zest
1 cup	cold butter, cubed

METHOD

cake:

Grease and line with parchment a 9" round cake pan.

In the bottom of an electric mixer beat the egg whites with the whisk attachment on medium speed until light and frothy, about 1 minute. Gradually add ¼ cup sugar and continue whisking until soft peaks form. Transfer the whites to another bowl and set aside. Add the egg yolks to the empty mixing bowl and beat on medium speed with the paddle attachment and slowly add the remaining ½ cup of sugar, lemon juice and zest. Beat until lightened in color and thick. With the mixer running, slowly drizzle in the olive oil in a steady stream. With the mixer on low speed add the flour, mixing until combined. Remove the bowl from the mixing stand. With a rubber spatula scrape the sides of the bowl and stir in a third of the egg whites to lighten the batter. Fold in the remaining egg whites in two additions, mixing gently until the mixture is combined. Pour into the prepared pan and bake at 350°F for 35-40 minutes. The top of the cake should just spring back when gently pressed.

blueberry compote:

Combine the sugar, zest and water in a medium saucepan and bring to a boil, dissolving the sugar. Cook for about 2 minutes until thick and then add the blueberries. Simmer gently until about half the blueberries begin to pop and the compote thickens. Pour into a bowl, remove the zest and chill.

olive oil ice cream:

In a saucepan bring the milk and cream just to a simmer. Meanwhile whisk the egg yolks until lightened in color. Add the sugar gradually and whisk until the mixture is pale and very thick. Slowly whisk in half of the hot milk and cream mixture then return to the saucepan and cook over a low heat, stirring constantly until the mixture thickens and coats the back of a wooden spoon. Strain through a sieve into a clean bowl. Cover the surface with plastic wrap and chill for several hours or overnight. When you are ready to freeze the ice cream, stir in the olive oil and freeze according to your ice cream maker's directions.

lemon curd:

Combine all the ingredients, except the butter, in a mixing bowl. Place the bowl over a pot of simmering water and stir constantly with a wooden spoon, or a heat proof spatula until thick. Remove from the heat, stir in the butter, mixing until it is melted and combined. Pour the mixture through a sieve into a clean bowl, cover the surface with plastic wrap and chill.

to serve:

Swirl lemon curd on the plate. Add a slice of cake and top with a scoop of ice cream and blueberry compote.

Mark Levy

After graduating in Catering and Hospitality in England, Mark Levy had a stint at the Inn at Perry Cabin, then transferred to its sister property, Keswick Hall. This was followed by Paris, where he worked with Michel Rostang, then to London doing high-end contract work for Roux Fine Dining. Next he was Chef de Partie at gastro pub The Bell. Mark continued on in the gastro pub universe, working at the Star Inn, the Running Horse, then finally on to Greg Nicholl's acclaimed 'pub,' The Russell, where he won the title of England's Gastro Pub Chef of the Year in 2007. He joined The Point in 2008.

Mark relishes the chance to cook for the guests of an eleven-room resort with no set menu: "I can't imagine anything more fun than constantly inventing approximately 36 dishes a week."

He thinks of his ingredients, his menus, and his guests: "They continuously raise the bar each night and expect an amazing meal. It is my aspiration to see no plates come back to the kitchen half-eaten. I like them squeaky clean."

The Point

The Point is a special place indeed set on the wooded shore of Upper Saranac Lake.

The Point, an Adirondack Great Camp, built for William A. Rockefeller, is a marvellous marriage of rustic simplicity and extraordinary luxury. Its eleven magnificent guest rooms are spread among four log buildings; here the silence and peace of the great North woods reign supreme. The Point is a study in delicious contrasts: the exceptional meals prepared by the kitchen, the blaze of the campfire on the edge of the dark lake, the fine art and antiques, most original to the camp, and the supply of snowshoes and skis for exploring the magical white forest. Enjoy gourmet picnic excursions, journeys through the rippling waters in gleaming mahogany boats, tasting menus of old cognacs, a staff that organizes each day according to the pleasure of the guests.

TRUFFLED HAMACHI TARTARE, AVOCADO, SOFT QUAIL EGG & AMERICAN CAVIAR

BY MARK LEVY

A fantastic fish of the highest quality.

Serves 4
Preparation time: 1 hour
Cooking time: 2-3 minutes

INGREDIENTS

truffled hamachi

9 oz hamachi
juice of 1 lemon
salt & pepper
1 tsp truffle oil
1 oz black truffle, grated + 32 truffle discs
4 radishes
picked chervil and anise hyssop leaves

quail eggs:

8 quail eggs
royal sterling American caviar

garnish:

1 avocado
8 cherry tomatoes
½ English cucumber
1 red pepper
red pepper oil

to serve:

1 handful of popcorn shoots

METHOD

quail eggs:

Boil the quail eggs for 2-3 minutes depending on their size, cool under cold water then peel, being very careful not to damage the egg. Top the eggs with caviar.

garnish:

Peel the avocado and cut some discs, gently grill them and set aside. Purée the rest of the avocado, season and chill. Blanch and peel the tomatoes, cut the cucumber into equal batons, finely dice the red pepper flesh and mix with some red pepper oil. set all this aside for when you finish the plate.

truffled hamachi:

Small dice the hamachi and mix with the grated truffle, lemon juice, salt, pepper and truffle oil, push this mix into a cutter, to make four portions. Surround with thin slices of the radish and stamped-out truffle discs. Top this off as shown, with the picked chervil and anise leaves.

to serve:

Sweep the avocado purée across the plate and arrange the garnish decoratively starting with the caviar topped quail eggs and finishing with the red pepper oil and popcorn shoots.

Chef's tip:

Only use top grade hamachi.

Serves 4
Preparation time: 2 hours
Cooking time: 3 hours

Planning ahead:
Prepare the lamb shoulder the day before to make life easier.

INGREDIENTS

lamb:

1 Colorado lamb shoulder, boned and rolled
1 8-bone Colorado lamb rack
½ cup lamb jus

Winter vegetables:

16 mini florets of green cauliflower
Brussels sprout leaves
16 carrots, cut into small cubes
16 cubes butternut squash
20 red pearl onions, peeled
4 shallots, roasted
4 turnips, cut into discs

to serve:

butter
2 qt picked spinach
½ cup onion purée
salt & pepper
1 cup black trumpet mushrooms
½ cup butternut squash purée
4 fingerling potatoes, cooked
chervil leaves
flour

ROAST RACK & BRAISED SHOULDER OF COLORADO LAMB, VIDALIA ONION PUREE & WINTER VEGETABLES

BY MARK LEVY

Some of the best lamb I have tasted.

METHOD

shoulder:

Seal and braise the lamb shoulder until tender, allow to cool in its liquid until cool enough to handle, remove any ties and wrap tightly in plastic wrap to form a cylinder, chill until required.

rack:

Trim the lamb rack, wrap each bone in aluminum foil to prevent burning, and seal over a medium-high heat. Transfer to the oven and roast for 8-10 minutes until pink. Rest well in a warm place.

Winter vegetables:

Blanch the cauliflower, sprout leaves, carrot, butternut squash, red pearl onions, shallots and turnips one at a time, refreshing them all in an ice bath. Dry and set aside for plating.

to serve:

Cut the chilled lamb shoulder into hockey puck-size pieces, dredge in flour and sauté on both side until crispy. Keep warm. Sauté the turnips, shallots, carrots and red pearl onions in a little butter. Do the same with the sprouts and spinach in a separate pan. Season the dish whenever you wish. Making sure everything is warm, including the purée, start to compose the dish, as illustrated. Make it as colorful and defined as possible with the black trumpet mushrooms, fingerling potatoes and chervil leaves. Finish with a few drops of lamb jus.

APPLE FINANCIER CAKE, CINNAMON MILKSHAKE, APPLE GELEE, SALTED CARAMEL SAUCE

BY CHARLENE SMITH

A big apple dessert in upstate New York.

Serves 4

Preparation time:	4 hours (including the time for the apple gelée to set)
Cooking time:	20 minutes

Special equipment:
3" high metal circular molds, small half moon fleximolds, ice cream machine

INGREDIENTS

apple financier cake:

5 tbsp	melted butter (browned)
4 tbsp	ground almond flour
6 tbsp	powdered sugar
4 tbsp	all purpose flour
2	whole egg whites
1 cup	minced apples (tossed with cinnamon sugar)

cinnamon milkshake:

1 cup	heavy cream
1 cup	whole milk
1	cinnamon stick
½ cup	granulated sugar
5	whole egg yolks

apple gelée:

4 cup	apple cider (or juice)
15	sheets of gelatin

salted caramel sauce:

1 cup	granulated sugar
¾ cup	heavy cream (warmed)
2 tbsp	unsalted butter
1 tsp	coarse sea salt

garnish:

powdered sugar
vanilla stick
mint leaf

METHOD

apple financier cake:

In a mixer combine the almond flour, all purpose flour, sugar and egg whites. Mix until completely combined and smooth. Melt the butter in a small pan until golden brown. Add to flour and egg white mixture until emulsified. Portion halfway up an oiled mold with batter, then place a small spoonful of apple mixture in the center, then fill the remainder of the mold with batter. Bake in a 350°F oven for about 15 minutes or until golden brown.

cinnamon milkshake:

In a saucepan combine the cream, milk, and cinnamon stick. Heat slightly and let it steep (about 30 minutes). Place the sugar and egg yolks into a small mixing bowl and whisk together. Bring the steeped cream up to a slight boil and gradually add to the yolk mixture, stirring constantly. Add the mixture back into the saucepan and bring to 180°F (or until it coats the back of a spoon). Pass through a strainer. Cool. Spin in an ice cream machine. Once spun, add ice cream in a blender with a ½ cup of cold milk, and set on low, just until it has combined.

apple gelée:

Place the gelatin in cold water to bloom. Heat the apple juice (or cider) up to a boil. Remove from the heat and add the bloomed gelatin. Position into small half moon flexi-molds and allow the geatin to chill for at least 3-4 hours. Once chilled, gently remove from molds and scoop a small amount of the gelée from the center of the half moon shapes. Fill two halves of the gelée with the thick caramel sauce and seal together. Set aside in a cooler.

salted caramel sauce:

In a heavy bottom saucepan gradually add sugar and caramelize until a light golden brown. Take off the heat and add warmed cream and butter. Add the salt, whisk until combined and chill.

to serve:

Place the milkshake in a tall shot glass and put on a large circular plate.

Garnish the apple financier cake with powdered sugar, vanilla stick and mint leaf, and set next to the shot glass. Place the apple gelée sphere on a small amount of bruinoise apple to balance. Place a quenelle of whipped cream appropriately on the plate.

David Daniels

The Wauwinet celebrates Nantucket's bountiful harvests from the sea and shore with its internationally acclaimed restaurant, Toppers. Using fresh local ingredients, Executive Chef David Daniels' signature cooking style is one of inspired simplicity. His innovative dishes celebrate the distinct, natural flavors of seasonal foods.

The Wauwinet

Built in 1860, The Wauwinet has the distinction of being one of the first hotels on the island of Nantucket.

With its tranquil harbors, endless stretches of beach, old manor houses, and beautiful gardens, the island of Nantucket is just 30 miles off the coast of Massachusetts. On the birthplace of Arthur Gordon Pym – hero of the novel of the same name by Edgar Allan Poe – stands The Wauwinet, a charming house covered in patinaed grey shingles. The freshly picked bunches of flowers in your room are characteristic of the attentiveness of the staff. Contemplate the splendid sunsets over Nantucket bay, relax or enjoy the water sports at the hotel's two private beaches, or indulge in massages inspired by local plants.

Serves 4
Preparation time: 15 minutes
Cooking time: 15 minutes

Special equipment:
Bain-Marie

INGREDIENTS

scallops:

½ cup	butter
20	Nantucket Bay or other small scallops, shells reserved
¼ cup	diced, rendered bacon
1 ½ cups	heavy cream
1 tbsp	diced chives
½ tsp	lemon juice
¼ cup	parmesan cheese, grated
salt & pepper	

parmesan foam:

1 cup	whole milk
1 tbsp	butter
1 tbsp	parmesan cheese powder
¼ cup	chicken stock

NANTUCKET BAY SCALLOPS IN OUR MEUNIERE

BY DAVID DANIELS

Nantucket Bay scallops are one of Nantucket's prized local bounties. Enjoyed hand harvested and commercially fished alike.

METHOD

scallops:

In a large skillet over a medium heat, melt the butter and sauté the scallops on one side until golden brown. Add the bacon and the cream. Bring to a boil and cook until the mixture coats the scallops. Add the chives, lemon juice, parmesan cheese, and salt and pepper to taste. Stir to combine.

parmesan foam

Combine all the ingredients and cook over a medium heat. Add to the bain-marie. Whisk with a small hand blender until foamy. Set aside.

to serve:

Place each scallop in a small, individual scallop shell, five per person. Top with the parmesan cheese foam.

Chef's tip:

Heat the parmesan foam to 125°F for ultimate effect.

SKILLET ROASTED DOVER SOLE, AUTUMN CHARD, FLAVORS OF BROWN BUTTER, LEMON & CAPERS

BY DAVID DANIELS

Classic Dover sole composed of modern techniques and flavors.

Serves 4
Preparation time: 20 minutes
Cooking time: 45 minutes

INGREDIENTS

Dover sole:

3	Dover sole, skinned with head removed, 1 lb each
1 cup	all purpose flour
1 tsp	salt
¼ tsp	white pepper
½ lb	unsalted butter
3 tbsp	capers
3	lemons, juiced
1 cup	canola oil

crust for Dover sole:

¼ cup	butter
½ cup	Panko breadcrumbs

vegetable composition:

¾ lb	baby spinach
¾ lb	rainbow chard, sliced with stem removed
10	cipollini onions, roasted and peeled
3 tbsp	olive oil

salt & pepper

cauliflower purée:

1 lb	cauliflower florets
3 cups	milk
3 tbsp	olive oil

salt & pepper

METHOD

Dover sole:

Combine the all purpose flour with salt and pepper. Dredge the Dover sole in the mixture. Shake off any excess mixture.

Place the oil in a heavy bottomed, oval sauté pan on a medium high heat and then add the Dover sole. Sauté to golden brown for 4 minutes, turn over and repeat on the other side. Place into a 400°F oven for 8 minutes. Remove the pan from the oven. Place the butter and capers into the pan and baste the fish for 1 minute. Finish with lemon juice and reserve the basting mixture. Remove the fish from the pan and set aside to rest for approximately 1 minute. Repeat the process for the other two fish.

To fillet fish from the bone, simply lift along the spine with a small utility knife or filleting knife and stack the filleted fish on top of each other.

crust for Dover sole:

Add the butter to a medium hot pan. Let it foam until the butter turns to a nut brown color. Remove from the heat and add the breadcrumbs. Mix thoroughly.

vegetable composition:

Add the olive oil to a large sauté pan on a medium heat. Sauté the chard, baby spinach and cipollini onions until soft. Add salt and pepper. Drain on paper towels, form into four equal piles and set aside.

cauliflower purée:

Combine the cauliflower, milk, salt and pepper. Simmer for 15 minutes, until soft. Place into a blender. Blend on high speed until smooth. Add olive oil to purée.

to serve:

Use a sauce spoon to create a pool of cauliflower purée in the middle of the plate. Place a pile of vegetable composition in the center of the cauliflower purée. Top each Dover sole fillet with some crust. Place the fillet in a crossed manner over the vegetable composition. Drizzle reserved sauce (basting mixture) over.

Chef's tip:

Ask your fish monger to skin the Dover sole for you.

Serves 6

Preparation time: 20 minutes

Cooking time: 40 minutes

Refrigeration time: 2 hours

Special equipment:

2 oz Mason jars

INGREDIENTS

crème brûlée:

½ cup	whole milk
1 ½ cups	heavy cream
4 tbsp	granulated sugar
5	egg yolks
1	vanilla bean (Tahitian), split lengthwise with seeds scraped out

raspberry compote:

1 cup	fresh raspberries
1 tbsp	sugar
1 tsp	red pepper juice

stewed figs:

8	black mission figs
1 tbsp	brown sugar

garnish:

8	thin slices of brioche toast
8	vanilla beans

VANILLA FIG CREME BRULEE, RASPBERRY COMPOTE, BRIOCHE TOAST

BY SERGE TORRES

This classic dessert has a hidden depth with the stewed figs, and the raspberry adds a lighter taste that sets off the rich cream beautifully. The Mason jar adds an interesting twist and will be the ultimate talking point at any event.

METHOD

crème brûlée:

Combine the milk, cream, sugar and vanilla bean in a small saucepan. Stir over a medium heat until it reaches boiling point. Set aside to steep until it cools.

Preheat the oven to 240°F.

In a separate bowl, whisk the egg yolks briefly. Add the cream mixture very slowly to the egg yolks, whisking well. Once blended, strain the mixture through a fine sieve. Pour the custard into 6 Mason jars, three-quarters full. Bake for 35-40 minutes, until the centers are softly set. Refrigerate for 2 hours.

raspberry compote:

Mix the raspberries, sugar and the red pepper juice. Lightly stew the mix for 5 minutes. Cool and reserve.

stewed figs:

Combine the sugar and figs over a medium heat for 5 minutes.

to serve:

Fill the remainder of each Mason jar with stewed figs. Sprinkle the top of each jar with sugar and torch to caramelize. Place the vanilla bean into the center of the brûlée. Position the raspberry compote opposite the brûlée in a sake cup. Add the thinly sliced toasted brioche.

Graham Gill

Born in the United Kingdom, Executive Chef Graham Gill discovered his passion for cooking in his early childhood. Trained at the Westminster Kingsway College, School of Culinary Art and Food Technology in London, Chef Gill gained his first practical experience working for the Savoy Group at The Connaught Hotel and The Berkeley Hotel. After continuing his European training in four and five star hotels and restaurants across the UK and Ireland, Chef Gill crossed the Atlantic Ocean and ventured to Bermuda, where he spent his first couple of years at the luxury Mandarin Oriental Elbow Beach and met and fell in love with his future wife, who brought him to Southern Vermont. Chef Gill is an excellent fit for the Windham Hill Restaurant with all of his international experience. He sources as many local products as possible for the menu and also has the pleasure of being able to harvest the bounty of the Inn's organic gardens.

Windham Hill Inn

Welcome to Windham Hill, a romantic place where the Summer nights offer up a magical spectacle and Fall reveals all the glorious colors of nature.

At the end of a country road, in the heart of 160 hectares of unspoilt nature, this elegant inn offers you exceptional views of the green mountains. Stroll among the pine and maple trees, watch the fireflies when night falls in the rolling hills of Vermont, admire the star-filled skies in the moonlight. Windham Hill Inn offers a haven of peace with its elegant rooms and suites and a cuisine showcasing seasonal produce from the garden that is sure to delight the most discerning of gourmets.

BUTTERNUT SQUASH & VERMONT CAMEMBERT RAVIOLI WITH PINE NUT & SAGE BEURRE NOISETTE

BY GRAHAM GILL

This dish was originally created by one of our international college interns as part of our on-going culinary training program. Adapted to become part of the menu, this is a great simple Winter dish.

Serves 8
Preparation time: 1 hour
Cooking time: 5 minutes

Planning ahead:
The pasta dough can be made in advance.

INGREDIENTS

ravioli filling:

1	medium butternut squash
1 tbsp	butter
⅛ cup	Vermont maple syrup
¼ tsp	cinnamon
½	small wheel Vermont Camembert cheese, finely sliced
salt & pepper	

ravioli dough:

1¾ cups	flour
5	egg yolks
1 tbsp	olive oil
1 tsp	salt

sage leaves:

1	bunch of sage leaves

pine nuts and sage beurre noisette:

1 tbsp	butter
1 tsp	pine nuts
½	chiffonard of sage leaves (shredded)

sage oil:

½	chiffonard of sage leaves (shredded)
¼ cup	olive oil
water	

METHOD

ravioli filling:
Cut the butternut squash in half, remove the seeds and score the surface with a knife. Add the butter, maple syrup, cinnamon and salt and pepper. Wrap each piece in aluminum foil and place on a baking sheet. Bake for 45 minutes to an hour at 350°F, until soft. Allow to cool. Scoop the flesh out of the skin and pass though a coarse sieve/strainer.

ravioli:
In a food processor, combine the flour, egg yolks, olive oil and salt. Pulse for 30 seconds or until the mixture has the texture of wet sand. Turn the mixture out onto a clean work surface and knead to form a dough. Knead for 2-3 minutes until pliable. Wrap in plastic film and rest in the refrigerator for 30 minutes. After resting, use a pasta roller or rolling pin to roll out the dough as thinly as possible into approximately 12" x 4" rectangular sheets. Cut the sheets into 4" x 4" squares (you will need two per raviolo, one for the base and one for the top - you should be able to make 16 ravioli). When you have all the squares of pasta ready, place one tablespoon of the filling in the center of the base of each square. Next, place a small slice of Camembert on top of the filling. Lightly brush water around the fillings. Now gently lift the other square of pasta and place on top of the fillings so that it exactly covers the base sheet. Press down to seal the layers of pasta around the base. Using a 3" fluted cutter, cut around each filling, making sure the edges are fully sealed.

sage leaves:
Using a deep fryer set to 365°F, add the sage leaves and cook for 1 minute or until crispy. Remove from the oil and place on a paper towel to drain off any excess oil.

pine nuts and sage beurre noisette:
Heat the butter in a frying pan heat until a light brown color. Add the pine nuts and shredded sage and cook for approximately 10 seconds. Remove the nuts from the pan and set aside.

sage oil:
Blanch the sage leaves in boiling water for approximately 10 seconds. Remove and place in a bowl of iced water. Remove and discard the stalks and add the leaves to a blender. Add the olive oil and blend for 5-10 seconds. Pour through a fine strainer, ready to serve.

to serve:
Boil a pan of seasoned water on the stove, add the ravioli and cook for 3-5 minutes (they should start to float when they are done). Remove from the water and place on a clean cloth to drain. Spoon the sage oil onto the front of the plate in a long line. Add the pine nuts at intervals along the line of oil. Place two ravioli behind the line and garnish each ravioli with a single deep fried sage leaf.

Chef's tip:
Ravioli can be made and frozen, but are always best served freshly made.

Serves 6
Preparation time: 1 hour
Cooking time: 10 minutes

INGREDIENTS

venison:

6 venison loin fillets, 5 oz each
salt & pepper

Brussels sprouts:

1 lb Brussels sprouts
4 oz chestnuts, peeled
1 tsp butter
salt & pepper

sweet potato purée:

1 lb sweet potatoes
1 pinch of nutmeg
dash of olive oil
salt & pepper

juniper berry jus:

2 cups veal stock
1 tbsp crushed juniper berries
salt & pepper

VERMONT HOLLAND FARM VENISON FILLET WITH JUNIPER BERRY JUS

BY GRAHAM GILL

Local Vermont venison is perfect for any Winter menu. The juniper berry sauce and sweet potato garnish prove to be the perfect match and contrast to the rich venison flavors.

METHOD

venison:

Season the venison fillets with salt and pepper and place to the side.

Brussels sprouts:

Wash the Brussels sprouts thoroughly with cold water and then slice into quarters. Add to a pan of boiling salted water and cook until al dente. Remove the sprouts from the water, strain and refresh under cold running water.

sweet potato purée:

Wash the sweet potatoes and then place on a piece of aluminum foil. Season with a dash of olive oil, salt and pepper, then wrap each potato with the foil. Preheat the oven to 350°F and then bake for 30 to 40 minutes, until soft. Allow to cool. Scrape out the inside of the potatoes, discarding the skins. Add the potatoes to a potato ricer and purée, seasoning with salt, pepper and a pinch of nutmeg.

juniper berry jus:

Add the veal stock and juniper berries to a pan, place over a medium heat and allow to reduce by half (approximately 15 minutes) and then strain into a clean bowl. Adjust seasoning if needed.

to serve:

Take the seasoned venison fillets and sear in a hot pan on both sides until rare (make sure the pan is hot before adding the fillets). Remove and rest for two minutes. Warm the sweet potato purée in a saucepan on a low heat on the stove. Sauté the Brussels sprouts in a hot pan with butter, add the chestnuts and a pinch of salt and pepper and cook for 2-3 minutes. Place a metal ring in the center of the plate and fill with the sweet potato purée. Thinly slice the venison fillet and arrange around and on top of the potato. Alternate the Brussels sprouts and chestnuts around the edge of the plate. Drizzle the juniper berry jus around the base of the venison and serve.

Chef's tip:

Be careful not to overcook the venison as it will become tough, medium rare is preferred.

Serves 6
Preparation time: 1 hour
Cooking time: 30 minutes

Special equipment:
Ice cream maker

Planning ahead:
The ice cream and pastry can be made a day in advance.

INGREDIENTS

sugar pastry:

8 oz	flour
5 oz	margarine or butter
2 oz	white granulated sugar
1	egg, beaten
1	pinch of salt

filling:

4	McIntosh apples
4	quinces
1 tbsp	butter
1 tbsp	maple syrup
1 tbsp	brown sugar
1	pinch of cinnamon
1	pinch of nutmeg

caramel pecan:

6	half pecans
4 oz	white granulated sugar
¼ cup	water

maple ice cream:

1 qt	heavy cream
6 oz	white granulated sugar
8	egg yolks
1	vanilla bean, split
¼ cup	Vermont maple syrup

VERMONT APPLE & QUINCE TART WITH MAPLE ICE CREAM

BY GRAHAM GILL

Whenever possible we source as many ingredients as we can straight from our garden here at the Inn, and this dish is a perfect example of that. The beautiful quince was used to give a different take on the traditional apple tart.

METHOD

sugar pastry:

Sift the flour and salt into a bowl. Cut the margarine/butter into cubes, add to the flour and lightly rub until a sandy texture. Make a well in the center of the flour. Pour the beaten egg and sugar into the well. Gradually incorporate with the flour and margarine until a smooth paste. Cover and allow to rest in the refrigerator for approximately 1 hour before using.

filling:

Peel and cut the applessnd quinces into quarters, remove the core from and cut into thin slices. Place the butter in a sauté pan and melt over a medium heat, then add the sugar and cook for 2 minutes. Add the sliced apples, maple syrup, cinnamon and nutmeg. Cook for a further two minutes then remove from the heat and cool.

Retrieve the pastry from the fridge, and roll out until approximately ⅛" thick. Cut six disks using a 3" pastry cutter. Rub six 3" flan molds with butter and line with the pastry. Start placing the apples in each mold, building a base up to the top. Finish with a layer of neatly arranged overlapping slices with the tips of the slices all pointing to the center of the tart.

caramel pecan:

Place the sugar in a saucepan and add the water, slowly bring to a boil over a medium heat until the sugar has fully dissolved. Turn up the heat and cook until it turns a golden brown color. Remove the pan from the heat and dip in a bowl of iced water to cool the caramel. Stick a Frill Pick into each pecan and dip into the caramel until coated. Slowly remove and draw up, creating a caramel strand from the nut. Leave to cool on the edge of a shelf with a weight on the pick so the caramel is free to hang down.

maple ice cream:

Add the cream and the vanilla bean to a pan and bring to the boil and then remove from the heat. In a bowl, whisk the sugar and egg together until light and fluffy. Whisk the cream into the eggs and sugar, then return to the stove. Slowly cook until it coats the back of a spoon. Pass through a strainer and allow to cool.

Pour the mixture into the ice cream machine and churn until it thickens. Remove and place into a storage container. Drizzle the maple syrup into the ice cream mix, stir and then freeze until needed (allow 4 hours to set).

to serve:

Bake the tarts at 350°F for approximately 18 minutes or until the pastry and apples are golden brown. Place each individual tart in the center of a bowl and add a quenelle of ice cream to the top. Garnish with the caramel pecan and any leftover caramel.

Chris Eddy

Chris Eddy is the Executive Chef at Winvian. Here he performs in a kitchen that caters to a highly sophisticated clientele that expect flawless presentations of the freshest possible ingredients. Chef Eddy calls his style "a la minute" which translates into cooking as little as possible until the last minute, thus capturing the freshness of the ultra high end ingredients that he uses.

Exposure to the international palate came early to Chef Eddy whose family traveled around the world. His belief is that every guest deserves to have meals prepared with what he calls "integrity, craftsmanship and a whole lot of love."

Before taking leadership of Winvian's culinary team of 10, he was a Sous Chef for both Alain Ducasse and Daniel Boulud; he also worked for Jean-Michel Bergougnoux. From these masters, and his French Culinary Institute training, his technique, he says, "is heavily ingrained with classic and southern French," with an emphasis on using local ingredients and artisanal products.

Winvian

Winvian is just two hours away from the buzz of New York and Boston. Within the green valleys and pristine lakes of the bucolic Litchfield Hills, Winvian is a unique hotel complex nestled in 45 hectares of lush grounds bordered by centuries-old maple trees.

A team of 15 architects was called upon to create the 19 original chalets, each with its own special design and atmosphere. Choose to stay in a 2 story treehouse perched 10 meters off the ground, in a lighthouse located in the midst of the forest, or perhaps a lodge built around a 100-year-old oak tree. On the agenda: relaxing in the romantic spa adjacent to the White Memorial nature preserve and Charles's pond, hot air ballooning, bike riding, croquet, bocce, horseback riding, fly fishing, race car driving among other unforgettable experiences.

PIGEON & FOIE GRAS SALAD

BY CHRIS EDDY

This pigeon salad makes for a perfect luncheon main course. The key to success in this dish is to maintain a nice balance of acidity via the vinegar in the sauce and the petite salad. Substitute for duck, chicken or whatever poultry you desire. This dish is an augmentation of the classic frisée lardon salad.

Serves 4
Preparation time: 2 hours
Cooking time: 12 minutes

Planning ahead:
The pigeon legs need to be cooked for 20 hours.

INGREDIENTS

- 4 pigeon breasts, cooked sous vide at 48°C/120°F for 30 minutes
- 4 pigeon legs, boned, seasoned and cooked sous vide at 55°C/150°F for 20 hours
- 8 duck gizzards confit, halved
- 4 chicken livers, seasoned
- 12 smoky lardons, blanched
- 4 portions of foie gras, 1½ oz each
- 4 quail eggs, cooked for approximately 3 minutes in boiling water, peeled then cooled
- sherry vinegar
- 2 garlic cloves, minced
- 1 large shallot, finely sliced (reserve a small amount for the frisée)
- 8 fl oz pigeon or chicken jus
- salt & pepper
- butter

to garnish:

- 4 small bunches of frisée salad
- 2 sprigs of fresh parsley
- Dijon mustard, to taste
- grapeseed oil, to taste
- sherry vinegar, to taste
- shallot (reserved from earlier)
- 4 croutons made from baguettes (sliced thinly then toasted until crisp)

METHOD

Heat three medium-sized pans over a medium heat and preheat the oven to 400°F. Season the foie gras and place in the first pan. Sear on both sides then cook in the oven for approximately 1 minute or until medium rare. Remove from the pan and keep warm.

Place the quail eggs in a small bowl filled with warm water. Season the pigeon breasts and sauté skin side down in the second pan to crisp the skin, approximately 5 minutes, then place in the oven for one minute.

In the third pan place a little butter and add the lardons. Render for approximately 2 minutes until crispy. Add the chicken livers, and gizzards and cook for an additional 2 minutes. Add the garlic and shallot and cook for 1 minute without browning. Deglaze with a dash of sherry vinegar then remove the chicken livers (cooked pink). Keep the livers warm.

Add the pigeon legs to the second pan, then add the jus. Cook until napant consistency (able to coat the back of a spoon), not too thick. Adjust the seasoning, set aside and keep warm.

to serve:

Place the frisée in a small bowl and toss with the mustard, sherry vinegar, grapeseed oil, shallot, salt and pepper. Place the sauce, livers, gizzards, lardons, and legs on the plate. Cut the eggs in half and add them. Slice the pigeon breasts and arrange decoratively with the foie gras and then sprinkle on the frisée and parsley. Top each plate with a toasted crouton.

NOCCHETTE WITH THE FLAVORS OF THE SEA

BY CHRIS EDDY

Nocchette is delicious light pasta that highlights fresh, delicate seafood. The flavor profile is and should be without much embellishment. Make sure to use plenty of broth. Use a great quantity of olive oil, and serve with crusty bread.

Serves 4
Preparation time: 3 hours
Cooking time: 20 minutes

Special equipment:
Pasta maker

INGREDIENTS

seafood:

1 ½ lb	lobster
4pt	salted water
1 lb	baby octopus
1-2 cups	white wine
6	shrimps
3 lb	mussels
1	small shallot, diced
2	cloves garlic, crushed
olive oil	
1	splash of vermouth
4	u16 scallops
8	uni roe pouches
1	small dollop of caviar
1	calamari sliced into thin rings
8 fl oz	reserved mussel liquid
28	saffron nocette (see recipe below)
28	squid ink nocette (see recipe below)

saffron nocchette:

1 lb	"00" flour
4 oz	semolina flour
3-4	whole eggs

approx 3½ oz hot water mixed with a large pinch of saffron then allowed to cool to room temperature

squid ink nocchette:

1 lb	"00" flour
4 oz	semolina flour
3-4	whole eggs
2 oz	squid ink mixed with 3 ½ oz water

garnish:

1 tbsp	parsley chiffonade
¼	preserved Meyer lemon peel, finely diced
chili flakes, to taste	
1	lemon, halved

METHOD

saffron and squid ink nocchettes (same instructions for both):

Mix either the saffron water or squid ink water with the eggs. Place the flours in the bowl of a mixer and mix on low speed using the paddle. Add the egg/water mixture gradually until the dough pulls clean from the bowl. Add more water if necessary in tiny increments. If made in a humid environment start with approximately 2½ fl oz of water and add more if necessary.

Pass the pasta through a pasta machine on # 10 four times, folding in half each time. Allow to rest for one hour. Roll out to the desired thickness. Cut out 1" circles. Lay a pencil down the center of the circle then take two opposite ends and bring them together over the pencil, pinching them together to form a 'closed taco' shape.

lobster:

Bring the salted water to a boil. Turn off the heat. Place the lobster tails and claws into the water. Cook the tails for approximately 4 minutes, then remove immediately. Remove the shells and cut in half lengthwise. Leave the claws in the water, and cook for an additional four to five minutes. The claw shells should be bright red. Crack the claw shells open and remove the meat without tearing.

baby octopus:

Only purchase tenderized baby octopus. Cook in a seasoned bouillon, or salted water at a medium simmer for approximately 45 minutes to an hour or until desired tenderness is achieved. Add a cup or two of wine if desired.

shrimps:

Remove the shrimps from their shells, and place in a shallow metal container. Salt generously and allow to brine for 10 minutes. Boil some water, then turn off the heat and allow to stand for 8 minutes. Pour the water over the shrimps to cover by ¾" then gently stir until the shrimps are cooked to desired doneness. I suggest approximately 3 minutes.

mussels:

Sweat the shallot and garlic in olive oil over a medium heat without browning. Add live mussels to the pot, add a splash of water, and a splash of vermouth and cover the pot tightly. Turn the heat to low, and gently shake the pan until the shells open. Strain the opened mussels, and reserve the cooking liquid. Remove the mussels from their shells.

scallops:

Cook for approximately 2 minutes until just opaque in the center.

to serve:

Place the pasta in water and cook for approximately 3 minutes. Meanwhile return the mussel broth mixture back to the heat and add the lobster, shrimp, octopus, and shelled mussels. Season as you wish. Gently cook until heated through. Add the pasta and calamari and cook for another minute or until the calamari is just cooked. Add more liquid if necessary to maintain a nice brothy consistency. Add oil or butter to your liking.

Place the pasta on a plate or in a bowl with the shellfish neatly arranged. Add the scallops and uni roe pouches then ladle over some broth. Finish with caviar, parsley, a pinch of lemon peel, chili flakes and more olive oil if desired. Squeeze your desired amount of fresh lemon juice over the pasta and enjoy.

FRENCH MACAROON WITH RASPBERRY & FROMAGE BLANC SORBET

BY CHRIS EDDY

A most colorful and attractive dish combining melt-in-the-mouth sorbet with crunchy macaroon.

Serves 20
Preparation time: 30 minutes
Cooking time: 1 hour

Special equipment:
Candy thermometer, acetate

INGREDIENTS

raspberry sorbet:

15 fl oz water
9 oz sugar
3½ oz atomized glucose
¼ oz stabilizer
2 lb 4 oz raspberry purée

fromage blanc:

11½ fl oz water
1 lb 8 oz sugar
11½ oz dry glucose
½ oz stabilizer
2 lb 4 oz fromage blanc

French macaroons: (or makes 80 bite-size macaroons)

1 lb 2 oz confectioner's sugar (10x)
1 lb 2 oz almond flour
¾ oz egg whites
food coloring (optional)
1 lb 2 oz sugar
8 fl oz water
6 oz egg whites

to serve:

pistachios, chopped
raspberries, halved
lime, strips of zest
candied fruits

METHOD

raspberry sorbet:

Make a syrup by adding the water and sugar to a saucepan and mixing together over a low heat until they are combined. Remove from the heat and add the glucose, stabilizer and raspberry purée, then purée with a hand blender until you have a smooth texture. Don't overturn the mixture – the texture is supposed to be nice and loose.

fromage blanc:

Make a syrup by adding the water and sugar to a saucepan and mixing together over a low heat until they are combined. Remove from the heat and add the glucose, stabilizer and fromage blanc and mix with a hand blender until you have a smooth, loose texture. Mix gently with the raspberry sorbet.

Make up cylinders with acetate to your desired size (the diameter should be the same as your intended macaroon width). Fill a piping bag with the raspberry sorbet/fromage blanc mix and fill the cylinders. Freeze and, when ready to serve, carefully unmold from the acetate cylinder.

French macaroons:

Preheat the oven to 275°F.

In a mixing bowl combine the confectioner's sugar, almond flour and ¾ oz egg whites. Add the food coloring if using. In a pan over a low heat cook the sugar and water together with the 6 oz of egg whites until it reaches 250°F on a candy thermometer. Remove from the heat and combine both mixtures to make the meringue, making sure it stays shiny and does not become too dry.

Place the mixture in a piping bag and pipe the macaroon lengths onto a parchment-lined baking sheet. Cook in the oven for approximately 12-15 minutes depending on size.

to serve:

Place a layer of chopped pistachios the width of your macaroon on a plate. Top with a macaroon followed by a cylinder and decorate with raspberries, lime zest strips and candied fruits.

Washington D.C.

In the land of opportunity there is one destination that stands out as a figurehead of the country – Washington D.C.

Officially known as Washington, District of Columbia, this unique capital is the essence of all things American. With historic landmarks such as the Washington Monument, Georgetown University and of course, The White House, it is understandable that Washington D.C. is highly acclaimed. A center for politics and banking this area of the States' is also home to the largest museum in America, The Smithsonian. It also holds the Kennedy Center and the historic Lincoln Memorial – making it a city awash with culture. The city's International Wine and Food festival entices food-lovers from all over the world and does not disappoint. With a global choice there is very little that Washington D.C. does not offer!

Damon Gordon

Executive Chef Damon Gordon, whose restaurants have added cachet to some of the nation's most illustrious hotels, heads the kitchens of Plume, The Jefferson's fine dining restaurant. This marks his return to the East Coast after a two-year turn in San Diego as Executive Chef of the critically acclaimed Damon Gordon's Quarter Kitchen at The Ivy Hotel.

For six years prior, Gordon built an impressive resume as Executive Chef of leading restaurants and hotels in New York City and Miami: Ono at Hotel Gansevoort, Mix, Royalton, and Miami's stylish Delano. A native of Great Britain, he spent his early career honing his culinary skills in the U.K.'s finest kitchens. They include Ian Schrager's Saint Martin's Lane, the Michelin-starred Quo Vadis and the three-Michelin-starred Waterside Inn.

The Jefferson

The Jefferson is the perfect place to explore Washington, its monuments, its art galleries and its theaters.

Situated just four blocks from the White House, its elegant decor is a tribute to Thomas Jefferson and draws inspiration from his great loves: Monticello and Paris. In the warm atmosphere in the restaurant Plume, one of the best in town, enjoy sophisticated seasonal cuisine. After a day spent sightseeing, relax with a good book in front of a roaring fire in the library, sip a delicious cocktail in the cosy lounge, savor a cigar on the terrace or have a rest in the spa with a vinotherapy treatment or massage. A wish? Just summon your private butler.

NOISETTES OF LAMB WITH BITTERSWEET EGGPLANT, NICOISE VEGETABLES, BLACK OLIVE INFUSED JUS

BY DAMON GORDON

This dish is a modern interpretation of 'ratatouille' with lamb, but executed with baby vegetables in a light and healthier fashion. I love taking dishes with a classic heritage and turning them into something pleasing to today's more enlightened palates.

Serves 4
Preparation time: 2 hours
Cooking time: 45 minutes

INGREDIENTS

lamb and eggplants:

2 loins of lamb (excess fat and sinew removed)
2 Chinese eggplants
Xéres (sherry) vinegar
honey
salt & pepper
olive oil
butter

vegetables:

1 whole garlic bulb + 1 clove, chopped
8 green beans
4 patty pan squashes
1 pt red grape tomatoes
1 pt duck fat
8 'mini' fingerling potatoes
8 green beans

black olive infused lamb jus:

lamb trimmings left over from the loins
4 shallots, peeled and chopped
2 cloves garlic, crushed
1 sprig of thyme
1 bay leaf
1 tsp black peppercorns
1 tsp black olive paste
4 fl oz white wine
4 pt 3½ fl oz veal jus

to serve:

4 black olives (Niçoise)
2 white marinated anchovy fillets (cut into 8 'diamonds')
8 small basil leaves

METHOD

lamb and eggplants:

For the eggplants remove the tops and slice lengthways, roughly ¼" thick, season with salt and pepper. In a frying pan heat some olive oil and fry the eggplant slices; when a light brown color deglaze with the vinegar and honey. Repeat the process for all the slices.

Season the lamb with salt and pepper and sear in a pan lightly on all sides.

When both the lamb and eggplants are ready lay the eggplants next to each other and then place the lamb loin on top. Wrap the eggplants around the lamb and then wrap the loin in plastic wrap and tie each end.

vegetables:

Blanch the green beans and patty pan squash in boiling salted water and refresh. Cut the squash in half and the beans into 'diamonds'.

Warm some of the duck fat and pour over the tomatoes in a shallow sauté pan. Cover with aluminum foil and 'confit' in a low oven for roughly 20 minutes or until the tomatoes are very tender.

Break the garlic into cloves, leave on the skin and follow the same process to 'confit' as for the tomatoes. but allowing the garlic to cook for roughly 45 minutes.

Remove the stones from the olives and cut into halves.

Roast the fingerlings in butter with thyme and garlic in a hot oven until cooked.

black olive infused lamb jus:

Heat a thick bottomed sauté pan and add the chopped lamb trimmings. Allow to evenly brown on all sides and then add the shallots, garlic and peppercorns. Cook for approximately 10 minutes, allowing the vegetables to brown also.

Pour out the excess grease and then deglaze with the white wine and allow to reduce by two-thirds.

Add the veal jus along with the thyme and bay leaf. Bring to a boil, skimming the excess fat off the top along the process. Once the sauce has come to a boil lower the heat and cook for 15-20 minutes. Remove from the heat and pass the sauce through a fine strainer. Put the sauce back into a clean pan and rapidly reduce by half. Once reduced place in a container over ice to cool.

to serve:

Bake the lamb in a hot oven to required taste. Medium rare will take roughly 13-15 minutes. Once cooked allow to rest for at least 6-7 minutes. Reheat the potatoes, tomatoes and garlic in the oven with some duck fat. Heat the required amount of lamb jus and add black olive paste to taste. The beans and squash should be reheated in an 'emulsion' of vegetable stock and butter with salt and pepper so the vegetables are shiny.

Slice the lamb into 1½" medallions, arrange the vegetables neatly along one side of the plate in alternate fashion and finish with the basil leaves, olive halves and anchovies.

Finish the medallions with some sea salt and spoon the lamb jus between the vegetables and noisettes of lamb.

FEUILLETE OF VEAL SWEETBREADS WITH SEASONAL MUSHROOMS, VANILLA BEAN VELOUTE

BY DAMON GORDON

The combination of sweetbreads and mushrooms with puff pastry is a classic, but this dish adds a contemporary twist via the style of execution. And the pairing of the vanillia with the sweetbreads elevates the dish to another level entirely.

Serves 4
Preparation time: 2 hours
Cooking time: 45 minutes

Planning ahead:
The sweetbreads need to be prepared in advance, and will keep for up to 3 days.

INGREDIENTS

sweetbreads:

12 oz veal sweetbreads
2 shallots, peeled
½ gal milk
salt & pepper
8 parsley stalks
½ cup white wine vinegar
1 sprig of thyme
bay leaf
¼ bunch flat leaf parsley, chopped
½ clove garlic, chopped
2 oz shallots, chopped to serve
4 oz butter
1 sheet puff pastry cut into 2" x ½" rectangles
1 egg for egg wash
flour
12 oz assorted seasonal mushrooms

vanilla bean velouté:

5 oz shallots, julienne
5 oz white button mushrooms
½ pt white wine
bouquet garni
1 pt chicken stock
½ pt veal stock
1½ pt heavy cream
2 vanilla beans
salt & pepper
1½ oz butter

to serve:

4 oz baby spinach
chervil, to garnish

METHOD

sweetbreads:

Rinse the sweetbreads under cold water and then cover with the milk and a pinch of salt for 12 hours. Remove the sweetbreads from the milk and rinse with cold water. Place the sweetbreads in a pan and cover with cold water, shallots, parsley stalks, thyme, bay leaf and vinegar. Season with salt and pepper. Place on a moderate heat and cook for approximately 30 minutes, being careful to not let the sweetbreads come to a boil. Remove the sweetbreads from the liquid and remove the membrane from the outside of the sweetbreads. Divide into four equal portions and then roll in plastic wrap to create a cylinder. Place into a blast chiller to rapidly cool and then store until needed.

Dice the mushrooms into small pieces, wash, drain and set aside until needed.

Cut the sheet puff pastry into the desired shape and then refrigerate again for 20 minutes. Brush the top of the puff pastry with egg wash and cook in a convection oven at 375°F for 15 minutes. Remove and cool on a wire rack.

vanilla bean velouté:

In a saucepot, bring the cream to a boil with the vanilla beans. Remove from the heat and cover the pan with plastic. Allow to steep for 15 minutes and strain through a chinois. Reserve. While the cream is steeping prepare the base for the sauce vin blanc. In a saucepot heat the butter over a medium heat and sweat the mushrooms and shallots. Add the bouquet garni and deglaze with the wine. Reduce the wine until almost dry and add the stocks. Reduce by half. Add the cream that has been infused with vanilla and reduce until the sauce almost coats the back of a spoon. Season with salt and pepper. Strain the sauce through a chinois and cool immediately.

to serve:

Dust each of the sweetbread portions with flour and cook in foaming fresh butter to caramelize the outside. Finish in the oven for 4-5 minutes.

Sauté the mushrooms with butter and finish with the chopped garlic and chopped shallots. Correct the seasoning and finish with chopped parsley.

Sauté the spinach and season with salt and pepper. Cut the pastry into three layers and layer two with the sautéed spinach and mushrooms. Make sure to leave a few mushrooms to garnish the plate. Slice the sweetbreads and place on top of the mushrooms and spinach. Put the one layer on top of the other to create the feuilleté and then place on to four plates, garnish around with the remainder of the mushrooms.

Correct the seasoning for the velouté and 'foam' with a hand blender. Pour some over each of the sweetbreads and pour the rest around the plate.

Place the top layer of puff pastry on each of the plates and garnish with picked chervil.

Serves 20
Preparation time: 2 hours
Cooking time: 30 minutes

Special equipment:
Stick blender, siphon

Planning ahead:
The chocolate pot de crème needs to be refrigerated for at least 3 hours.

INGREDIENTS

bitter cocoa sorbet:

9½ oz	Valrhona Manjari 64%
3¾ oz	cocoa powder
2 pt	water
9½ oz	sugar

chocolate guanaja 70% espuma:

9 oz	whole milk
4 oz	Valrhona Guanaja 70%
1 oz	caster sugar
2 oz	egg whites

white chocolate macaroon:

4½ oz	almond powder
8 oz	powdered sugar
4 oz	egg whites
2 oz	sugar
6 oz	white chocolate
2½ oz	cocoa butter

chocolate pot de crème:

1 pt	whole milk
1 pt	whipped cream
1 oz	honey
13 oz	Valrhona Guanaja 70%
8	egg yolks
5½ oz	sugar

CHOCOLATE VARIATION

BY DAMON GORDON

The Chocolate Variation is an exciting dish in the sense that it utilizes several different chocolates and then combines them using both classic and modern execution. The result is a dish that is as arresting to the eyes as it is pleasing to the mouth.

METHOD

bitter cocoa sorbet:

Bring the water and sugar to a boil, set aside and then incorporate the cocoa powder and chocolate. Bring back to the boil stirring continuously.

Strain, set aside and freeze and hold at -65°F.

chocolate guanaja 70% espuma:

Bring the milk to the boil with the sugar. Pour gradually into the melted chocolate and stir with a rubber spatula to create a shiny and elastic core, the sign of a well started emulsion. Add the egg whites, process with a stick blender then pour into cream siphon canister. Add two cartridges of NO gas and maintain between 105°-120°F.

white chocolate macaroon:

Melt the white chocolate and set aside along with the cocoa butter. Whip the egg whites with the sugar to stiff peaks and then fold in all the other ingredients. Pipe the size of a 'dollar' coin on parchment paper. Leave out for 15 minutes and then cook at 140°F for 15 minutes. Allow to cool. Before serving, fill with melted chocolate and cocoa butter mixture.

chocolate pot de crème:

Bring the milk and the cream to a boil, remove from the heat and add the honey. Whip the egg yolks with the sugar and then pour in the milk/cream mixture and pasteurize to 185°F, set aside then strain on top of the chocolate, whip until a smooth texture is reached then pour into molds and refrigerate for 3 hours minimum.

to serve:

Fill shot glasses with chocolate guanaja. Unmold the pot de crème. Take a long plate and spread some melted chocolate along its length. Arrange all four elements of the dish attractively on top.

Virginia

Sweet Virginia – no other state could be so historically privileged. Virginia is American to the core and known as the 'Mother of Presidents' for eight US presidents having been born in the state.

The Blue Ridge Mountains look out peacefully over the valleys below and take in the historical tales that unfold before them. From colonization to Civil War, Virginia has seen it all, but history is not forced upon you in this golden state. White tailed deer grace the land and the Chesapeake Bay is home to fish and crab galore, and who could forget the American Osprey and Bald Eagle who also make their home in this area of the states.

Patrick O'Connell
Grand Chef Relais & Châteaux

Patrick O'Connell, a native of Washington, D.C., is a self-taught chef who pioneered a refined, regional American cuisine in the Virginia countryside. Considered to be one of the best chefs in the world, Patricia Wells of The International Herald Tribune hails O'Connell as "a rare chef with a sense of near perfect taste, like a musician with perfect pitch." Alain Ducasse said, "I have long admired Patrick O'Connell and always appreciate what he does at The Inn at Little Washington, one of the best restaurants in the United States ..."

Patrick has evolved and refined many of the dishes from his childhood, making them relevant in a new century while keeping their soul intact – building a culinary bridge between past and future.

His commitment as an Ambassador of American Cuisine has led him to become the current President of North American Relais & Châteaux delegations.

Both Patrick and The Inn at Little Washington have enjoyed enormous national and international recognition. He is a best-selling cookbook author, a successful guest speaker and has made numerous television appearances.

The Inn at Little Washington

PAN-SEARED MAINE DIVER'S SCALLOP WITH CARAMELIZED ENDIVE, LEEK PUREE & SHAVED BLACK TRUFFLE

BY PATRICK O'CONNELL

This is a sensual and colorful way to serve sea scallops in combination with crunchy, bittersweet endive. The presentation makes the scallop look as if it just washed up on the shore, the natural briny sweetness of the scallop is accentuated by the leek purée.

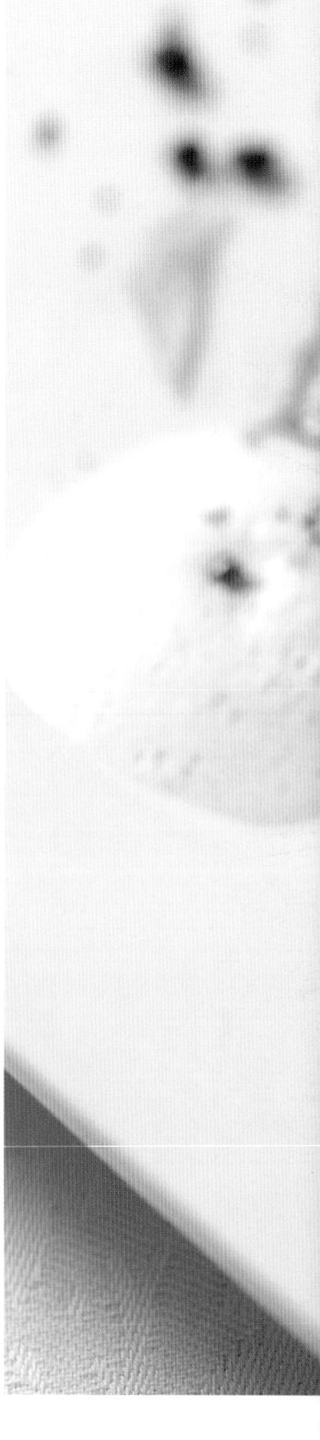

Serves 6
Preparation time: 45 minutes
Cooking time: 20 minutes

Planning ahead:
The veal sauce reduction can be made up to 3 days in advance.

INGREDIENTS

veal sauce reduction:

- 1 cup veal stock demiglace
- ½ cup chicken stock

leek purée:

- 2 tbsp unsalted butter
- 4 cups chopped leeks, thoroughly cleaned
- 1 cup spinach, to taste
- salt & sugar, to taste

parmesan froth:

- ½ cup water
- 1 tbsp unsalted butter
- ½ cup freshly grated, good quality parmesan
- salt, to taste

endive:

- 3 endives, split in half lengthwise
- 1 tbsp unsalted butter
- ¼ cup sugar
- ¼ cup unseasoned rice wine vinegar

to serve:

- 6 large, fresh Maine diver's sea scallops
- 2 tbsp clairified butter or grapeseed oil
- grey salt
- 1 tbsp cracked black peppercorns
- 1 tbsp cracked red peppercorns
- 20 celery heart leaves
- black truffle (optional)

METHOD

veal sauce reduction:

In a small heavy bottomed saucepan, over a medium heat, bring the veal stock to a boil and reduce it by half. Add the chicken stock and return to a boil. Reduce the stock mixture by approximately a third and remove from the heat. The veal sauce can be stored in the refrigerator for up to 3 days, just gently warm for use.

leek purée:

In a large sauté pan over a medium-low heat, melt the butter, add the cleaned leeks and cook them until soft and translucent but not browned. Add the spinach and cook until the spinach has wilted. Remove from the heat. Purée the leeks and spinach together in a blender, adding a little cold water or ice if necessary. Pass through a fine mesh strainer and season with salt and sugar. The purée can be held in the refrigerator until ready to serve and rewarmed.

parmesan froth:

Combine the water and butter in a small, heavy bottomed saucepan. Gently heat the mixture over a low heat until just barely simmering. It is important that the froth does not come to a boil. Remove from the heat, whisk in the parmesan cheese and adjust the seasoning with salt. Keep at room temperature until ready to serve.

endive:

Score the heart of each endive in half in a criss-cross pattern. Melt the butter in a large sauté pan over a medium-high heat. Add the endive halves, flat side down, and cook for 2-3 minutes or until golden brown. Flip over and cook for another 2-3 minutes or until the second side has browned. Add the sugar and vinegar, and cook until the liquid has thickened into a glaze. Set aside and keep warm until ready to serve.

to serve:

In a sauté pan, heat the clarified butter or grapeseed oil over a medium-high heat. Add the scallops to the hot oil and and cook until they are golden brown on both sides, about 2 minutes per side. Take care not to overcook. Spoon a few tablespoons of the leek purée onto the center of each of six warmed plates. Using a small offset spatuula, spread the purée until it is about 6" long. Drizzle a little of the veal sauce in the center of the leek purée. Place a piece of endive, fanning the leaves, flat side up on the purée. Slice the scallops into thirds lengthwise exposing the pearly white center. Fan the scallops across the endive. Vigorously whisk the parmesan froth until a foam forms like a cappuccino, spoon the foam across the plate. Sprinkle the scallops with grey salt. Lightly dust the plate with peppercorns, and a few celery leaves. Top with freshly grated black truffle if desired.

MEDALLIONS OF RABBIT LOIN WRAPPED IN PANCETTA SURROUNDING A LILLIPUTIAN RABBIT RIB ROAST RESTING ON A PILLOW OF RUTABAGA PUREE

BY PATRICK O'CONNELL

Rabbit can be a challenge to cook because the delicate, little loins can dry out so quickly while the leg meat usually requires a long braising to be tender. This method involves fusing two rabbit loins together by wrapping them in pancetta and forming them into a kind of sausage by twisting them together in plastic wrap and slowly cooking them in a circulating water bath. The loin becomes wonderfully flavorful and stays moist. It is then unwrapped, seared, brushed with mustard, rolled in breadcrumbs and finished in the oven. The tiny 'rib roast' garnish is simply seared, coated with mustard and breadcrumbs and finished in the oven for a minute or two. The legs of the rabbit can be saved for another dish.

Serves 4

Preparation time: 40 minutes

Cooking time: 20 minutes

Special equipment:

Circulator bath

Planning ahead:

The breadcrumbs can be made in advance and stored in an airtight container. The purée can also be prepared in advance.

INGREDIENTS

rabbit:

4 saddles of rabbit

12 slices of pancetta, thinly sliced

salt & pepper, to taste

veal sauce:

4 qt veal stock

salt & pepper, to taste

chicken stock reduction:

3 qt chicken stock

2 tsp Dijon mustard

salt & pepper, to taste

breadcrumbs:

2 tbsp butter

2 tbsp garlic, finely chopped

1 cup panko breadcrumbs

salt & pepper, to taste

4 tbsp parsley, finely chopped

vegetables:

12 baby carrots, cleaned and peeled (tops left on)

6 baby yellow turnips, cleaned and peeled (tops left on)

rutabaga purée:

2 large rutabagas, peeled and diced

3 tbsp butter

¼ cup maple syrup

1 pinch of cayenne pepper

salt, to taste

to serve:

3 tbsp butter, divided

⅓ cup vegetable or grape seed oil

2 tbsp Dijon mustard

METHOD

rabbit:

Cut the saddle crosswise between the third and fourth ribs. Divide into two miniature rib roasts. Trim and french the bones. Repeat for the remaining saddles. Hold in the refrigerator until ready to use.

Separate the remaining loins from the bones and trim the silverskin.

On a piece of plastic wrap lay three slices of pancetta vertically so they overlap slightly. Season two loins with salt and pepper, lay side by side and roll them up in the pancetta. Wrap the rolled loins tightly in plastic, tying off both ends like a sausage. Place the four wrapped loins in a circulator bath and poach them at 63°C/145°F for 5 minutes. Remove from the water bath. Let them come to room temperature and refrigerate until ready to use.

veal sauce:

In a large saucepan over a medium heat, reduce the stock until it coats the back of a spoon. Skim the stock during the reduction as necessary. Season with salt and pepper, and refrigerate until ready to use.

chicken stock reduction:

In a large saucepan over a medium heat, reduce the stock until it coats the back of a spoon. Skim the stock during the reduction as necessary. Whisk in the Dijon mustard, season and refrigerate until ready to use.

breadcrumbs:

Melt the butter in a skillet over a medium heat. Add the garlic and sauté for one minute. Add the breadcrumbs and sauté until golden brown. Season with salt and pepper. Add the parsley, stir to combine and remove from the heat. Allow the breadcrumbs to cool completely. They may be stored in an airtight container until ready to use.

vegetables:

Blanch the vegetables in boiling, salted water until just tender. Shock immediately in cold water, drain and hold in the refrigerator until ready to use.

rutabaga purée:

Cook the rutabagas in boiling, salted water until tender. Drain for 5 minutes in a colander. Combine the cooked rutabaga, butter, maple syrup and

cayenne in a food processor and purée until smooth. Add a little water if the purée seems too thick. If desired, for an extra silky texture, pass the purée through a fine mesh chinois. Add salt to taste and more cayenne if necessary. The purée can be kept warm for several hours or refrigerated and re-warmed before serving.

to serve:

Preheat the oven to 375°F. Reheat each of the sauces. In an 8" skillet, heat the oil over a medium high heat. Remove the loins from the plastic wrap and add them to the pan. Cook, turning frequently, until the pancetta is browned and crispy and the loins are warmed through. Remove from the oil, drain and let rest. Pour off all but 2 tablespoons of oil and return to a medium high heat. Season the rib roasts with salt and pepper and sear in the hot oil. Cook for 1 minute on each side and then remove them from the pan. Allow them to rest with the loins.

Reheat the baby vegetables in a little simmering water. Drain and add 1 tablespoon of butter, tossing to coat. Keep warm.

Brush the loins and the rib roasts with a very thin coat of mustard and roll them in the toasted breadcrumbs. Place them in the oven for 1 minute to crisp the crumbs.

Meanwhile, drizzle both sauces around the plate. Surround with the baby vegetables. Place a dollop of the purée in the center of the plate. Remove the loins and rib roasts from the oven. Place the rib roasts on top of the purée. Slice each of the loins into 3 medallions. Arrange the medallions in a triangle around the purée. Serve immediately.

Serves 6

Preparation time: 40 minutes
Cooking time: 1 hour 30 minutes

Special equipment:
Ice cream machine

Planning ahead:
The chocolate curls take a bit of practice but can be made well in advance and kept in the freezer. the ice cream needs to be put into frozen dishes and returned to the freezer several hours before serving.

INGREDIENTS

mint ice cream:

2 cups	whole milk
2 cups	heavy cream
1 cup	sugar
¼ lb	fresh peppermint (about 2 bunches)
8	egg yolks
2 tbsp	crème de menthe

chocolate ribbons:

¼ lb	finest quality semi-sweet chocolate

A CHOCOLATE MINT FANTASY

BY PATRICK O'CONNELL

This is a dazzling presentation and a wonderfully refreshing ice cream that you will definitely want to add to your ice cream making repertoire.

METHOD

In a 2-qt heavy-bottomed saucepan, combine the milk, cream, sugar and peppermint over a medium heat. Bring to the boil, then remove from the heat and allow to steep for approximately one hour or until the cream mixture has a peppermint flavor. Remove the peppermint. Bring the cream mixture back to a simmer.

Place the egg yolks in the top of a double boiler or in a large stainless steel bowl and slowly whisk in the hot cream mixture. Set the mixture over a pot of simmering water and whisk until the mixture thickens enough to coat the back of a spoon. Remove from the heat and strain through a fine mesh sieve. Stir in the crème de menthe. Chill in the refrigerator, then freeze in an ice cream machine according to the manufacturer's instructions.

chocolate ribbons:

Roughly chop the chocolate and place in a stainless steel bowl. Place the bowl over a pot of barely simmering water, making sure that no moisture comes in contact with the chocolate. Stir the chocolate occasionally until it is about half melted. Remove from the heat and whisk until all of the chocolate has melted and is very smooth.

Using a metal cake spatula, spread a quarter of a cup of the melted chocolate out onto the back of a cookie sheet. The chocolate should be only ⅛" to 1/16" thick. Place the cookie sheet in a freezer for about 30 seconds to allow the chocolate to set slightly and just begin to dry. Using a knife, cut the chocolate into 2" wide ribbons. Using a wide putty knife or metal pastry scraper held at a 45° angle scrape the ribbons off the cookie sheet, forming irregularly shaped curls. Place the chocolate curls in the freezer to solidify for a few more seconds. Cover and store the curls in a sealed container in the freezer until ready to serve.

to serve:

Several hours before serving, smooth the mint ice cream into the wells of frozen soup plates or serving bowls and return them to the freezer. Just before serving, remove the ice cream and the chocolate curls from the freezer and mound the curls on top of the ice cream.

Dean Maupin

An Albemarle County native, Executive Chef Dean Maupin was fascinated by cooking at an early age. His culinary dreams started at his grandfather's fruit stand in Crozet, Virginia. He pursued his newfound passion with internships, including one with the acclaimed Albemarle Baking Company. Next he graduated from the Greenbrier's renowned four-year culinary apprenticeship program, then headed on a westward journey to Tra Vigne Restaurant, where he learned from Chef Carmen Quagliatta. The call of the Blue Ridge then brought Chef Dean back to his home and roots, where he became Chef of Charlottesville's highly acclaimed Metropolitan Restaurant. He was soon hired as Chef de Cuisine of Keswick Hall's Fossett's Restaurant. Chef Dean's career experiences and unique talents made him a perfect choice for his current position leading the culinary team at Clifton. Here, he wins fans nightly with his remarkable and remarkably delectable creations. His hallmark simplicity and culinary integrity, combined with his unwavering commitment to using the very best products available, have helped to cement Clifton's reputation as one of the restaurant-heavy Charlottesville region's premier eateries.

Clifton

There is no doubt that you will fall under the spell of this part of the world when you stay in this lovely historic hotel built in 1799 – just like the three early presidents and founding fathers of the United States.

For it was in the Charlottesville Blue Ridge Mountains that Thomas Jefferson, James Madison and James Monroe built their homes. Clifton is set in 100 acres of woods, and the hotel prides itself on its understated elegance with its charming interior design and the warm beauty of its rooms and sites. Here, the murmur of the nearby Rivanna River, the gentle gurgle of the fountains and the soothing sounds of nature will surround you. On the program of this official trip: visiting historical residences (Monticello, Ashlawn-Highland and Montpelier) and renowned vineyards, a culinary cabaret at our Chef's Table, a game of croquet and refreshing dips in the infinity pool.

Serves 4
Preparation time: 1 hour
Cooking time: 12 minutes

INGREDIENTS

bass and chèvre tortellinis

4	striped bass fillets, 6oz each, skinned
3 oz	olive oil
4 oz	chèvre
8	fresh pasta rounds, 4" in diameter, rolled as thin as possible
1	lemon, for juice

sea salt & fresh ground black pepper, to taste

black truffle vinaigrette:

1	egg yolk
1 tbsp	dijon mustard
3 tbsp	sherry vinegar
1 tbsp	shallots, minced
1 cup	canola oil
1 oz	black truffle, minced

salt & pepper to taste

to serve:

12 oz	cooked and shaved beets, any variety
2 oz	pea tendrils
1 oz	shallots, thinly shaved
1 oz	chives, thinly shaved
4 oz	black truffle vinaigrette

CHESAPEAKE BAY STRIPED BASS, BEET CARPACCIO, CHEVRE TORTELLINI, BLACK TRUFFLE VINAIGRETTE

BY DEAN MAUPIN

A robust and whimsical dish utilizing the freshest Chesapeake Bay fish paired with the earthy flavors of beets, truffles and goat cheese.

METHOD

bass and chévre tortellinis:

Place ½ oz of chèvre into the center of each pasta round, lightly brush the edges with a little water, then fold as tortellinis. Place into the fridge. Bring a pot of water to a boil.

Heat a sauté pan over a medium-high heat. Brush a bit of olive oil onto the bass fillets then season with salt and pepper. Add a little olive oil to the sauté pan then place the fish in gently, sear for two minutes, then flip and allow the fish to finish over a low-medium heat for another 3-4 minutes. Remove the fish from the pan onto a paper towel to drain, then squeeze a bit of lemon over each fillet.

Drop the tortellinis into the boiling water and cook for 2-3 minutes, remove and reserve warm for plating.

black truffle vinaigrette:

Whisk together the egg yolk, vinegar, dijon mustard and shallots. Slowly whisk in the canola oil to create an emulsion, add the black truffle, then season with salt and pepper.

to serve:

To plate the final dish, arrange the sliced beets onto the four plates, add blobs of black truffle vinaigrette, then place the bass in the center. Arrange the tortellinis on top of the bass, then mix the pea tendrils and shaved shallots together with a touch of olive oil and lemon. Place the pea tendril salad on top of the bass and serve at once. Garnish with the chives.

SHENANDOAH VALLEY DUCK & SEARED FOIE GRAS WITH SWEET POTATO & HUCKLEBERRY JUS

BY DEAN MAUPIN

Utilizing a nearby farm's Fall bounty, a rich and luxurious dish composed of some of the finest ingredients the Shenandoah Valley has to offer.

Serves 4
Preparation time: 1 hour 30 minutes
Cooking time: 20 minutes

INGREDIENTS

duck breast and foie gras

4 skinless duck breasts
4 pieces of foie gras, 2 oz each
olive oil
salt & pepper

sweet potato:

2 medium-sized sweet potatoes, approx 10 oz, baked, peeled and mashed
2 tbsp butter
1 tbsp maple syrup
1 pinch of salt & pepper

huckleberry jus:

1 cup red wine vinegar
¾ cup sugar
6 oz huckleberries
6 oz rich duck stock or veal stock
1 bay leaf
1 stick of cinnamon
salt & pepper, to taste

METHOD

sweet potato:

Mash all the ingredients together, reserve warm.

huckleberry jus:

In a sauce pot add the vinegar and sugar and reduce by three-quarters. Add the huckleberries, bay leaf, cinnamon stick and stock. Reduce by half. Season with salt and pepper. Reserve warm.

duck breast and foie gras:

Rub the duck breasts with olive oil and season with salt and pepper. Heat a saute pan over medium heat, add a bit of olive oil, then the breasts. Gently sear on one side for 3-4 minutes, then flip and sear the other side for 3-4 minutes. Remove from the pan and allow to rest.

Put another pan on the stove and heat to medium-high intensity. Season the foie gras with salt and pepper and place into the dry pan. Allow to sear for 1-2 minutes then flip and turn the heat off. Leave the foie gras in the hot pan to finish cooking.

to serve:

Divide the sweet potato among four plates, Slice the duck breast thinly, then place on top of the sweet potato. Top with the seared foie gras then finish the plate with the huckleberry jus.

VANILLA BEAN MOUSSE & HAZELNUT-MILK CHOCOLATE BAR WITH RASPBERRY CRUNCH & CARAMEL

BY DEAN MAUPIN

Pure decadence, creamy, salty, crunchy, chocolatey, nutty... what else is there to say!

Serves 8
Preparation time: 1 hour + 2 hours for chilling
Cooking time: 15 minutes

Planning ahead:
The chocolate base and mousse elements need to be made the day before.

Special equipment:
1½" diameter, 6" in length metal tube

INGREDIENTS

hazelnut-milk chocolate base:

4 oz	milk chocolate
7 oz	feuilletine
8 oz	hazelnut paste
1 oz	butter

vanilla bean mousse:

2 cups	heavy cream, whipped stiff and chilled
6	sheets of gelatin, bloomed in ice water
4 cups	milk
1	vanilla bean, scraped
¾ cup	egg yolks
4 oz	sugar

raspberry crunch:

2 cups	fresh raspberries

tuile:

1¾ cup	sugar
1 cup	all purpose flour
1	orange, zest
¾ cup	orange juice
6 oz	melted butter

caramel sauce:

1½ cups	sugar
⅓ cup	water
1 tsp	salt
2 cups	cream
2 oz	butter

METHOD

hazelnut-milk chocolate base:

Melt the chocolate over a double boiler, then whisk in the butter. Fold in the hazelnut paste and mix well, then fold in the feuilletine and mix well. Spread out evenly in a 8" x 8" dish with 3" deep sides. Allow to set.

vanilla bean mousse:

Bring the milk and vanilla bean to a boil. Whisk together the yolks and sugar, temper the hot milk into the sugar and yolk mixture. Pour back into the pot over a low heat and stir until thickened. Whisk in the gelatin sheets, then strain into a bowl. Allow to cool to room temperature. Once cool fold in the whipped cream, then pour over the hazelnut base and place into the fridge. Allow to set up for 6 hours.

raspberry crunch and tuile:

Mix together the sugar, flour and zest with a whisk, add the melted butter, then the orange juice and mix well. Allow to chill for 2 hours.

Once set, preheat the oven to 350°F. Place 1 tablespoon of the mix onto a silpat, and repeat seven times, being sure to leave 6" of space between each scoop to allow for spreading. Bake until golden brown. Remove from the oven and while they are still hot place a metal tube in the center, gently roll warm tuile around the tube and allow to set up, then gently remove the tube from tuile and repeat.

caramel sauce:

In a heavy gauge sauce pot add the sugar and water. Allow to cook until a dark amber color is reached. Remove from the heat and very carefully whisk in the cream, butter and salt. Reserve warm until use.

to serve:

Slice the vanilla mousse and hazelnut-milk chocolate into 1½" x 5" pieces. Place onto a plate. Place a raspberry stuffed tuile on top, and drizzle caramel sauce over.

Colin Bedford

A native of England, Colin Bedford began his career at the Castle Hotel in Taunton as Commis Chef. In pursuit of his desire to see other cultures and experiences, Colin moved to Niagara on The Lake, Canada and worked at the Prince of Wales Hotel where he was soon promoted to Junior Sous Chef. In 2005 Colin was recruited to Fearrington as Executive Sous Chef and then in late 2008, Colin assumed the role of Executive Chef of the Fearrington House Restaurant.

Colin continues to grow The Fearrington House's commitment to 'Farm-to-Table' cuisine, maintaining partnerships with local farmers, and using some of the finest produce and ingredients in the region and in our own gardens.

The Fearrington House
Country Inn & Restaurant

This is a made-to-measure retreat for lovers of good food, fine wine and gracious hospitality.

The farm-like setting with white facades, rocking chairs, lush landscaping and intimate courtyards will transport you to a place far away from the ordinary. Inspired by their travels abroad, R.B. Fitch and his late wife transformed a central North Carolina farm into a charming, elegant village, replete with shops, restaurants and the award-winning Fearrington House Inn and Restaurant. It is situated near one of the country's most dynamic research and venture capital hubs – the Research Triangle region encompassing Raleigh and Durham. You can discover the Jordan Lake nature preserve and nearby Chapel Hill, home to the nation's oldest state university among author readings, spa treatments, shopping and customized wine dinners.

Serves 4
Preparation time: 48 hours
Cooking time: 2 hours

Planning ahead
The veal breast needs to be cured 36 hours in advance and then cooked for a further 6 hours before preparing the rest of the dish.

INGREDIENTS

veal:

1	veal breast
1 lb	kosher salt
9 oz	granulated sugar
2 oz	pink salt
1 oz	crushed black pepper
1	bulb of garlic
½ oz	thyme
duck fat	

apple & vanilla chutney:

3	Granny Smith apples, diced
3	shallots, minced
1 cup	white wine
⅓ cup	Champagne vinegar
⅓ cup	granulated sugar
1	vanilla bean
1	bay leaf

sunchoke purée:

8 oz	peeled sunchokes
2	shallots
1 cup	heavy cream
3 cups	milk
3	lemons
¼ tsp	xanthan gum
2 tbsp	butter

truffle velouté:

3 ½ oz	shallots
3 ½ oz	celery
3 ½ oz	fennel
2	cloves garlic
12 fl oz	white wine
12 fl oz	white port
8 ½ fl oz	Madeira
3 pt	white chicken stock, reduced by half
4 pt	heavy cream, reduced by half
1	bay leaf
½ oz	thyme
2 cups	black truffle juice
4 tbsp	truffle peelings
truffle oil	

to serve:

1	bunch of salsify
1	Savoy cabbage
12	scallops
4 tbsp	truffle trimmings
truffle oil	
butter	
4	sprigs of thyme
lemon wedges	

SEARED SCALLOPS, CONFIT VEAL BREAST, APPLE & VANILLA CHUTNEY, SUNCHOKE PUREE & TRUFFLE VELOUTE

BY COLIN BEDFORD

A wonderfully impressive play on 'surf and turf' the confit veal is relatively simple to prepare ahead of time. It has a good balance of flavor and texture – the scallops are sweet and veal breast adds an element of saltiness. The acid in the vanilla and the apple chutney brings the dish together – perfect for any dinner party. The flavor combination is also wonderful for pairing wines.

METHOD

veal:

To cure the veal breast combine all the ingredients, except the duck fat, and liberally season, place in a container and refrigerate for 36 hours. Then wash and cover with duck fat in a roasting pan and cover with foil. Place in an oven at 250°F and cook for 6 hours. Allow to cool, remove from the fat and press.

apple & vanilla chutney:

Sweat the shallots without any color. Add all other ingredients apart from the diced apples and begin to reduce. Sauté the apples in a hot pan with oil until they start to turn translucent. This will stop them from going brown. Add to the shallot mixture and reduce until tacky, then chill.

sunchoke purée:

Place the sunchokes in lemon water. Then remove from the water, and combine with all the other ingredients, except for the xanthan gum, and cook until tender. Strain and purée, adding back some of the cooking liquid as needed. Add the xanthan gum, and butter adjust the seasoning and chill.

truffle velouté:

On a medium-high heat sweat the shallots, celery, fennel and garlic with the bay leaf and thyme until soft without color. Deglaze with the wine, port and Maderia, and reduce the alcohol until it smells sweet. Add the stock and reduced cream, and continue to reduce until the required consistency. Finish with the truffle juice.

to serve:

Peel and then blanch the salsify. Shave the Savoy cabbage and blanch. Cut the veal breast into a square which is just a little bit bigger than a scallop. Have a pan slowly warming on a burner. Take another pan and sear the breast then place in the oven to keep warm. Sauté the salsify until golden brown and begin to warm the cabbage and the velouté. Season the scallops, place in a preheated oiled pan and begin to brown. After 2-3 minutes flip the scallops, adding butter, thyme and lemon, squeezed from the wedges and then remove from the heat. Remove the veal from the oven. Arrange the drained cabbage on the plate, drag the purée across the plate, and distribute chutney in piles around the cabbage. Place a cube of veal at one end of the cabbage with a scallop on top and place the other two on the cabbage. Place salsify around the scallops, add truffle oil and trimmings to the sauce, then sauce around the scallops and garnish.

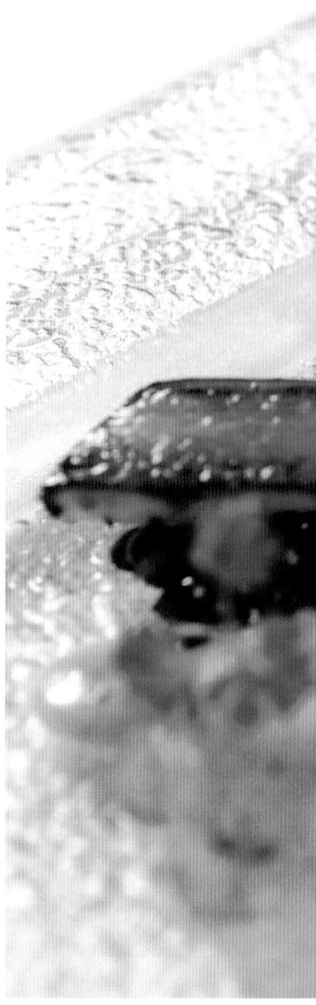

SMOKED PORK SHANK WITH CAULIFLOWER PUREE, BELUGA LENTILS, TRUFFLE OIL, CINNAMON & CIDER SAUCE

BY COLIN BEDFORD

Pork is a regional staple of the South and considered somewhat of a comfort food. This dish is our twist on the local pulled pork BBQ that is famous in North Carolina.

Serves 6
Preparation time: 38 hours
Cooking time: 25 minutes

Special equipment:
Deep fat fryer

Planning ahead:
The shanks should be prepared in brine the day before. They then need to be smoked for 4 hours and cooked 6 hours.

INGREDIENTS

smoked pork shanks:

12 pork shanks

pork brine step 1:

16 pt water
35 fl oz red wine vinegar
2 salt
1¾ brown sugar
3½ oz pink salt
1 head of garlic
2 oranges, zest
2 bay leaves
1 bunch of thyme
2 tsp black pepper

pork brine step 2:

4 cups apple cider
2 carrots, roughly chopped for mirepoix
2 onions, roughly chopped for mirepoix
1 head of celery, roughly chopped for mirepoix
1 head of garlic, halved
2 pieces sage
2 pieces rosemary
2 bay leaves
1 parsley, freshly chopped
brown chicken stock

pork brine step 3:

2 cups duck fat
1 cup sherry vinegar
1 cup honey
4 tbsp whole grain mustard
Bayonne ham

cinnamon and cider sauce:

1 carrot
3½ oz shallots
2 celery sticks
1 leek
4 garlic cloves
2 oz thyme
1 bay leaf
3 pt apple cider, reduced by half
2 pt white port, reduced by half
6 pt dark chicken stock, reduced by half
2 3" cinnamon sticks

cauliflower purée:

1 head of cauliflower
4 cups milk
2 tbsp butter
¼ tsp xanthan gum
salt & pepper

Beluga lentils:

1 cup Beluga lentils
1 carrot
2 stalks of celery
1 yellow onion
¼ oz fresh thyme for bouquet garni
½ oz parsley stalks for bouquet garni
2 pieces bay leaf for bouquet garni
3 garlic cloves
1 cup vegetable stock
2 tbsp shallots, chopped
1 tbsp parsley, chopped
1 tbsp butter

cauliflower beignet:

8 oz self raising flour
12 fl oz beer
1 tbsp poppy seeds
carbonated water
12 cauliflower florets, blanched
salt & pepper

to serve:

kale, blanched
beech mushrooms
butter
micro greens

METHOD

pork brine step 1:

Bring all the ingredients to a boil except the aromatics. Once the sugar has dissolved add the aromatics and then chill the brine. Pour over the shanks and refrigerate for 24 hours.

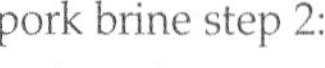

pork brine step 2:

Preheat the oven to 275°F. After 24 hours remove from the shanks from the brine and rinse. Cold smoke the pork for up to 4 hours. After smoking, caramelize the pork by searing in a high heat pan. Place in a pan with the apple cider and cover with brown chicken stock. Add the mirepoix, garlic, sage, rosemary and bay leaves. Cover and cook in the oven for 6 hours.

pork brine step 3:

Once you are able to move the bones freely the shank will be cooked. Allow to reach room temperature. Pick all the meat off the bones. Heat the duck fat, sherry vinegar, honey and mustard, use this to add any extra moisture and to adjust the seasoning.

Lay cling film out on the table about 4 ft in length. Place another piece just above the first one, overlapping them both by 2". Place the picked pork at the front of the cling film and roll up tightly to a 2" diameter, tying at each end. Reserve in the fridge until needed.

Lay the same amount of cling film down. Place the Bayonne ham down on the film, overlapping each piece, the same length as the rolled pork. Remove the cling film from the pork and lay the pork down on the ham and roll up in the new cling film, tying the ends again and placing it in the fridge.

cinnamon and cider sauce:

Brown the carrot, celery and shallots. Then add the leek, garlic and aromatics and cook for a further 5 minutes. Deglaze with the reduced port and apple cider and bring to a boil, skim and simmer. Add reduced stock and continue to reduce until you reach the require consistency.

cauliflower purée:

Cook the cauliflower, remove from the heat and add the milk, butter and xanthan gum, season to taste and purée in a blender.

Beluga lentils:

Put all the ingredients in a pan, cover with 3 times the amount of water and bring to a boil and simmer for 20-25 minutes. Once cooked strain, pick out the cooking aromatics and reserve.

cauliflower beignet:

To make the batter combine the flour, poppy seeds and seasoning, then add the beer, whisking constantly. Adjust the viscosity by adding the carbonated water.

to serve:

Preheat the oven to 350°F. Cut the pork to the desired portion size, sear and place in the oven for 8-10 minutes. Warm the cauliflower purée. For the beignets, take the blanched cauliflower florets, dust them with flour and then dredge them through the batter and into a fryer on 325°F. Cook until golden brown. Warm up the lentils in some vegetable stock and diced shallots, and also begin to warm up the blanched kale. Have a pan on high heat so you are able to sauté the mushrooms until golden brown, then finish with butter and season. Remove the pork from the oven, and bring everything up to serving temperature including the sauce. Arrange on plates and garnish with micro greens.

Chef's tip:

Blanching the kale prior to serving with 1 teaspoon of baking soda in the water will cook the green faster while maintaining its color.

DARK CHOCOLATE SOUFFLE, CHOCOLATE SAUCE & VANILLA ICE CREAM

BY COLIN BEDFORD

The Chocolate Soufflé has been the iconic item on the menu at the Fearrington House for 30 years. It was introduced by then guest chef Edna Lewis and featured on the cover of *Gourmet* magazine in April of 1984 and is still today a favorite dessert of our guests.

Serves 8
Preparation time: 1 hour
Cooking time: 8-12 minutes

Special equipment:
Ice cream machine

Planning ahead:
The ice cream can be made in advance.

INGREDIENTS

vanilla ice cream:

1 pt	whole milk
10 fl oz	heavy cream
4½ oz	granulated sugar
5 oz	trimoline
5	egg yolks
2	vanilla beans

soufflé base: (makes extra)

14 oz	100% chocolate
1 pt	whole milk
1 oz	all purpose flour
1 oz	butter

chocolate sauce:

10 oz	100% chocolate
3½ cups	granulated sugar
1 qt	heavy cream

soufflé:

2 cups	egg whites
1	pinch of sugar

METHOD

vanilla ice cream:

Infuse the vanilla beans into the milk by bringing to a boil. Combine the yolks, sugar, and trimoline. Temper the milk onto the egg mixture then return to the heat until the mixture will coat the back of a spoon. Strain and then add the cream, mix thoroughly and churn.

soufflé base:

Bring the milk to a boil. Melt the butter in a big enough pan to be able to take all the milk. Have the chocolate weighed out in the bowl on a mixer. Add the flour to the butter and make a roux, then pull both pans off the heat. Add the hot milk gradually to the roux, constantly whisking to prevent lumps. Once all the milk is incorporated put it back on the heat and boil. Once boiled remove from the heat and allow to cool for about 10 minutes. Add to the chocolate on the mixer, beat until smooth. Place in a container and keep warm.

chocolate sauce:

Bring the cream to a boil, add the sugar and chocolate. Using a hand blender mix until all the chocolate has melted and the sugar dissolved. Place in a jug and keep warm.

soufflé:

Whisk 2 cups of egg whites and once they start to get frothy add a pinch of sugar then whisk until thick. Meanwhile have 10 oz of soufflé base in a bowl. The rest of the soufflé base can be reserved in the fridge for 5 days for additional soufflés, creating eight servings per 10 oz batch. Once the egg whites are stiff, beat a third of the whites into the chocolate base, then fold the additional whites in carefully. Fill to the top of a sugared ramekin, scrape flat, run your thumb around the lip and blowtorch the top. Cook for 8-12 minutes, turning at the mid point.

to serve:

When the soufflé is ready, dust with powdered sugar, and serve with vanilla ice cream. Break the top of the soufflé with a spoon and pour in some chocolate sauce.

Robert Carter

As Executive Chef and Partner of Peninsula Grill, Robert Carter has received widespread acclaim for his sophisticated southern cuisine, defined by a simple approach that bolsters the essence of each ingredient to create extraordinary layers of flavor. Robert's contemporary menu and presentation at the award-winning 125-seat Peninsula Grill have earned the restaurant a national following as the pre-eminent culinary destination in Charleston.

After graduating from the prestigious Johnson & Wales University, Carter charted a gastronomic journey that included an apprenticeship with Victor Gielisse in Dallas. He then took his first Executive Chef position at The Inn at Blackberry Farm. In 1991, during his tenure as Executive Chef for Café Marquessa in Key West, Carter met hospitality entrepreneur Hank Holliday and the two began developing plans for a fine dining restaurant at Holliday's historic Planters Inn, South Carolina's only Relais & Châteaux hotel.

When Peninsula Grill opened in 1997, *Esquire* magazine named it one of the 'Best New Restaurants in America'. Since that time, Carter and Peninsula Grill have garnered numerous other national accolades.

Planters Inn

The Planters Inn is located in the very heart of Charleston's famed Historic District and was originally built in 1844.

Dating back three centuries, the City of Charleston is one of the best-preserved architectural treasures in the United States and is the birthplace of the Charleston dance – made famous by Josephine Baker. The meticulously restored colonial homes lining its charming streets are an eloquent reminder of its joyous and long history and the city still has all the charm that it owes to its multi-ethnic European origins. With their ornate landscaping and fountains, the courtyard and verandas of the Planters Inn create an urban oasis where guests can relax to a serenade of jazz, while sipping delicious cocktails and tasting the generous regional American cuisine of the nationally-acclaimed Peninsula Grill.

BOURBON-GRILLED JUMBO SHRIMP WITH CREAMED CORN SAUCE & GREEN ONION HORSERADISH HUSHPUPPIES

BY ROBERT CARTER

Shrimp is an abundant crop in Charleston and when the shrimp are running it's a great time to grill these jumbo shrimp. We take the low-brow hushpuppy to new heights by spiking them with horseradish and serving them with grilled jumbo shrimp...the large puppy makes for a great boat to serve the shrimp in and the smaller fritters add crunch and texture to the dish. The sweetness of the fresh corn balances with the cornmeal in the puppies and enhances the shrimp as well.

Serves 6
Preparation time: 1 hour
Cooking time: 30 minutes

Special equipment:
Fry-Daddy or other small deep fat fryer

INGREDIENTS

shrimps:

36	jumbo shrimps, peeled and deveined, but tails left on
1 tbsp	garlic, minced
1½ tsp	freshly ground black pepper
1 tbsp	fresh basil, chopped
½ cup	olive oil

Bourbon butter:

4 oz	unsalted butter
1 tbsp	light brown sugar, firmly packed
1 tbsp	Bourbon
1	pinch of kosher salt
1	pinch of freshly ground black pepper

creamed corn sauce:

3	large ears of fresh yellow corn
5 tbsp	unsalted butter
¾ cup	onions, chopped
1¾ tsp	garlic, minced
1 cup	heavy whipping cream
⅓ cup	milk
¾ tsp	fresh thyme, chopped (fresh basil or oregano may be substituted)
1½ tsp	kosher salt
¼ tsp	white pepper
1	pinch of cayenne pepper
1	pinch of freshly grated nutmeg

green onion horseradish hushpuppies:
(makes 36)

1 cup + 1 tsp self raising flour
1 cup + 1 tsp yellow cornmeal

2 tbsp	sugar
½ tsp	kosher salt
¼ tsp	white pepper
2	eggs
1 cup	buttermilk
2 tbsp	unsalted butter, melted
½ cup	prepared horseradish
¼ cup	white part of a green onion, finely chopped
¼ cup	green part of a green onion, finely chopped

peanut oil, for frying

risotto:

2 tbsp	olive oil
2 tbsp	garlic, minced
1	onion, chopped
1 cup	Arborio rice
3 cups	chicken stock or shrimp stock, hot
2 cup	corn kernels
3 tbsp	roasted red peppers, diced
2 tbsp	butter
2 tbsp	parmesan cheese

METHOD

shrimps:

Combine the garlic, pepper, basil and olive oil, add the shrimps, cover, and marinate them for 1 hour in the refrigerator.

Bourbon butter:

Melt the butter in a small saucepan over a medium-high heat. Add the sugar, Bourbon, salt and pepper and cook for 3 to 5 minutes, or until the mixture comes to a foam. Set aside.

creamed corn sauce:

Cut the corn kernels off the cobs. You will need 2½ cups of kernels. Using a knife, scrape the cobs over a bowl to extract their 'milk'. Reserve. Heat 4 tablespoons of the butter in a large sauté pan over a medium-high heat until foaming. Add the onion and garlic and sauté, stirring occasionally, for about 2 minutes, or until soft. Add the corn kernels, stir well, and sauté for 2 minutes more. Do not brown. Add three-quarters of the cup of cream, the milk, 'corn milk', thyme, salt, pepper, cayenne pepper and nutmeg and stir well. Put half of this mixture in a blender and pulse just enough to cut up the corn. Remove, and put the other half in the blender. Purée this well, adding up to 2 tablespoons of the cream if necessary. Combine the two mixtures. Combine the corn with the remaining 2 tablespoons of heavy cream in a heavy-bottomed saucepan and bring them to a boil. Slowly stir in the remaining tablespoon of unsalted butter.

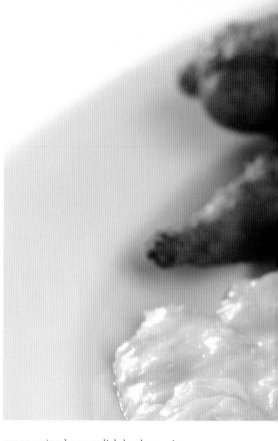

green onion horseradish hushpuppies:

Combine 1 cup of flour, 1 cup of cornmeal, the sugar, salt and pepper and mix well. Whisk together the eggs, buttermilk, butter and horseradish. Stir the wet ingredients into the dry ingredients. Fold in the green onions and let set for 15 minutes.

Heat the oil to 350°F. When hot, test a hushpuppy. When the consistency is correct, it should go to the bottom without breaking up. If it does break apart, add the remaining teaspoons of flour and cornmeal to the batter. Once they pass the consistency test, you may begin to fry the hushpuppies. Put several in the fryer but don't

crowd them or the temperature of the oil will drop and the hushpuppies will become greasy. Fry for 3 to 4 minutes, stirring them a little to make them brown evenly. They are done when they turn a nice golden brown. Place the hushpuppies on paper towels to drain. You may keep them warm in a 200°F oven when they are all fried.

risotto:

Sauté the garlic and onion in the olive oil. Add the Arborio rice. Slowly stir in one-quarter of the stock into the rice mixture. Stir constantly until the liquid is absorbed.

Repeat with another quarter of the stock. Add the corn to the rice mixture. Repeat with the last two additions of the stock. After all the stock is added and absorbed, fold in the red peppers, butter and parmesan cheese.

to serve:

Prepare a hot grill or grill pan. Working with 6 shrimps at a time, lay the shrimps flat, side by side, and all turned the same way. Push 2 skewers through each set of six, sliding 1 skewer through at the point that the meat and tail meet and the second skewer through the other end. This will keep the shrimps from twisting on the skewer. Grill the shrimps for 2 to 3 minutes per side, basting them with the Bourbon butter several times, and again when they come off the grill. Be careful not to overcook. Serve immediately with the risotto, some creamed corn sauce and the green onion horseradish hushpuppies.

Chef's tip:

At the Peninsula Grill, we also have a fancier version of the hushpuppies: Lobster-Basil Hushpuppies. To make these, simply omit the green onion and horseradish and replace them with ½ cup of chopped cooked lobster meat and ¼ cup chopped fresh basil.

Serves 4
Preparation time: 1 hour
Cooking time: 30 minutes

LOW COUNTRY OYSTER STEW WITH WILD MUSHROOM GRITS

BY ROBERT CARTER

There is nothing sweeter than fresh shucked oysters that have been harvested from your backyard. Many a night in the Low Country there have been oyster roasts along the marshes while the sun is setting. Brown Oyster Stew is a classic Low Country dish that we have enhanced with smoked bacon, garlic and basil – then in the style of gumbo we put a nice helping of wild mushroom grits in the middle instead of rice.

INGREDIENTS

oyster stew:

2 tbsp	smoked bacon, ¼" diced
¼ cup	Vidalia or other sweet onion, diced
½ tsp	garlic, minced
2 tbsp	mixed red, green and yellow bell peppers, finely diced
1¼ cups	dark chicken stock
¼ cup	heavy whipping cream
2 tbsp	fresh basil, chopped
1	pinch of freshly ground black pepper
½ pt	fresh oysters with their liquor (about 20)

wild mushroom grits:

4 tbsp	unsalted butter
¼ lb	button or cremini mushrooms, cleaned with a damp paper towel, stems removed and caps quartered
¼ lb	shiitake mushrooms, cleaned with a damp paper towel, stems removed and caps sliced into ⅛" slices
¼ cup	dark chicken stock
½ tsp	kosher salt
1 tsp	freshly ground black pepper
3½ cups	water
1 cup	heavy whipping cream
2 tsp	garlic, minced
1 tsp	kosher salt
¼ tsp	white pepper
1 cup	stone-ground white grits
1 cup	milk
¼ cup	Asiago cheese, grated

METHOD

oyster stew:

In a medium saucepan over a medium-high heat, sauté the bacon for 3 to 4 minutes, or until the fat is rendered and the bacon is beginning to brown. Add the onion, garlic and peppers, reduce the heat to medium, and sauté for 2 to 3 minutes, or until the vegetables are translucent. Add the stock and cream and simmer, stirring occasionally, for 2 to 3 minutes, just to thicken slightly. Add the oysters and basil and simmer for 1 to 2 minutes, or until the oysters are just beginning to set and are slightly curled around the edges. Stir in the pepper.

wild mushroom grits:

Heat 2 tablespoons of the butter in a medium saucepan over a medium-high heat until foaming. Add the button mushrooms and sauté for 1 minute. Add the shiitakes and mix well. Increase the heat to high, add the chicken stock, salt and pepper, and cook over a high heat for 2 to 3 minutes, or until all the liquid is evaporated. Set aside.

In a medium heavy-bottomed saucepan over a high heat, bring the water, cream, the remaining 2 tablespoons of butter, garlic, salt and pepper to a boil. Stir in the grits and bring back to a boil, stirring constantly. Reduce the heat to medium-low and simmer, stirring frequently, for about 20 minutes, or until the grits are tender. If the grits need more liquid, whisk in some of the milk. Fold in the cheese and mushrooms and set aside in a warm place.

to serve:

Divide the grits between four warm soup bowls. Spoon the oyster stew around the grits, making sure that each serving gets its share of oysters.

LEMON MERINGUE CAKE

BY CLAIRE CHAPMAN

Serves 12
Preparation time: 1 hour 30 minutes
Cooking time: 45 minutes

Special equipment:
Blow torch

Planning ahead:
The lemon curd can be made several days in advance. The cake needs to be chilled overnight.

A twist on an all time favorite, this meringue cake adds a twist of elegance and beauty. Blueberries are abundant in the Low Country in the Summertime and go nicely with the tartness of the cake.

INGREDIENTS

vanilla cake:

4½ cups	all purpose flour
1½ tbsp	baking powder
½ tsp	salt
3 cups	sugar
6	eggs
1 lb	butter
1½ cup	cream
1½ tbsp	vanilla extract
1 tsp	canola oil

almond sponge cake: color paste

2 oz	butter
2 oz	powdered sugar
2 oz	all purpose flour
2 oz	egg whites
2-4	drops yellow food color

almond sponge:

3	eggs
3 oz	powdered sugar
3 oz	almond flour (you can substitute all purpose flour for this)
¾ oz	all purpose flour
¾	butter, melted butter
3	egg whites
1 tbsp	granulated sugar

lemon syrup:

1 cup	water
1 cup	sugar
½	lemon, squeezed

lemon curd:

1 ⅛ cup	granulated sugar
4	whole large eggs
4	large yolks
¾ cup	lemon juice
1	lemon, zest
10 oz	soft butter
2 tsp	powdered gelatin
½ cup	soft butter, for final assembly

blueberry compote:

1 pt	fresh or frozen blueberries
¼ cup	brown sugar
½	lemon, squeezed
2 tbsp	Madeira

Italian meringue:

4	large egg whites
1 ⅛ cup	granulated sugar
⅛ cup	water

METHOD

vanilla cake:

Preheat the oven to 325°F. In a mixer cream the butter and sugar well, add the oil and vanilla extract. Add the eggs on medium speed, one at a time. Scrape down the bowl. Mix all the dry ingredients together and sift well. Add alternately with the cream, scraping down in between. Pour the batter into a sprayed 9" x 3" round deep cake pan. Bake until a toothpick comes out clean, approximately 45 minutes.

almond sponge cake: color paste

Cream the butter and sugar together, then add the flour. Slowly add the whites to form a smooth paste, then add the food color. Spread a very thin layer of this paste onto a silicone baking sheet, then take a small spatula and create a wave pattern by removing the paste in some areas. Place this mat on a baking sheet and freeze.

almond sponge:

Preheat the oven to 325°F. Place the first four ingredients in a mixer bowl and whip with the whisk attachment until thicker, approximately 10 minutes. Add the melted butter. Remove from the machine. Place the whites and sugar into a clean mixing bowl and whisk until soft peaks. Fold the meringue into the egg/flour batter. Spread the batter gently over the frozen paste. Bake immediately until lightly golden and when it springs back to the touch, approximately 15-25 minutes. Cool, flip over and gently peel off the silicone mat.

lemon syrup:

Bring all the ingredients to a boil and cool.

lemon curd:

Place the first five ingredients over a double boiler and whisk until the mixture thickens. While thickening the curd, bloom the gelatin in a little water. Remove the bowl from the heat and slowly whisk in the 10 oz butter. Melt the gelatin gently in the microwave and whisk into the thickened curd mixture. Place in a container, cover and allow to cool to room temperature before using. You can also refrigerate the curd at this point and make several days ahead of using. To finish the curd for assembly - place the curd in the mixer with the whip attachment and slowly whip in ½ cup of soft butter until the curd comes to a thicker consistency.

blueberry compote:

Cook all the ingredients together for 15-20 minutes until the mixture thickens.

Italian meringue:

Bring the sugar and water to a boil and continue to boil until the bubbles pop slowly, at around 248°F. Whisk the whites in a mixer until just beginning to form soft peaks, then carefully pour the hot syrup down the side of the bowl, turn the speed up and whip until it forms shiny stiff peaks.

cake assembly:

Using a 10" loose bottom 3" high round cake pan, lightly spray the pan and dust with sugar – this will help release the cake. Cut the very top of the round 9" vanilla cake off and then cut the remaining cake into three even layers. Set aside.

Cut two strips of the almond sponge cake 2½" high, and wrap the strips of cake around the inside of the cake pan; you will need two to complete the ring. Place a layer of cake on the base of the pan and brush with lemon syrup.

Place the lemon curd in a piping bag and pipe a ring around the edge of the cake, knock the pan on the counter to eliminate air bubbles. Place more lemon curd in the center of the cake and spread evenly.

Place the second cake layer on the curd and repeat the steps until all the layers are in the cake and top the last layer of cake with the remainder of the lemon curd. This should now be even with the top of the almond sponge. Place cling film over the top and chill overnight.

to serve:

When you are ready to serve the cake, un-mold from the pan and place on a serving platter. Top the cake with the Italian Meringue and lightly torch to a golden color using a blow torch. Allow the cake to sit out for at least 15 minutes so that the flavors come through when eating. Serve with the blueberry compote.

Chef's tip:

Any remaining paste from the almond sponge may be frozen for future use. If you do not wish to use the almond sponge you can assemble this cake in a 9" round pan and cover the entire cake in the meringue.

Tennessee

The home of country music and of course the King himself, Tennessee is the birthplace of modern music.

Boasting country, blues and rock and roll on its set list, and Elvis, Jonny Cash and Jerry Lee Lewis on its stage, the 'volunteer state' offers a great place to entertain in the forms of Nashville and Memphis. If that wasn't enough, take in the ambience of the Great Smoky Mountains, the Cumberland Plateau with its dense, lush countryside or revel in the humid temperature of the lowlands overlooking the Mississippi river. So, eat like the King in Tennessee and enjoy the Southern hospitality.

Adam Cooke
Grand Chef Relais & Châteaux

Adam Cooke is Chef de Cuisine of The Barn at Blackberry Farm. His culinary influence began when his family moved from Northern California to the Sierra Nevada Mountains to a farm in the valley. His memories of milking cows, gathering eggs, and picking fruit from the cherry trees as a young boy still impact his culinary endeavors.

From Montana to Nantucket, Adam moved through restaurants and the New England Culinary Institute, all the while identifying his own style. During this time, his work with Chef Martha Beuser, formerly of San Francisco's Zuni Café and Chez Panisse, led him to find an early enthusiasm for the sourcing of local and sustainable foods.

Adam joined the Blackberry Farm team in 2005 and has now opened the newest restaurant at Blackberry, The Barn. He works directly with Blackberry's team of artisans to create dishes using seasonal produce and herbs found in the Blackberry Farm gardens, fields and forests, ensuring a taste of East Tennessee in every course. In 2009, Adam was named a Grand Chef Relais & Châteaux.

Blackberry Farm

This traditional farm is deep in Tennessee and offers a chance to return to nature and rediscover life's simple pleasures. Guests are treated to a steady flow of deliciously fresh produce all year round as part of the 1700 hectares of land set aside for farming.

In addition to vegetables, cheese, herbs, honey, cider and much more are all produced right here. Established ties with local gardeners and tradespeople mean that Blackberry Farm's team of Chefs offers a menu that respects the authenticity of the flavors and the integrity of the products. The result is simple and delicious recipes accompanied by excellent wines. If you want to you can become really involved in life at the farm indulging in a spot of gardening and cheese making. Alternatively you can go fly fishing, explore the region on a Harley-Davidson or by horse-drawn carriage, not to mention the variety of beauty treatments available.

ENDIVE, ESCARGOT & BENTON'S BACON TART

BY ADAM COOKE

This is an easy but impressive starter or middle course. We use Wild Burgundy Escargot. Endive is easy to find these days, just look to make sure the tips are not browning and that the heads feel dense and heavy for their size. Benton's bacon is a very smoky country style bacon with addictive qualities.

Serves 4
Preparation time: 30 minutes
Cooking time: 12 minutes

Special equipment:
Four 3" ramekins or tart molds
Ring cutter that fits the opening of your ramekins
Sheet pan

INGREDIENTS

pastry rounds:

1	box puff pastry or 1 lb fresh made puff pastry

tarts:

3	heads white Belgian endive
1 lb	Benton's bacon, small diced
1	white onion, small diced
3	cloves garlic, minced
1	bunch parsley, minced
4	branches thyme, leaves picked, branches discarded
20	pieces Wild Burgundy Escargot
12	pieces wild mushrooms (chanterelle, abalone, hen of the woods, porcini)
1 cup	hazelnuts
1	shallot, minced
10	chives, minced
½ cup	extra virgin olive oil

Salt & pepper

METHOD

pastry rounds:

Roll the chilled dough to ¼" thickness and dock thoroughly with a fork. Cut into 3" rounds and move to a sheet pan and refrigerate while building the tarts.

tarts:

Bring a large saucepot of water to a boil.

Trim the root end of the endive and remove the large outer leaves and set aside. Cut crosswise to remove smaller tips, pull apart and set aside. Small dice the base of the endive.

In a large sauté pan at medium heat add the bacon and begin to render. When the bacon has taken some color and looks evenly browned remove half of the bacon fat and add the onion to the pan. Reserve the fat to grease the ramekins. Cook for 2 minutes. Add the garlic and diced endive base. Cook for one minute. Add the escargot, parsley, thyme and cook until all is warmed through and the vegetables are completely cooked. Correct the seasoning with salt and pepper, and reserve.

Fill a medium mixing bowl with ice and water. Dunk the large endive leaves in the boiling water for 30 seconds to soften and remove to iced water. Drain thoroughly. Rub the ramekins with the bacon fat, line with the softened outer leaves and fill with the escargot filling.

Toss the wild mushrooms in 3 tablespoons of olive oil, salt and pepper. Place on a baking sheet.

Bake puff pastry circles at 350°F until golden brown, about 10 minutes. Warm the tarts in the same oven for the same amount of time, baking the mushrooms also.

Make a mignonette by combining hazelnuts, the remaining olive oil, minced shallot, and minced chives. While everything is cooling toss the small endive tips in the mignonette.

to serve

Place the puff pastry rounds on the tarts and turn out. Place on a plate decorated with wild mushrooms, endive tips and hazelnut mignonette. Serve warm.

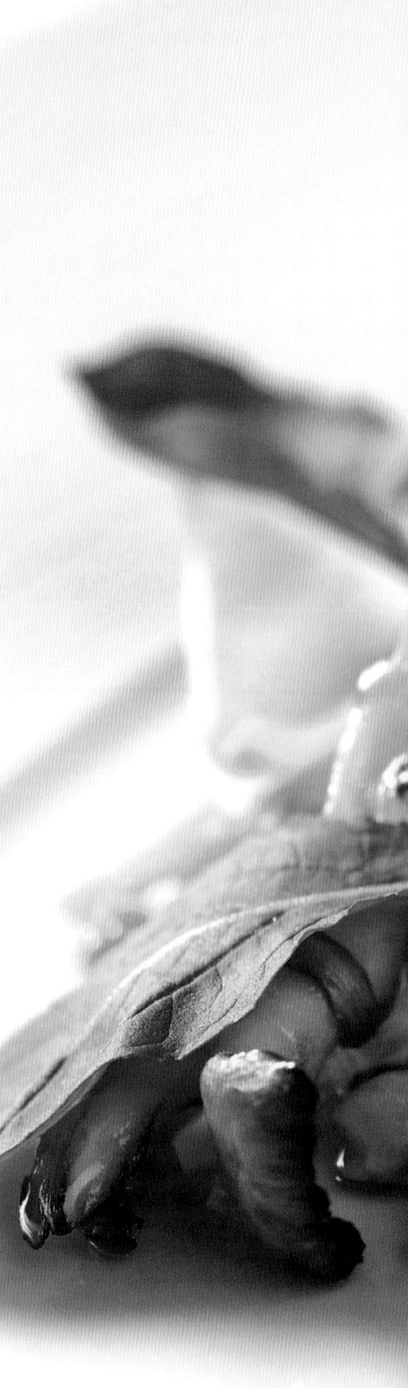

OLIVE OIL POACHED STURGEON, NEW CROP POTATO, CAVIAR & WATERCRESS

BY ADAM COOKE

Sturgeon's high fat content lends nicely to a 'confit' method of cooking, a method in which meats are cooked and actually preserved in fat. We use olive oil for flavor here as our cooking fat, and to balance this cooking method, a nearly raw salad of radishes and slightly acidic pickled onion and spicy watercress and, in our opinion, caviar is always a good idea.

Serves 4
Preparation time: 1 hour
Cooking time: 30 minutes

INGREDIENTS

sturgeon:

1 lb sturgeon fillet
6 cups olive oil
½ cup salt
½ cup sugar
1 lemon, zest
¼ cup fresh horseradish
fresh herbs

new crop potatoes:

1 lb baby new potatoes
mixed fresh herbs

dill and potato mousseline:

1 Yukon gold potato
1 cup crème fraîche
1 tbsp dill, minced
1 cup milk
1 tbsp whole grain mustard

pickled pearl onions:

1 red pearl onion
1 cup red wine vinegar
1 cup water
½ cup sugar
pickling spice

garnish:

olive oil
salt
½ lb caviar, American sturgeon Roe
fresh watercress, arugula or other spicy greens.
baby radishes

METHOD

sturgeon:

Mix salt, sugar and zest from the lemon and ¼ cup fresh grated hoarseradish. Spread the mixture over the sturgeon and let cure for 15 minutes. Rinse and dry well. Place the sturgeon in a flat pot or baking dish and cover with oil and fresh herbs. Place in an oven at 250°F and cook for about 20 minutes or until soft when pierced with a knife. Rest in the oil at room temperature.

new crop potatoes:

Place the new potatoes in a similar dish, cover with herbs, and cook until tender when pierced with a knife.

dill and potato mousseline:

Peel and small dice the Yukon gold potato and simmer in milk until very soft. Pass through a fine mesh sieve or food mill. Season and loosen to a creamy consistency with crème fraîche. Add the minced dill, and the whole grain mustard and reserve.

pickled pearl onions:

Peel the onions. Bring to a boil the red wine vinegar, 1 cup of water, ½ cup of sugar and the pickling spice. Add the onions and boil for 1 minute then remove from the heat to cool to room temperature. Quarter the onions to make petals.

to serve:

Spoon a line of potato mousseline across the plate. Halve and toss the new potatoes in olive oil and salt and arrange on the plate. Slice the sturgeon and place in the middle of the plate. Quenelle a generous portion of caviar on top of the sturgeon. Place red onion petals among the potatoes and place watercress around the plate. Serve cool.

ORANGE MOUSSE WITH CRANBERRY JAM

BY ADAM COOKE

Our idea for this dessert spawned from a love for the combination of our great homemade yogurt and Josh Feathers' Grain and Nut Cereal. The crunchy streusel topping goes beautifully with the creaminess of the mousse.

Serves 4
Preparation time: 1 hour
Cooking time: 30 minutes

INGREDIENTS

cranberry jam:

12 oz	frozen cranberries
1 cup	granulated sugar
½ cup	orange juice
1	orange zest
1 cup	water

orange mousse:

9 oz	heavy cream
9 oz	cream cheese
¼ oz	gelatin, melted
2½ oz	sugar
3½ oz	egg yolks
½ oz	orange zest

crispy streusel topping:

1½ cups	oats
½ cup	all purpose flour
4 oz	brown sugar
¼ tsp	salt
¼ tsp	baking soda
1 tsp	cinnamon
4 oz	melted butter

orange cranberry sauce:

½ cup	cranberry jam (left over from above)

orange juice

METHOD

cranberry jam:

In a saucepan combine the cranberries, granulated sugar, orange juice, orange zest and water. Bring the mixture to a boil, then reduce the temperature to a simmer. As you continue cooking, make sure you stir often, so the jam does not burn. Cook until the mixture sticks well to a spoon, or place a small amount on a plate and place into the freezer. Check the jam in a minute or two, and if the jam is set it is done. Allow to cool completely before using. You can pass the jam through a food mill if you do not prefer having the cranberry skins in the jam.

orange mousse:

Whip the cream to soft peaks and reserve in the fridge. Melt the cream cheese very slowly on a double boiler. Once it is melted whisk in the sugar, egg yolks and orange zest. Return over the double boiler and whisk until the mixture is very hot to the touch. Make sure you are stirring the mixture, so it does not curdle. Strain immediately, add in the melted gelatin and fold in the soft whipped cream. Place into a piping bag and pipe into an acetate lined mold. Smooth the top and place into the freezer. Once the mousse is frozen, top with a thin even layer of jam. Immediately remove the plastic, leaving a smooth surface. Store in the refrigerator until required, but not more than 12 hours before you need it.

crispy streusel topping:

Combine in a mixing bowl the oats, all purpose flour, brown sugar, salt, baking soda and cinnamon then add the melted butter. Once it is all combined spread evenly onto a sheet tray and bake at 350°F until golden brown and crispy. Let it cool and place on top of the jam.

orange cranberry sauce:

Place the cranberry jam in a mixer, stream in orange juice one tablespoon at a time, until the mixture is a sauce consistency. You can either strain the sauce or leave it chunky.

to serve:

Add a stripe of sauce to one side of the plate. Place the mousse to the other side and scatter some more streusel topping around.

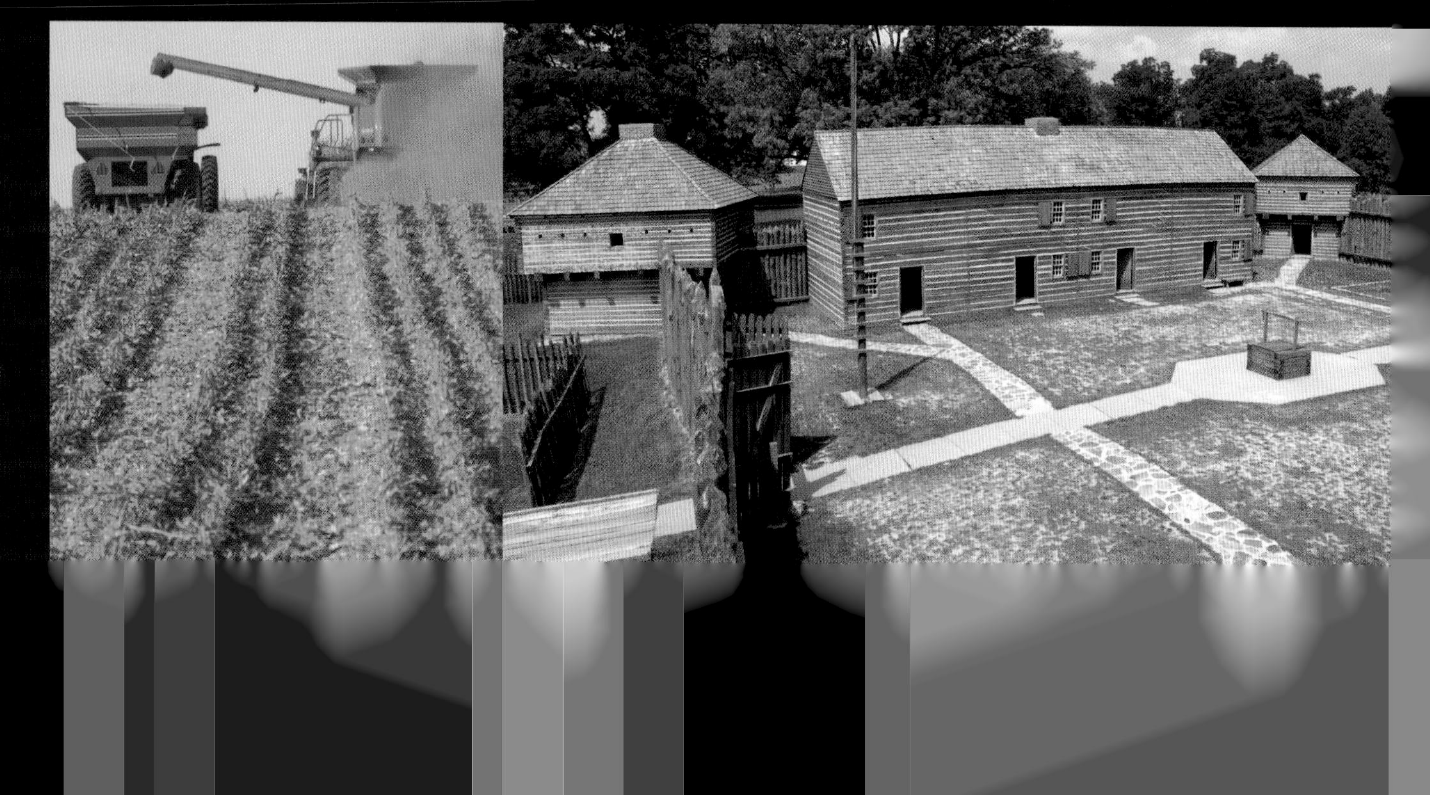

Illinois

Illinois – a state with it all. Sometimes known as the Lincoln State, this area of the U.S. is home to the bright lights of Chicago and the woody greens of Fort Massac State park. Its cornfields, dairy products and soybeans are the argicultural outputs of choice in this state.

Windy city Chicago offers a mixture of extremes from gastronomic artistic creations to the ultimate in deep-dish pizzas. With Chicago's cultural sights, Springfield's Lincoln's Tomb and Fort Massac State Park relaxed outdoor ventures make Illinois an easy-to-please favorite.

Jean Joho
Grand Chef Relais & Châteaux

With celebrated restaurants in Chicago, Las Vegas and Boston, Chef Joho's culinary passion knows no bounds; his soul is deeply at home in the kitchens that he loves. His talent can be measured in accolades, prestigious awards, thriving restaurants, fiercely loyal patrons and signature dishes that continue to set the standards for dining.

His formal training began as a 13-year-old apprentice for Paul Haeberlin of the famous L'Auberge de L'Ill in Alsace, France and continued in kitchens in France, Italy and Switzerland. By the age of 23, Joho was the chef at a two-Michelin-star restaurant. While studying at the Hotel Restaurant School in Strasbourg he immersed himself in the hotel and restaurant business, as well as the arts of pastry, cheese and wine.

Today Joho is known for having made an indelible mark on the culinary world with his exquisite French cuisine. His body of work is elegant, creative and deeply personal. Joho continues to thoughtfully handpick the famed wine selections at each of his restaurants: Everest, Brasserie Jo and Eiffel Tower Restaurant.

Everest

This stylishly decorated restaurant offers breathtaking views and flavors. Chief/proprietor Jean Joho embodies the American dream.

This Frenchman from Alsace is now one of the most respected chefs on the continent after coming to the United States almost 25 years ago. Like a symbol of his success and the giddy heights that his cuisine has reached, Everest is situated on the 40th floor of the Chicago Stock Exchange. Jean Joho endlessly reinvents the great classics of French cuisine. His hallmark is to combine noble products like foie gras or caviar with the humble potato and turnip to create delicious surprises. In honour of his homeland, wines from Alsace also star in many of his recipes such as his Wasserstriwela smoked Arctic Char on a bed of paprika-infused sauerkraut or Casco Bay Sea Scallops with Belgian chicory, Melfor and Gewurztraminer.

ROASTED MAINE LOBSTER WITH ALSACE GEWURZTRAMINER BUTTER & GINGER

BY JEAN JOHO

This is the only dish that has remained on the menu at Everest for 20 years. It is a perfect match for Alsace Gewurztraminer – a wine that is often difficult to marry with food.

Serves 4

Preparation time: 45 minutes
Cooking time: 20 minutes

INGREDIENTS

4 lobsters, 1 lb each
2 oz clarified butter
salt & fresh black pepper
1 tsp fresh ginger, julienne
1 cup Alsace Gewurztraminer Vendanges Tardives
5 oz butter
cayenne pepper, to taste
lemon, zest, to taste

to serve:

Romaine lettuce
lobster butter
fresh herbs

METHOD

Blanch the lobsters each for 30 seconds.

Preheat the oven to 375°F. Preheat a roasting pan with the clarified butter. Add the lobsters and roast for 10-15 minutes. Season with salt and pepper. Add the ginger. Halfway through the cooking time deglaze with the wine. Remove the lobster from the heat and let it rest for 5 minutes. Remove the lobster meat from the shell and keep warm on a plate.

Pour the sauce reduction from the roasting pan into a small saucepan and emulsify with the butter. Season with salt, cayenne and lemon zest.

to serve:

Sauté the lettuce and place on a warm serving dish. Top with the lobster, and dress with lobster butter and fresh herbs.

Chef's tip:

The lobsters must be properly cooked and should be accompanied with a great Alsace Gewurztraminer Vendanges Tardives wine.

CREPINETTE OF WILD STURGEON & CABBAGE

BY JEAN JOHO

Wild sturgeon from the Columbian River is a perfect substitute for meat. If desired, you may substitute halibut.

Serves 4
Preparation time: 1 hour 30 minutes
Cooking time: 15 minutes

Special equipment:
Butcher's twine

INGREDIENTS

sturgeon:

1½ lb wild sturgeon fillet, cleaned
fine slices of Prosciutto ham
choucroute, Alsace style

Pinot Noir sauce:

1 tsp shallots, chopped
1½ cups Pinot Noir
1 tsp chicken jus
1 tsp fresh butter
salt & pepper

to serve:

vegetables of your choice

METHOD

sturgeon:

On a cutting board lay out some cling film. Cover three-quarters of the film with the slices of Prosciutto ham. In the center spread out ½" thick the choucroute. Season the sturgeon and place on top of the choucroute, then coat evenly the top part of the fillet with more choucroute. Fold the prosciutto over the top and do the same with the cling film. Tie firmly and maintain both ends with butcher's twine. Keep in the refrigerator for half an hour.

Pinot Noir sauce:

In a saucepan, sweat the shallots then add the Pinot Noir and bring to a syrupy consistency. Add the jus and butter. Season to taste.

to serve:

Preheat the oven to 425°F. Remove carefully the wrapped fillet of sturgeon from the saran wrap and lay on a roasting rack. Put in the oven for 15 minutes. Let rest for 5 minutes, then slice. Garnish the bottom of warm plates with the Pinot Noir sauce, add the sliced sturgeon, and serve with vegetables of your choice.

Chef's tip:

Substitute according to your taste the sturgeon for wild halibut.

GOLDEN STAR APPLE BEIGNET, ROSE HIP COULIS, FROMAGE BLANC GLACE

BY JEAN JOHO

This recipe is a new interpretation of a classic apple beignet. I have a great farmer in Michigan who grows heirloom apples. Rose hips are extremely popular in Alsace.

Serves 4
Preparation time: 1 hour
Cooking time: 10 minutes

Planning ahead:
The batter needs to be mixed the night before.

Special equipment:
Thermometer

INGREDIENTS

beer batter:

2 cups	all purpose flour
1	pinch of salt
1	pinch of sugar
2	egg yolks
10 oz	beer
1 tsp	canola oil

golden star apple beignet:

frying oil
4 golden star apples
sugar, to taste
Alsace kirsch eau de vie, to taste
3 egg whites
cinnamon sugar

to serve:

rose hip coulis
kirsch and cheese ice cream

METHOD

beer batter:

Mix all the ingredients together and set aside overnight.

golden star apple beignet:

Preheat the frying oil to 375°F on a thermometer. Peel and core the apples and cut with a small knife into a spiral. Sprinkle with a touch of sugar and the kirsch.

Whip the egg whites to soft peaks and fold into the batter. Coat each apple in batter and fry until golden brown. Set on paper towels to drain. Sprinkle with cinnamon sugar.

to serve:

Garnish a serving platter with the rose hip coulis. Place a beignet on top and serve with the ice cream.

Chef's tip:

You can substitute the golden star apples with any other crisp apples.

Wisconsin

Typically known as the dairy state, Wisconsin has been historically the biggest producer of cheese in the United States, and is a close runner-up in the production of milk and butter.

However it is the state's production of cranberries, oats, corn and of course cows that really marks it on the map as a destination for local produce. But the emphasis on nature and locality doesn't stop there – roam through dense forests, walk the scenic trails or visit cities such as Milwaukee with its American Indian past. Wisconsin's beautiful surroundings such as its popular lakes, forests and red rocks ensure that it makes an impression on many a visitor.

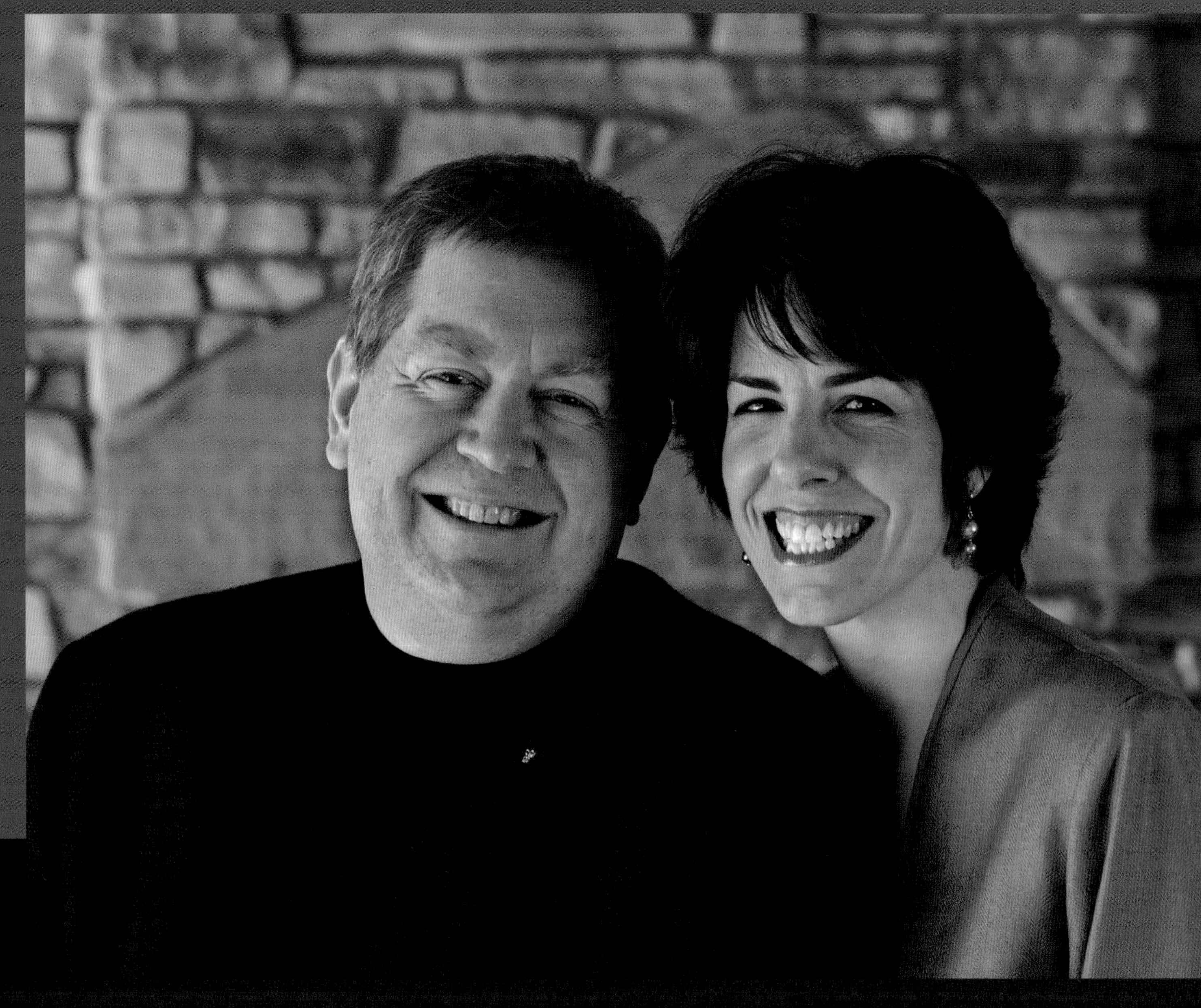

Dan & Lisa Dobrowolski

Born and raised in the Midwest, and exposed to chef's training and great restaurants in their youths, Canoe Bay owners Dan and Lisa Dobrowolski delight in excellent ingredients, gathered and presented with care. This husband and wife team uses the word 'organic' in describing their approach to both architecture and food at Canoe Bay. "Whereas Frank Lloyd Wright is our primary inspiration in architecture, Alice Waters' Chez Panisse restaurant is our original inspiration in dining," says Dan. "Our chefs' approach is simple: source the Midwest's finest indigenous, naturally raised foods – including from our own extensive gardens – and showcase them in a delicious, natural style."

Canoe Bay

This hotel is a refuge for the most romantic souls.

Set on the banks of a wild and untouched lake, Canoe Bay plunges you into a preserved and enchanting part of Wisconsin where the simple pleasures – strolling through the woods, swimming in the lake, dining in the wine cellar, sampling great vintages – will shape your days. Forget cars and other modern means of transport ... here your vehicle is a canoe. This hotel offers a different rhythm, another way of looking at things, appreciating the time on your hands and feeling at one with nature. The lakeside terraces invite you to gaze at the view, daydream, or read, and the cedar interiors, flooded with light, soothe the senses.

ROASTED BEET & HERBED CHEVRE SALAD WITH BUTTERMILK VINAIGRETTE

BY CANOE BAY

Roasted beets have a sweet flavor that pairs perfectly with the characteristic tartness of chèvre. Try adding gold beets for additional color or mix Bull's blood beet into your micro green mixture for red congruity.

Serves 4
Preparation time: 45 minutes
Cooking time: 45 minutes

INGREDIENTS

salad:

4	medium red beets
6 oz	soft chèvre
¼ cup	blend of chopped parsley, dill, chervil, tarragon and chives
½ lb	fresh microgreens or lettuces
½ cup	buttermilk vinaigrette
oil	
salt & pepper	

vinaigrette:

1½ cups	grapeseed oil
½ cup	buttermilk
2 tbsp	apple cider wine vinegar
2	egg yolks
1	medium shallot, minced
1	clove garlic, minced
4	sprigs of dill, finely chopped
salt & pepper	

METHOD

salad:

Preheat the oven to 350°F. Coat the beets lightly with oil, salt and pepper. Roast in the oven for 25 minutes. Remove the beets from the oven and place in a steamer for approximately 15-20 minutes, or until easily pierced with a knife. (If you do not own a steamer, you can mimic one by bringing 1" of water to a boil in your largest stock pot and setting a metal colander or strainer inside. Place a lid on top.)

Allow the beets to cool briefly then, using a kitchen towel, slide the skins off. Using a melon baller, cut the beets into small globes and reserve the remainder of the beets for another purpose. Place the chèvre in a small bowl and mix thoroughly with the herbs and salt and pepper to taste. Roll the chèvre into small balls approximately the size of the beets. Toss the beets with a little olive oil and salt and pepper to taste.

vinaigrette:

In a mixing bowl, whisk together the egg yolks, vinegar, buttermilk, shallot, garlic and dill. While whisking vigorously, slowly drizzle the oil into the buttermilk mixture. Add salt and pepper to taste and adjust with additional vinegar if necessary.

to serve:

Stack the beets on a plate intermittently with the chèvre balls. Coat the greens lightly with the vinaigrette, salt and pepper to taste, and place alongside the beet and chèvre stack. Decorate the plate with additional vinaigrette.

Chef's tip:

You can toss the beets with the buttermilk vinaigrette ahead of time, which gives them a soft pink look.

BATTER-SEARED WALLEYE WITH HARICOTS VERTS, NATIVE-HARVESTED WILD RICE & SWEET CORN PUREE

BY CANOE BAY

Wisconsin is known for its abundant walleye population in many of the state's lakes. We like the golden color and crunch imparted by a light batter on the firm, white flesh of this classic Midwestern catch.

Serves 4
Preparation time: 1 hour 15 minutes
Cooking time: 10 minutes

INGREDIENTS

walleye and batter:

2 lb	fresh walleye, filleted
½ cup	breadcrumbs
½ cup	all purpose flour
½ cup	flavorful but light-bodied ale (nut browns and red ales work quite well)
¼ cup	grapeseed or canola oil
salt & pepper	

haricots verts:

½ lb	fresh haricots verts (green beans)
1 tbsp	butter
salt & pepper	

wild rice:

1 cup	native-harvested wild rice (if this type of wild rice is not available in your area, substitute your favorite rice pilaf recipe)
2 cups	vegetable stock
1 tbsp	butter
salt & pepper	

sweet corn purée:

1 cup	fresh sweet corn
1 cup	heavy cream
1	medium shallot, diced
1	clove garlic, diced
1 tbsp	grapeseed or canola oil
2	small limes, juice
¼ tsp	cayenne pepper

METHOD

walleye and batter:

Combine the breadcrumbs, half of the flour and the ale into a thick slurry. Season with salt and pepper thoroughly. Add salt and pepper to the remaining flour and place on a platter. Heat the oil in a large frying pan over a medium high heat. Dredge both sides of the walleye in the flour. Using a pastry brush, paint one side of the walleye fillets with the batter. Fry batter side down until golden brown – approximately 2 minutes – then flip. Remove the pan from the heat and allow the fish to finish cooking for approximately 2 minutes. Remove from the pan and allow to drain on a wire rack.

haricots verts:

Bring a large pot of heavily salted water to a boil. Toss in the haricots verts and cook until just beginning to soften. This should take somewhere between 2-4 minutes depending on the thickness of the beans. Remove from the water and immediately plunge into ice water. Once cool, remove from the ice water and set aside. When assembling the dish, quickly warm the beans in a saucepan with the butter, salt and pepper to taste, and serve.

wild rice:

Place the wild rice and stock together in a saucepan. Bring to a boil and immediately turn to a simmer. Simmer until thoroughly cooked, approximately 30 minutes, and then drain off any excess liquid. Mix in the butter and salt and pepper to taste.

sweet corn purée:

Heat the oil in a saucepan on a medium high heat. Sauté the shallot until translucent – approximately 2 minutes – then add the garlic. After one minute, add the corn and heat until the corn just begins to brown. Add the cream and bring the mixture to a boil, then immediately remove from the heat. Add the juice and cayenne pepper and then transfer the mixture into a blender. Blend on high speed for about 2 minutes.

Pass the mixture through a fine mesh strainer. Season with salt and pepper to taste (this requires a bit more salt than expected).

to serve:

Place a mound of rice on the plate, top with the walleye, spoon some purée to the side and serve with the green beans.

'CANOE BAY S'MORES' WITH CINNAMON ICE CREAM & CANDIED BLACK WALNUTS

BY CANOE BAY

The homemade marshmallow makes all the difference in this recipe, especially after torching – which gives it that toasty, campfire flavor.

Serves 6
Preparation time: 2 hours
Cooking time: 45 minutes + 4 hours cooling time

Planning ahead:
The cake needs to be made at least 4 hours in advance.

Special equipment:
Sugar thermometer, ice cream maker, blow torch

INGREDIENTS

flourless chocolate cake:

7 oz	dark chocolate
⅓ cup	water
4½ oz	granulated sugar
4 ½ oz	butter, room temperature
3	eggs

marshmallow:

8	gelatin sheets (silver) or 3 tbsp powdered gelatin
½ cup	cold water
1 lb	granulated sugar
2 oz	glucose syrup
½ cup	water
4	egg whites

Graham cracker fry bread:

1 cup	Graham cracker crumbs
½ cup	all purpose flour
¼ cup	brown sugar
1 tsp	baking soda
1 cup	milk

frying oil, e.g. canola or pan spray, as needed

cinnamon ice cream:

1 cup	granulated sugar
1 cup	whole milk
2	cinnamon sticks
6	egg yolks
2 cups	heavy cream, chilled
1	pinch of salt

candied black walnuts:

1 cup	black walnuts
1 tsp	grapeseed (or canola) oil
2 tbsp	brown sugar

METHOD

flourless chocolate cake:

In a medium sauce pan, bring the water and 3 oz of the granulated sugar to a boil. Remove from the heat, then add the chocolate. Stir until the chocolate is fully incorporated. Add the butter, stirring until fully incorporated. Whip the eggs and remaining 1½ oz of granulated sugar together in a mixing bowl on high speed for approximately 3 minutes. Gently fold into the chocolate.

Preheat the oven to 350°F. Pour the batter into six buttered individual 3" molds, or into a small removable bottom pan. Place the molds in a water bath and bake for approximately 30 minutes (35-40 minutes for a large single pan), or until the cake has set. Remove from the oven and allow to cool in the refrigerator for about 4 hours before using.

marshmallow:

Rehydrate the gelatin sheets in ½ cup of the cold water. Prepare a cooling pan by taking a half-sheet tray and placing a well-oiled piece of parchment paper inside it. Oil an additional sheet of parchment for the cover and set aside. Combine the sugar, glucose syrup and remaining ½ cup of water in a medium saucepan and bring to a boil. While the sugar mixture is coming to a boil, use a double boiler to melt the gelatin mixture.

In a mixing bowl, whip the egg whites to stiff peaks. Turn off the mixer. When the sugar mixture hits 242°F, remove from the heat. At medium speed in the mixer, slowly add the sugar syrup into the egg whites, pouring the liquid onto the side of the mixing bowl to avoid splattering. Once incorporated, add the gelatin mixture in the same manner. Turn the mixer up to high speed and whip until the whole mixture is smooth and fluffy. Using an oiled spatula, spread the mixture onto the sheet tray lined with parchment. Place the other parchment sheet over the top of the mixture and press down with a weight to create a flat, even surface. Set aside and allow to cool for 1 hour. When ready to use, remove the top parchment sheet and cut out desired shapes, using either a cutter or knife dipped in powdered sugar to prevent sticking.

Graham cracker fry bread:

Combine all the dry ingredients into a large mixing bowl. Add milk until you achieve a thick batter. Heat a frying pan over a medium heat. Coat the pan with frying oil or pan spray, then spoon the batter into 3-4" wide discs. When the first side has fried to golden brown, flip and fry the opposite side. Remove from the pan, place on paper towel to cool.

cinnamon ice cream:

Bring the sugar, milk, salt and cinnamon to a simmering boil over a medium high heat in a small saucepan. Place the egg yolks into a separate saucepan. Slowly drizzle the infused milk into the egg yolks, whisking vigorously. When fully incorporated, return the mixture to the heat. Transfer the cinnamon sticks into the new mixture. Whisk constantly, heat until a light custard consistency has been achieved. Be careful not to overheat, as this cooks the egg. Pass the entire mixture through a fine mesh sieve and into the chilled cream. Place into your ice cream maker and follow its specific instructions.

candied black walnuts:

Preheat the oven to 350°F. In a small bowl, coat the walnuts with the oil and then coat with brown sugar. Heat in the oven for 5-7 minutes until the walnuts begin browning on the inside. Remove from the oven and set aside.

to serve:

Preheat the oven to 350°F and reheat the fry bread on cookie sheet or foil for 3 minutes. Place on a plate. Unmold the chocolate cake over the fry bread. Place a marshmallow shape on top of the cake and torch the top to golden brown. Crush the walnuts and place a small pile alongside 'S'mores'. Place a scoop of ice cream on top and serve.

Chef's tip:

For a more whimsical presentation, try piping store-bought marshmallow topping from a pastry bag in swirls on top of the chocolate. Torch for a burnt look, but expect the marshamallow to ooze down the side a bit.

California

California Dreamin', Hotel California, the sunny state has its fair share of references – and being a visitor's dream it has fair reason to be so well known.

The state with the highest population and the largest reputation, California is home to some of the largest cities in the U.S. Los Angeles, San Francisco and San Diego all reside in this part of the west coast, as in California, everything is done in extremes. Home to the highest mountain and lowest valley in America, its entertaining cities are paralleled with cool vineyards and sleepy towns. The Napa Valley region in the north of the state boasts rare and endangered species as well, of course, as world famous wine.

Karsten Hart
Grand Chef Relais & Châteaux

Originally from Baton Rouge, Karsten Hart's mother is German and his father Sicilian. The influence of the South is apparent in his personal cuisine – the effect of two years spent in Germany and Sicily are exemplified by his culinary diversity.

While attending Louisiana State University Karsten worked in various restaurants to support his schooling. He then moved to the culinary Mecca of San Francisco where he attended and graduated with honors from California Culinary Academy. In 2000 Karsten returned to Louisiana to serve as the Windsor Court Hotel Sous Chef. In 2002 he joined the culinary team of Chef James Overbaugh at California's prestigious Estate by the Elderberries. Under his creative direction Karsten demonstrated his fine talents and in 2006 was promoted to Executive Chef. He continues to make owner Erna's Elderberry House a top culinary destination.

Karsten Hart is deeply committed to procuring all produce and meat products for his menu from local farmers. As the person who guides the Estate's culinary direction, he proudly carries forth Erna's long tradition of gastronomic excellence.

Château du Sureau

You will love this majestic château, reminiscent of the finest châteaux in Europe.

It is ideally placed to explore the magnificent waterfalls and granite domes of Yosemite National Park – one of America's most spectacular natural sites. Château du Sureau's elegant interior, featuring guest rooms named after fragrant herbs and flowers, is resplendent with fine antiques, tapestries and artwork. Chef, Karsten Hart, showcases the freshest Californian produce in sophisticated, flavorful dishes, enhanced by a dash of the Mediterranean, and accompanied by the region's finest wines.

SALAD OF BABY GEM LETTUCE, SHAVED WINTER SQUASH, YELLOW CARROT VINAIGRETTE, ROSEWATER EMULSION

BY KARSTEN HART

This salad is a representation of some of the best organic ingredients that California has to offer. The natural sweetness in the yellow carrots makes a great vinaigrette.

Serves 4
Preparation time: 30 minutes
Cooking time: 2 hours

Planning ahead:
The roulade can be prepared in advance as it needs to chill for at least 3 hours.

Special equipment:
Immersion blender

INGREDIENTS

yellow carrot vinaigrette:

1 cup reduced yellow carrot juice
1 tbsp acacia honey
1 pinch of cinnamon
1 pinch of allspice
1 tbsp rice wine vinegar
1 lemon, juice
1 tsp thyme, chopped
1 tsp extra virgin olive oil
salt & freshly ground pepper

shaved trumpet squash:

2 cups trumpet squash, peeled and sliced into ribbons
1 tsp shallots, minced
1 tbsp acacia honey vinegar
½ tsp olive oil
salt & freshly ground pepper

rosewater emulsion:

3 cups fat-free milk
1 cup heavy cream
1 cup dried hibiscus flowers
few drops of soy lecithin
2 tbsp rosewater

to serve:

4 heads of baby gem lettuce
salt & pepper

METHOD

yellow carrot vinaigrette:

Combine the carrot juice, honey, spices, vinegar, lemon juice and thyme in a stainless steel bowl. Slowly whisk in the olive oil. Season to taste.

shaved trumpet squash:

Place all the ingredients in a stainless steel bowl. Mix together. Season to taste.

rosewater emulsion:

In a small sauce pot place the milk, cream and hibiscus flowers over a low heat and simmer for 20 minutes. Strain into a clean sauce pot. Add the lecithin and rosewater. Incorporate with a whisk to combine.

to serve:

Rinse the gem lettuce and trim the bottoms. Place a head of lettuce in the center of four plates. Arrange the shaved squash within the leaves of the lettuce to mimic a flower. Drizzle the vinaigrette over the lettuce and around the plate. Season with salt and pepper. Using an immersion blender, foam the rosewater emulsion. Spoon over the lettuce and around the plate.

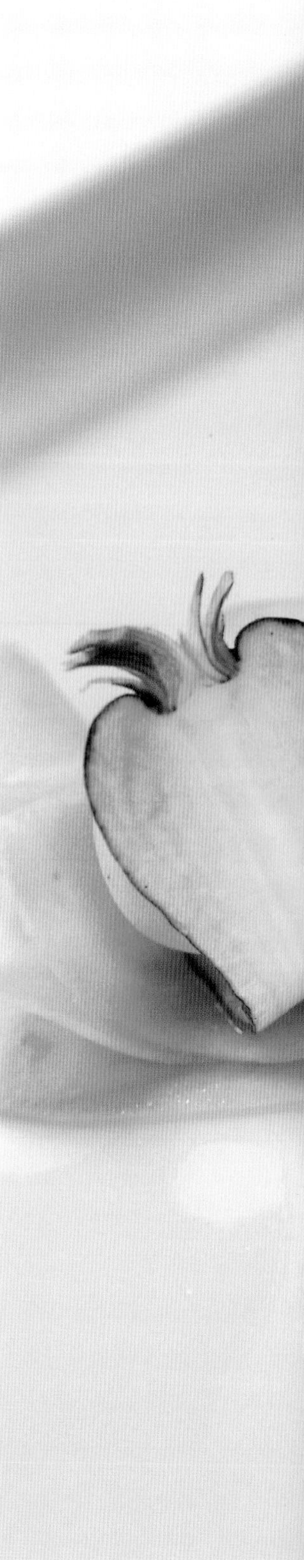

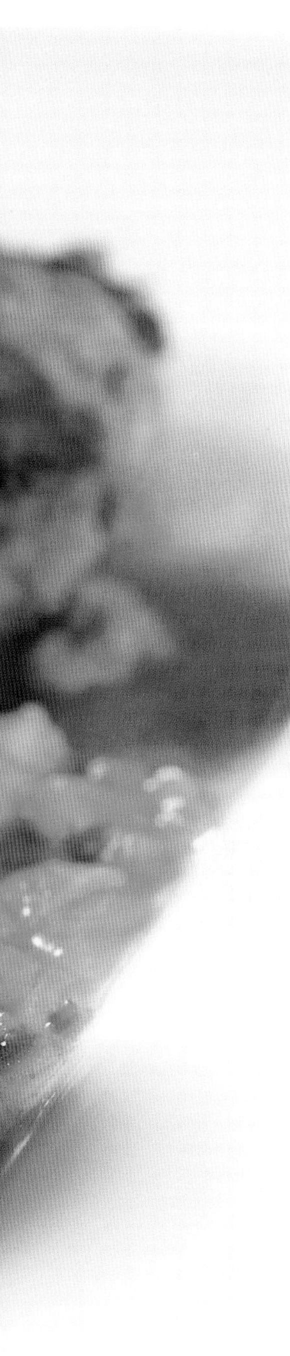

GULF SHRIMP CIOPPINO WITH SHRIMP 'SPAETZLE', RED PEPPER ROUILLE

BY KARSTEN HART

We played with the idea of replacing the traditional Austrian spaetzle dough with shrimp mousseline and adding it to a popular San Francisco dish cioppino.

Serves 4
Preparation time: 1 hour 30 minutes
Cooking time: 1 hour

Special equipment:
Spaetzle maker

INGREDIENTS

cioppino:

1 tsp	butter
1 tbsp	Andouille, ground
½	yellow onion, diced
2	red bell peppers, diced
2	tomatoes, peeled, seeded and diced
¼ cup	Vermouth
1 qt	shrimp stock
½ cup	basil, chopped

salt & freshly ground pepper

shrimp spaetzle:

1 lb	gulf shrimp, chopped
1	shallot, peeled and sliced
½	garlic clove, peeled and sliced
½ tsp	curing salt
1 tbsp	thyme, chopped
1	lemon, zest
2	egg whites
½ cup	heavy cream

salt & freshly ground pepper

red pepper rouille:

4	red bell peppers
4	cloves garlic
1 tbsp	olive oil for rubbing the peppers and garlic
1 small	Russet potato
1 cup	extra virgin olive oil

salt & freshly ground black pepper

to serve:

crispy bread

METHOD

cioppino:

In a saucepan add the butter, Andouille, yellow onion and red bell peppers. Sweat. Deglaze the pan with the tomatoes and Vermouth. Add the shrimp stock and simmer for 20 minutes. Season to taste.

shrimp spaetzle:

Pre-chill a food processor in the freezer. Mix the shrimp with the shallot, garlic, curing salt, thyme and lemon zest and place in the freezer for 5 minutes. Place half of the shrimp mix into the bowl of the processor. Blend until smooth. Add a proportional amount of egg whites (if you have used half of the shrimp use half of the egg whites), and continue processing until the egg whites are completely emulsified into the meat. Slowly drizzle in proportional amounts of cream while the food processor is still running. Adjust the seasoning and test for flavor/texture by poaching a quenelle of this mousseline in seasoned simmering broth. Transfer the mousseline to a stainless steel bowl over an ice bath. Repeat with the remaining ingredients.

In a 4 quart pot, bring 2 quarts of water to a boil. Squeeze the mousseline through the cup of a spaetzle maker and add to the boiling water. Remove the spaetzle from the water once they have risen to the surface.

red pepper rouille:

Preheat the oven to 400°F. Rub the bell peppers with the oil and roast until blistered. Remove from the oven, place in a bowl and cover with plastic, allowing the skins to steam. Remove the skins, stems and seeds. Rub the garlic with oil, place in a sauté pan, cover with foil and add ½" water to the bottom of the pan. Roast in the oven until completely soft. Remove and cool. Cut in half and press out the garlic meat. Mash and reserve. Thoroughly bake the potato in the oven. Remove and cool.

Combine the peppers, garlic, and potato in the bowl of a food processor. Purée completely. Slowly add the olive oil while the machine continues to run until a creamy emulsion is formed. Season to taste.

to serve:

In a sauté pan gently heat the cioppino and shrimp spaetzle. Place the cioppino in four small bowls, serve with crispy bread and the red pepper rouille.

Chef's tip:

It is very important when making the mousseline for the meat to remain very cold to ensure proper binding.

POACHED WHITE VEAL LOIN, ANGUS BEEF TENDERLOIN, OXTAIL CONSOMME, CORN JUICE & TRUFFLES

BY KARSTEN HART

I really like the idea behind this dish. Beef and veal roulade, a combination of new and old. Traditional technique and modern technique. It's a fun dish.

Serves 4
Preparation time: 45 minutes
Cooking time: 3 hours

Special equipment:
Immersion blender

INGREDIENTS

veal and beef:

1 veal loin
1 beef tenderloin
veal and beef roulade:
2 tbsp transglutaminase
1 tbsp water
¼ cup white truffle oil
2 tbsp thyme, washed and chopped
1 tbsp black truffle, washed and minced
salt & freshly ground black pepper

oxtail consommé:

4 qt beef stock
2 cups Zinfandel wine
10 oxtails, roasted
reserved beef and veal scraps, roasted
5 tomatoes, cut in half and grilled
8 yellow onions, cut in half and grilled
5 large portobello mushrooms, grilled
2 leeks, sliced and caramelized
3 carrots, diced and caramelized
2 celery sticks, diced
3 garlic cloves, chopped
10 black cardamoms
¼ cup hibiscus, dried
2 tbsp fennel seeds
1 tbsp coriander seeds
5 sprigs of rosemary
10 sprigs of thyme
10 sprigs of oregano
10 sprigs of marjoram
2 lb lean beef, chopped in a food processor
15 egg whites
salt & freshly ground pepper

clarified corn juice for the spheres:

9½ oz cold corn juice
½ tsp agar agar, powder
21 oz cold corn juice
salt & white pepper

sodium alginate bath:

2 qt water
10 tbsp sodium alginate
1½ tsp sodium citrate

to finish the corn spheres:

8.8 oz clarified corn juice
2 tsp calcium lactate
1½ tsp glucose

confit Yukon potato bases:

2 Yukon gold potatoes
1 qt duck fat
2 cloves garlic, peeled
1 bay leaf
10 sprigs of thyme
5 black peppercorns
1 lemon, peel

to serve:

confit potato balls (made with a melon baller), blanched and tossed with butter, parsley, salt and pepper
parsley leaves
chervil leaves
corn kernels
shaved black truffles
beech mushrooms, marinated with truffle oil, lemon juice, salt and pepper

METHOD

veal loin:

Using a sharp butcher's knife carefully remove the loin and tenderloin from the bone. Remove the silver skin and fat. Cut the veal loin in half lengthways. Remove the tail portion of the tenderloin and reserve all scraps for the consommé.

beef tenderloin:

Carefully remove the silver skin, fat and the chain connected to the side of the tenderloin. Reserve all scraps. Remove the head and tail of the tenderloin leaving only the center. Slice the center in half lengthways.

veal and beef roulade:

In a small bowl with a whisk thoroughly incorporate the transglutaminase and water to from a paste. Using a sharp knife cut the beef tenderloins so they are the same length as the veal loins. Spread the paste on the inside of one veal loin and the inside of one beef tenderloin and place both pasted sides together. Wrap the veal and beef together in plastic wrap to form a roulade. Repeat this process with the other veal loin and beef tenderloin. Place in the refrigerator for at least three hours. Remove from the plastic wrap and season each roulade with truffle oil, thyme, black truffle, salt and pepper. Wrap each roulade in plastic wrap then aluminum foil to form a roulade. To cook the roulades poach in water measured at 270°F for medium, checking the temperature after 10 minutes. This is usually not enough time but a good point to see what the internal temperature is (at this point it is usually about 190°F). Place back in the water for an additional 2-4 minutes. This will usually raise the temperature to 230°F. Allow the beef to rest until the internal temperature reaches 270°F. Remove from the plastic/aluminum and slice into three ¼" medallions for each entrée.

oxtail consommé:

In a large stock pot add all the ingredients except the lean beef, egg whites and seasoning. Place over a low heat. In a stainless steel bowl mix the lean beef and egg whites thoroughly. Pour the beef mixture into a stock pot and incorporate with a whisk. Bring the broth to a simmer slowly. Once the raft floats to the top cut a hole to allow the broth to simmer without breaking the raft. Simmer for 1-2 hours. Remove from the heat and strain through a coffee filter. Season to taste.

clarified corn juice spheres:

In a small sauce pot combine 9½ oz cold corn juice with the agar agar powder. Bring to a simmer, whisking constantly. In a stainless steal bowl drizzle the warm corn juice into the cold corn juice, whisking constantly until the agar forms small 'curds'. Place the contents in a chinois lined with cheese cloth and gently squeeze the liquid out. Season with salt and pepper.

sodium alginate bath:

In a small soup pot, combine all the ingredients and bring to a simmer. Blend thoroughly with an immersion blender. Keep the alginate bath warm and reserve for later.

to finish the corn spheres:

Combine all the ingredients in a small pot over a low heat. Bring to a simmer and purée with an immersion blender. Using a squeeze bottle fitted with a wide tip, fill 15 small hemisphere molds with the corn liquid and place into the freezer. Once the corn spheres are completely frozen place in the sodium alginate bath to encapsulate (this will keep the center liquid and the outside solid). Reserve the spheres for later.

confit Yukon potato bases:

In a small sauce pot combine all the ingredients and gently simmer until the potatoes are cooked through. Slice the potatoes ¼" thick.

to serve:

Preheat four large soup bowls. Place one potato base in the center of each bowl. Place three ¼" medallions of veal-beef roulade on top of each potato base. Ladle the hot consommé into each bowl. Garnish the broth with potato balls, herb leaves, corn spheres, corn kernels, beech mushrooms and shaved black truffles.

Chef's tip:

Do not remove the portobello mushroom gills as they will add color to the broth.

Thomas Keller

Grand Chef Relais & Châteaux

Thomas Keller, one of the most recognized American chefs working today, is as renowned for his well-honed culinary skills as he is for his ability to establish a restaurant that's both relaxed yet exciting. Good food coupled with a memorable social and sensual experience has always been Keller's focus.

Keller opened The French Laundry in 1994 and later brought his distinct style to Manhattan with the opening of Per Se in 2004. Today, these restaurants are two of the most treasured dining establishments in the U.S. Both have been internationally recognized, with Keller the only American-born chef to hold multiple 3 star ratings from the prestigious *Michelin Guide*.

Keller's casual dining restaurants include Bouchon (Beverly Hills, Yountville, Las Vegas), Bar *Bouchon* (Beverly Hills), Bouchon Bakery (Yountville, Las Vegas, NYC), and Ad Hoc (Yountville).

In addition to his restaurants, Keller is the author of the award-winning *The French Laundry cookbook, Bouchon,* and *Under Pressure*. Keller released a fourth cookbook, *Ad Hoc at Home*, in the fall of 2009, which is a *New York Times* Best Seller.

The French Laundry

With the herbs and vegetables straight from the garden, don't be surprised by the freshness that bursts in your mouth.

At the heart of Napa Valley, Thomas Keller, who also welcomes guests in New York with his Per Se restaurant, has established one of the best tables in California. Thomas Keller's technique has become so famous that Pixar studios called upon his expertise when making the film Ratatouille. You may not get a chance to taste it in his restaurant The French Laundry, but the revisited ratatouille served at the end of the film is his invention. Working closely with Chef de Cuisine, Timothy Hollingsworth, and the best producers in the region, he and his team concoct voluntarily minimalist dishes, where products such as oysters and truffles are savored in a series of scripted mouthfuls. The idea behind this 'sequencing' of the meal is to multiply the surprises in a restaurant that renews its menu every day.

Serves 4
Preparation time: 1 hour
Cooking time: 5 minutes

INGREDIENTS

Japanese hamachi:

4 oz hamachi belly
lime salt

Meyer lemon:

2 tbsp Meyer lemon zest, brunoise
simple syrup

cipollini onions:

4 cipollini onions

garnish:

crème fraîche
lime salt (4 parts Maldon salt, 1 part microplane lime zest)
4 tsp Californian white sturgeon caviar

CALIFORNIAN WHITE STURGEON CAVIAR

BY THOMAS KELLER

Every meal at the French Laundry begins with caviar. It signals the start of a celebration and pairs beautifully with champagne.

METHOD

Japanese hamachi:

Thinly slice the belly on a bias and season with lime salt.

Meyer lemon:

Cook the lemon zest in simple syrup until translucent.

cipollini onions:

Start the onions in cold water and bring to a boil; cook until tender. Half onions and caramelize the cut faces.

to serve:

Arrange the hamachi, lemon and onions on a plate. Place a teaspoon of caviar onto the hamachi. Garnish with the créme fraîche and lime salt.

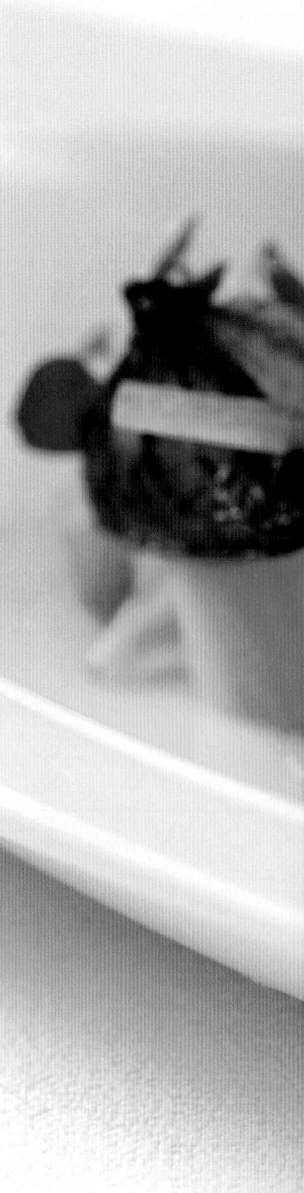

Serves 4
Preparation time: 1 hour
Cooking time: 5 minutes

INGREDIENTS

white quail:

4	quail breasts, airline
4	leg and thighs
1	bunch of thyme
3	cloves of garlic, crushed
4	½ tbsp butter

oil, as needed
dark quail stock, as needed
sherry vinegar
salt & pepper

pommes darphin:

7 oz	Kennebeck potatoes, parboiled, cooled and grated
½ oz	cornstarch
½ oz	extra virgin olive oil
½ oz	black truffle, finely chopped

salt, to taste
canola oil, for frying

sauce périgourdine:

¾ cup	veal stock
1 tbsp	black truffle, chopped
1 tsp	white truffle oil

salt

green asparagus:

10	asparagus spears

chicken stock, as needed
clarified butter, as needed
salt, to taste

quail egg:

4	quail eggs

to serve:

black truffle, shaved

WOLFE RANCH WHITE QUAIL

BY THOMAS KELLER

While the quail from local producer Wolfe Ranch may be the centerpiece of this dish, each element is designed to carry and complement the delicate flavor and aroma of black truffle.

METHOD

white quail:

Remove the bone from the legs and trim off any sinew. Season legs and breast. With breast skin-side down, place a piece of butter in the center and cover with a leg, in the style of a sandwich. Wrap the quail in caul fat, leaving wing bone on the breast exposed. Brown in oil and transfer to a pot with dark quail stock. Glaze, basting often, until cooked to desired taste. Finish with butter and a splash of sherry vinegar.

pommes darphin:

Preheat the oven to 300°F. Par-bake the potatoes on a bed of salt, until just fork tender. Cool quickly. On a large-hole box grater, grate the potatoes into a bowl. Season with salt and olive oil. Sift in the cornstarch. Carefully mix by hand, maintaining a grated texture. Finish with the chopped truffle and press into a plastic-lined quarter sheet pan. Place another quarter sheet pan on top and press down with a weight. Allow to cool completely. When cold, punch out circles with a 1" ring cutter. Fry in oil at 375°F and season with salt.

sauce périgourdine:

Combine the veal stock and chopped black truffle. Reduce to a sauce consistency and finish with the oil and salt.

green asparagus:

Carefully peel the asparagus, maintaining a round shape. Tie in bundles of five with butcher's twine. Place into an ice bath. Blanch in a large pot of salted water, ensuring the water does not lose its boil, until tender. Shock in ice water immediately. Portion appropriately and heat in chicken stock, clarified butter and salt.

quail egg:

Cook sunny-side up in a nonstick pan and trim using a 1" ring cutter, taking care not to puncture the yolk.

to serve:

Spoon sauce onto the plate. Plate the quail and arrange bias-cut pieces of asparagus alongside the meat. Place a round of pommes darphin on the plate and top with the trimmed quail egg, taking care not to rupture the yolk. Garnish with shaved black truffle.

Chef's tip:

Fresh black truffles are available to purchase from late October through March. They are better at maintaining their flavor and aroma than white truffles, so suitable substitutes may be found frozen or canned.

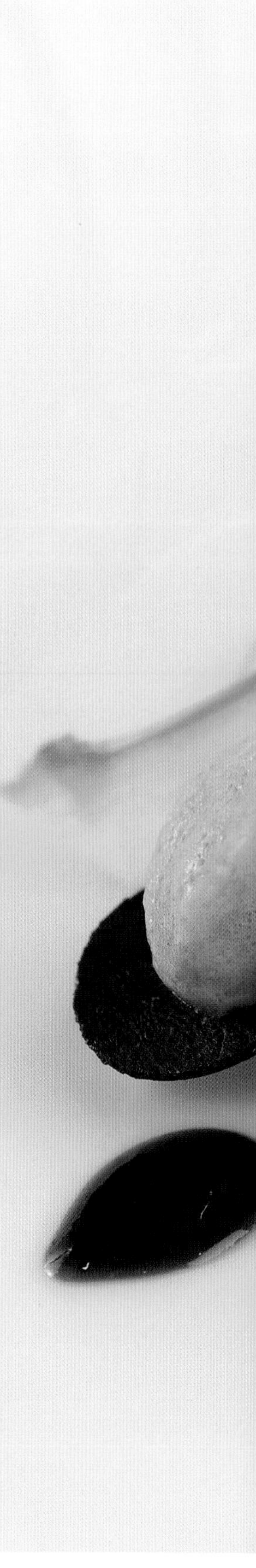

BAKEWELL TART

BY COURTNEY SCHMIDIG

Courtney Schmidig, The French Laundry's Pastry Chef, first encountered the Bakewell Tart at William Curley's shop outside of London. The memory of his rendition was the inspiration for this interpretation.

Serves 4
Preparation time: 2 hours 40 minutes
Cooking time: 30 to 40 minutes

Special equipment:
Ice cream machine, candy thermometer

Planning ahead:
All components can be made ahead of time and assembled to order.

INGREDIENTS

pâte brisée:

9 oz all purpose flour
5 oz cold butter, cubed
1 oz sugar
1 whole egg

almond frangipan:

6 oz almond paste
6 oz sugar
6 oz butter, softened
4 whole eggs, at room temperature
3 oz cake flour
1 lemon, zest
¾ tbsp rum

huckleberry jam:

2 cups granulated sugar, or to taste
1 tbsp + 1 tsp pectin
4 cups huckleberries
¼ cup water
1 tsp lemon juice

crème fraîche sherbet:

2 lb crème fraîche
2 oz sugar
4¼ cups buttermilk
12 oz corn syrup
salt, to taste

honey tuile:

2½ oz soft butter
3½ oz powdered sugar
2½ oz honey
3½ oz all purpose flour
2 egg whites, room temperature

garnish:

fresh huckleberries
powdered sugar
roasted Marcona almonds

METHOD

pate brisée:

Using the paddle attachment on a mixer mix the flour and butter until the chunks are pea-sized. Add the sugar and egg, and mix until combined, followed by the flour. Roll the brisée in between two pieces of parchment paper to fit a quarter sheet pan, achieving a thickness of ⅛". Dock the dough with a fork so that steam pockets do not develop underneath it. Chill for 30 minutes.

almond frangipan:

Mix the sugar and almond paste in the mixer with the paddle attachment for 10 minutes on low speed. Add in the following order: butter, eggs, cake flour, lemon zest and rum.

huckleberry jam:

Combine the sugar and pectin in a small bowl, mixing well. Combine the huckleberries, pectin mixture and water in a large saucepan. Attach a candy thermometer to the pan and bring to a simmer over a medium-high hear, stirring occasionally to dissolve the sugar. Reduce the heat and simmer until the mixture reaches 215°F-220°F. Remove from the heat, taste and adjust with sugar if needed. Add the lemon juice.

to assemble the Bakewell tart:

Preheat the oven to 350°F. Partially bake the rolled dough to a light brown color and allow to cool. Spread a layer of huckleberry jam over the cooled dough. Pour 1½ lb of frangipan on top of the jam, return to the oven and bake to a medium-dark brown color or until a knife inserted in the middle comes out cleanly. Allow to cool for about an hour and then cut into rectangles (you will have tart left over).

crème fraîche sherbet:

Warm the corn syrup and sugar until it is at a liquid consistency. Slowly pour this sugar mixture over the crème fraîche and buttermilk while whisking. Season to taste with salt and strain. Freeze in an ice cream machine.

honey tuile:

Preheat the oven to 350°F. To make the batter cream together the butter, sugar, honey and flour then mix in the egg whites. Spread the batter on a silpat as thinly as possible. Bake until the batter is a golden brown. While the tuile is still warm, break off pieces and form into abstract shapes.

to serve:

Sprinkle the powdered sugar over the Bakewell tart. Place on a plate, spoon over the fresh huckleberries and almonds. Add a scoop of crème fraîche sherbet and top with a honey tuile.

Chef's tip:

For both the jam and the garnish, any fresh berry in season can be substituted for the huckleberries. Make sure the frangipan is at room temperature before spreading it over the brisée and jam.

Gary Danko
Grand Chef Relais & Châteaux

Gary Danko is recognized as one of America's most talented and respected chefs. Danko combines classical training with focuses on French, Mediterranean, and regional American cooking. Danko is dedicated to using seasonal, locally grown and raised foods. He forged close relationships with artisanal cheese, meat, and produce suppliers long before other chefs.

Danko was reared in the small town of Massena in upstate New York. Cooking was learned at his mother's knee. His father, an architect and builder, launched Danko's interest in restaurants. Although Danko received his formal training at the CIA, he credits his study under Madeleine Kamman with refining his skills and developing the approach that embodies his personal cooking style today.

Beringer hired him as Executive Chef in 1985. He then took the helm at Chateau Souverain, where Danko's achievements first attracted national acclaim. He then became the Chef of the Dining Room at The Ritz-Carlton, San Francisco, but left there in 1996 to work on a cookbook and to lay the groundwork for his own restaurant – Gary Danko.

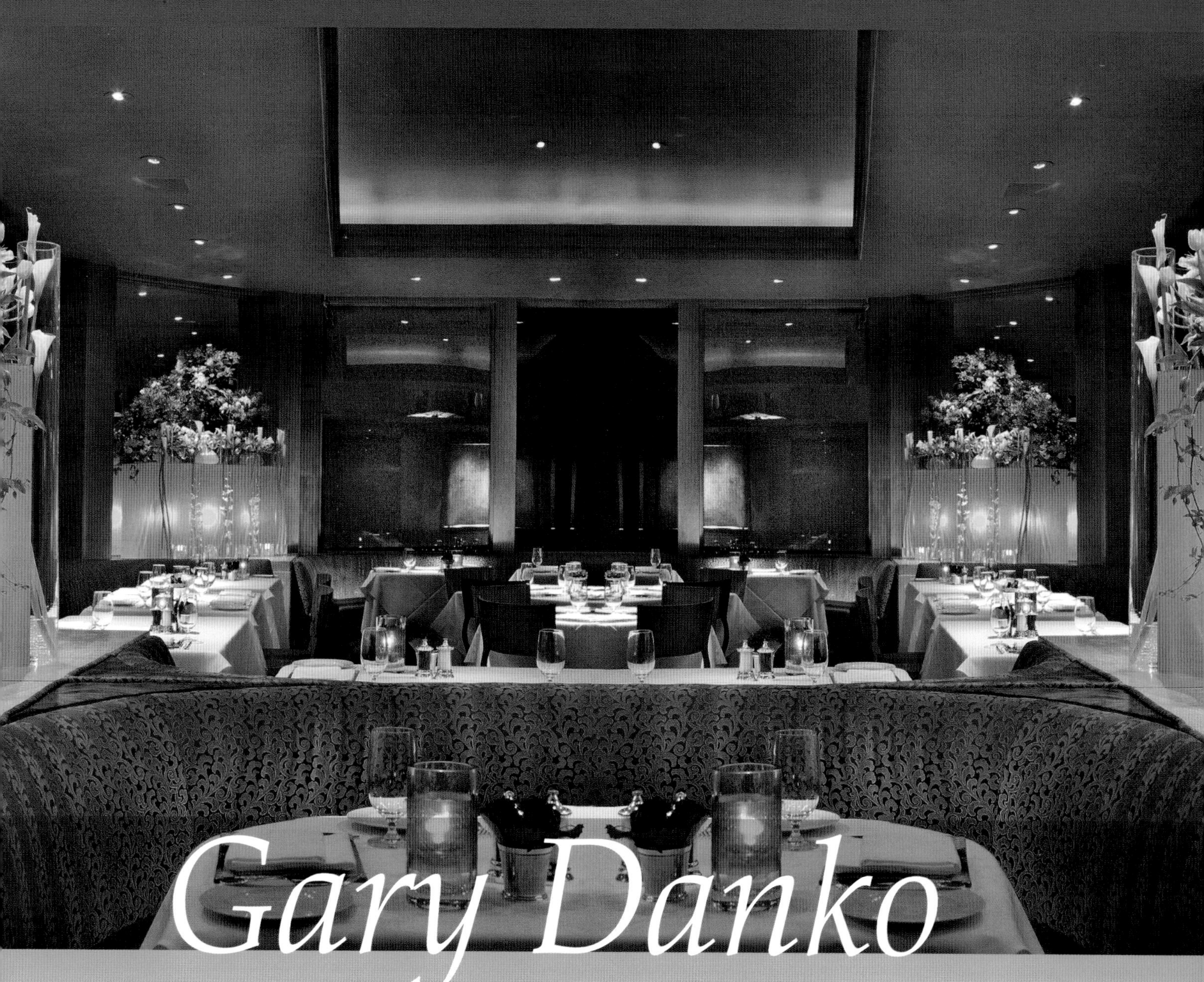

Gary Danko

Described as the ambassador of contemporary American fine dining, the cuisine of Gary Danko draws on culinary traditions from around the world.

Roast quail stuffed with morels, leeks and pine nuts, steamed shellfish with a Thai curry, seared sea scallops with Spring vegetables. Using seasonings from Asia and India, he adds a pinch of audacity to his French-style precision and technique. The results are sublime and balanced, often showcasing strictly seasonal flavors such as his foie gras served with cherries in Spring and roast figs in Fall. The food is pure sophistication, to be savored in an intimate and welcoming ambience – taupe walls enhanced by modern paintings – in one of San Francisco's trendiest districts.

BRANZINI FILLETS WITH FENNEL PUREE, SAFFRON, ORANGE & BASIL

BY GARY DANKO

The texture of a crispy skinned branzini and the juxtaposition of a creamy fennel purée, the orangey tang of the saffron sauce and briny olive make this a pleasure to look at and to eat.

Serves 6
Preparation time: 35 minutes
Cooking time: 20 minutes

Planning ahead:
The spinach and fennel purées should be made in advance and refrigerated until needed.

INGREDIENTS

branzini:

1½ -2 lb boneless branzini or red snapper fillets, cut into 6 portions weighing 3-4 oz each; score the skin with a cross mark
clarified butter or vegetable oil for cooking the fish

saffron sauce:

1 shallot, peeled, minced finely
½ cup dry white wine
½ cup clam juice
½ cup fish fumet
¾ cup orange juice
1 pinch of saffron
1 bay leaf
1 sprig of thyme
¼ cup heavy cream
6 tbsp butter
1 tbsp basil, chopped
1 tsp chives, sliced thinly
salt

fennel purée:

2 large bulbs of fennel, chopped
1 star anise
1 tbsp butter
½-1 cup fish fumet or water
½ cup potato purée (see recipe below)
½ cup spinach purée (see recipe below)
salt, to taste

potato purée:

1 lb large red or yellow Finn potatoes, peeled
6 tbsp unsalted butter, cold
salt, to taste

spinach purée:

12 oz bag of cleaned spinach leaves
salt

garnish:

18 orange segments
2 red peppers, peeled and cut into ½" diamonds, sautéed until tender
9 Niçoise olives, pitted and cut in halves

METHOD

branzini:

Remove any scales from the fish and clean off any bones, leave the skin on. Cut into desired size portions. Refrigerate covered until needed.

saffron sauce:

In a saucepan combine the shallot, wine, clam juice, fumet, orange juice, saffron, bay leaf and thyme. Bring to a boil, reduce to a simmer and cook until reduced to one-third. Add the cream and return to the boil. Whisk in the butter to taste (this sauce is a simple reduction emulsion sauce – make sure that your sauce reduction base is hot but not boiling when you emulsify the cold butter into the sauce). Strain through a fine chinois. Season with basil, chives and salt to taste. Keep warm while you cook the fillets.

fennel purée:

In a saucepan melt the butter and sauté the fennel and anise until translucent, about 5 minutes. Add enough fish fumet to just barely cover the fennel: cook until tender and all liquids have concentrated into the fennel - there should be no browning. Remove the star anise and purée in a blender, adding small amounts of liquid only if necessary. Strain through a medium sieve to remove any fibers and obtain a thick purée. Just before cooking the fish, mix hot potato purée with the fennel purée and add enough spinach purée to obtain a bright green purée. Season with salt to taste. This should be combined and reheated at the last minute.

potato purée:

Place the potatoes and enough water to cover in a saucepan. Bring to a boil and salt the water to taste. Cook until the potatoes are easily pierced with a fork. Drain and while very hot run through a food mill with butter. Season to taste with salt. Keep hot in a bain marie water bath until ready to serve. You can use more or less butter depending on your dietry needs. Just before serving check or correct the consistency. If it is too thick, thin with a small amount of boiling, salted water to result in a potato purée that is still mounding when placed on the plate.

spinach purée:

Blanch the spinach in boiling water for 30 seconds. Plunge into ice water until cold. This will set a bright green color. Drain and purée in an electric blender and add salt to taste.

to serve:

Heat a cast iron skillet or a rolled steel pan over a medium heat. Put a small quantity of clarified butter or vegetable oil in the pan. Place the fish in the hot oil, skin side down and cook over a medium high heat. The skin should be golden brown before turning; this will take about 3 minutes. Turn over and cook until golden, then salt the fillet. Arrange on a bed of fennel purée. Spoon the sauce around the plate. Garnish with the orange segments, peppers and olives.

ROAST QUAIL STUFFED WITH WILD MUSHROOMS
BY GARY DANKO

Quail is an underutilized game bird that is very tender and easy to cook. Buy birds that are semi-boneless with only the leg bones remaining. The quails are marinated briefly. A simple mushroom ragout is made and stuffed into the cavity. The quails are then reshaped and tied to hold their shape while cooking. The quails are browned until golden and finished cooking either on top of the stove or in the oven.

Serves 6
Preparation time: 20 minutes
Cooking time: 20 minutes

Planning ahead:
The quails may be marinated a day in advance. The mushroom ragout should be made ahead and chilled before stuffing the birds. The polenta is best made ahead of time and held in a hot water bath. It may need to be thinned with hot water before serving.

INGREDIENTS

quails:

6 quails, semi-boneless
vegetable oil for cooking the quails
2 cups rich chicken or veal stock
1 tbsp unsalted butter

marinade:

2 tbsp Cabernet Sauvignon or Pinot Grigio
½ tsp garlic, minced
½ tsp kosher salt
2 tsp Dijon mustard
¾ tsp dried thyme
¾ tsp coriander, ground
2 tbsp olive oil

mushroom ragout:

½ lb wild mushrooms of choice, cleaned and sliced
2 tbsp olive oil or butter
1 clove of garlic, minced
1 tbsp parsley, chopped
salt & pepper

polenta:

4 tbsp olive oil
¼ cup onion, minced
1 cup large cracked polenta
5 cups water
2 tsp kosher salt

METHOD

marinade:
Combine all of the ingredients and store them in the refrigerator until they are needed.

mushroom ragout:
In a sauté pan heat the olive oil or butter over a medium high heat. Stir in the mushrooms and cook until limp and juices are rendered and leave a light syrup. Stir in the garlic, parsley, salt and pepper to taste. Cool completely. This should be made ahead and chilled before stuffing the birds.

quails:
Remove the wing tip from the quails and brush each with the marinade. Place in a bowl or plastic bag, refrigerate and let marinate for a few hours (this may be done a day ahead). Stuff each quail with cold mushroom ragout. Reform each quail to look like a plump bird. Tie with butcher's twine to hold its shape. Refrigerate until ready to cook.

Preheat the oven to 350°F. In an 8" nonstick sauté pans heat 1 tablespoon of vegetable oil over a medium heat. Brown the quails quickly and lightly. Place in the oven and roast for 10-15 minutes until cooked as desired. Salt and pepper the quails and remove to a warm serving platter. Drain any excess fat from the pan. Deglaze with stock and reduce to a glaze. Whisk in 1 tablespoon butter and season with salt to taste. Spoon this sauce over the quails and serve.

polenta:
Preheat the oven to 350°F. In an ovenproof saucepan, heat the olive oil. Stir in the onion and sauté over a medium heat until translucent, about 5 minutes. Stir in the polenta and coat with olive oil, cooking long enough to heat the polenta through. Whisk in boiling water (measured after the boil) and return to a boil and season. Place uncovered in the oven for 50-60 minutes or until most of the water is absorbed. There should be a thin layer of oil floating on the top. Remove from the oven and whisk until well blended. Finish the polenta with some fresh herbs, butter or heavy cream, if you wish.

to serve:
Serve the quails and sauce on a bed of soft polenta and surround with seasonal vegetables or on dressed fresh salad greens, such as arugula, watercress, frisée or Belgian endive with extra virgin olive oil and vinegar.

Chef's tip:
If you would like a slightly higher end dish you can fold in some cubes of raw foie gras into the mushroom stuffing. You may also extend your mushrooms by incorporating ½ cup or so of cooked, cooled cous cous. Make sure you season accordingly with salt. For the polenta this is a method of cooking in an oven which saves you all the time generally required for stirring polenta. You can also cook it in a slow cooker or a crock pot.

ROAST CARAMEL PEARS WITH GINGERBREAD, NUTMEG ICE CREAM TRUFFLES

BY GARY DANKO

This dish is a classic combination of American flavors: warm caramel roasted pears and spiced gingerbread served alongside a nutmeg flavored ice cream truffle – a play on warm and cool. Although there are three components to this dish you may serve it simply as caramel pears on a slice of gingerbread, either with whipped cream or vanilla ice cream.

Serves 6

Preparation time:	The three separate components take 25 minutes each
Cooking time:	1 hour 20 minutes

Special equipment:
Ice cream machine

Planning ahead:
The nutmeg ice cream can be made in advance.

INGREDIENTS

roast caramel pears:

6	large Bartlett pears, perfectly ripe
¾ cup	brown sugar
½ cup	apple cider, as needed

gingerbread:

2 cups	all purpose flour
2 tsp	baking soda
1 tsp	ground cloves
1 tsp	ground ginger
½ tsp	nutmeg, grated
¾ tsp	salt
3	large eggs
1 cup	sugar
1 cup	molasses
½ cup	corn oil
1 cup	boiling water

nutmeg ice cream truffles:

1½ cups	heavy cream
1½ cups	milk
½	vanilla bean, split
½ tsp	nutmeg, grated
¼ tsp	salt
10	egg yolks
1 cup + 3 tbsp sugar	
1½ cups	heavy cream

garnish:

mint

METHOD

roast caramel pears:

Preheat the oven to 350°F. On a 12½" x 16½" sturdy aluminum sheet pan spread the brown sugar. Peel, halve and core the pears. Lay the cut side down onto the brown sugar. The pears should snugly fit into the pan. Bake in the oven until the pears are tender and their juices have formed a light caramel syrup. If the pan is dry add a little apple cider to help dissolve the sugar. Turn the pears over and bake for 5-10 more minutes. The results should be golden pears with a nice caramel syrup. Cool. They may be served like this or molded.

To mold the caramel pears, in a 4-5 oz ramekin or mold arrange two halves of pears. Press firmly on them to compress and take on the shape of the mold. Place a round of gingerbread on top of the pears. Wrap each mold in plastic wrap. Reserve the syrup.

gingerbread:

Preheat the oven to 350°F. In a large bowl combine the flour, baking soda, cloves, ginger, nutmeg and salt. In a separate bowl combine the eggs, sugar, molasses, oil and boiling water. Stir the liquids into the dry ingredients. Pour into a 9" cake pan with a bottom that has been lined with parchment paper. Bake in the oven until a skewer comes out clean, about 35-45 minutes. Cool. Cut in half horizontally into ½" thickness. Cut into 6" x 3" rounds or large enough to just fill the top of ramekins.

Preheat the oven to 300°F. Place all the scraps and trimmings from the gingerbread on a sheet pan and place in the oven. Bake for 20 minutes or until they are dry. You may also let them air dry and finish in a warm oven. They should be completely dry. In a food processor grind into fine crumbs. Store covered until needed.

nutmeg ice cream truffles:

In a saucepan combine 1½ cups of cream, milk, vanilla bean, nutmeg and salt. Place over a medium heat and bring to just under a boil.

Meanwhile in a thick-bottomed non-reactive saucepan combine the egg yolks and sugar. Gradually whisk the hot cream into the egg yolk-sugar mixture. Cook over a medium heat, stirring constantly, until the mixture starts to thicken and lightly coats the back of a spoon. Do not allow the mixture to boil. Add the remaining 1½ cups of cream. Strain and cool completely, overnight if desired. Freeze in an ice cream machine of choice. Store in the freezer until needed.

To make the truffles form the ice cream into 1½" balls and roll in the crumbs. Hold the 'truffles' in the freezer until serving time.

to serve:

Preheat the oven to 325°F. Place individual plastic wrapped molded pears on a sheet pan in the oven. Let them warm for 25-30 minutes. Once they are heated through hold until serving time. Remove the plastic and invert the molded pear onto a plate. Warm the reserved syrup and spoon a tablespoon over the pear, and arrange a frozen 'truffle' alongside. Garnish with mint and serve.

Joachim Splichal

Grand Chef Relais & Châteaux

Joachim Splichal's culinary approach emphasizes a playful yet perfectionist style and his enthusiasm for California's abundant resources translates into wildly innovative and elegant dishes. Born and raised in Spaichingen, Germany, Splichal traveled to Holland at 18 to work in the hospitality industry. Soon thereafter, he relocated to Switzerland and began developing culinary skills that were later perfected at La Bonne Auberge, a three -Michelin-star restaurant in Antibes, France. Splichal continued to hone his talents at the legendary L'Oasis in La Napoule and later joined forces with Jacques Maximin, who later became his professional mentor. He worked alongside the master chef for four years at the Chantecler restaurant in the Hotel Negresco in Nice, France. Arriving in the United States in 1981, Splichal assumed Executive Chef duties at the Regency Club, then opened Seventh Street Bistro and finally Max Au Triangle, where his memorable meals were the talk of Los Angeles. Based upon his vision of unique restaurants emphasizing fresh, seasonal ingredients and unparalleled service, in 1989 he opened Patina Restaurant.

Patina

Californian cuisine is infused with European influences in this elegant restaurant with its pure and modern decor.

Inside the huge Walt Disney Concert Hall – a steel complex of venues at the heart of Los Angeles – the renowned German Chef Joachim Splichal has created one of the city's most prized tables. The trademark of Patina is fresh seasonal products highlighted by sophisticated presentations. The flavors are distinct in each dish, sweet or salty, but are always magnified by herbs, exotic spices or bursts of acidity such as in the grilled Scottish salmon with baby artichokes and blood orange, or the Mediterranean loup de mer with minestrone and pesto croutons. The caviar guéridon and the variety of cheeses are two other reasons to visit this prestigious address.

Serves 4
Preparation time: 1 hour
Cooking time: 36 minutes

Special equipment:
Rectangle cake frame 5" x 2" x 1½"

Planning ahead:
The lobster oil and citrus terrine can be made in advance, and you can cook the lobster beforehand.

INGREDIENTS

lobster:

4	Maine lobsters, 1¼ lb each
1 tbsp	black peppercorns
4 tbsp	rock salt

citrus terrine:

⅛ cup	white balsamic vinegar
⅛ cup	simple syrup
4 sheets	of gelatin
1	navel orange
1	blood orange
1	ruby red grapefruit
1	oro blanco grapefruit
1	tangerine
1	cara cara orange

fleur de sel black peppercorns

lobster oil:

4	cleaned and quartered lobster heads
2 cups	blended oil
1	large shallot
2	garlic cloves
1 tbsp	tomato paste
1	fennel stick
¼	star anise
1 tsp	coriander seeds
1	slice ginger
1	orange, peel
1	lemon, peel
1	sprig of thyme

lobster salad:

4	lobster trimmings and knuckles, chopped
1 tsp	tarragon, chopped
1 tsp	tarragon mustard
2 tsp	lobster oil (see recipe above)
1 tbsp	endive, small diced
1	pinch of espelette pepper
½ tsp	lemon juice

salt

garnish:

1 tbsp	coriander seeds, crushed
2	Belgian endives
1 tbsp	citrus juice (leftover from the terrine)
1	pinch of fleur de sel

black peppercorns, freshly ground
extra virgin olive oil

CHILLED MAINE LOBSTER SALAD, CALIFORNIA CITRUS SEGMENTS, ENDIVE, CRUSTACEAN ESSENCE

BY JOACHIM SPLICHAL & TONY ESNAULT

This refreshing salad incorporates elements from Chef Joachim's classic 'Quartet of the Sea' into a delightful starter for every meal.

METHOD

lobster:

Bring a large pot of water to a boil and add the black peppercorns and rock salt. Once the water is at a rapid boil, emerge the whole live lobsters for 6 minutes. After 6 minutes, remove the lobsters and let cool. Once cooled, proceed to clean them. Use the knuckles and trimmings for the lobster salad. Cut the tails into six medallions per lobster. Rinse and quarter each head and reserve for the oil.

citrus terrine:

Cut all of the citrus fruits into segments, reserving the juice for serving. In cold water, bloom the gelatin until soft. In a small pan, combine the vinegar and simple syrup until hot (not boiling) and melt the gelatin in the liquid. Toss the citrus segments into the gelatin mixture and pour into the rectangle mold. Crack black pepper on top and let sit until hard. Cut the terrine into 12 pieces and set aside until you are ready to serve.

lobster oil:

In a hot pan with 3 tablespoons of blended oil, roast the lobster heads without color. Add the shallot and garlic to the pan, and sweat until soft. Add the tomato paste and cook while stirring for about 5 minutes. Add the spices, herbs and peels and cover with the blended oil. Let steep for 30 minutes and then strain and cool.

lobster salad:

Chop the lobster trimmings and knuckles to medium dice. In a small bowl, whisk together the tarragon, mustard, lemon juice, lobster oil, Espelette pepper and salt until emulsified. Add the chopped lobster and endive to the mix, combine well and set aside until you are ready to serve.

to serve:

Brush the lobster medallions with the lobster oil and season with salt and pepper. Cut the tips off the endives, season with black pepper corns and toss in a bowl with the citrus juice, olive oil. Brush the citrus terrine slices with extra virgin olive oil and sprinkle the fleur de sel on to the terrine. Serve arranged attractively on a cold plate immediately.

PRIME BEEF TENDERLOIN, CONTRAST OF CAULIFLOWER, 'SAUCE AU POIVRE VERT'

BY JOACHIM SPLICHAL AND TONY ESNAULT

Inspired by California's abundant and local variety of vegetables, this hearty entrée is both comforting and delicious.

Serves 4
Preparation time: 20 minutes
Cooking time: 15 minutes

Planning ahead:
The beef sauce, and lemon confit can be prepared in advance.

INGREDIENTS

beef tenderloin:

4 medallions of beef tenderloin, tied, 7 oz each
salt & freshly ground black peppercorns
3 tbsp grapeseed oil
1 oz butter
1 garlic clove
1 sprig of thyme

lemon confit:

2 lemons
1 sugar cube

white cauliflower:

1 small head of white cauliflower
1 tbsp butter, unsalted
2 tbsp caper brine
1 tbsp chervil, chopped (reserve stems for the sauce)
1 tbsp tarragon, chopped (reserve stems for the sauce)
salt & pepper

green, orange and purple cauliflowers:

1 small head of purple cauliflower
1 small head of orange cauliflower
1 small head of green cauliflower
2 tbsp extra virgin olive oil
1 tbsp sherry vinegar
salt & pepper

sauce au poivre vert:

12 oz beef trimmings
2 tbsp grapeseed oil
1 tbsp butter, unsalted
2 cups chicken stock
2 tbsp cognac
½ cup heavy cream
2 large shallots, sliced
3 garlic cloves, peeled and crushed
1 cup white wine
6 parsley stems
3 sprigs of thyme
1 tbsp green peppercorns

METHOD

lemon confit:

Remove the peel of one lemon without the pith. Place the peel in a pan and cover with cold water. Once the water comes to a boil, strain and repeat three times. Take another saucepan and bring the juice from both lemons and the sugar cube to a boil. Add the blanched lemon peel to the liquid, bring to a boil and cook until very tender. Once the lemon is cooled, finely chop.

white cauliflower:

Remove the florets from the white cauliflower and chop finely. In a hot sauté pan, add the butter and heat until browned. Add the white cauliflower and sauté without color until cooked. Deglaze with the caper brine. Once cooked, add the chopped chervil, tarragon and lemon confit. Season with salt and pepper.

green, orange and purple cauliflowers:

Slice the cauliflowers lengthwise into ¼" pieces, separate by color. In a hot pan, sear the orange and purple cauliflower in 1 tablespoon of olive oil on both sides. Season with salt and pepper. Once cooked, remove the orange cauliflower from the pan. Add a dash of sherry vinegar to the purple cauliflower; reduce and remove the cauliflower from the pan. For the green cauliflower, toss in a bowl with 1 tablespoon of olive oil, remaining sherry vinegar and salt and pepper.

sauce au poivre vert:

In a hot pan, sear the beef trimmings in the grapeseed oil and butter until golden brown. Add the shallots, parsley stems, chervil stems, tarragon stems, garlic and thyme. Deglaze with the cognac and reduce until dry. Deglaze again with the white wine and reduce until dry. Add the chicken stock and bring to a boil. Let simmer for half an hour. Strain into a new pan, bring back to a boil. Add a tablespoon of heavy cream and the green peppercorns.

beef tenderloin:

Preheat the oven to 400°F. Season the beef with salt and black peppercorns. In a very hot pan, sear both sides of the beef in grapeseed oil until golden brown, place in the oven and cook until the desired temperature. Once the desired temperature is reached, place back in the pan adding butter, garlic and thyme. Using a large spoon, glaze the beef with the foamy butter. Let rest for five minutes and serve.

to serve:

Arrange the cauliflower on a hot plate, alternating the different colors. Add some sauce and top with slices of beef tenderloin and serve immediately.

ROASTED PINEAPPLE, EXOTIC FRUIT, ALMOND CAKE, COCONUT MALIBU ICE CREAM

BY JOACHIM SPLICHAL & TONY ESNAULT

Inspired by America's favorite dessert of cake and ice cream, Chefs Joachim and Tony incorporate tropical flavors to provide a light and tasty ending to a Patina meal.

Serves 4
Preparation time: 15 minutes
Cooking time: 3 hours

Special equipment:
Pacojet, dehydrator, microplane, rectangle mold 10" x 5"

Planning ahead:
The roasted pineapple, ice cream, almond cake batter, and dry pineapple chips can all be made in advance.

INGREDIENTS

roasted pineapple:

1	pineapple, peeled and cut in eights length wise
1	vanilla bean
2 cups	sugar
¼ cup	water

almond cake:

1 cup	almond paste
⅓ cup	melted butter
2	whole eggs
⅛ tsp	vanilla extract

coconut Malibu ice cream:

2 cans	coconut milk
8 oz	sugar
1 tsp	lime juice
1 tsp	Malibu rum

tapioca sauce:

¼ cup	coconut milk
⅓ cup	milk
1 tsp	sugar
2 tsp	tapioca
1 tsp	butter

pineapple chips:

1 cup	sugar
1 cup	water
4	thin slices of pineapple

garnish:

1	mango
1	Hawaiian papaya
1	kiwi
3	coquitos
1 tbsp	napage (clear glaze)
1	passion fruit
1	lime zest

METHOD

roasted pineapple:
Preheat the oven to 350°F. In a medium cocotte make a dry caramel with the sugar, add the vanilla bean, and deglaze with the water. Add the pineapple, cover and put in the oven for 3 hours or until it is a caramel color. Once cooked let it cool down, then chop finely to make a compote.

almond cake:
Preheat the oven to 350°F fan. In a mixer mix the almond paste with the paddle until soft, add the melted butter, add the eggs one at a time then add the vanilla extract. Let it sit in a refrigerator then, using a pastry bag and a rectangle mold, pipe the mix in a flat shape on a baking sheet and then bake for 10 minutes.

coconut Malibu ice cream:
In a sauce pot heat the coconut milk and the sugar until the sugar melts. Cool it down then mix with the rest of the ingredients put the mixture in Pacojet containers and freeze. Overnight, right before you need it spin in the Pacojet.

tapioca sauce:
In a sauce pot bring to a boil the milk, coconut milk, and sugar, add the tapioca and move to a lower temperature, mixing constantly until the tapioca is cooked, then add the butter. Cool down and fix the consistency if necessary with milk.

pineapple chips:
In a sauce pot put the sugar and the water, bring to a boil and set aside. Put the slices of pineapple in the sugar and water mixture, arrange them in the tray of the dehydrator and let them dry for at least 24 hours until crisp.

garnish:
Cut the mango in thin slices, the papaya in small batons, kiwi in small dice and, using a mandoline, slice the coquitos and toast them in the oven for 1 minute. Mix some napage with the lime zest.

to serve:
Spread the pineapple compote over the cake and cut in rectangles 1½" x 5". Serve on a room temperature plate topped with the fruits to garnish. Add sauce and ice cream topped with a pineapple chip.

Chef's tip:
If you don't have a dehydrator you can use the oven at a low temperature instead.

Christophe Grosjean

Christophe Grosjean's love of cuisine began at his grandmother's farm in Burgundy, France, where every meal she made was created using the ingredients she harvested. At the age of 16, a friend invited him to cook at his restaurant. After two years, Christophe embarked upon a 'tour de France' where he traveled from province to province, studying various techniques and ingredients.

He was mentored by only the finest chefs in Michelin-starred restaurants. This journey came to a close at Le Jardin des Sens. Here he learned every detail of execution from preparation in the kitchen to the perfect service each time. Desiring more international experience, he moved to California and landed in the kitchen at Bernardus Lodge. At 26, he acquired the Chef de Cuisine position. After eight years of experimenting with the products of the Monterey area, he was able to adapt his French style of cooking to a cleaner, simpler taste. He's found his niche here at the L'Aubergine restaurant, cooking his exciting, unaffected and pure French cuisine adapted to Californian style.

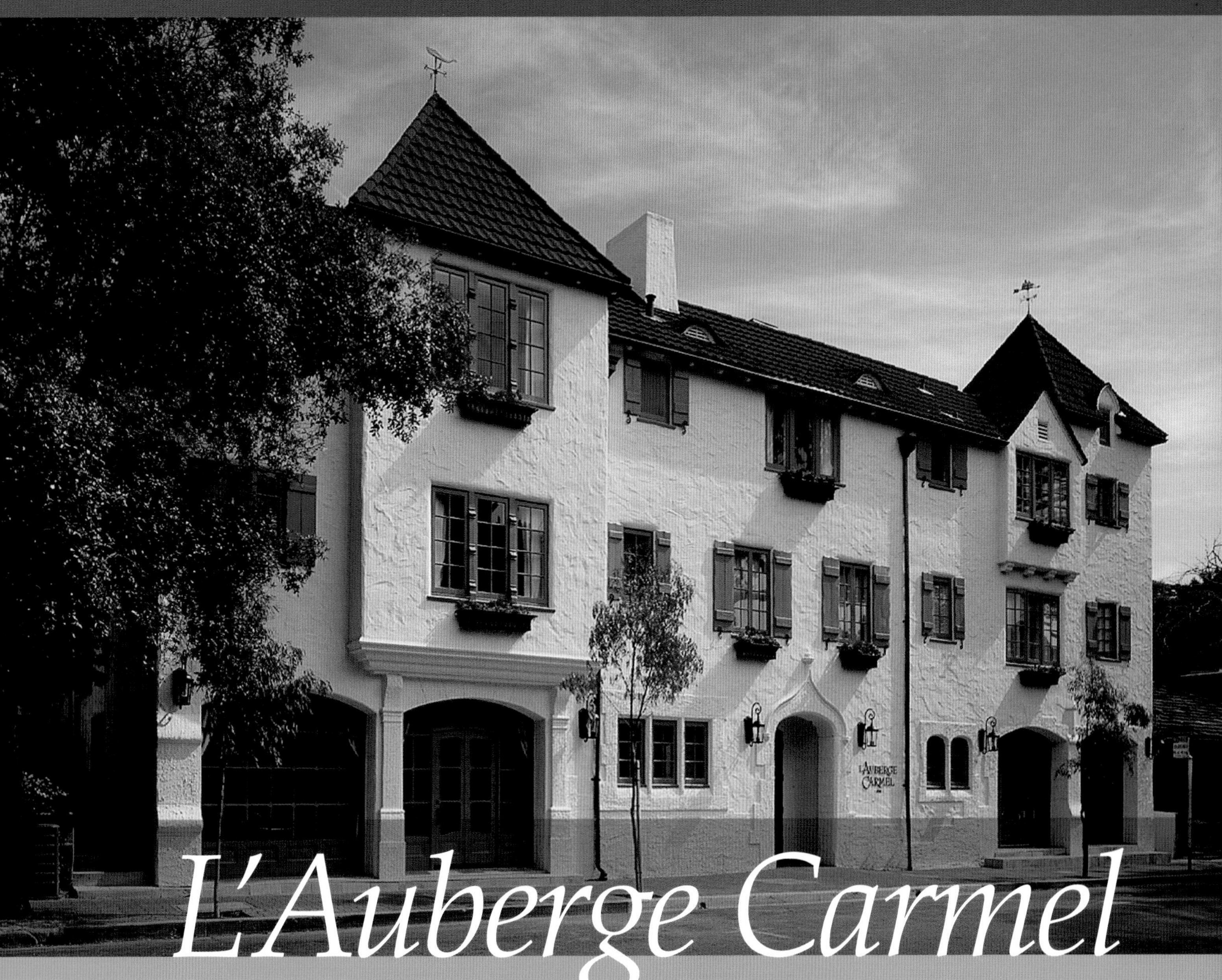

L'Auberge Carmel

It was in front of the stunning scenery of Big Sur that Henry Miller said that he learnt to pray. Drop your bags at a romantic hotel, L'Auberge Carmel, which was built in 1929.

In the little village of artists of Carmel-by-the-Sea it is the ideal base to take the time to meditate in front of the immensity of the cliffs which seem to plunge down into the ocean. Halfway between San Francisco and the coast of Santa Barbara, inhabited by seals, whales and other marine mammals, the village – where Clint Eastwood was once mayor – will charm you with its many art galleries and pebble beaches. The interior designer Kathleen Fink has decorated it with the most beautiful antiques and fabrics from Europe. Delicious cuisine, a wine cellar with over 4,500 bottles, massages and a short stroll to Carmel beach will give this address a special place in your heart, in the footsteps of the author.

DUNGENESS CRAB, HEIRLOOM BEETS, HAAS AVOCADO

BY CHRISTOPHE GROSJEAN

This dish is very popular at L'Auberge Carmel because it's mixing the ocean, right here, and one of the sweetest vegetables – they are very colorful and have a beautiful shape.

Serves 6
Preparation time: 1 hour 30 minutes
Cooking time: 1 hour 30 minutes

INGREDIENTS

crab:

2 whole Dungeness crabs
court bouillon, as needed
1 bulb fennel, diced
2 sheets phyllo dough
breadcrumbs

beets:

1 bunch of chiogga beet
1 bunch of golden beet
1 bunch of red beet
canola oil, as needed
vinegar, as needed

avocado:

2 haas avocado
2 limes, juice from both, lime from one
salt, to taste

ginger emulsion:

2 egg yolks
2 limes, juiced
salt & pepper
1 tbsp diced ginger
½ cup extra virgin olive oil

lime vinaigrette:

2 lime, zest
2 tbsp extra virgin olive oil

to serve:

3 tbsp maltodextrin
2 tbsp bergamot oil
micro herbs, to garnish

METHOD

crab:

Preheat the oven to 400°F. Separate the legs from the body of the crabs and cook them for 4 minutes in a court bouillon. Then cook the bodies for 12 minutes.

beets and avocado:

Place in an ice bath and when cool, pick out the meat. Roast the beets in the oven with canola oil and vinegar, covered with foil, until tender. Purée the avocado, then season with lime juice and salt. Take the lime zest and emulsify it with the extra virgin olive oil.

ginger emulsion:

To make the ginger emulsion emulsify all ingredients together. Mix the crab meat with the fennel and the ginger emulsion. Roll it in phyllo dough, then roll in breadcrumbs to make a cromesqui. Season the beets and the crab legs with lime vinaigrette.

to serve:

Blend some maltodextrin and bergamot oil until it becomes a fine powder and use to decorate and give another texture to the dish. Fry the cromesqui and serve with the beets, crab legs and garnish with micro herbs.

MONTEREY BAY SPOT PRAWNS, PEAS, BOTTARGA SAUCE

BY CHRISTOPHE GROSJEAN

This dish is very popular because it uses the star shellfish of the bay of Carmel. The prawns are harvested very deep, every day, and brought alive to the restaurant. The combination of the sweetness of the peas and the crunchy texture of the prawns gives a very Spring-like spirit to the menu.

Serves 6
Preparation time: 30 minutes
Cooking time: 20 minutes

Special equipment:
Vacuum sealing bag

INGREDIENTS

18 prawns
3 lb sugar snap peas
1 lb parsley root, peeled
salt
10 fl oz fish stock
bottarga
butter
lime, juice
1 oz pea shoots, to garnish

METHOD

Separate the heads of the prawns from the tails and peel them. Extract the bigger peas from the pod. Blanch the large peas and the left over pods. Place the peeled parsley root in a vacuum sealing bag with salt and butter. Cook at 158°F for 45 minutes. Place in an ice bath. Dice the prawns. Reduce the fish stock with bottarga and butter, blend and add a couple of drops of lime juice.

to serve:

Sear the prawns (cook medium rare). Dice and fry the parsley root. Warm the peas with butter, add the fried parsley root. Arrange on a plate and garnish with the pea shoots.

Serves 8
Preparation time: 45 minutes
Cooking time: 30 minutes

Special equipment:
Ice cream machine, Airtight container, Cryovac machine, dehydrator

Planning ahead:
All components can be made ahead of time, but the carrot croquant and cream cheese ice cream must be made in advance.

INGREDIENTS

cream cheese ice cream:

21 oz	cream cheese
10 oz	yogurt
3 oz	milk
3 oz	trimolene
3 oz	simple syrup
3 oz	glucose

yuzu coulis:

7 oz	water
2 oz	sugar
½ oz	agar agar
7 oz	yuzu juice

carrot croquant:

10 oz	carrot purée
1 oz	powdered sugar
2 oz	isomalt
½ oz	glucose syrup

carrot purée:

3 large carrots, peeled and diced
simple syrup, to taste

gingerbread:

9 oz	butter, soft
9 oz	brown sugar
5 oz	sugar
1	egg
1 oz	milk
½ oz	cinnamon, ground
1	pinch of salt
17 oz	flour
½ oz	baking soda

herb garnish:

micro cilantro
wood sorrel
rosemary flowers

CARROT & CREAM CHEESE ICE CREAM

BY RON MENDOZA

Inspired by traditional carrot cake flavors, this is a much lighter version that plays with various textures. The cream cheese ice cream is aerated in a cryovac machine but could just as easily be scooped. Yuzu juice has a more fragrant aroma but could be substituted with a mixture of lemon and lime juices. It's a very successful dessert because our guests can find, on reading the menu, a very American comfort dessert, but we deconstructed it and use a new technique to make it lighter.

METHOD

cream cheese ice cream:

Bring to a boil the trimolene, simple syrup, and glucose. Pour over the cream cheese, yogurt, and milk. Blend until smooth. Cool overnight. Process in an ice cream machine, then in a FoodSaver storage container. Process in a Cryovac machine until fully aerated. Return the ice cream to a freezer for 3 hours.

yuzu coulis:

Combine the water, sugar, and agar agar. Bring to a boil. Simmer for 1 minute. Remove from the heat, and blend in the yuzu juice. Pour into a tray and chill for 1 hour. Place this gel in a blender and blend until smooth. Strain and reserve.

carrot croquant:

Combine all the ingredients, place in a saucepan and simmer on a medium heat for 5 minutes until the sugars have melted. Chill, and reserve overnight. Spread on a nonstick mat and dry in a dehydrator for 24 hours. Break into irregular pieces and reserve in an airtight container.

carrot purée:

Boil the carrots until tender, then drain. Blend with the syrup to taste until thick and smooth. Chill, and reserve.

gingerbread:

Preheat the oven to 325°F. Sift together the cinnamon, salt, flour, and baking soda. Cream the butter and sugars. Add the egg followed by the milk, then add in the dry ingredients. Mix until a smooth paste is made, then spread on a parchment-lined baking sheet. Chill for 30 minutes. Bake for 20 minutes, then cool and grind in a food processor. Reserve.

to serve:

Place a spoonful of gingerbread crumbs on a plate. Spoon several dollops of carrot purée around the plate. Drizzle with yuzu coulis. Remove the cream cheese ice cream from the container, place on the plate and add more gingerbread crumbs. Garnish with the herbs and broken pieces of carrot croquant.

Robert Curry

Chef Robert Curry received his degree from the Culinary Institute of America in New York, although perhaps the most predominant influence on his work was his training with Michel Richard and Alain Giraud at Citrus. After traveling the world and cooking under Alain Ducasse, Michel Rostang and other renowned chefs, he was lured to Napa Valley where he has earned a reputation as one of 'Wine Country's' finest chefs.

Chef Curry's cooking style reflects his extensive experience in the traditions of both his native California and France. His menus showcase organic ingredients from a bounty of local markets, farmers and purveyors. Curry says, "To have the product at its peak, you have to have a connection with the farmer." Curry's cuisine displays the natural diversity and rich ingredients of Napa Valley accented with Mediterranean flavors.

With a Michelin star to his name for his California-influenced French cuisine, Robert Curry oversees all culinary aspects of Auberge du Soleil, where he is Executive Chef.

Auberge du Soleil

French restaurateur Claude Rouas has created a discreet and elegant hotel hidden among a grove of olive trees that evoke his love of Provence in the South of France.

Situated at the heart of the Cabernet-Sauvignon, Merlot and Chardonnay vines of Napa Valley, the 15,000 bottle wine cellar promises an oenophile's journey to wine heaven as you watch the sun set on the horizon. A handful of cottages perched on the hillside offer spacious 'maisons' with private terraces where aged French oak floors, colorful chenille fabrics, abstract paintings and fireplaces create an air of romance. The Mediterranean-inspired cuisine features the very best of the region. The spa which also draws its cue from the land, proposes treatments based on grapes, olives, herbs, flowers, mud and minerals.

Serves 4
Preparation time: 50 minutes
Cooking time: 1 hour

ARTICHOKE SALAD, BLOOD ORANGE, RICOTTA & PICKLED MUSTARD

BY ROBERT CURRY

This salad speaks to the season – fresh artichokes, citrus and wild arugula is quintessentially wine country.

INGREDIENTS

blood oranges:

3 blood oranges
1 artichoke, tournée cut
1 qt grapeseed oil
salt

steamed artichokes:

3 large artichokes, tournée cut
½ onion, peeled and diced
½ carrot, peeled and sliced
¼ bunch of thyme
1 lemon, juice
1 head of garlic, halved
1 bottle (75cl) of dry white wine
1 tbsp black peppercorns
¼ cup extra virgin olive oil
2 cups chicken stock
2 tbsp kosher salt
1 bay leaf

lemon dressing:

4 oz lemon juice
1 tbsp Dijon mustard
3 oz pure olive oil
2 oz extra virgin olive oil
1 lemon, zest
salt, to taste

pickled mustard seed vinaigrette:

2 tbsp pickled mustard seeds (see recipe below)
1 tbsp shallots, minced
1 tbsp chives, minced
¼ cup extra virgin olive oil
2 tbsp sherry vinegar
salt & freshly ground black pepper, to taste

pickled mustard seeds:

½ cup mustard seeds
¾ cup water
¾ cup rice wine vinegar
¼ cup sugar
1½ tsp salt

to serve:

1 shallot, peeled and minced
1 bunch of chives, minced
¼ lb sheep's milk ricotta
1 baby fennel bulb, shaved
12 wild arugula leaves
salt & freshly ground black pepper, to taste

METHOD

blood oranges:

Peel and slice the blood oranges. Heat the grapeseed oil to 300°F. Fry the slices of artichoke until crispy. Drain on paper towels and season with salt.

steamed artichokes:

Place all the ingredients in a small pot. Cover with a clean towel. Simmer until the artichokes are easily pierced with a knife, then into quarters.

lemon dressing:

In a small mixing bowl add the mustard and half the lemon juice. Slowly whisk in the oils to emulsify. Add the remaining lemon juice and the zest. Season to taste with salt.

pickled mustard seed vinaigrette:

Mix all the ingredients. Season to taste with salt and pepper.

pickled mustard seeds:

Place all the ingredients in a small pot. Simmer until the mustard 'pops' and is no longer crunchy, about 40-50 minutes. Add extra water as necessary to ensure the mustard is just covered with liquid.

to serve:

Place three slices of orange on each of four plates. In a bowl dress the quartered artichokes with the chives, shallots, dressing, salt and pepper. Place three artichokes on each plate, with some ricotta between them. Garnish with fennel and arugula. Sauce the plates with the vinaigrette.

WILD STRIPE BASS, DELTA ASPARAGUS, GNOCCHI, MEYER LEMON COULIS, BLACK OLIVE VINAIGRETTE

BY ROBERT CURRY

Usings seasonal ingredients is important in any dish, but when it comes to Wild Stripe Bass it is critical. To complement the robust flavor of the bass serving it with a combination of asparagus and citrus makes this the perfect dish to begin our Spring season.

Serves 4
Preparation time: 1 hour 15 minutes
Cooking time: 10 minutes

INGREDIENTS

bass:

4	wild striped bass fillet, 5 oz each
1 qt	grapeseed oil
20	asparagus, peeled and blanched in salted boiling water
1 oz	chicken stock
3 oz	butter
12	squid tentacles

Maldon salt & freshly ground black pepper, to taste

Meyer lemon coulis:

1	onion, peeled and diced
2 tbsp	extra virgin olive oil
12	Meyer lemons, juice and zest
½ cup	sugar
10	threads of saffron

potato gnocchi:

1 lb 10 oz	Russet potatoes, baked in their jackets and passed through a tamis
4 oz	all purpose flour, sifted
½ oz	salt
2 tbsp	extra virgin olive oil
1	egg
1 oz	chicken stock
3 tbsp	butter

salt & pepper

black olive vinaigrette:

½ cup	pitted nicoise olives, with brine
2 tbsp	lemon juice
¼ cup	sugar
1 tsp	glucose
¼ cup	banyuls vinegar
¼ cup	extra virgin olive oil

garnish:

12	sunflower sprouts

METHOD

bass:

Heat the grapeseed oil to 140°F. Season the bass with salt and pepper. Poach it with the squid tentacles in the grapeseed oil. Drain on paper towels. Glaze the asparagus in a sauté pan with the chicken stock and butter. Season to taste with salt and pepper.

Meyer lemon coulis:

In a small pot sweat the onion in the olive oil. When tender add the lemon juice, sugar and saffron. Reduce until slightly thickened. Purée in a blender with the zest. Pass through a chinois. Reserve hot.

potato gnocchi:

In a mixing bowl make a well out of the potatoes. Place the egg in the well. Drizzle olive oil over the potatoes. Sprinkle the flour and salt on the potatoes. Gently mix until the dough comes together. On a floured surface divide the dough into four pieces, then roll it into cylinders and cut into 1" pieces. Roll off the tines of a fork on to a floured sheet pan. Cook 12 gnocchi in non-salted boiling water until they just start to float. Glaze in a sauté pan with butter and stock, then season with salt and pepper.

black olive vinaigrette:

Blend the olives with the lemon juice until smooth to make a purée. Caramelize the sugar with the glucose. Whisk in the olive purée. Pass through a chinois and chill. Whisk in the vinegar and add the olive oil.

to serve:

Swipe four warm plates with Meyer lemon coulis. Divide the asparagus and the gnocchi among the plates. Add the fish and divide the squid tentacles among the plates. Sauce over with the black olive vinaigrette. Garnish with the sunflower sprouts. Finish the squid tentacles and bass with Maldon salt.

ROASTED WHITE CHOCOLATE & BERGAMOT MOUSSE, ANGOSTURA PUFF PASTRY, SEVEN CITRUS ACCOMPANIMENTS

BY PAUL LEMIEUX

Serves 8
Preparation time: 1 hour 30 minutes
Cooking time: 2 hours 30 minutes

Special equipment:
Ice cream maker, dehydrator, microplane, chocolate spray gun

Planning ahead:
The mousse needs to be frozen overnight. The pastry needs to rest for a total of 4 hours 30 minutes.

This dish is a very original preparation of white chocolate mousse. The sweet white chocolate and intense citrus make this an inventive and seasonally inspired combination of flavors.

INGREDIENTS

roasted white chocolate mousse:

5½ oz	white chocolate
7 oz	heavy whipping cream
1	sheet of gelatin, bloomed
1	egg yolk
½ tsp	salt
1 tsp	bergamot, zest
1 oz	bergamot, juice
1	egg white
½ oz	plain grain sugar
3 oz	crème fraîche

chocolate spray:

12 oz	white chocolate
3 oz	cocoa butter

Meyer lemon sorbet:

16 oz	Meyer lemon, juice
18 oz	sugar
16 oz	warm water
1	pinch of salt

puff pastry Angostura:

22 oz	flour
1 tsp	salt
2 tsp	vinegar
9 oz	cold water
2½ oz	melted butter
2 oz	Angostura bitters
16 oz	cold butter

Angostura syrup (1 tbsp Angostura bitters to 1 tbsp simple syrup)

candied kumquats:

1 lb	kumquats
10 oz	water
5 oz	sugar

Buddah's hand citron powder:

1	citron
8 oz	water
3 oz	sugar

to serve:

blood orange slices
mandarin supremes
ruby red grapefruit supremes
1 microplaned lime zest

METHOD

roasted white chocolate mousse:

Roast the white chocolate under a salamander until golden brown. Place the gelatin, egg yolk, salt, zest and juice on top of the roasted chocolate. Boil 4 oz of the cream and pour on top of the chocolate, stir to emulsify. With a mixer fitted with a whisk attachment, whip the egg white on high speed until frothy. Slowly add the sugar and whip until medium peaks form, then fold into the chocolate mixture. Combine the remaining 3 oz of cream and crème fraîche, whip to medium peaks, and fold into chocolate mixture. Pipe the mixture into 2" x 2" ring molds lined with acetate. Freeze overnight. Once frozen, remove from the mold and remove the acetate.

chocolate spray:

Melt the white chocolate and the cocoa butter to 110°F add to spray gun. Flock mousse with chocolate spray and spray according to manufacturers spray gun instruction. Reserve.

Meyer lemon sorbet:

Dissolve the sugar in the water. Add the juice and salt. Process the mixture in an ice cream maker according to the manufacturer's instructions.

puff pastry Angostura:

Mix the flour, salt, water, vinegar, bitters and melted butter in a mixer on a low speed with a paddle attachment. Mix for 1 minute or until the mixture is crumbly. Remove from the bowl and kneed by hand until the dough comes together. Form the dough into a ball and rest for 30 minutes. Pound out the dough to make a 10" square. Cut a cross into the top of the dough and use a rolling pin to roll outward – the center should be 1" thick. Place the cold butter block in the center of the dough and fold the flaps over so that all the butter is completely covered. Sheet dough to 2" in thickness, give a double turn. Repeat. Rest the dough for 2 hours. Repeat. Rest the dough for a further 2 hours, then divide it into three equal parts. Sheet to 1", rest. Cut into 4" strips, then cut each strip into ¾" slices, placing them cut-side down onto a silpat baking mat. Bake at 350°F for 8 minutes. Brush with Angostura syrup.

candied kumquats:

Trim the top and bottom off the kumquats. Slice into ¼" rings, then remove and discard the center. Place with the sugar into a pot of water. Simmer for 45 minutes, or until tender.

Buddah's hand citron powder:

Peel the citron and blanch the zest in water. Shock the citron in ice water. Blanch the citron again in water and sugar. Simmer until tender. Strain and place in a dehydrator. When dry, pulverize to make a powder.

to serve:

Place the mousse on a plate at 2 o'clock. Decorate with the lime zest. Put the grapefruit supremes at 10 o'clock, the mandarin supremes at 3 o'clock and the blood orange slices between 4 and 5 o'clock. Add the kumquats in front of the mousse. Place a line of citron powder near the grapefruit supremes and a small quenelle of sorbet on the mandarin supremes. Finish with two puff pastry slices by the mousse and sorbet.

Christopher Kostow

A Michelin-starred chef before the age of 30, Christopher Kostow takes a thoughtful approach to food that belies his age. Masterfully blending contemporary French cuisine with the farm-to-table tradition, Kostow creates a transcendent experience for diners every night at The Restaurant at Meadowood.

Kostow, a Chicago native, trained in kitchens far and wide: from a Paris bistro to the Michelin-starred Le Jardin des Sens in Montpellier. Upon returning to the States, Kostow worked as sous chef under Daniel Humm in San Francisco. He soon became top toque at Chez TJ in Mountain View, California, garnering the restaurant many accolades including two-Michelin-stars and a coveted spot on *Food & Wine* magazine's list of Top Ten Dishes of the Year in 2007.

Upon arriving at Meadowood in February of 2008, Christopher maintained two Michelin stars, was nominated for Best Chef, Pacific by the James Beard Society and named one of *Food & Wine* magazine's Best New Chefs 2009. In February of 2010, Christopher garnered a rare four stars in the *San Francisco Chronicle*.

Meadowood Napa Valley

The Napa Valley is one of the most prestigious wine-producing areas in the United States due to its Mediterranean climate and extremely fertile soil.

It has a viticultural heritage dating back to the 19th century. At Meadowood, you will find yourself at the heart of a unique tasting journey, starting with the estate's very own wine educator, who loves to share his passion. And for culinary delights 'The Restaurant at Meadowood' is one of the best in the region. The cosy lodges, guestrooms or suites with patios and views of the trees or the fairways – everything comes together to ensure sweet dreams among Redwoods, California 'LiveOak' trees, Big Leaf Maple trees and Douglas Fir.

Serves 4
Preparation time: 3 hours
Cooking time: 5 minutes

INGREDIENTS

5 oz	braised sweetbreads
1 oz	heavy cream
2 oz	chicken breast
1	sheet cooked pasta

farro:

5 oz farro
water, as needed

truffle broth:

10 oz	water
½ oz	black truffle
3 oz	maitaki mushroom
1 oz	carrot
1 oz	celery
1 oz	onion
1 oz	truffle brine
1 oz	white wine

garnish:

sautéed mushrooms
lettuces
edible flowers

SWEETBREAD CANNELONI WITH TRUFFLE BROTH, MAITAKE MUSHROOMS & PUFFED FARRO

BY CHRISTOPHER KOSTOW

In this dish we take flavors traditionally associated with heaviness and richness and put an elegant, light spin on them.

METHOD

In a food processor, combine the chicken and cream and mix to a smooth paste. Chop the cooked sweetbreads and mix with the chicken. Using the pasta sheet, roll the sweetbread mixture into a tube. Simmer to set the chicken mixture.

farro:

Cook the farro in water until very well done. Rinse under cold water and allow to dry. Once dry, fry in oil at 350°F until puffed.

truffle broth:

Combine all the ingredients in a pot and simmer until flavorful.

to serve:

Place some broth in a bowl, add a canneloni and spread around the farro. Finish with sautéed mushrooms, lettuces and edible flowers.

SLOW COOKED SQUAB BREAST WITH CARROTS & PISTACHIO

BY CHRISTOPHER KOSTOW

By poaching the squab with some spice, we are able to cut through the strong game flavors. The carrots, chocolate, citrus and pistachio are reminicent of a traditional Mole.

Serves 2
Preparation time: 3 hours
Cooking time: 5 minutes

Special equipment:
Cryovac machine

INGREDIENTS

1	squab breast
½ tsp	paprika
1 tbsp	butter

carrot purée:

5 oz	carrots, sliced
10 oz	carrot juice
1 oz	ginger

pistachio purée:

5 oz	pistachio
10 oz	water
3 oz	sugar

METHOD

Cryovac the squab, butter, and paprika in a vacuum bag. Poach in a 135°F water bath. Once the breast is medium rare, remove from the water and sear skin side down until crisp. Let rest before slicing.

carrot purée:

Cook the carrot and ginger in the carrot juice. Once tender, process in a blender until smooth.

pistachio purée:

Combine the ingredients in a pot and simmer until the pistachios are tender. Process the ingredients in a blender until smooth.

to serve:

Serve the squab breast with the carrot and pistachio purées. Garnish with vegetables and herbs as desired.

Serves 6
Preparation time: 4 hours
Cooking time: 2 hours

Special equipment:
Ice cream machine

INGREDIENTS

pâte sucrée:

10 oz	butter
6 oz	sugar
2	eggs
14 oz	all purpose flour
1 oz	cornstarch

bergamot curd:

10 oz	bergamot juice
1/8 tsp	agar agar
11 oz	sugar
11 oz	egg yolks
11½ oz	butter

yogurt sorbet:

7 oz	water
4 oz	glucose
4 oz	sugar
1 oz	lemon juice
20 oz	yogurt
1/8 tsp	stabilizer

TASTING OF CITRUS

BY CHRISTOPHER KOSTOW

We serve this dish during the height of citrus season in California so as to highlight the incredible bounty of our nearby orchards.

METHOD

pâte sucrée:

Cream the butter, sugar and eggs. Combine with the dry ingredients and knead lightly. Roll into a thin sheet and bake in a 350°F oven until golden. Cut and place into a prepared sheet tray.

bergamot curd:

Place the butter, sugar, eggs, and agar agar in a pot and cook until the mixture coats the back of a spoon. Place the mixture in a blender, and blend in the butter. Pour over the pâte sucrée and allow to set.

yogurt sorbet:

Boil the water, stabilizer, sugar and glucose together. Add the mixture hot to the yogurt and lemon juice. Chill and process in an ice cream machine.

to serve:

Slice the tart, add a quenelle of yogurt sorbet and garnish with assorted citrus fruits.

C. Barclay Dodge

Executive Chef C. Barclay Dodge has more than 20 years experience in the restaurant business. He has cooked professionally at prestigious restaurants, including Encantado Resort in Santa Fe, New Mexico, Restaurant Mogador and Renaissance Restaurant in Aspen, CO; Stokes Adobe in Monterey, CA; and Bix Supper Club and Bistro Roti in San Francisco, CA.

Dodge trained at the California Culinary Academy in San Francisco, CA and received culinary training in both the United States and Europe with apprenticeships at acclaimed restaurants such as Jean Georges and Daniel in New York; El Bulli in Roses, Spain; and Can Gaig in Barcelona, Spain. He was also a James Beard Guest Chef for Restaurant Mogador in 2003 and is a DiRoNA award winner.

'Coastal Ranch' is Dodge's creation specifically for Rancho Valencia, a showcase of the market-fresh vegetables available in the neighborhood. He also incorporates free-range meats and local seafood, intertwining these fresh, seasonal California ingredients with his extensive travel experience.

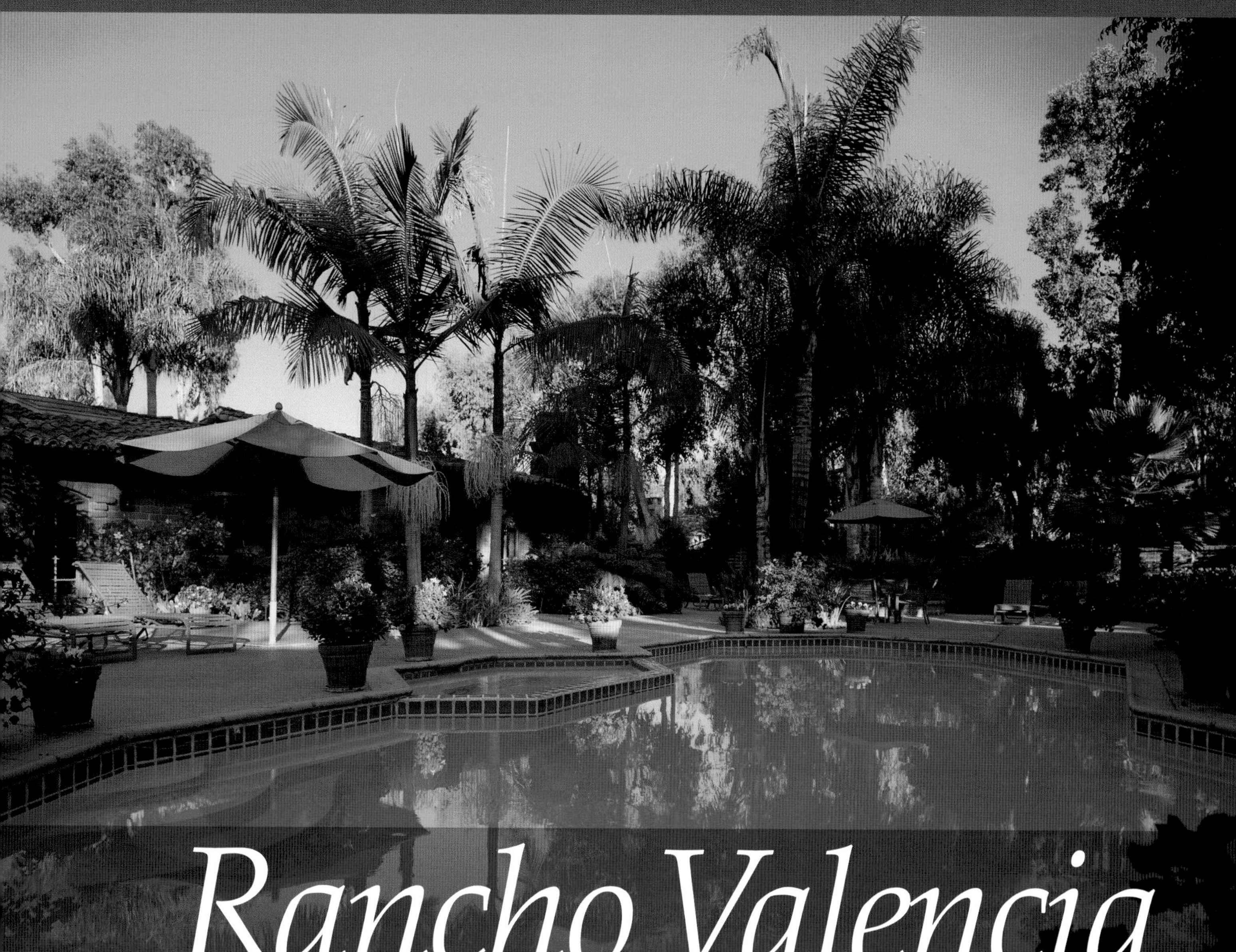

Rancho Valencia

This Spanish colonial-style complex stands in 16 hectares of grounds set on the hillside, among the eucalyptus and orange trees, cacti and hibiscus and is near the chic beaches of La Jolla and Del Mar.

Inside the tiled roof bungalows, there are treasures of craftsmanship including hand-painted Mexican pottery and Berber rugs on the floors. The spa with its Latin influences can be found in an ochre-colored building. Here, you can take a bath in a private garden and choose the formula to suit your mood: 'tonic' with orange, tangerine and black pepper; 'anti-stress', with sandalwood and lavender; or 'relaxing', with basil, pine and lemon. Couples will love the treatment rooms for two and the massages with bergamot and terracotta. Soak up the sun, discover San Diego and its historic Gaslamp Quarter famous for the gas lanterns that continue to illuminate the night and enjoy walking, tennis and golf.

OVEN ROASTED SALMON & BLACK CORN RAVIOLI WITH POBLANO FRITTER, SHELLFISH CHORIZO & LOBSTER-TORTILLA SAUCE

BY C. BARCLAY DODGE

Working in San Diego, and being so close to the border of Mexico you find an abundance of Latino influenced cuisine. It is hard not to pick up on your surroundings and cook some of the local fare ... when in Rome. This dish captures just a bit of the delicious world only 30 minutes south of Rancho Valencia.

Serves 4

Preparation time: 2 hours

Cooking time: 25 minutes

Planning ahead:

The pasta dough needs to rest for a few hours

Special equipment:

Butchers twine

INGREDIENTS

salmon:

4	fillets of salmon, 6 oz each
2 tbsp	clarified butter
salt	

black corn filling:

½ cup	creamed corn, best quality grocery store brand (I say grocery store brand because of the great reminiscent flavor of childhood this product has.)
¼ cup	huitlacoche (optional - can be difficult to find, check a specialty Mexican market)
⅓ cup	heavy cream
1	dash of Worcestershire sauce
1	dash of tabasco sauce (or more to desired taste)
1	pinch of salt
1	pinch of white pepper
3	leaves of gelatin, previously bloomed in cold water

ravioli dough:

1 cup	all purpose flour
3	egg yolks
1 tsp	squid ink (optional)
1 tbsp	water (or more as necessary if the dough is dry)
1 tbsp	virgin olive oil
¼ tsp	salt

poblano fritter:

6 oz	masa flour
3 cups	chicken stock
1 ½ tsp	salt
1	poblano chili, roasted, peeled, deseeded and cut into small dice
3 tbsp	scallions, finely sliced crosswise
1	pinch black pepper, freshly ground
3 cups	oil (canola or peanut oil) for frying

shellfish chorizo:

6 oz	fresh shrimp, peeled and deveined
½ tsp	each of finely chopped garlic and pimento (smoked Spanish paprika)
1	pinch of cayenne
½ tsp	salt

lobster tortilla sauce

1 tbsp	butter
1	corn tortilla, 6"-8" in diameter
1 cup	canola or corn oil, for frying
⅓ cup	yellow onion, small dice
3	cloves garlic, minced
2 tsp	harissa (or any available chili paste)
¼ tsp	chili powder
½ tsp	each of ground cumin, freshly ground black pepper, salt
1	pinch of dry oregano
6	sprigs of fresh cilantro, chopped
½ tbsp	lime juice, freshly squeezed
1 cup	crushed tomato
2 cups	lobster stock
1	dash of sherry vinegar

METHOD

black corn filling:

Bring the creamed corn and cream to a boil. Season with the Worcestershire sauce, tabasco, salt and white pepper. Add the huitalacoche to the mix, purée well in a blender and pass through a chinois. Check the seasoning.

Let cool off a bit and add the bloomed gelatin. Stir in well. Pour the creamed corn mixture into ice cube trays and freeze.

ravioli dough:

Combine the salt and flour together and put into a mixing bowl with a paddle or dough hook attachment. Blend together the water, squid ink and olive oil. Process/knead the flour on low and add the egg yolks one-by-one. Then add the squid ink mixture and process/knead for a few minutes. Add any necessary water if needed so the pasta is not too dry. Wrap in plastic and refrigerate for a few hours.

Roll the dough out very thin. Once rolled out cut the dough into four pieces 3½" x 3½" and blanch in simmering salted water for 90 seconds. Remove from the water and shock the pasta in a bowl of cold water. (Excess pasta not portioned can be wrapped up well and frozen for another time.)

assembling the ravioli:

Lay each square piece of cooked pasta onto your work surface and place a frozen cube of the corn filling in the center. Fold over the sides of the pasta around the filling to form a purse. Wrap in plastic wrap and refrigerate until ready to use.

poblano fritter:

In a small saucepan heat the chicken stock. Once it comes to a boil, slowly add the masa stirring the whole time. Cook for approximately 15 minutes over a low heat until the corn meal is cooked, stirring frequently. Fold in the poblano chili and scallions. Remove from the heat, and season with salt and pepper. Pour the masa mixture out onto a shallow plate about a ¼" thick, and let cool in the refrigerator. Once cool cut into 2" x 4" pieces.

shellfish chorizo:

In a food processor roughly chop the shrimp, add the garlic, salt, pimento and cayenne and continue to process to a rough paste. Place

the mix in a piping bag and pipe a long sausage about 1½" in diameter on a sheet of plastic wrap. Roll the plastic wrap tightly around the shrimp, and twist the ends securely and tie off with butcher's twine at the ends so that the shrimp resembles a sausage link. Repeat with the remaining shrimp. Poach the shrimp in simmering water for about 8 minutes. Remove and cool in the refrigerator until ready to use.

lobster tortilla sauce:

Fry the tortillas in oil until golden and crispy. Once cooked, crush and break up the tortillas.

Heat a medium saucepan over a medium flame. Add the butter, yellow onions and garlic and sweat for a few minutes. Add the crushed tortillas, the harissa, the spices, oregano and salt and cook for 10-15 minutes over a medium soft flame. Cook until a light caramelization is achieved. Add the cilantro and lime juice and continue cooking for five minutes longer. Add the crushed tomato, reduce the flame to low and simmer for 30 minutes. Add the lobster stock, bring to a boil and immediately reduce to a simmer, and cook for 30 minutes longer. Remove from the heat and add the sherry vinegar. Purée in the blender until smooth and pass through a chinois. Check the seasoning and cool down immediately.

to serve:

In a hot sauté pan or black iron skillet heat the clarified butter. Season the salmon with salt, lay flesh side down in the pan and sear until lightly golden brown. Flip the salmon over and place in a 350°F-400°F oven and cook for a few minutes until the center of the fish is slightly warm.

For the fritter, heat the oil in a pan suitable for frying until very hot (approximately 350°F) and fry each piece of masa until golden brown. Remove from the oil and place on a few paper towels to drain, season with a little salt.

Place the ravioli on a small buttered baking sheet and place in a hot oven for a minute or two. You only want to warm the ravioli through, thus melting the gelatin.

Warm up the shellfish chorizo in the same pan as the ravioli and heat until warm.

Warm the sauce in a saucepan and reserve for plating.

to finish:

Place a spoonful or two of lobster tortilla sauce across the plate. Set the fried poblano fritter beside the sauce. The roasted salmon sits on top of the fritter and the warm corn ravioli on top of the salmon. Lay three slices of shellfish chorizo in front of the salmon and garnish with petit cilantro leaves across the chorizo. Serve immediately.

BRAISED BEEF SHORT RIB & RED WINE GLAZED SHALLOTS WITH ACORN SQUASH PUREE & COCOA BORDELAISE

BY C. BARCLAY DODGE

This dish has many years' cooking behind it, techniques and flavors learned from years in the kitchen. It is a grounding and satisfying dish that is well suited as an appetizer in the Winter and Fall months.

Serves 4
Preparation time: 4 hours
Cooking time: 3 hours

Special equipment:
Siphon with N_2O charge

Planning ahead:
The ribs need to be prepared in advance and left overnight.

INGREDIENTS

braised beef short ribs:

1 ½ lb	beef short ribs, boneless
salt	
1	yellow onion, sliced
½	carrot, peeled & sliced
1	rib of celery, sliced
3	cloves garlic, crushed
1 tsp	tomato paste
3	sprigs of thyme
3	sprigs of parsley
½	tsp black pepper, toasted
¼"	cinnamon stick, toasted
½	star anise, toasted
1	bay leaf
½ cup	red wine
1 tsp	salt
1 quart	water
1 cup	demiglace

red wine glazed shallots:

15	whole shallots, peeled
2 cups	cabernet sauvignon wine
1 tsp	sugar
1	pinch of salt
1	sachet of 1 tsp black pepper, 1 bay leaf and thyme

acorn squash purée:

5 oz	acorn squash, roasted (weighed after roasting)
4 oz	cream, scalded
1 tbsp	butter
¼ tsp	salt
¼ tsp	star anise, finely ground
½ tbsp	dark moscovado sugar

cocoa bordelaise:

½ cup	Cabernet Sauvignon
1 tsp	black peppercorns, lightly roasted
3	sprigs of fresh thyme
2 cups	veal demiglace
2 oz	bittersweet chocolate 66%

Garnish:

2 tbsp	chives, freshly chopped
4	tufts watercress, fresh
2 tbsp	cocoa nibs

METHOD

braised beef short ribs:

Remove any excess fat from the short ribs. Season with salt, cover and refrigerate overnight. The next day sear on both sides achieving a nice caramelization to the meat, then transfer to a braising pan.

In a hot sauté pan with a little oil add the carrots, onion and celery and cook until caramelized. At this point add the tomato paste, garlic and spices and cook for a few minutes longer. Add the herbs and deglaze with the red wine, then add to the braising pan with the short ribs. Pour in the water and demiglace and season with the teaspoon of salt. Cover loosely with foil and bring to a boil over a high flame, then transfer to a 325°F oven for 1 hour, remove the foil and cook for 2 hours longer or until tender.

Strain the liquid from the short ribs through a chinois, then put the short rib back into the hot braising liquid and let cool. Once cool, remove from the liquid and portion into four equal portions. Reserve the liquid to reheat the short rib at the time of serving.

red wine glazed shallots:

In a shallow stainless steel saucepan add all the ingredients and reduce the wine over a medium flame by 80%. Transfer to a 350°F oven and continue cooking until the wine has reduced and glazed the shallots. Finish by stirring in a little whole butter, check the seasoning and keep warm until ready to serve. The shallots should be well glazed with the reduced wine and dark red in color.

acorn squash purée:

Split the acorn squash in two and scoop out the seeds. Lay the squash cut side down on a buttered parchment lined sheet pan and bake at 350°F-400°F until tender.

Scoop out the meat of the squash and weigh out 10 oz for the recipe.

Purée the hot squash and the other ingredients in a blender until very smooth. Check the seasoning. Pass through a chinois. Then pour the purée into a siphon and apply one charge. Keep warm in a bath of hot water (do not hold in boiling water, but rather water that is hot to the touch).

cocoa bordelaise:

Reduce the wine with peppercorns by 90% (to a thick syrup). Add the demiglace and reduce to a consistency to coat the back of a spoon. Finish with the fresh thyme, stir in the chocolate and strain through a fine chinois. Keep warm until ready to serve. (You may also refrigerate and reserve for a few days until ready to use.)

to serve:

Reheat the short ribs in the braising liquid until hot. Expel a few tablespoons of acorn squash purée from the siphon into the center of four plates. Set a portion of short rib on top of the acorn squash. Nape the short ribs with the cocoa bordelaise and some of the cocoa nibs. Reheat the shallot, place three pieces around the outside of each plate and glaze with the red wine syrup that comes off the shallots. Garnish each plate with a small tuft of watercress and freshly chopped chives on top of the short ribs and serve immediately.

CHOCOLATE & HAZELNUT MOUSSE WITH HAZELNUT BRITTLE, TOASTED MARSHMALLOW

BY C. BARCLAY DODGE

A subtle blend of hazelnut and chocolate makes this classic pairing of flavors a real winner with guests. Set off with the smooth caramel and toasted marshmallow, this dish is the ultimate in melt-in-the-mouth indulgence.

Serves 4
Preparation time: 2 hours
Cooking time: 20 minutes

Planning ahead:
The hazelnut brittle can be made in advance and stored in an air tight container.

INGREDIENTS

gianduja mousse:

4 oz milk chocolate gianduja
2 tsp butter
3 tbsp cream
1 egg yolk
¼ tsp powdered gelatin
6 oz cream, whipped to soft peaks

crust:

½ cup Graham cracker crumbs
1 tbsp sugar
3 tbsp butter, melted and cooled slightly

marshmallows:

1 tbsp powdered gelatin
⅓ cup water
½ cup corn syrup
⅔ cup sugar
1 tsp vanilla
salt, to taste

Graham cracker tuile:

2 egg whites
¾ cup powdered sugar, sifted
1 tsp vanilla extract
¼ tsp salt
⅓ cup Graham cracker crumbs
¼ cup all purpose flour
5 tbsp butter, melted

caramel sauce:

1 cup sugar
3 tbsp corn syrup
½ cup cream
¼ cup butter
2 tbsp crème fraîche
smoked sea salt, to taste
¼ cup water

hazelnut brittle:

¾ cup sugar
¼ cup corn syrup
4 oz hazelnuts, blanched
2 tsp butter
1½ tsp baking soda
1 pinch of salt

to serve:

melted chocolate

METHOD

gianduja mousse:

Sprinkle the gelatin over 1 tablespoon of cold water and set aside. Melt the gianduja with the butter and cream over a double boiler. Add the egg yolk. Melt the gelatin mixture and add to the gianduja. Fold in the whipped cream and pour into the 3" ring molds. Refrigerate until firm.

crust:

Combine the crumbs and the sugar. Add the butter and mix until well combined. Divide the crust between the ring molds and press onto the mousse, making the top as flat as possible.

marshmallows:

In a small saucepan sprinkle the gelatin over the water and let sit for 5 minutes. Add the sugar and stir over a low heat until the sugar dissolves. Combine the gelatin mixture, corn syrup, ¼ teaspoon of salt and vanilla in the bowl of the mixer and whip for about 15 minutes, or until peaks form. Spread into a bread pan lined with plastic wrap. Allow to cool at room temperature for at least 2 hours before cutting. Once firm, cut with a sharp knife wetted with some warm water. Set aside until needed.

Graham cracker tuile:

Whisk together the egg whites, powdered sugar, vanilla extract, and salt. Add the Graham cracker crumbs and flour. Add the butter and stir until well combined. Refrigerate for 20 minutes before using. Spread the paste onto a slipat lined baking sheet in the desired shape and at 325°F for about 10 minutes.

caramel sauce:

Combine the sugar and corn syrup with the water. Bring to a boil and cook to medium amber. Remove from the heat. When the bubbles have dispersed, add the cream, butter,

crème fraîche, and salt. Stir until smooth, over heat if necessary.

hazelnut brittle:

Combine the sugar and corn syrup with the water and bring to a boil. When the sugar is dissolved, add the hazelnuts. Continue to cook, stirring frequently, over a medium-high heat until the sugar reaches 300°F. Remove from the heat and add the butter, baking soda, and salt. Stir well and pour onto a buttered baking sheet. Once the brittle has cooled, break into small pieces and store in an airtight container until needed.

to serve:

Decorate the plate as desired with caramel sauce, melted chocolate, and hazelnut brittle. Remove the mousse from the ring molds by either using a blow torch or warm water to heat the metal ring and push the mousse out. Place onto the plate and top with the chopped hazelnut brittle. Toast one marshmallow for each mousse with a blow torch or quickly under the broiler in the oven. Place on the mousse over the brittle. Garnish with a Graham cracker tuile dusted with powdered sugar.

Montana

Big skies, big mountains, big rivers – Montana has it all! Nicknamed the 'Treasure State', this part of the United States is full of natural treasures.

From crystal glaciers to emerald forests Montana is made for those who love nature and wide open spaces. Well known for ranching, trout fishing and skiing, there is no shortage of things to do. The site of the Battle at Little Bighorn gives a historical visiting point, while the state makes the most of its three entrances to Yellowstone National Park. So settle down, pull on your boots and get ready to take on the open spaces of Montana, the US state gone wild.

Jacob Leatherman

A native of Cincinnati, Ohio, Jacob Leatherman found his calling to cuisine while an English student at Ohio State University. He enrolled in the French Culinary Institute in New York City and embraced his new career with passion. Upon graduation he worked in French restaurants in Cincinnati and soon found a desire to move to the Rocky Mountains. He took a position as Sous Chef at the Home Ranch, a Relais & Châteaux Resort, in Clark, Colorado.

In 2005 Jacob joined Triple Creek as Executive Sous Chef. Jacob quickly became a major contributor to the restaurant, bringing his wealth of knowledge and creativity to our dining services. In February 2006 he was named Executive Chef, a role in which he continues to excite guests with his refined contemporary cuisine. Jacob believes the most flavorful cuisine is made simply with the best, highest quality products. As he always says, "After love, cuisine is the most important part of life."

Triple Creek Ranch

The pleasures may change with the seasons but the program is always intense at Triple Creek Ranch.

In Summer, slip your boots into the stirrups, don your cowboy hat and set off to explore the rugged scenery of Montana with its white water torrents, conifers and prairies full of wild flowers. In Winter, put on your skis and glide down the slopes of the Rockies or enjoy a romantic couple's massage. The homemade cookies are a small clue to the hospitality of William and Leslie McConnell and the way they will look after you during your stay. An exceptional address that immerses you in the wild America of Westerns, and offers an intense moment of excitement for those who dare to go rafting down the Salmon River – the famous 'River of No Return'.

BLODGETT CREEK SLOW ROASTED PORK BELLY WITH POACHED QUAIL EGG, TRUFFLED BEETS & PASSION FRUIT REDUCTION

BY JACOB LEATHERMAN

Serves 8

Preparation time: 2 days
Cooking time: 3 hours

Planning ahead
The pork belly should be placed in the brine and chilled for 2 days.

INGREDIENTS

5 lb	fresh pork belly, trimmed

brine:

1 gal	water
3 cups	apple cider
4	whole cloves
½ cup	kosher salt
½ cup	brown sugar
10	Tellicherry peppercorns, crushed

beets:

1	beet
4	fresh basil leaves, chopped
1 tsp	fresh lemon juice
2 tbsp	olive oil
½ tbsp	truffle oil

salt & pepper, to taste

passion fruit reduction:

1 cup	passion fruit purée
¼ cup	white chicken stock
1	kaffir lime leaf
1	sprig of fresh thyme

quail eggs:

8	quail eggs

salt & pepper
white wine vinegar

This pork belly is from the Bitterroot Valley, 30 minutes from Triple Creek Ranch. The farmer who raised the pigs is named Bosco and the pigs rest and eat in an apple orchard which adds character and wonderful flavor.

METHOD

brine:

Place all the brine ingredients in a sauce pot, bring to a simmer and turn off the heat. Let the brine cool to room temperature. Place trimmed pork belly in the brine. Chill for 2 days.

After 2 days, take the pork out of the brine and pat dry. Preheat oven to 350°F. Place the pork belly on a wire rack, fat side up, then place that on a sheet tray. With a paring knife score the fat diagonally. Season with salt and pepper. Place the pork in the oven. Check after 2 hours and rotate the tray. Check in another hour. Pork should feel very soft and melty. The skin should be crispy and a golden brown. Take the pork out of the oven and let rest for at least 30 minutes.

beets:

Season the beet with 1 tablespoon of olive oil, salt and pepper. Oven should be at 450°F. Wrap the beet with aluminum foil and place in the oven. After 45 minutes, poke the beet with a paring knife – it should be very tender. Take the skin off the beet while still warm. Slice the beet into very thin rounds and place in a mixing bowl. Add basil, lemon juice, remaining olive oil, truffle oil, salt and pepper. Toss the beets gently and set aside for the flavors to marry.

passion fruit reduction:

Place all the ingredients in a saucepan and onto a medium-high heat. Bring to a simmer and reduce by half. Take off the heat, and season with salt and pepper. Take out the kaffir lime leaf.

quail eggs:

Poach the quail eggs and drain over paper towel, and season with salt and pepper. Poach in slowly simmering water and a splash of white wine vinegar.

to serve:

Place the pork belly on the plate, top with the beets, quail egg and pour over some passion fruit reduction.

PAN-SEARED GOLDEN TROUT WITH SALSIFY SALAD & CAPER BROWN BUTTER SAUCE

BY JACOB LEATHERMAN

Serves 4
Preparation time: 1 hour
Cooking time: 20 minutes

Planning ahead:
The salted capers need to be soaked for several hours and drained.

INGREDIENTS

1 golden trout, whole and gutted
2 tbsp olive oil
2 tbsp butter
1 fresh lemon, juice
2 tbsp salted capers (make sure they have been soaked for several hours and drained)
3 tbsp fresh parsley and chives
salt & pepper

salsify salad:

2 salsify roots
1 piece of bacon, cut into strips and cooked until crispy
1 bunch of celery leaves (the nice tender pale ones)
3 white anchovies, chopped
3 tbsp fresh parsley, chopped
8 lemon supremes (cut out from around the white membrane of the lemon)
olive oil
salt & pepper

The trout we use are farm raised, but some do swim wild in high mountain alpine lakes.

METHOD

Preheat the oven to 375°F. Put a sauté pan on a high heat. Season the trout liberally with salt and pepper. Put olive oil in the pan – the oil should be smoking before carefully placings the trout in the pan. Cook on one side for about 5 minutes until the skin is a nice brown, then flip the trout onto the other side. Add the butter to the pan and place the pan and trout in the oven. The fish will take 15 minutes to cook. Take out of the oven and place the cooked trout onto a cutting board to rest. Put the same pan back on a medium heat. Add the lemon juice, capers and the fresh herbs, and finish with salt and pepper to taste.

salsify salad:

Peel the salsify and season with olive oil, salt and pepper. Place in a roasting pan and put into a 400°F oven. The salsify should be fork tender and nicely caramelized. This will take about 20 minutes. Cut the salsify into ¼" coins. Add these to a mixing bowl along with the bacon, celery leaves, parsley, anchovies, and lemon supremes. Toss with olive oil, and salt and pepper.

to serve:

Place the trout on a plate top with salsify salad, and caper juice from the sauté pan.

PAIN D'EPICE & CARAMEL NAPOLEON WITH MARINATED PEARS & NOUGATINE ICE CREAM

BY CHRISTOPHER WHITTEN

A classic Napoleon with a Triple Creek twist, this dish is sure to impress all those that are served it. Pain D'Epice literally translates as spiced bread, or gingerbread, and paired with the smooth caramel and cool nougatine ice cream this is a dish that really excites the senses.

Serves 6
Preparation time: 25 minutes
Cooking time: 1 hour 15 minutes

INGREDIENTS

pain d'épice:

9 oz	all purpose flour
9 oz	honey
4½ oz	milk
½ tsp	baking soda
1 ½ oz	candied orange zest, diced
½ oz	almonds, sliced and toasted
1 tsp	ground ginger
½ tsp	ground cinnamon
1	pinch of five spice
¼ tsp	salt

caramel supreme:

6 oz	turbinado sugar
2 oz	water
17 oz	heavy cream
4 oz	egg yolks
3	gelatin sheets
4 oz	whipped cream

ice cream base:

18 oz	milk
18 oz	heavy cream
7 oz	egg yolks
3 oz	sugar

nougatine:

12 oz	sugar
5 oz	water
10 oz	glucose
10 oz	almonds, sliced and toasted

pears and poaching liquid:

1	75cl bottle Cabernet Sauvignon
8 oz	water
8 oz	sugar
½	orange, zest
1	cinnamon stick
6	Bosc or D'Anjon, not too ripe

METHOD

pain d'epice:

Butter a 4"x 8" loaf pan. Preheat the oven to 350°F. Boil the milk and honey, let sit aside until it reaches room temperature. Add the remaining ingredients and bake for approximately 45 minutes.

caramel supreme:

Combine the sugar and water in a medium saucepan and let it caramelize. Add the heavy cream while stirring to deglaze. Whisk half of the mixture into the egg yolks and return to the pot, cooking to 185°F. Add the soaked gelatin and strain into an ice bath. Allow to cool and fold in the whipped cream. Place in a mold and freeze until needed.

ice cream base:

Boil together the milk, cream and sugar. Whisk into the egg yolks and return to the pot. Cook to 185°F while stirring and strain into an ice bath.

nougatine:

Cook the sugar, glucose and water to caramelize. Mix in the almonds and pour the mixture onto a parchment sheet and allow to cool.

pears and poaching liquid:

Heat together all ingredients, except the pears, and bring to a simmer. Poach the pears until almost tender and let stand until cool.

to serve:

Slice and toast the pain d'épice into the desired shape. Layer the pain d'épice and caramel supreme into a napoleon. Thinly slice the pears and shingle them on the plate. Place the napoleon on top of the pears. At the last minute, fold the crushed nougatine into the ice cream and serve.

Colorado

The distinguished horizon of Colarado's Rocky Mountains looks out over what can only be described as outdoors country.

Skiing, mountain biking and walking, Colorado has the highest altitude of the United States so the natural high plus the amazing views make a perfect reason to visit. The state's well-known background of oil mining and fossil beds together with the UNESCO site rock dwellings make it clear that the land has a history to tell. To get a better view of things Colorado's largest and longest running balloon festival paints the perfect setting. Sit back as you enjoy Palisade peaches, tender bison or a Rocky Mountain oyster as the sun sets.

Clyde Nelson

Clyde Nelson has been the Executive Chef at The Home Ranch for the past 20 years. His New Western cuisine has always set the standard and is emulated throughout the dude ranch kingdom. Now a guest's culinary experience rivals the horseback ride as a reason for a dude ranch vacation.

Raised in Connecticut, Nelson earned a Wildlife Ecology degree from the University of Vermont. He apprenticed with Anton Flory for four years in Stowe, Vermont before staging in Innsbruck, Austria. He returned to the United States to be chef at several mountain lodges in Vermont and Colorado before settling at The Home Ranch.

Clyde takes the typical dude ranch meal and makes it exquisite. He is especially fond of grilling; his grilling tip is to use charcoal, be patient, allow the coals to 'ash-up'. Heavily season the meat, use plenty of salt. Sear directly over coals on all sides, then spread the coals and finish on a higher level indirectly.

The Home Ranch

Admire stunning views of the Rockies from your cosy room and the magnificent hand-hewn log lodge – mountains made famous by so many great Westerns.

As you gallop horseback across the splendid terrain, transport yourself to another world: you are the cowboy. Back at the ranch, dive into the pool or try your hand at fly-fishing, and enjoy a remarkable breakfast, lunch and dinner prepared under the direction of the chef.

CRISPY SMOKED TROUT OVER A POTATO & LARDON SALAD WITH SHERRY THYME VINAIGRETTE

BY CRAIG SINGER

Living only a few steps away from some of the best trout fly-fishing in the United States, we have a love for fresh trout at the Home Ranch.

Serves 4-6
Preparation time: 1 hour
Cooking time: 35 minutes

Planning ahead:
The trout can be smoked up to 2 days in advance.

INGREDIENTS

2	rainbow trout fillets or 4 brook trout fillets

brine:

1½ cups	water
2 tbsp	kosher salt
1 tbsp	brown sugar
1 tbsp	whole pepper corn mélange
1	garlic clove
1 tbsp	fresh ginger, grated
3	sprigs of fresh thyme
1	bay leaf

potato salad:

2	Yukon gold potatoes
¼ cup	pancetta, small dice (rendered, reserve the fat)
2 tsp	grain mustard
1 tbsp	parsley, chopped
1 tsp	ver jus
salt & pepper	

vinaigrette:

1 tbsp	sherry vinegar
¼ cup	olive oil
1 tsp	thyme, chopped
1 tsp	shallot, brunoise
1 tsp	garlic, minced
1 tsp	Dijon mustard
salt & pepper	

garnish:

1	bunch of mache
1	slice of oven-dried speck

METHOD

brine:

Combine all the ingredients in a small saucepan and bring to a boil. Remove from the heat and cool. Submerge the trout fillets in the brine, skin side up, for 1½ hours. Rinse and pat dry.

Cold smoke the trout below 100°F for 45 minutes (depending on the smoker). This can be done up to 2 days in advance.

potato salad:

Preheat the oven to 375°F and roast the potatoes for an hour or until they are soft to the touch. Peel and then smash lightly with a fork until the potatoes are chunky. Add in the remaining ingredients along with half of the reserved fat from the pancetta and season with salt and pepper to taste.

vinaigrette:

Combine the sherry vinegar, thyme, shallot, garlic, and Dijon mustard. Then slowly whisk in the olive oil. Season to taste with salt and pepper.

to serve:

Quickly sear the smoked trout, skin side down in a hot pan with the remaining pancetta fat until the skin is crispy (about 1 minute). Remove from the pan, and drain over paper towel. Place a small mound of potato salad on a plate, and top with the trout and mache, oven-dried speck and drizzle with some vinaigrette.

Serves 4
Preparation time: 30 minutes
Cooking time: 2 hours

Planning ahead:
Salt your meat liberally 1-3 days ahead. This improves flavor and succulence.

BEEF (OR BUFFALO) SHORT RIBS BRAISED IN BEER WITH CREAMY SOFT SAGE POLENTA & ROASTED WINTER VEGETABLES

BY CLYDE NELSON

Hearty, delicious and succulent braised meats are an ideal fit to our Winter menus. They're also received well by our guests on our cold mountain evenings in Spring and Fall. We strive to feature locally raised organic meats and poultry, and actually raise beef cattle and hogs on ranch. We also try to accompany our center-of-the-plates with locally grown organic produce from our Alpine valley, as well as vegetables from our ranch gardens and greenhouse.

INGREDIENTS

ribs:

4	beef (or buffalo) short ribs (about ¾ lb each)
salt & freshly ground pepper	
¼ cup	flour for dusting the meat
½ lb	carrots, chopped in half pieces
2	medium onions, quartered
4	medium garlic cloves
1 cup	chopped tomatoes
2	bay leaves
4	sprigs of thyme
4	sage leaves
1 tbsp	coriander seeds wrapped in cheesecloth as a sachet
2-3 cups	beef or chicken stock (or water)
1	bottle of dark beer
1	small dried chili arbol

vegetables:

2	Yukon gold potatoes cut into thick wedges
1	turnip, peeled and cut into thick wedges
2	carrots, peeled and cut into 1½" sections, thick sections cut in half lengthwise
2	parsnips (cut the same as the carrots)
½ cup	pearl onions, blanched and peeled
2 tbsp	olive oil
salt & freshly ground pepper	

creamy soft sage polenta:

3 cups	water or chicken stock
1 cup	milk
1 cup	polenta or stone ground cornmeal
6 tbsp	unsalted butter
2 tbsp	fresh parmesan cheese, grated
1 tbsp	chopped fresh sage
salt	

METHOD

ribs:

Preheat the oven to 350°F. Season the ribs with salt and pepper and dredge in flour, shaking off excess flour. Heat an oven-proof casserole with the oil and brown the ribs on all sides over a medium high heat, 4-5 minutes on each side. When brown, add the carrots and onions and cook for 5 minutes until the vegetables start to caramelize. Add the garlic, then 1 minute later add the chopped tomatoes, bay leaves, thyme, sage, coriander, stock, beer, and chile. Mix well. Cover tightly and place in the oven for two hours. Remove from the oven, take the ribs out of the stock and strain the cooking juices through a sieve into a bowl or pot. Discard the vegetables. Skim the fat off the surface of the braising juices and return the juices to the casserole. Return the ribs to the pan. Continue to cook on top of the stove slowly if the ribs are still tough (they should easily separate from the bone). Either cook with the lid on or off depending upon the quantity and thickness of your braising juices. You may want to reduce the amount of sauce until the correct consistency.

vegetables:

Preheat the oven to 325°F. Toss the potatoes, turnip, carrots, pearl onions and parsnips with the olive oil, and season with salt and pepper. Place on a sheet pan and roast for 45-60 minutes, or until tender.

creamy soft sage polenta:

Bring the water or chicken stock and milk to a strong simmer in a heavy saucepan. Add salt. 'Rain-in' the polenta, incorporating with a whisk to prevent lumps. Reduce the heat and stir with a wooden spoon. Cook the polenta for 10-15 minutes until it thickens. Stir in the butter, sage, and cheese. Serve immediately.

to serve:

Skim off any more fat from surface of the rib sauce. Spoon the polenta into a pasta bowl or rimmed dinner plate. Place a rib on top of the polenta. Arrange some of the vegetables in the bowl. Spoon the sauce over the vegetables and a little over the ribs.

Chef's tip:

The same basic procedure for the roasted vegetable preparations can be used to make an appealing Summer or Winter buffet or served dinner side dish. In Summer we use a combination of vegetables such as zucchini, eggplant, red and yellow peppers, chilis, garlic, shallots, fennel, cherry tomatoes and mushrooms; in Winter various root vegetables, squashes and fennel. Toss with plenty of fresh herbs and oil. Roast on a sheet pan in one layer but at a higher temperature, 425°F, for a shorter time 10-15 minutes. Remove from the oven and place the vegetables in a bowl. Cool at room temperature and toss with more herbs, a splash of balsamic or sherry vinegar and more extra virgin olive oil. Our guests love this!

For any leftover polenta, while it is still warm spread smoothly into a cake pan ⅜" to ½" thick. Chill. Cut into sticks or squares. Either dust the sections with flour and fry until crispy, 3-4 minutes each side, or oil and grill on the barbecue for 5 minutes on each side. Serve with a spicy tomato sauce or roasted red bell pepper sauce.

WARM PALISADE PEACH & BLACKBERRY COBBLER WITH CARAMEL PECAN ICE CREAM

BY CLYDE NELSON

At the ranch our guiding principle is 'always fresh from scratch'. Our cobbler is served warm right out of the oven and the ice cream is made that day. Palisade peaches are grown at high altitude in the intense Summer sun. They're the sweetest we've ever had.

Serves 4-6
Preparation time: 30 minutes
Cooking time: 20-45 minutes

Special equipment:
Ice cream machine

cobbler batter:

1 cup	all purpose flour
¾ tsp	baking powder
⅛ tsp	salt
¾ cup	granulated sugar
8 oz	unsalted butter, at room temperature
2	large eggs, at room temperature
1 tsp	vanilla extract

filling:

4-6	large ripe peaches
1-2 cups	blackberries
¾ cup	sugar
⅓ cup	flour
1 tbsp	cinnamon
2 oz	Bourbon whiskey

caramel pecan ice cream: (makes 1½ pt)

6	large egg yolks
⅔ cup	sugar
1 tbsp	water
1½ cups	milk
1½ cups	heavy cream
1 cup	pecans, chopped and toasted

METHOD

cobbler batter:

Sift together the flour, baking powder and salt; set aside. Cream together for several minutes the butter and sugar until light and fluffy. Add the eggs and vanilla and continue to mix until incorporated. Add the dry ingredients in batches to the butter mixture. Mix with a wooden spoon until just smooth. Set aside.

filling:

Preheat the oven to 350°F. Lightly butter six 8 oz ramekins or one 2 quart casserole dish.

Bring one 2 quart pot of water to a boil. Score an 'X' on the peach skin on the non-stem end. Plunge the peaches into boiling water for 30 seconds. Remove and plunge the peaches into ice water. Drain. Peel away the skin. Slice the peaches into ¼" sections. Toss together the sliced peaches and blackberries with the sugar, flour and cinnamon in a mixing bowl. Add the Bourbon. Spoon the filling into the ramekins or baking dish and top with the batter, spreading it evenly to cover. Bake the ramekins for 20-25 minutes or for the casserole dish 30-45 minutes or until browned, the cake set and the fruit bubbly. Let cool slightly before serving.

caramel pecan ice cream:

Combine the sugar with the water in a heavy bottomed pot over a medium heat. Heat the sugar until it turns dark amber in color and just begins to smoke. While the sugar is heating whip the egg yolks at high speed in the bowl of a countertop mixer until light. Stir the milk into the caramel sugar. Pour a third of the caramel into the egg yolks and let them continue to whip. Bring the rest of the caramel to a boil. Add the egg mixture and whisk over a medium heat until thick. Transfer to a bowl.

Pour the cream into the saucepan and stir with a rubber spatula, scraping any remaining caramel off the sides of the pan before it has a chance to harden. Add the cream to the egg mixture and let it cool. Freeze in an ice cream machine and add pecans just before it has finished freezing.

to serve:

Serve the cobbler with the ice cream.

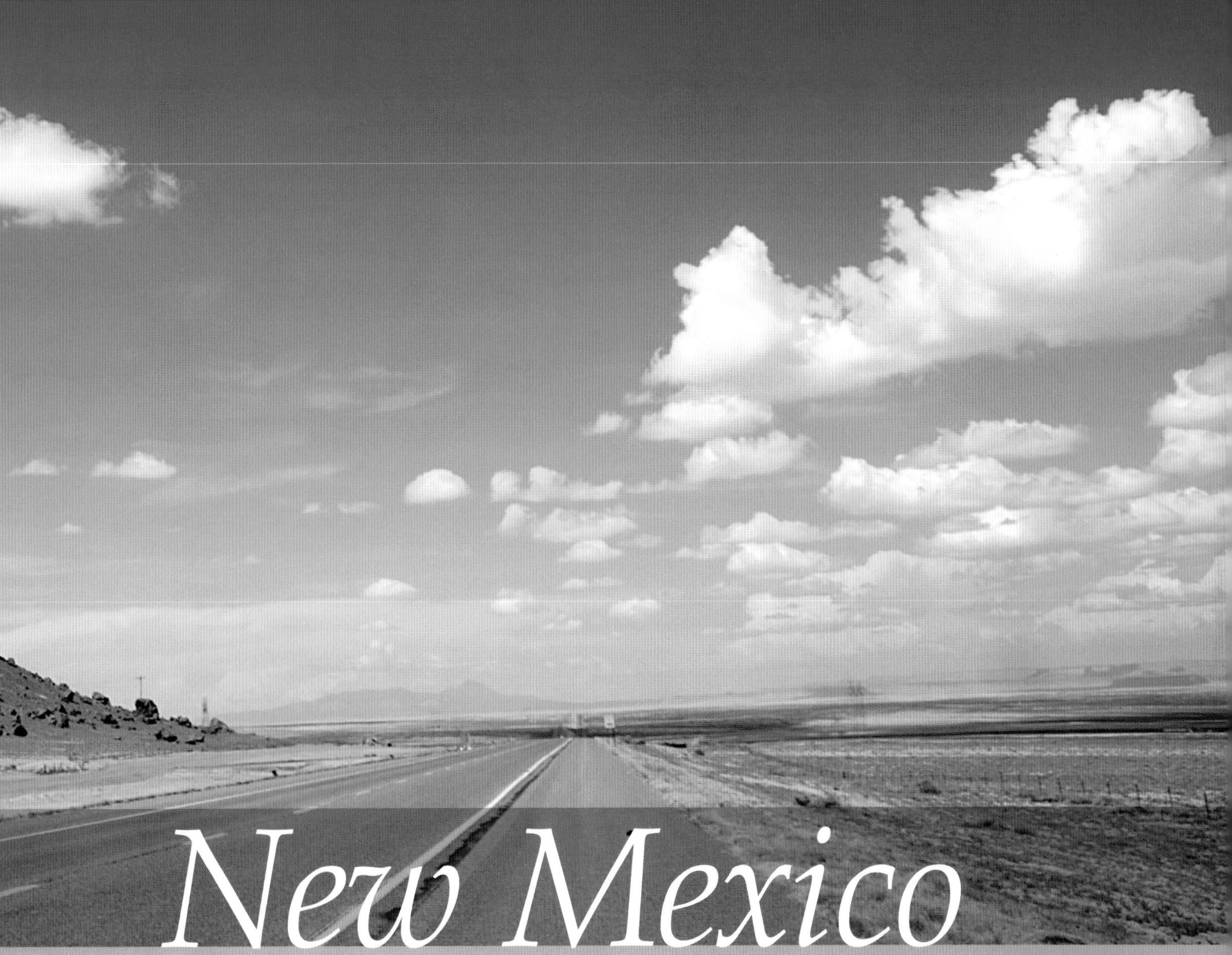

New Mexico

Journey along the famous Route 66 through New Mexico and reflect on the desert landscape before you as it makes its way to land of a different nature in this southern state.

New Mexico is a mix, with the north of the state a home to forest-life while the south is cactus central. Towns such as Santa Fe are home to art galleries and Spanish architecture, while those such as Roswell and Albuquerque offer a metropolitan dream. With a population mix of Hispanic, Mexican, Anglo and American Indian, New Mexico is teaming with cultural heritage. Indulge in the shade in one of the states many Catholic churches, or bask in the heat of one of New Mexico's chili dishes. Otherwise known as the 'Land of Enchantment' it is easy to see why this state has been given such a name.

Michael Roybal

Michael Roybal was born and raised in 'the land of enchantment', Santa Fe, New Mexico, a few doors away from the now famous Pink Adobe.

Michael began his career in the business early, at the age of 14, working as a porter at The Pink Adobe. Gaining hands-on experience, his passion grew as he studied, learned, applied and perfected techniques, mastering the positions of his fellow chefs.

Michael continued to work at several restaurants in the fast growing food mecca of Santa Fe, while he pursued a degree in Business Management. Michael decided to return to The Pink Adobe in 1980, joining forces with the legendary Rosalea Murphy, founder of The Pink Adobe.

Rosalea and Michael worked closely together defining a fusion of Cajun Creole and authentic Native American cuisine. Michael has collaborated on two Pink Adobe cookbooks; he has been featured in several publications and appeared on the Food Network.

Working closely with local farmers, ensuring the freshest ingredients, Michael Roybal continues to create a truly unique dining experience in Santa Fe, New Mexico.

The Inn of the Five Graces

Located in the historic district of Santa Fe, The Inn of the Five Graces combines luxury with an aura of mystery.

With an ethnic decor enhanced by East Indian and Tibetan antiques, oriental carpets and nomadic textiles combined with Southwest architecture, the interiors feature many handcrafted pieces as well as spectacular tile mosaics. Santa Fe is the second oldest town in the U.S. and is still very much influenced by its Indian and Spanish heritage. It possesses that true 'Pueblo' charm, with its narrow streets, patios and typical ochre-colored houses. It is above all a town of art and culture where you can also enjoy a private concert at the opera house or discover the works of numerous painters and sculptors. Passionate about this land with its wealth of Indian legends, the owners invite you to embark on a sensory voyage to fully savor this melting pot of cultures and colors. One of the possibilities: take lessons with a professional photographer and capture the incredible beauty of the landscapes.

Serves 4
Preparation time: 30 minutes
Cooking time: 30 minutes

Planning ahead:
Everything can be made a day ahead of time but I recommend slicing the beets, tomatoes and basil right before serving.

INGREDIENTS

2	heirloom tomatoes
2	large beets
1 tbsp	extra virgin olive oil

goat cheese:

5 oz	goat cheese
½ tsp	fresh lemon juice
1	green onion tops, thinly sliced
1	pinch of salt

Champagne vinaigrette:

⅓ cup	extra virgin olive oil
1 tbsp	Champagne vinegar
1 tsp	shallot, minced
1	pinch of salt

garnish:

4	basil leaves chiffonade (thinly sliced)

ROASTED BEET & HEIRLOOM TOMATO SALAD WITH GOAT CHEESE, CHAMPAGNE VINAIGRETTE & BASIL CHIFFONADE

BY MICHAEL ROYBAL

During Summer the local farmers' market is flourishing with beautiful produce bursting with flavors. This colorful salad, a Summer favorite, is proof of that.

METHOD

Preheat the oven to 400°F. Place the beets on a baking sheet, rub with olive oil and roast in the oven until just soft, about 30 minutes. Remove from the oven, allow to cool then peel and slice into ¼" slices. Also slice the tomatoes into ¼" slices.

goat cheese:
Combine all the ingredients and mix well.

Champagne vinaigrette:
Place all the ingredients in a medium bowl and whip until infused.

to serve:
Lay the heirloom tomatoes and roasted beet slices on chilled plates, alternating and overlapping them in a fan pattern, about three slices of each per serving. Place small dollops of goat cheese spread out over the beet and tomato slices, drizzle with the Champagne vinaigrette and garnish with the basil chiffonade.

STEAK DUNIGAN WITH SAUTEED MUSHROOMS, GREEN CHILI, BROCCOLINI & BUTTERNUT SQUASH

BY MICHAEL ROYBAL

This meat dish has been a classic at The Pink Adobe for over 20 years, it's timeless and everybody loves it.

Serves 4
Preparation time: 1 hour
Cooking time: 30 minutes for the chili and 10-20 minutes for the steaks depends on desired temperature.

Special equipment:
Grill or broiler

Planning ahead:
The green chili can be made a day ahead of time and reheated before serving.

INGREDIENTS

steaks:

4	New York steaks, 10 oz each
4 tbsp	charcrust (hickory smoked rub)

green chili sauce:

16 oz	green chili roasted, peeled and chopped
¼ cup	yellow onion, chopped
½ tbsp	butter
⅓ cup	tomatoes, diced
½ tsp	garlic, minced
½ tsp	cilantro, chopped
¼ tsp	ground oregano
¼ tsp	ground cumin
½ tsp	salt

sautéed vegetables:

8 oz	broccolini
8 oz	butternut squash
1 tbsp	blended oil
1 tsp	garlic, minced
salt & pepper	

sautéed mushrooms:

2 cups	sliced mushrooms
2 tbsp	butter
2 tbsp	fresh lemon juice

METHOD

green chili sauce:

In a medium saucepan, cook the onion over a medium heat until transparent. Add the garlic and cook until fragrant, about 30 seconds. Add the remaining ingredients, mix well and simmer for 15 minutes. Keep warm until ready to serve.

sautéed vegetables:

Preheat the oven to 400°F. Peel the butternut squash and cut in half vertically, clean out the insides and cut into 1" cubes. Place on a baking sheet, wet with oil and roast in the oven until just soft, 10-15 minutes. Remove from the oven and cool.

Place the broccolini in boiling water for 1 minute, then into an ice bath for 1 minute. Cool. Remove from the bath and drain.

While the steaks are grilling, sauté the vegetables in a pan with oil until just hot, add the garlic and cook for 1 minute more.

sautéed mushrooms:

While the steaks are grilling, sauté the mushrooms in a fry pan with butter over a medium heat until the mushrooms are soft. Turn off the heat and stir in the lemon juice.

to serve:

Preheat the grill. Rub both sides of the steaks with the charcrust. Grill or broil the steaks to the desired temperature, turning once. Spoon the sauce on to plates as a bed for the steak. Add the steak and top with the sautéed mushrooms. Place the other vegetables next to the steak.

TRES LECHES CAKE WITH DULCE DE LECHE, KAHLUA & OAXACAN MOCHA CHOCOLATE

BY MICHAEL ROYBAL

This timeless rich dessert has a special creminess that just melts in the mouth. Sweet and delicious, what more could you want?

Serves 4
Preparation time: 15 minutes
Cooking time: 1 hour and 2 hours 30 minutes for dulce de leche

Special equipment:
8" x 8" baking pan or can be made in a muffin pan

Planning ahead:
The tres leches cake and dulce de leche can be made the day before.

INGREDIENTS

cake:

¾ cup	all purpose flour
½ tsp	baking powder
¼ cup	unsalted butter
½ cup	white sugar
3	eggs
¼ tsp	vanilla extract

tres leches:

1 cup	whole milk
7 oz	sweetened condensed milk
6 oz	evaporated milk

whipped cream:

¾ cup	heavy cream
¼ cup	sugar
½ tsp	vanilla extract

dulce de leche:

4 oz	sweetened condensed milk

garnish:

2 tbsp	kahlua
2 tsp	oaxacan chocolate shavings
4	raspberries
mint leaves	

METHOD

cake:

Preheat the oven to 350°F. Sift the flour and baking powder together and set aside. Cream the butter and sugar together until fluffy. Add the eggs and the vanilla extract, and beat well. Add the flour mixture to the butter mixture and mix until well blended. To prepare the pan, smear with butter and then coat with flour, discarding any excess. Pour the batter into a prepared pan, cook for 30 minutes, remove from the oven and pierce the cake several times with a fork, then allow to cool.

tres leches:

Combine the whole milk, condensed milk, and evaporated milk, mix well, pour over the cooled cake and allow to soak in.

whipped cream:

In a medium mixing bowl combine the cream, sugar and vanilla extract. Whip on high with a hand mixer until whipped firm.

dulce de leche:

Place the condensed milk in a small double boiler and boil on low, stirring occasionally until it becomes a caramel color, about 2 hours. Allow to cool to room temperature.

to serve:

Portion the cake. 'Scribble' the plates with the dulce de leche. Spoon the kahlua on the center of the plate. Place the cake on the kahlua, and top with cream whipped with the sugar and vanilla extract. Finish with the shaved chocolate and garnish with raspberries and mint leaves.

Texas

Austin, Houston and Dallas, each of these cities is synonymous with Texas – The Lone Star State. Proudly independent, Texas's spirit remains strong, after all it is the largest state in the US after Alaska.

The state's prairies, swamps, cities and woods offer no shortage of sights, with views such as the El Capitain peak, grazing Long Horn cattle and the state's famous oil wells. Texas' State Fair brings in the crowds from miles around, while Austin hosts more music venues than anywhere else in the States. Whether it's a cattle drive, cowboy demonstration or even taking in a football game, Texas is the place to be. Wind down with Texas' smooth blend of Southern style and revel in the influence of this mighty state.

Jason Robinson
Grand Chef Relais & Châteaux

In addition to its perfect union of 300 acres of rich Texas soil and a temperate climate, The Inn at Dos Brisas boasts a passionate commitment to sustainable farming and to the personalities behind the finest produce. The individual who most sets it apart from the growing trend of farm-to-table is Grand Chef Jason Robinson, who literally walks the refined, simple but sophisticated, seasonal ingredients from his organic garden to the table.

"When I told my dad I wanted to go to culinary school, he wisely suggested I get a job in a restaurant kitchen first," Jason recalls. Before long, he found himself manning the grill at the Fog City Diner in Las Vegas and assisted in the opening of the Chicago Fog City Diner. Jason then moved to Tru, followed by Goodfellas.

Jason went on to join Doug Bosch, a true Texan who owns Dos Brisas. To experience a dish by Jason fashioned in the spirit of the sustainable agricultural movement is one of the most memorable moments to be had at The Inn at Dos Brisas.

The Inn at Dos Brisas

Live the life of a wrangler, surrounded by horses and vistas of rolling hills at this elegant ranch deep in the Texas countryside.

You stay in one of only four private casitas within the 120 hectares of this ecological property with its elegant interiors featuring leather and silky fabrics. You can enjoy unforgettable treks on horseback, and the land supplies fresh produce for the talented Grand Chef Jason Robinson. The extraordinary breakfasts are the moment to plan your day and it's a tough choice between swimming in the pool, organic gardening lessons, trap shooting, treks, therapeutic treatments, fly fishing and all of the other activities of a gentleman-farmer.

WAGYU SHORT RIB CARPACCIO, HORSERADISH CHANTILLY, SOURDOUGH CROSTINI

BY JASON ROBINSON

This is pure Texas raised beef, the short rib is seared on the outside and cut really thin for high flavor. Wagyu is really high in Omega 3 and is really good for you while the marble texture of the beef just melts in the mouth.

Serves 4-6
Preparation time: 1 hour
Cooking time: 5-10 minutes

INGREDIENTS

Wagyu carpaccio short rib:

1 lb boneless Wagyu short rib, trimmed and cleaned
fleur de sel
cracked pepper

horseradish chantilly:

½ cup heavy whipping cream
2 tsp crème fraîche
salt & pepper, to taste

Worcestershire gastrique:

½ cup Worcestershire sauce
¼ cup honey
2 tbsp red wine vinegar

sourdough crostini:

1 loaf of sourdough bread
¼ cup extra virgin olive oil
salt & pepper, to taste

fried leeks:

½ cup leeks, julienne of white and light green parts only
2 cups frying oil
salt, to season

garnish:

gherkin pickles
fresh chervil

METHOD

Wagyu short rib carpaccio:

In a sauté pan over a high heat sear the short rib on all sides. Remove from the pan. Using a sharp slicing knife slice as thinly as possible approximately nine slices per person.

horseradish chantilly:

Combine all the ingredients in a bowl and whip with a whisk until stiff peaks form. Season with salt and pepper to taste.

Worcestershire gastrique:

Combine all the ingredients and reduce in a small pan over a low heat by 75% until it is a thick like syrup. Cool and reserve

sourdough crostini:

Preheat the oven to 400°F. Slice the sourdough into thin slices, approximately five to seven slices per person. Brush with olive oil. Season with salt and pepper to taste. Bake for 5-7 minutes until golden brown and crisp.

fried leeks:

Heat the oil to 250°F. Fry the leeks until light golden brown and crisp. Season with salt to taste.

to serve:

Place the sliced beef in a shingle formation on a plate. Season with fleur de sel and cracked pepper. Add dollops of chantilly, and a spoonful each of the gastrique, crostini and fried leeks. Garnish with the gherkins and chervil.

MAINE LOBSTER, SWEET PEA PUREE, POTATO FONDANT, VANILLA GRAPEFRUIT BEURRE BLANC

BY JASON ROBINSON

Spring inspired this dish, Texas is known for its ruby red grapefruits hence why we included it, while the pea gives sweetness and texture and the butter adds a beautiful richness – perfect for lobster.

Serves 4-6
Preparation time: 90 minutes
Cooking time: 5-15 minutes

Special equipment:
Blender

INGREDIENTS

lobster:

4–6	Maine Lobsters, 1½ lb each
½ cup	onions, chopped
½ cup	celery, chopped
½ cup	carrot, chopped
2 tbsp	thyme
2 tbsp	black peppercorns
1 cup	white wine
12 cups	water

pea purée:

1 cup	English peas out of the shell (frozen peas are fine if fresh ones are not available)

salt & pepper, to taste

potato fondant:

1 lb	Fingerling potatoes, peeled into little football shapes
2 tbsp	vegetable oil
2 tbsp	butter
1	clove garlic, smashed

grapefruit reduction:

2 cups	ruby red grapefruit juice
½ cup	sugar
1	vanilla bean, split

vanilla grapefruit beurre blanc:

2	shallots
1 tsp	thyme
1	vanilla bean
½ cup	white wine
½ cup	ruby red grapefruit juice
1 lb	butter

salt & pepper

METHOD

lobsters:

Sweat the mirepoix (onions, celery, carrots) over a low heat in a stock pot. Add the thyme, and peppercorns to bloom in the heat of the pan. Deglaze with the white wine and reduce until almost dry. Cover with water and bring to a boil. Tear the claws and tail off the lobster bodies. Place the claws in the boiling liquid for 5 minutes. Add the tails and continue cooking for 5 more minutes. Remove from the liquid and crack out of the shells.

sweet pea purée:

Boil the peas in lightly salted water until tender. Blend on high until smooth. Salt and pepper to taste.

potato fondant:

Over a medium heat in a large sauté pan, add the oil and potatoes and cook to a golden brown color. Strain off the oil. Add the garlic and butter, reduce the heat to low and cook until tender.

vanilla grapefruit reduction:

Reduce the grapefruit juice, sugar and vanilla over a low heat for approximately 15 minutes to a syrup like consistency.

vanilla grapefruit beurre blanc:

In a medium saucepan over a low heat, combine the shallots, thyme, white wine, vanilla bean and grapefruit juice and reduce until almost dry. Slowly whisk in the butter over a low heat and strain through a fine sieve. Season with salt and pepper to taste.

to serve:

Place a large spoon of pea purée in the center of the plate. Place the potatoes around the edge of the purée. Place the lobster on top. Finish with some beurre blanc and grapefruit reduction. Garnish with flowering pea tendrils.

NOT YOUR MAMMA'S RICE PUDDING

BY JASON ROBINSON

This dish was inspired by ingredients from the garden, we were experimenting in the kitchen and I wanted to make a dish where the rice pudding flavor is an emulsion flavor with beautiful roasted pineapple for color, rather than the typical type of rice pudding that your mother used to give you.

Serves 4-6
Preparation time: 1 hour
Cooking time: 3-4 hours

Special equipment:
Ice cream machine

INGREDIENTS

roasted pineapple:

1	pineapple, green removed, skin on
¼ cup	olive oil
salt	

beet ice cream:

2	large red beets, cooked and sliced
1 cup	heavy cream
1 cup	milk
1 tsp	lavender blossoms
4	egg yolks
⅓ cup	sugar

rice pudding emulsion:

¼ cup	Jasmine rice
¼ cup	sugar
1	pinch of salt
1 cup	whole milk
½	vanilla bean
½ cup	half & half

lavender sugar cookie:

1 cup	all purpose flour
¼ tsp	baking powder
1	pinch of salt
⅓ cup	butter
⅓ cup	sugar
1	egg
1 tbsp	milk
1 tsp	lavender blossoms
sugar, to sprinkle on top	

garnish:

micro cilantro leaves

METHOD

roasted pineapple:

Preheat the oven to 275°F. Toss the pineapple in olive oil and salt. Cover and roast for 3-4 hours in the oven until soft. Uncover and refrigerate for 1 hour. Remove the skin and core, then set aside.

beet ice cream:

Bring the beets, cream, milk and lavender blossoms to a boil and infuse for 30 minutes. Strain off the beets and return the liquid to a boil. Temper the yolks and sugar into the cream and cook until the mixture thickens. Strain through a fine sieve and cool in an ice bath. Spin in an ice cream machine.

rice pudding emulsion:

Combine the first 5 ingredients in a saucepan on a medium heat until the rice is cooked, making sure to stir frequently. Transfer into a blender and blend until the rice is no longer visible. Strain through a fine sieve, add the half & half and refrigerate until needed.

lavender sugar cookies:

Heat the milk and infuse the lavender blossoms for 15-20 minutes. Combine the flour, baking powder and salt, and sift. Using a mixer with a paddle attachment mix the butter and sugar until creamy. Add the egg, then add the dry ingredients. Strain the milk and add. Wrap the bowl and refrigerate for one hour.

Preheat the oven to 350°F. Roll out on a floured surface and cut out circles 1½" in diameter. Sprinkle sugar on top and bake for 8-10 minutes until golden brown.

to serve:

Slice five thin pieces of pineapple and lay out on the left side of the plate. Place a lavender sugar cookie on the right side and place a scoop of beet ice cream directly on top. Froth the rice pudding emulsion and spoon around the plate. Garnish with the micro cilantro leaves.

Chad Martin

Chad Martin joined the elegant Hotel St. Germain in 2000 as Sous Chef to the then Executive Chef Sharon Hage. Martin accepted the Executive Chef position in 2001. During his tenure, the dining room at Hotel St. Germain has been awarded Five Stars for both Food and Service by the *Dallas Morning News*, which said, "nothing we put in our mouths – not a bite, not a spoonful – was less than exquisite ... an unbroken arc of old-world hospitality and charm". The Dining Room has been named "The Most Romantic Restaurant" in Dallas by *Gourmet* magazine.

Martin began his culinary career studying at The Culinary Institute in Dallas. After three years at The Adolphus Hotel's French Room he moved to New York to perfect his techniques in French cuisine at the famous Café Boulud where he worked under Chef Andrew Carmellini.

Martin's skill and technique in French cuisine plus his attention to every detail and his artist's eye are evident in his menu at Hotel St. Germain.

Hôtel St Germain

Recently classified as a historical landmark, Hôtel St Germain was built in 1906 as a private residence for a prominent local family.

Truly a cosmopolitan retreat, Hotel St Germain is merely steps away from the bustle of the Dallas Center for the Performing Arts, the Winspear Opera House and Meyerson Symphony Center. It has the sumptuous allure of a French hotel with exceptional old world service, thoroughly modern amenities and memorable fine dining. The gracefully appointed interiors combine to evoke the haunting, exotic beauty of 19th century New Orleans. Hôtel St Germain is a true European urban sanctuary, which offers a unique destination experience, where fine dining and the art of gracious living are celebrated and are a personal reflection of the proprietors' French heritage.

Serves 4-6
Preparation time: 1 hour
Cooking time: 15 minutes

Special equipment:
Two different-sized silver bowls, 2 pairs of shellfish pliers, oyster knife, clam knife

Planning ahead:
Purchase the seafood fresh, on the day of serving. Serve with cocktail sauce, remoulade, mignonette, and lemon wedges

INGREDIENTS

1	lobster, 2 lb
12	littleneck clams
12	fresh oysters
1 lb	fresh shrimps, large
3	lemons
2 qt	water
1 cup	celery, chopped (reserve the leaves for garnish)
½ cup	onion, chopped
2 tbsp	Old Bay seasoning
salt	

CHILLED SEAFOOD DISPLAY

BY CHAD MARTIN

This is a popular dish that is usually served to a small intimate group of guests in our New Orleans-themed courtyard, while sipping on Champagne.

METHOD

Bring salted water, celery, onion, Old Bay seasoning and juice of one lemon to a boil and cook for 5 minutes. Poach the shrimps in seasoned water for 4 minutes, remove and chill. Return the seasoned water to a boil and poach the lobster for 7 minutes, remove and chill. Open the oysters and clams and chill on ice. Cut one lemon into wedges for serving and the remaining lemon in half for garnish.

Once chilled, peel the poached shrimps and separate the lobster tail and claws/knuckles from the body. Split the tail in half lengthwise and then into half across for four equal portions.

to serve:
Fill both of the silver bowls with crushed ice and place the smaller one atop the larger bowl. Arrange the oysters, clams, and lobster pieces on the ice and line the edge of the bowl with the shrimps. Place the shellfish pliers in the ice for cracking the lobster claws and knuckles.

Chef's tips:
When purchasing seafood, ask your local seafood attendant for a bag of crushed ice for presentation. Provide plenty of linen napkins or paper towels for your guests, and even offer wet towels to clean with.

ROASTED LAMB CHOPS WITH EGGPLANT-CHIPOTLE BREAD PUDDING, BACON-WRAPPED FRENCH BEANS, CREOLE MUSTARD GLACE DE VIANDE

BY CHAD MARTIN

Lamb (or lamb chops) is an everyday item found on the menu at Hôtel St Germain. The accompaniments change seasonally.

Serves 4
Preparation time: 1 hour 30 minutes
Cooking time: 30-40 minutes

Planning ahead:
For the bread pudding tear apart and dry the bread on a counter-top a day ahead.

INGREDIENTS

roasted lamb chops:

1	2 lb lamb rack, julienne
1 tsp	thyme, chopped
1 tsp	rosemary, chopped
salt & freshly cracked pepper	
2 tbsp	olive oil
1	clove garlic

bacon-wrapped French beans:

8 oz	French beans, yellow or green
4	slices of smoked bacon
1 tbsp	olive oil
1 qt	water
salt & pepper	

eggplant and chipotle pepper bread pudding with Texas ricotta:

3 cups	dry French loaf, crusts removed, torn into bite-sized pieces
1 tbsp	unsalted butter
1 tbsp	olive oil
1	shallot, minced
1	clove garlic, minced
2 tbsp	celery, brunoise
1	small purple eggplant, peeled, cut into 1" dice
2	canned chipotle peppers in adobe sauce, seeds removed and diced
½ cup	heavy whipping cream
1 cup	chicken stock or canned broth
1	egg
1 tsp	fresh basil, chiffonade or chopped
½ tsp	cumin powder
2 tbsp	ricotta cheese

creole mustard glace de viande:

2 cups	veal stock
1 cup	red wine
1 tbsp	creole mustard

garnish:

basil leaves

METHOD

roasted lamb chops:

Preheat the oven to 350°F. Season the lamb rack on all sides with salt and pepper, then set aside. Heat the oil in a heavy-bottomed skillet on a medium-high heat until it just begins to smoke. Sear the lamb rack in hot oil on all sides until a nice brown crust forms, add the garlic clove to the pan and swirl for one minute before you remove the lamb. Remove the lamb rack from the pan, allow to cool to the touch and rub the chopped thyme and rosemary into the skin. Place the lamb in the oven and cook to the desired temperature, approximately 8 minutes for medium rare. Remove the lamb from the oven and allow to rest for 5 minutes before slicing.

bacon-wrapped French beans:

Bring the water to a boil with 1 teaspoon of salt. Have ready a bowl of ice water to cool the beans. Blanch them in boiling salted water for 2 minutes, and immediately shock in ice water to cool. Remove the beans from the water and dry with a towel. Separate into four equal bunches and wrap each bundle with a strip of bacon. Heat the oil in a skillet over a medium heat and cook the bacon-wrapped beans on all sides until the bacon is crispy. Season with salt and pepper.

eggplant and chipotle pepper bread pudding with Texas ricotta:

Preheat the oven to 350°F. Place the dried bread cubes into a bowl, large enough for mixing the remaining ingredients. Butter a small glazed earthenware dish and set aside. In a heavy-bottomed skillet, heat the butter and olive oil over a medium-high heat until the butter begins to foam. Add the shallot, garlic, and celery to the pan and sauté until translucent. Add the chunks of eggplant and cook until they begin to caramelize, stirring frequently. Add the chipotle to the eggplant mixture, followed by the cream and chicken stock. Turn the heat off and whisk in the egg. Pour the mixture over the bread pieces and mix together with basil and cumin. Season with salt and pepper and fold in the ricotta cheese. Pour the final mixture into a buttered dish and bake in the oven until browned on top. Cool briefly.

creole mustard glace de viande:

Heat the red wine in a 1 quart saucepan over a medium-high heat until reduced by a quarter. Add the veal stock and reduce to 1 cup and until it coats the back of a spoon. Whisk in the creole mustard.

to serve:

Fry the basil leaves in hot oil until they stop popping (stand back!) and remove with a slotted spoon. Place hot eggplant bread pudding in the center of the plate. Slice the lamb chops between the ribs and cross two chops on the plate, leaning against the bread pudding. Lean a bundle of beans against the bread pudding and spoon the creole mustard in front of the lamb chops. Garnish with the fried basil.

Chef's tip:

Cool the bread pudding overnight, unmold, and cut into triangles or other desired shapes before reheating and serving. Add smoked shredded chicken to the mixture and enjoy as a full meal.

Serves 12
Preparation time: 2 hours 30 minutes
Cooking time: 1 hour

Special equipment:
Three 9" round cake pans buttered and floured and lined on the bottom with parchment paper, candy thermometer

Planning ahead:
Make the cake one day ahead of time, wrap and cool for easier slicing without tearing.

DOBERGE CAKE

BY CHAD MARTIN

An elegant dessert brought originally to New Orleans from Europe, the Doberge Cake is available at Hôtel St Germain for any special occasion, either in the hotel or in the guest's home. It is often the choice for luncheons, teas, bridal showers, and even small weddings.

INGREDIENTS

vanilla cake:

2 cups cake flour
1 ¾ cup all purpose flour
2½ tsp baking powder
1 cup unsalted butter, semi-softened
3 cups granulated sugar
¾ tsp salt
1 tbsp pure vanilla extract
1 cup egg whites (reserve the yolks for the buttercream, below)
1½ cups milk

buttercream:

3 cups sugar
12 egg yolks
2 lb unsalted Butter, semi-softened
2 tsp pure vanilla extract
1 tsp almond extract
1 tbsp lemon, zest
1 cup water

chocolate ganache:

3 cups bittersweet chocolate, chopped or pistols (coin shapes)
3 cups heavy cream
1 tbsp corn syrup

garnish:

raspberries, or edible flowers

METHOD

vanilla cake:

Preheat the oven to 350°F. In a large bowl sift the flours together with the baking powder, then set aside. In the bowl of a standing mixer, cream the butter and sugar with the mixing paddle until light and fluffy, then incorporate the salt and vanilla extract. Turn the mixer to low and gradually add the egg whites until incorporated. Alternately add the milk and the flours a little at a time until incorporated and continue to mix for another 30 seconds. Divide the mixture among the three prepared pans and bake in the oven for approximately 45 minutes or until a toothpick inserted comes out clean. Allow the cakes to cool on a wire rack in the pans before inverting them and cooling them overnight in a refrigerator. Once cool, slice each cake horizontally into three layers, totaling nine layers.

buttercream:

In a heavy-bottomed saucepan, add the water and the sugar, then cook over a medium-high heat until the temperature reaches 240°F on a candy thermometer. Meanwhile, place the egg yolks in the bowl of a standing mixer and whip on high speed until light and fluffy. Lower the speed of the mixer to medium and slowly drizzle the hot sugar-syrup into the yolks. Continue to whip the egg-sugar mixture on a medium speed until it is cool. Begin whipping the butter into the egg mixture a chunk at a time until it is all incorporated and the buttercream has thickened and has body (sometimes you must refrigerate the entire mixture, in the bowl, and allow to cool more before continuing to mix and emulsifying begins). Incorporate the vanilla and almond extracts and zest.

chocolate ganache:

Place the chocolate in a large stainless steel bowl. In a heavy-bottomed saucepan, heat the cream until it begins to simmer around the edges. Pour over the chocolate and allow to sit for a few minutes. Whisk the chocolate and cream together until smooth and then incorporate the corn syrup. Keep in a warm place to prevent solidifying.

to serve:

Begin with a layer of cake that came from the bottom of one of the cake pans (this will ensure a flat and level bottom for the cake). Spread an even layer of buttercream over the layer and continue with the remaining layers (it is important to make sure that every layer matches up all the way around the edges for a nice sharp edge).The top layer should again be one of the three bottoms of cake taken from the pans, flat side up. Spread the remainder of the buttercream around the sides of the cake and smooth out as much as possible. Refrigerate the cake on a wire rack until the buttercream hardens, about 30 minutes. Remove the cake from the refrigerator and pour the ganache over the top of the cake. Allow to pour down the sides using a hot spatula to smooth it out. Cool the cake again and repeat with another layer of ganache. Cool, garnish as desired, and bring to room temperature before slicing and serving.

Eastern Canada

With its French influence it is no surprise that Eastern Canada is famed for its quaint, peaceful lifestyle and authentic European architecture.

Eastern Canada is also home to the legendary Niagara Falls – a sight to behold as over 4 million cubic feet of water pass over the edge. While the Hudson Bay is home to many a polar bear, the villages around the area are sparse but Eastern Canada offers many other areas to visit. With provinces such as New Brunswick, Ontario, Québec and Nova Scotia there is no shortage of culinary destinations to visit. Peaches and cheeses are local foods of choice, and there is always elk if you prefer something a little more exciting.

Jonathan Gushue
Grand Chef Relais & Châteaux

Jonathan Gushue, Executive Chef of Langdon Hall, is no stranger to working in an award-winning environment.

Jonathan trained at Georgian College, and after schooling he took his culinary skills worldwide, with stints in Japan and London. In 1988 he returned to Canada and his hometown of St. John's, where he became Sous Chef at The Fairmont Newfoundland Hotel. He then moved to Vancouver, where he was able to refine his skills with Sous Chef positions at the Wedgewood Hotel and then the Four Seasons.

Jonathan has been at Langdon Hall since November 2005 and has a passion for French-inspired cuisine. His creativity at Langdon Hall comes from the surrounding rich farmland, which provides both inspiration and rich ingredients. He incorporates the region's deep Mennonite heritage into his cooking, while experimenting with traditional specialties such as hams, sausages, and double-smoked bacon alongside fresh-picked local corn, peaches, cherries and other seasonal produce. Right at his doorstep are local farmers and a network of artisan producers in addition to Langdon's own vegetable garden.

Langdon Hall

Country House Hotel & Spa

Just an hour and a half drive from Toronto and the Niagara area, this is the address for those who love beauty. Epicurean and romantic are the best words to describe Langdon Hall.

Romantic with its gracious interiors of warm tones, silky fabrics and wood panelling detail, its tranquil grounds and gardens, where one can sit under a century old elm tree sipping fine wine or relax by the lily pond reflecting the elegant lines of the manor. And epicurean with its exceptional cuisine. In the kitchen, every detail counts for young Chef Jonathan Gushue, who even makes his own butter and, as a result, each meal is an unforgettable moment. As a devotee of French cuisine, his favourite ingredients include truffles, foie gras, frogs' legs, snails and artisanal cheeses all of which he turns into sophisticated compositions that match the elegance of the setting. For added relaxation, the spa offers the very best in body and beauty therapies.

Serves 6
Preparation time: 45 minutes
Cooking time: 20 minutes

Planning ahead:
The stock can be prepared a day in advance.

INGREDIENTS

lobsters:

6	lobsters
8 oz	unsalted butter, cut into pieces
1	sprig of thyme
3	shallots, minced
1 pt	white wine
1	clove garlic, crushed
1 tsp	coriander seeds, crushed
salt	

lobster stock:

6	lobster bodies
1	onion, chopped
1	celery stick, chopped
1	garlic bulb, split
1 pt	white wine
1 tbsp	sugar
1	lemon, sliced
1 tsp	coriander seeds
10	black peppercorns

apple purée:

1 tbsp	butter
3	Warsaw apples, peeled, seeded and diced
1	pinch fleur de sel
1	vanilla bean, split
1 tsp	ground black pepper
salt	

boulanger potato:

1 pt	lobster stock (see recipe below)
3 tbsp	butter
1	sprig of thyme
salt & pepper	
18	1-2" barrels cut from a Roseval potato
18	double smoked bacon lardons
18	baby red onions

gem lettuce emulsion

1 tbsp	butter
3	shallots, sliced
1½ oz	ginger, julienned
2	cloves garlic, sliced
2½ oz	double smoked bacon, minced
1 pt	white wine
1 pt	35% cream
3½ oz	sea scallop or trim, not abductor, mussels
2	heads of baby gem lettuce or romaine hearts, cut into chiffonade

BUTTER BRAISED NEWFOUNDLAND LOBSTER

BY JONATHAN GUSHUE

Being from Newfoundland I always want to have a lobster dish on our menu when available. The lobster from the Grand banks of Newfoundland is so sweet due to the frigid waters. That sweetness provides a unique strength that allows lobster to lend itself to many varying flavors.

METHOD

lobsters:

Cook the lobsters in boiling salted water for 3 minutes and refresh in salted ice water. While the lobsters are cooling you can start your butter baste. Combine the wine, coriander seeds, thyme and shallots in a suitable saucepan and reduce by one-third. Pull from the heat and stir in the butter piece by piece until totally combined. Season with a pinch of salt. Transfer to a heat proof container and wrap with plastic wrap to prevent a skin forming. Store in a warm place until needed. Remove each lobster from its shell, reserving the bodies for the stock. Cover and refrigerate until needed.

lobster stock:

Combine all the ingredients in a pot and just cover with water. Add a pinch of salt and bring to the boil. Simmer for 20 minutes and set aside to cool without straining. Ideally strain the next day after refrigerating, but the stock may be strained after 2 hours. Freeze what you do not need.

apple purée

Foam the butter in a pan and add to it the apples, fleur de sel and split vanilla bean. Cover and set the burner to the lowest setting. Simmer for 12 minutes. Set aside to cool for 5 minutes. Remove the vanilla bean and blend to a smooth purée. Season with salt and pepper.

boulanger potato:

Add the butter, and thyme to the lobster stock. Season with salt and pepper. Bring to a simmer and add the potato barrels. Cook for 5 minutes from the boil. Remove from the stock and let cool. To the same stock-butter emulsion add the baby onions and simmer for 12 minutes. After 8 minutes add the bacon. When the onions are soft remove from the heat and allow to cool in the liquid. Reserve the liquid to reheat the boulanger.

gem lettuce emulsion:

Foam the butter and add the shallots, ginger, garlic and bacon. Sauté on a low heat without color for 5 minutes. Add the white wine and reduce by two-thirds. Add the cream and bring to a boil. Pull from the heat and, working in batches while still very hot, start adding the scallops and lettuce a little by little. Push this mixture through a fine mesh sieve.

to serve:

To finish warm the lobster in the butter baste over a low heat. While waiting for your lobster, you can separately warm the purée, boulanger and the gem lettuce emulsion. Check for seasoning. Remove the lobster and potato boulanger from their stocks, drain and place around a shallow plate. Enliven the gem lettuce emulsion with a couple of pulses of a hand blender then add to the plate with the purée as shown.

PIGEON & FOIE GRAS A LA PRESSE

BY JONATHAN GUSHUE

This dish is a tip of the hat to our local farms and farmers. There are so many great producers of heirloom vegetables and outstanding poultry in our area it is hard to just focus on a couple.

Serves 4
Preparation time: 1 hour
Cooking time: 2 hours

Special equipment
Sous vide machine (optional), blender

Planning ahead
The pigeon/foie gras and pickled shallots need to be made 1 day in advance.

INGREDIENTS

pigeon and foie gras:

2 squab pigeons
9 oz foie gras, split on the width
2 tbsp duck fat
1 tbsp truffle oil
1 tbsp cognac
1 tbsp Madeira
salt & pepper

pickled shallots:

2 shallots, sliced to ⅛"
3½ fl oz red wine vinegar
1 fl oz honey

confit legs:

4 pigeon legs, from above
1 tbsp kosher salt
2 cloves garlic
2 sprigs of thyme
2 star anise
½ pt duck fat

pumpkin purée:

½ sugar pumpkin
2 tbsp olive oil
2 cloves garlic, crushed
3½ oz Idiazábal cheese, grated
3 tbsp butter, unsalted
salt & pepper

pigeon jus:

2 pigeon carcasses
1 tbsp olive oil
2 shallots, sliced
3 cups chicken stock
1 star anise
2 cloves garlic, crushed

leeks:

2 King Richard leeks, cut into barrels, white only
2 tbsp butter, unsalted
1 pinch sugar
1 pinch kosher salt
3½ fl oz white wine

cromesqui:

1 large shallot, minced
4 oz minced chicken breast
meat from confit legs (see recipe below)
1 tsp cepe powder
2 oz cooked foie gras trim, minced
1 oz bacon slab, minced
2 tsp thyme leaves
1 tsp coriander seeds, cracked
1 clove garlic, minced
2 tbsp veal jus
1 tbsp Madeira
1 tbsp butter
salt & pepper

cromesqui breading:

1 egg, beaten
1 tbsp olive oil
3 oz all purpose flour
5oz dried breadcrumbs
2 tbsp parmesan cheese, grated
oil for frying

ice wine vinaigrette au jus:

1½ fl oz ice wine
1 fl oz extra virgin olive oil
1 tbsp banyuls vinegar
1½ fl oz reduced pigeon jus (see recipe below)
1 tsp truffle oil

METHOD

pigeon and foie gras:

Remove the breasts from the pigeons, skin and set aside. Do the same with the legs and chop the carcasses for the pigeon jus. Marinate the breasts with half of the quantity each of the duck fat, truffle oil, Madeira and cognac. Season with salt and pepper. Marinate the foie gras the same way. Wrap and refrigerate.

Sandwich the foie gras between two pigeon breasts. Wrap both of the sandwiches tightly in plastic wrap and place in the fridge to set. It is best to sous vide the breasts on the highest setting. In lieu of a sous vide machine wrap tightly in plastic once more and square with three pieces of twine. Poach in 65°C/150°F water for 75 minutes. Let cool in the liquid and place in the fridge overnight or for 12 hours.

pickled shallots:

Bring the vinegar and honey up to a boil and add the shallots. When you notice even the slightest shimmer or shimmering of the sides remove the shallots from the liquid and cool. Then combine the two again (best done the day before).

confit legs:

Dress the legs with the salt, garlic, thyme and star anise. Allow to marinate for three hours. Wipe off the salt and confit in the fat for 1-1 hour 30 minutes or until soft. Allow to cool in the fat for optimal flavor. Pick the meat from the bone, shred and set aside.

pumpkin purée:

Rub the pumpkin in olive oil, crushed garlic, salt and pepper. Roast in a 350°F oven for 45 minutes or until soft. Allow to cool for 10 minutes, and then scrape into a blender with the Idiazabal and butter. Blend, then season with salt and pepper. Set aside to cool to room temperature.

pigeon jus:

Slowly pan roast the pigeon carcasses in olive oil until cooked through (about 25 minutes). Add the shallots, chicken stock, star anise and garlic to the pan. Cook for 30 minutes. Strain and reduce quickly to two-thirds of a cup, skimming occasionally.

leeks:

Foam the butter in a shallow pan. Add the sugar and salt. Dissolve. Then add the leeks and wine. Cook covered for 6 minutes or until soft. Remove from the liquid to cool.

cromesqui:

Sauté the shallot in butter for 2 minutes. Set aside to cool. When cool combine with all remaining ingredients. Season with salt and pepper. Place in the refrigerator to stiffen up. Form into chestnut-size balls and place in the freezer. When firm bread the cromesqui by combining the beaten egg with the olive oil and mixing the parmesan and breadcrumbs together. Roll the ball into the flour, shaking off the excess, then into the egg, followed by the breadcrumb and parmesan mixture. Fry in oil until golden, then keep warm. They will keep their heat for up to 15 minutes.

ice wine vinaigrette au jus:

Incorporate all the ingredients but do not emulsify. You are looking for a split vinaigrette. Serve at room temperature.

to serve:

Slice the pigeon in two length-wise. Season with salt and pepper on the cut side and rub with olive oil. Present next to the leek rounds with a spoonful of the pumpkin purée to one side. Put a few slices of the pickled shallots on the plate and top with a cromesqui. Spoon some of the vinaigrette around and serve.

CITRUS CRAQUELIN - TEMPLE ORANGE SORBET & HAZELNUT PRALINE

BY JONATHAN GUSHUE

For me citrus is the ultimate in refreshment. So crisp and clean. Big flavor with a nice clean finish. Can't imagine a better way to end a great meal.

Serves 10
Preparation time: 1 hour
Cooking time: 1-1 hour 30 minutes

Special equipment:
Ice cream machine, hotel pan, food processor

INGREDIENTS

citrus cream:

2	gelatin leaves, with water to bloom
5 fl oz	citrus juice (orange, lemon and lime)
1 tsp	each of orange, lime and lemon zests
6 oz	sugar
10½ oz	butter
5 fl oz	water
4	eggs

Grand Marnier craquelin:

3½ oz	icing sugar
1 fl oz	Grand Marnier
1 oz	all purpose flour
2 oz	hazelnuts, sliced
1½ oz	butter

temple orange sorbet:

16	temple oranges (mandarins if not available)
10 oz	caster sugar
2½ fl oz	liquid glucose
8½ fl oz	water

hazelnut praline:

5 oz	crushed hazelnuts
5 oz	sugar
1 oz	glucose
1 fl oz	water

orange chips:

3	oranges sliced 1/16" thickness
5 fl oz	water
6 oz	sugar

citrus fruit garnish:

20	grapefruit segments
20	navel orange segments

edible flowers

METHOD

citrus cream:

Line a 12" x 8" hotel pan with cling film. Soak the gelatin. Combine the citrus juice, zests, three-quarters of the sugar, water and butter in a pot. Heat it up to 104°F, stirring all the time. Whip the eggs with the rest of the sugar until thick and lemon colored. Pour the warm citrus mixture onto the egg mixture. Whip it then pour it back into the pot. Bring to the boil and whisk continuously until thickened. Remove from the heat, then add the gelatin. Stir until dissolved. Pour into the hotel pan and chill until set. Please note that this recipe makes more than is required to compensate for trimming precise rectangles.

Grand Marnier craquelin:

Melt the butter then add the icing sugar. Whip until creamy. Whisk in the Grand Marnier then fold in the flour. Set aside to rest for about 1 hour. Preheat the oven to 350°F. With an offset spatula, spread the craquelin mixture onto a silpat or piece of parchment. Sprinkle with the sliced hazelnuts. You will need a 14" x 10" rectangle. Bake until golden, 15 minutes approximately. Pull from the oven. Gently slide the parchment with tuile onto a flat surface. With a pizza cutter, cut 20, 4" x 2½" rectangles. Wait 5 minutes to cool before handling.

temple orange sorbet:

Juice the oranges and reduce by one-third to make a syrup. Combine the sugar, glucose and water together and bring to a boil for the stock syrup. Set aside to cool. Mix the two syrups together. When cool, spin in an ice cream machine.

hazelnut praline:

Heat the sugar, glucose and water in a heavy based saucepan until it reaches 300°F. Pull from the heat and add the hazelnuts. Pour onto a lightly oiled tray and let cool. Break into medium-sized pieces, add to a food processor and crush to a crumble-like consistency.

orange chips:

Combine the sugar and water and bring to the boil to make a syrup. Reduce the heat. Poach the orange slices in the syrup until translucent. Drain thoroughly and place the orange slices on parchment or silpat. Be sure they are round. Whatever shape you lay them at is the shape they will stay. Cook at 175°F for approximately 2 hours or until crisp.

to serve:

Cut the cream into 3" x 1" pieces. Press a piece of the craquelin on each side of the cream and place to the side of the plate. Mound a tablespoon of the praline onto the plate to use as a bed for a spoon of the sorbet. Place an orange chip on the sorbet. Garnish the plate with citrus segments, extra praline and edible flowers.

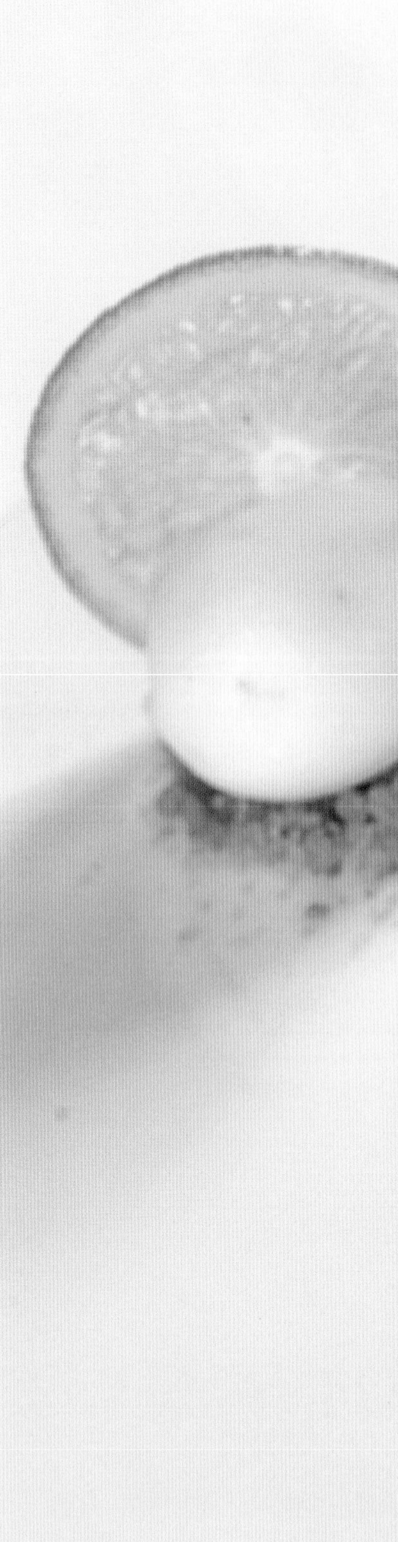

Anne Desjardins and Emmanuel R. Desjardins

Anne Desjardins & Pierre Audette
Grand Chef Relais & Châteaux

In 1979, Anne Desjardins and Pierre Audette became restaurateurs and transformed a charming cottage in Sainte-Adèle into a bistro. They added a small contemporary hotel and garden in 1987, and in 2006 a Nordic Spa, mingling perfectly with the creek and the mountain behind.

Anne, self-taught in cuisine, has always been passionate about food, freshness, authenticity and terroir. In the 1980s she attended renowned Chef's seminars in France, and became fully involved in a network of Québec's farmers and agricultural officials to promote seasonal and local products. Elegant cuisine du terroir became her signature.

Pierre takes wine-tasting courses, and encourages the role of sommeliers and wine pairing to bring an added dimension to the fine dining experience at the hotel.

In 1998, eldest son Emmanuel joined the kitchen brigade after completing his culinary scholarship. Highly skilled and innovative, he is now a partner, the Chef de cuisine, a true contributor to the spirit that has made the reputation of the enterprise.

Cooking with four hands is the new strength of L'Eau à la Bouche.

L'Eau à la Bouche

Hôtel-Spa-Restaurant

This pretty Laurentides residence is surrounded by pine trees facing the ski slopes. "Everything started rather simply. We couldn't afford the services of a Grand Chef so I took the plunge," says Chef Anne Desjardins.

In 1979, Anne and her husband, Pierre Audette, probably had no idea that their inn would become such a resounding success. A proud ambassador of Québec cuisine, this former geographer showcases the best regional produce, in harmony with the seasons, adding her own personal touch like the St. Lawrence rock crab with celery, cucumber, daikon, Thai basil and Vietnamese white pepper. In addition to these culinary delights, experience the Nordic spa with original offerings like maple sap treatments, iced baths purified with salt water, and a Finnish cedar sauna.

FRESH DUCK FOIE GRAS CREME BRULEE, CRANBERRY PUREE, APPLE BRUNOISE, CELERY SHOOTS & BALSAMIC VINEGAR

BY ANNE DESJARDINS & EMMANUEL R. DESJARDINS

A divine all-seasons appetizer.

Serves 4
Preparation time: 30 minutes
Cooking time: 40 minutes

Special equipment:
Blowtorch, digital thermometer

INGREDIENTS

duck foie gras crème brûlée:

8 oz duck foie gras, fresh
8 oz 35% cream
1 egg yolk
1 whole egg
few drops of lemon juice
salt, to taste

cranberry purée:

2 oz apple juice
2 oz dry cranberries
¼ tsp white peppercorns

apple brunoise:

½ fresh Empire apple
few drops of lemon juice
1 pinch of celery seeds

to serve:

brioche, thinly sliced
sugar (enough to caramelize)
aged balsamic vinegar
celery shoots or tender leaves from a stick of celery

METHOD

duck foie gras crème brûlée:

Preheat the oven to 250°F.

In a small pot, mix the cream with the yolk and the whole egg. Continue to stir, and bring the temperature to 150°F. Remove from the heat and let the temperature descend for 1 minute.

Put the foie gras in a mixer and pour in the egg and cream mixture. Add the salt and a few drops of lemon juice, and mix well. Pass through a chinois (fine sieve).

Put plastic wrap in a square mold 6" x 6". Pour in the foie gras cream. Cook in a bain-marie for 40 minutes. Remove from the oven. Let it rest and cool down in the fridge.

cranberry purée:

Bring to a boil the apple juice, cranberries and peppercorns. Let rest for 10 minutes. Purée in a mixer and reserve.

apple brunoise:

Just a few minutes before serving cut and core an apple. Cut half of it in thin slices and dice into very small cubes. Add a few drops of lemon juice and celery seeds.

to serve:

Toast the slices of brioche slightly. Reverse the crème brûlée over a wooden board and cut into six rectangles. Keep in the fridge until ready to serve, then sprinkle the top of each with sugar and caramelize with the blowtorch.

Place on cold plates. With a spoon add the cranberry purée, diced apple, and a slice of brioche, make a stripe with the aged balsamic vinegar and garnish with celery shoots/leaves.

Chef's tip:

We suggest that you buy the brioche from your preferred pastry shop.

LOIN OF VENISON, ELDERBERRY & GINGER SAUCE, ROASTED BEETS, CHERVIL ROOT PUREE

BY ANNE DESJARDINS & EMMANUEL R. DESJARDINS

A favorite at L'Eau à la Bouche in Winter. A venison mix with tasty but unusual vegetables, berries and spices.

Serves 4
Preparation time: 45 minutes
Cooking time: 10 minutes

INGREDIENTS

roasted beets:

8 oz beets (red and yellow)
1 tbsp olive oil
1 tbsp ginger, freshly grated
salt, to taste

chervil purée:

1 small potato
8 oz chervil root (or tuberous chervil)
3 tbsp butter
salt, to taste

venison:

4 red deer venison loin, 8 oz each
1 tbsp butter
1 tbsp olive oil
salt, to taste

elderberry and ginger sauce:

2 tbsp fresh ginger
1 shallot, minced
2 tbsp elderberry jam
1 tbsp red wine vinegar
1 cup red wine
1 cup game or veal stock
3 tbsp elderberries, fresh or frozen

garnish:

sprout of beet

METHOD

roasted beets:

Preheat the oven to 400°F.

Place aluminium foil in a sheet pan, pour in the olive oil, add the raw and unpeeled beets, and sprinkle with salt and ginger. Close the foil tightly and cook until done. Remove from the oven, let the beets cool down but not until completely cold, peel, cut in half and keep warm.

chervil purée:

Boil together the potato and chervil until soft, strain well. Purée them, adding butter and salt. Reserve in a warm place.

venison:

In a hot pan, add the butter (reserving a little for finishing the sauce), oil, and salt and sear the four pieces of venison for 3 minutes each side. Remove them from the pan and reserve in a warm place.

elderberry and ginger sauce:

In the same pan, add the minced shallot, ginger, and elderberry jam, and cook for 1 minute.

Deglaze with the red wine vinegar, add the red wine, boil for 2 minutes, add the stock and let cook until reduced by half. Pass through a sieve, put back in a pot over a low heat and add the elderberries with a little piece of butter and salt.

to serve:

Put the purée and beets on the plates, add the piece of venison, pour over the sauce and garnish with the beet sprout.

Chef's tip:

If you do not find chervil root (or tuberous chervil) you could substitute by using celeriac instead.

MAPLE SYRUP PARFAIT, STRAWBERRY GRANITE & JELLY, SUMMER EDIBLE FLOWER PETALS

BY ANNE DESJARDINS & EMMANUEL R. DESJARDINS

A sweet and fruity Summer dessert, a touch of tradition with some of what nature in the Laurentians produces best.

Serves 6

Preparation time:	1 hour 20 minutes + marinating and freezing time
Cooking time:	45 minutes

Special equipment:
Digital thermometer

Planning ahead:
This dish is best made 1 day in advance as the parfait and granité need to freeze

INGREDIENTS

strawberry jelly and strawberry granité:

2 cups	fresh strawberries
1 cup	maple syrup
1 tsp	lemon juice + a few drops
2½	gelatin sheets

whole wheat crust (Graham style):

5 tbsp	whole wheat flour
5 tbsp	regular white flour
½ tsp	ground star anise
½ tsp	baking powder
3 tbsp	unsalted butter
1 tbsp	maple syrup

maple parfait:

1 cup	pure maple syrup
3 tbsp	maple liquor (Ruffin, Val Ambré or Muscat)
4	egg yolks
5 oz	35% cream

garnish:

fresh diced strawberries and fresh edible flowers like calendula, carnation, centaurée

METHOD

strawberry jelly and strawberry granité:

Remove the stems of the strawberries. Pour the maple syrup over them and let them marinate for 3 hours. Drain the strawberries, reserving the juice.

For the jelly, boil 1 cup of the reserved strawberry juice with a few drops of lemon juice. Remove from the heat, add the gelatin (previously soaked in cold water), mix and pour into a shallow pan. Store in the fridge.

For the granité, mix the marinated strawberries and remaining juice in the blender, add 1 teaspoon of lemon juice, pour into a shallow pan, and place in the freezer.

whole wheat crust (Graham style):

Preheat the oven to 375°F.

In the bowl of a mixer, mix together all the ingredients with the pulse button until well mixed but not too compact. Press the dough into the bottom of a parchment lined 6" x 6" square pan. Place in the oven and cook for 10 minutes. Remove from the oven and let it cool.

maple parfait:

Bring to a boil the maple syrup and liquor until it reaches 242°F on the thermometer. While it boils beat the egg yolks rapidly. Continue beating then, when the maple syrup mix has reached the right temperature, pour it very slowly in a thread on to the beaten eggs. Continue beating until the mix has cooled down.

Beat the cream to soft peaks and incorporate carefully into the egg mixture. Pour over the cooled crust and place in a freezer for at least 6 hours.

to serve:

Remove the maple parfait from the freezer and cut into six rectangles. Grate the granité with the tip of a fork, place in a nice verrine shooter glass. Cut the jelly into little cubes.

On cool plates place the elements of the dessert and garnish with fresh morsels of strawberry and petals of the edible flowers.

Chef's tip:

Organic honey from your area could make a nice substitute for the maple syrup. Graham crackers could be an alternative for the crust of the parfait.

Yvan Lebrun
Grand Chef Relais & Châteaux

Yvan Lebrun was born in Brittany, Cancale, to a dressmaker mother and a marine father. At 14 years old he had his first contact in the kitchen, cooking in a house of Saint-Malo, The Métairie de Beauregard, alongside its Chef-Owner, Jacques Gonthier.

In 1986 Yvan arrived in Québec as second-in-chief at the Hilton in Québec with Jean Soulard, a real inspiration. Yvan says, "I kept my French philosophy while adapting my style in Québec. The result is a French traditional cuisine with a distinctive taste of Québec."

At the Hilton Yvan met Rolande Leclerc, who was 'maitre d'hôtel' for the dining room, The Croquembroche. Together in 1990 they decided to open their own restaurant, Restaurant Initiale.

In 2006 Restaurant Initiale was admitted into Relais & Châteaux, this recognition of quality allows the restaurant to greatly enhance its visibility around the world.

Restaurant Initiale Inc.

Originally from the little fishing village of Cancale in Brittany, Yvan Lebrun and his partner Rolande, have created one of the best restaurants in North America.

Yvan Lebrun's motto is 'simplicity and precision'. His love of food and the pure delight of his guests spurs him on to combine the very best of French and Québec culinary tradition. Here, hearts of palm are made into flour, dandelion honey becomes a smooth ice cream, maple syrup appears regularly in harmonious creations and, of course, oysters have a starring role.

Serves 4
Preparation time: 1 hour
Cooking time: 1 hour 30 minutes

LOBSTER TAIL, WHITE BISQUE, HARICOTS 'COCO', LEEKS & SALICORNE GREMOLATA

BY YVAN LEBRUN

This is a beautiful mix of pastel colors. The white haricot beans blend perfectly with white leeks, and together they set off the pink of the lobster. Not only this but it has amazing flavor.

INGREDIENTS

white bisque:

2	female lobsters, 1½ lb each, heads and shell, tails and coral (roe) reserved
2	white leeks, cubed
8 oz	white mushrooms
2 oz	shallots, thinly sliced
4	garlic cloves
2 cups	sweet white wine
4 cups	chicken stock
1	branch of thyme
1	branch of tarragon
2	bay leaves
1 tbsp	fennel seeds, roasted and ground
1 cup	35% cream

lobster tails:

2	reserved lobster tails
2 oz	unsalted butter
1	pinch of cayenne pepper
1	pinch of paprika
1	pinch of curry powder
1 tbsp	banyuls vinegar

white haricots 'coco':

4 oz	fresh haricots 'coco' e.g. lingot
4 cups	water
1	onion
1 tsp	sugar
2 oz	butter
1 tbsp	olive oil

pancake of coral:

reserved coral roe
same weight of 35% cream, kept cold
white pepper, to taste

leeks and salicorne gremolata:

2	white portions of leeks
1½ cups	vegetable stock
2 oz	salicorne, blanched
1 oz	olive oil
1	lemon, zest
1 tbsp	parsley, chopped

fresh pepper

garnish:

dill flowers
spice powder

METHOD

white bisque:

Concassé the head and shell in a casserole dish, then add the vegetables and herbs, white wine and chicken stock, and cook for around 30-40 minutes. Skim and strain. Mix with the cream. Reserve.

lobster tails:

In a marmite (tall cooking pot) warm some water, and cook the lobster for 2 minutes 30 seconds. Refresh and remove the shell. Reserve the tails in the fridge.

white haricots 'coco':

In a casserole, cook all the ingredients together until the beans are cooked. Reserve.

pancake of coral:

Mix the coral, cream and white pepper. Pass through a fine sieve. In a nonstick frying pan, cook four pancakes and roll them up.

leeks and salicorne gremolata:

Clean the leeks and cook gently with the vegetable stock in a covered pan. In a bowl, mix the salicorne, parsley, lemon zest, pepper and olive oil. Drain the leeks and chop finely. Combine with the salicorne mix.

to serve:

Cook the lobster tail slowly in melted butter for around 5-6 minutes. Add the spices. Deglaze with the banyuls vinegar and cut into medallions. Stir the bisque.

Drain the haricots 'coco' and add a spoon of bisque. Serve on four plates, each with some haricots 'coco', leeks and salicorne gremolata, a pancake coral, and some bisque. Top the beans with the lobster tail. Decorate with dill flowers and spice powder.

VEAL SIRLOIN WITH JERUSALEM ARTICHOKES, NUTS, MUSHROOMS & VINAIGRETTE VIANDEE WITH ANCHOVIES

BY YVAN LEBRUN

An amusing range of flavors are all in this dish. Salty anchovies set off the tender veal. This mix is a soft and tasty taste explosion!

Serves 4
Preparation time: 1 hour
Cooking time: 1 hour 30 minutes

Planning ahead:
The veal jus should be prepared a day in advance.

INGREDIENTS

veal jus:

½ lb parure of veal roast (trimmings)
1 lb roast veal bones
4 oz carrots, chopped
4 oz onions, cubed
2 oz celeriac branch, cubed
3 garlic cloves
1 cup tomatoes, chopped
½ oz thyme
1 bay leaf
1 tsp white pepper
8 cups vegetable stock
4 cups water
2 cups red wine
1 oz olive oil

veal sirloin:

1 lb veal sirloin
2 oz green olives, sliced thinly
2 oz anchovies in oil, unsalted
4 oz unsalted butter
2 oz olive oil
salt & pepper

Jerusalem artichokes:

¾ cup Jerusalem artichokes
4 cups vegetable stock
salt
sugar
lemon juice

nuts:

4 oz wild hazelnuts
2 oz water
2 oz sugar

wild mushrooms:

4 oz cepe mushrooms
4 oz pied bleu mushrooms
4 oz lactaire mushrooms
4 oz armillaire mushrooms
2 oz salted butter
vinaigrette viandée (see recipe below), to serve

vinaigrette viandée:

½ cup veal juice reduction (see recipe above)
1 oz anchovies, unsalted
1 oz peanut oil
2 oz sherry vinegar
1 tbsp Dijon mustard

to serve:

4 green cabbage leaves, blanched and cooked with warm butter
lemon thyme

METHOD

veal jus:

In a marmite (tall cooking pot), roast the vegetables and herbs, add the bones and parure. Add the red wine, vegetable stock and water. Cook for 4 hours (slowly). Add the olive oil and pepper. Strain and reserve 2 cups.

veal sirloin:

Preheat the oven to 350°F. Fix the piece of veal on to a board: make a few slits and stuff with anchovies and green olives. Roll up and tie securely. Seal with butter and olive oil in a frying pan. Then cook in the oven for 15 minutes. Reserve.

Jerusalem artichokes:

Clean and brush the artichokes then cook slowly on top of the stove with the vegetable stock, salt, sugar and lemon juice. Drain after cooking and reserve.

nuts:

In a casserole dish add the water and sugar, bring to a boil and add the nuts. Cook for 2-3 minutes.

wild mushrooms:

Brush and peel the mushrooms (make sure you clean the foot very well). Cut into halves, cook with butter but be careful to not overcook.

vinaigrette viandée:

Add to the veal jus the anchovies, peanut oil, vinegar and mustard, and mix together.

to serve:

Preheat the oven to 200°F and cook the veal sirloin for around 5 minutes. Re-warm the Jerusalem artichokes, mushrooms and nuts in a frying pan with a touch of the vinaigrette viandée. Take plates and on each put some mushrooms, artichokes, nuts and cabbage leaves, and place a slice of sirloin on top. Pour over the vinaigrette. Add lemon thyme as a garnish.

Serves 4
Preparation time: 1 hour
Cooking time: 2 hours

Special equipment:
Ice cream maker

INGREDIENTS

apples:

4	Courtland apples
4 oz	butter
2 oz	maple syrup
2 oz	dry cider

crispy maple bread:

8 oz	sugar
2 oz	maple sugar
1	egg white
1 oz	hazelnut powder

cranberry sorbet:

2 cups	cranberry juice (natural and unsweetened)
¾ cup	sugar
1 cup	dried and ground cranberries
1 tsp	stabilizer

green tomato confit:

1 lb	green tomatoes, cubed
1	lemon, zest
8 oz	sugar

yogurt sauce:

1 cup	yogurt
2 tbsp	ice cider
½	vanilla pod

spicy bread:

1	bay leaf
1	pinch each of salt, cinnamon, anise, ground cloves, pepper, cardamom, ginger
1	orange, zest
1 tbsp	yeast
3 oz	low flour
4 oz	spelt flour
3 oz	whole milk
1	egg, beaten
6 oz	honey

cider jelly:

1 cup	ice cider
4	leaves of gelatin

cider caramel:

reserved apple juice
1 cup 35% cream

APPLES WITH CRISPY MAPLE BREAD, CRANBERRY SORBET, GREEN TOMATO CONFIT, YOGURT SAUCE, CIDER JELLY & CIDER CARAMEL

BY YVAN LEBRUN

Local produce is always high on the agenda for our dishes. These are simple ingredients but with this preparation they are transformed into something extraordinary.

METHOD

apples:

Preheat the oven to 275°F. Remove the apple cores then put the apples into a pan with the butter, maple syrup and cider. Place in the oven and cook for around 1½ hours. Pour off the juice of the apples sometimes during cooking and reserve. Remove the apples from the oven and reserve.

crispy maple bread:

Preheat the oven to 300°F. Mix all the ingredients in a bowl. Spread on a silpat. Cook in the oven until it has a nice color, approximately 10 minutes.

cranberry sorbet:

Boil the cranberry juice with the sugar. Add the dried cranberries and the stabilizer. Mix and put in an ice cream maker.

green tomato confit:

Mix the green tomatoes with the zest of lemon and sugar. Cook in a pan until it is like a jam.

yogurt sauce:

Mix the yogurt with the ice cider and vanilla pod, and freeze.

spicy bread:

Preheat the oven to 300°F. Mix all the dry ingredients together then add the milk slowly, followed by the honey and egg. Cook in a nonstick cake pan for 30 minutes. Remove from the oven and let cool.

cider jelly:

Put the gelatin leaves in cold water to soften. Cook a quarter of the cider with the gelatin. Mix with the rest of the cider. Strain and pour into a bowl.

cider caramel:

Take the reserved apple juice and add the cream. Mix and cook, then keep warm.

to serve:

Break up the crispy maple bread into pieces and put onto four plates. Place an apple skin on each piece of crispy maple. Spoon around 1 teaspoon of green tomato confit. Add a cube of cider jelly, a touch of yogurt sauce and one quenelle of cranberry sorbet. Dip a cube of spicy bread in the caramel cider and add to the plate.

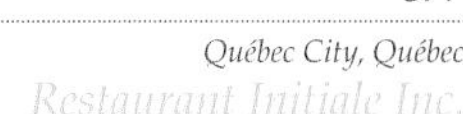

Normand Laprise
Grand Chef Relais & Châteaux

Normand Laprise is well-known in New York gastronomic circles, ever since his debut in 1996 at a James Beard Foundation dinner featuring his cuisine.

When Cena Restaurant was launched in May of 1998, it seemed that the whole of New York was enamoured of his 'cuisine du terroir du Québec' and above all of his mastery of textures and tastes. While Executive Chef of Cena until July of 1999, Normand Laprise continued to head up Toqué!, which was founded in 1993, in association with his colleague Christine Lamarche.

Since that time, Normand Laprise has become known around the world. Invited to Bermuda, as well as Tokyo, Hong Kong and Bangkok, he has cooked side by side in the kitchens of Charlie Trotter and of Ken Oringer. He has shared his own kitchen in Montreal with some of the best chefs in the world, including Xavier Pellicer (Abac, Spain), Tetsuya Wakuda (Tetsuya's, Australia) and Daniel Boulud (Daniel, USA).

Toqué! is a recipient of the 5 Diamond Award from both the CAA and the AAA.

Restaurant Toqué!

With its light-filled dining room and its contemporary atmosphere, the restaurant Toqué is the meeting place for gourmets in search of new flavors to share with friends right in the heart of Montréal.

The Chef, Normand Laprise, is far from being a solitary artist. He supports local suppliers and farmers through his cuisine, true artisans of taste who help turn his culinary experiences into truly great moments of discovery. Vegetables, wild herbs, seafood, wild mushrooms, edible flowers, duck, beef, lamb, fish... The finest products from Québec are featured with photos of the various dishes displayed on the menu. Accompanied by a superb, audacious wine list. The taste of Québec in all its freshness!

PRINCESS SCALLOP CEVICHE, CANTALOUPE MELON & WASABI

BY NORMAND LAPRISE

Serves 4
Preparation time: 30 minutes + 6 hours for foam to set
Cooking time: N/A

Special equipment:
Cream whipper with 2 gas cartridges, melon baller (½" diameter)

Planning ahead:
The wasabi foam can be made the day before or it needs to set in the fridge for a minimum of 6 hours.

We are lucky enough to receive these beautiful princess scallops 12 months a year from Eastern Canada. These scallops are the heartbeat of a concept we developed served as a ceviche, and into oil, water, and foam. When Summer starts we serve it with melon and coriander, in the fall with apple and wasabi, in the Winter with buckthorn berries and Christmas tree, and in the Spring with Japanese plums and almonds.

INGREDIENTS

wasabi foam:

1 gelatin sheet
⅓ cup lime juice
⅔ cup water
½ tube of wasabi paste
salt, to taste

melon juice:

½ cantaloupe melon, pieces
lime juice

princess scallops:

8 princess scallops
1 tbsp shallots, finely minced
1½ tsp lime juice
2 tbsp extra virgin olive oil
8-10 tsp cantaloupe melon juice (see recipe below)
24 cantaloupe melon balls
basil oil
salt & pepper, to taste
micro greens

METHOD

wasabi foam:

Bloom the gelatin in cold water for a few minutes. Blend together the lime juice, water, and wasabi paste using a hand mixer. Season with salt to taste. Warm a quarter of the finished liquid until just hot. Squeeze excess water from the gelatin and whisk into the hot liquid. Once dissolved, incorporate the rest of the liquid into the hot mixture and whisk well. Put into the whipper and charge with the gas. Leave in the fridge to set for at least 6 hours.

melon juice:

Juice the melon pieces and strain through a fine sieve. Depending on the taste of the juice, adjust with a small amount of fresh lime juice to add a little bit of acidity.

princess scallops:

Shuck the princess scallops – remove the guts as well as the dark membrane surrounding the scallop. Remove from the shell, rinse under cold water and pat dry. Slice each scallop horizontally into three equal pieces and set aside. Scrape the inside of the shell (the deeper one) and scrub well of any residue, then rinse well.

to serve:

Place the scallops in a bowl and add the extra virgin olive oil, lime juice, shallots, and season well with salt and pepper to taste. Mix gently with a spoon until well coated.

Place the eight cleaned shells on a tray. In each shell, arrange three slices of scallop and add 1 teaspoon of melon juice and two drops of basil oil. Continue by placing threemelon balls in each as well. Garnish with a sprig of micro greens and finish with a touch of wasabi foam. Serve immediately.

Serves 4
Preparation time: 2 hours
Cooking time: 1 hour - 1 hour 30 minutes

INGREDIENTS

vegetables:

raw cucumbers
raw carrot slices
raw radish slices
raw tomatoes
raw litchi tomatoes
ground cherries
fresh strawberries
fresh raspberries
baby lettuce
micro greens
cooked and roasted mini beets
blanched green and yellow string beans
sautéed chanterelles
crispy shiso

vinaigrette:

3-4 tbsp Chardonnay vinegar
1 tsp honey
2-3 tbsp extra virgin olive oil, to serve
salt, to taste

green onion foam:

2 bunches of scallions
3 cups cold water
1 tsp soy lecithin
salt

whelks:

16 medium to large whelks
2 tbsp extra virgin olive oil
3 tbsp butter
3 tbsp minced shallots
salt & pepper

MELI-MELO OF VEGETABLES

BY NORMAND LAPRISE

This is a dish that always appears at the peak of the Summertime on Toqué!'s menu. It brings together all the fresh fruits and vegetables of the season. The best way to make this dish is by taking a trip to the market and see what kind of goodies the farmers have to offer.

METHOD

vegetables:

Cook each vegetable as desired depending on the type available. For instance, blanch the green beans in salted boiling water for 2-3 minutes depending on their size. To roast the beets, wrap each washed beet (with peel on) in aluminum foil and cook in a an oven preheated to 350°F for 1-1 hour 30 minutes depending on size as well. The chanterelles can be sautéed in extra virgin olive oil and a few teaspoons of butter and seasoned with salt and pepper. For the raw items, cut according to type as well. Be creative and try to use different cooking and slicing techniques to make the plate more interesting.

vinaigrette:

Mix the honey with the Chardonnay vinegar and season with salt.

green onion foam:

Blanch the scallions in boiling water, remove and squeeze out as much excess water as possible. Blend with the 3 cups of cold water and season with salt. Add the lecithin and blend well with a hand blender. Set aside.

whelks:

Leave the whelks under cold running water for about an hour or so. Put in a large pot and cover with salted water. Boil for 45 minutes. With the help of a small fork, remove each whelk from the shell. Clean under running water, removing all the guts and leaving just the muscle. Cut each muscle in half and continue to clean with water, rinsing very well. Drain well on a towel. Heat the olive oil and butter in a large pan. Add the whelks and season with salt and pepper. Sauté until heated through. Just before removing from the pan, add the shallots, toss and serve.

to serve:

In a large bowl, very carefully toss the vegetables with some vinaigrette and extra virgin olive oil, and season with salt and pepper. Carefully place the different vegetables on the plate and then follow with the fruits and whelks. Finish by emulsifying the green onion mixture with a hand blender and spoon some foam on the plate.

Serves 4
Preparation time: 1 hour
Cooking time: 3 hours

Special equipment:
Ice cream maker or pacojet

Planning ahead:
The strawberry crisps and dacquoise can be prepared in advance.

INGREDIENTS

strawberry sorbet:

1 lb	fresh strawberries, cleaned and halved
4½ oz	sugar

strawberry purée:

1 lb	fresh strawberries, cleaned and quartered
½ cup	sugar

strawberry crisps:

1 ½ cups	strawberry purée (see recipe above)
1	egg white

strawberry chips:

15-20	medium to large strawberries
2 cups	simple syrup

dacquoise:

1 cup	sugar
2	egg whites
½	vanilla pod

whipped cream:

1½ cups	heavy cream
1 tbsp	sugar

vanilla syrup

½	vanilla pod
1 cup	simple syrup

to serve:

12	strawberries, quartered

STRAWBERRIES: DRY SALAD, FRESH & FROZEN

BY NORMAND LAPRISE

The dry salad comes from a long way. We have been playing with those words 'dry salad` to develop all kinds of funky ideas. In this case, we get 100% of the strawberries into your mouth, which make you appreciate the two months of the year when they are in season.

METHOD

strawberry sorbet:

Mix the strawberry halves with the sugar and macerate overnight. Then purée in a blender and pass through a fine sieve. Churn in an ice cream maker or pacojet.

strawberry purée:

Macerate the strawberries overnight with the sugar. Blend all together in a blender and pass through a fine sieve. Reserve.

strawberry crisps:

Preheat the oven to 225°F. Blend the purée and egg white together until well incorporated. Spread a thin layer of mixture onto two silpats. Cook in the oven for 20-30 minutes until the top is dry. Then, peel off the silpat, flip over on to a parchment sheet and continue to dry in the oven until crisp. Keep in an airtight container.

strawberry chips:

Preheat the oven to 225°F. Slice the strawberries thin with the help of a very sharp knife. Dip each slice in the simple syrup and arrange on a silpat. Cook in the oven for 25 minutes and turn each one over very carefully. Continue to cook in the oven until the slices are crisp and dry.

dacquoise:

Preheat the oven to 225°F. Scrape the vanilla out of the pod and mix with the sugar. Whip the egg whites and gradually add the sugar. Continue to whip until stiff peaks are formed. Divide the mixture on to four parchment sheets. Cover with another parchment sheet and roll flat with the help of a rolling pin until thin. Cook in the oven for 12 minutes. Immediately remove from the parchment paper and keep in an airtight container.

whipped cream:

Whip the cream and lightly sweeten with the sugar. Whip until soft peaks are formed.

vanilla syrup:

Over a low heat, infuse the simple syrup with the vanilla pod. Strain, cool and reserve.

to serve:

Using a piping bag, pipe some of the sweetened cream on to the plate. Mix the fresh strawberries with a little bit of vanilla syrup. Spread a few strawberries around the cream, and follow by covering with the strawberry crisps, strawberry chips and dacquoise. Drizzle with the vanilla syrup and finish with a quenelle of strawberry sorbet.

François Blais

The Executive Chef of Panache, François Blais, has quickly gained a reputation for culinary excellence and innovation. His creative approach to reviving our region's traditional dishes has revealed his enormous talent.

After solid training and many years of experience in such celebrated restaurants as the Laurie Raphaël, the Auberge du Canard Huppé, La Pinsonnière (Relais & Châteaux) and L'eau à la Bouche (Relais & Châteaux) as well as the Auberge du Mange Grenouille, François Blais insists that his unique interpretation of traditional cuisine was inspired by visiting the Auberge Saint-Antoine.

Nostalgic for your grandmother's shepherd's pie? François Blais will serve you an updated version made with bison, venison or lamb. "Panache revives those traditional Québec classical dishes from our childhood memories, but adds that light touch that our more sophisticated contemporary tastes require," he says.

While thumbing through *La Cuisine Raisonnée*, and other recipe collections of old Québec secrets, he was inspired to reinvent such dishes as his sweetbread stew, mashed Yukon gold potatoes, macaroni and cheese, the old favourite bread-and-butter pudding, and maple-iced doughnuts.

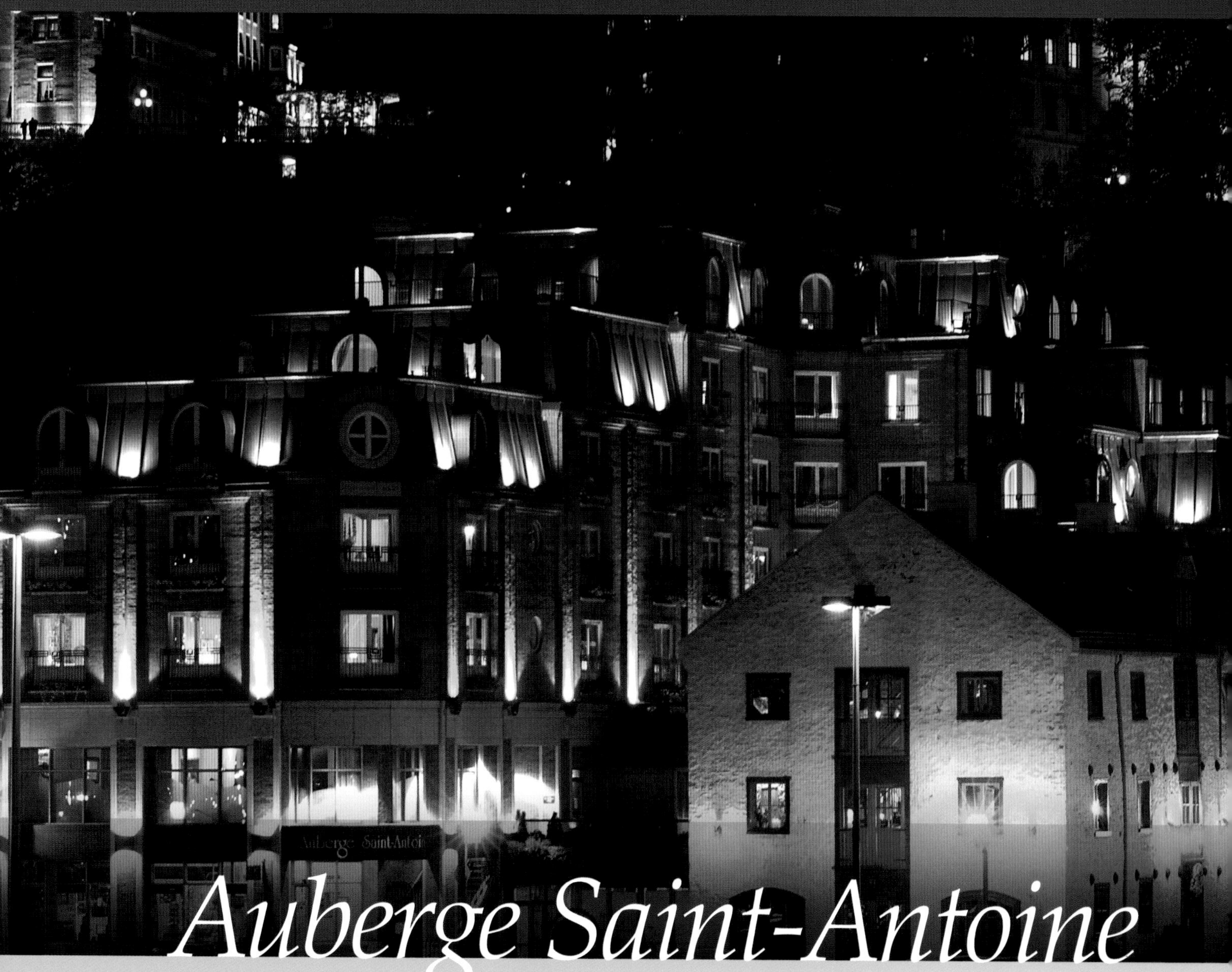

Auberge Saint-Antoine

With its irresistible charm and gourmet cuisine, the Auberge Saint-Antoine is nestled in the heart of Québec, the first city to be founded in North America.

"The impression made upon the visitor by this Gibraltar of America: its giddy heights, its citadel suspended, as it were in the air, its picturesque steep streets and frowning gateways, and the splendid views which burst upon the eye at every turn, is at once unique and lasting ...," wrote Charles Dickens on the subject of Québec city. The Auberge Saint-Antoine is a perfect place to stay to share in the writer's wonderment. This Vieux-Port hotel stands on a unique archaeological site. When it was built, many relics from French and English colonial times were discovered. Today, they adorn the chic, wood and cast iron designer interiors of this museum location.

PAN-SEARED CANADIAN DIVER SCALLOP WITH BACON & MAPLE FOAM

BY FRANCOIS BLAIS

Bacon and scallop is a common combination, but adding a little maple syrup will increase the sweetness from the scallop. It's a perfect match, especially in Québec!

Serves 4
Preparation time: 45 minutes
Cooking time: 30 minutes

INGREDIENTS

scallops:

3 tbsp	butter
4	big diver scallops or off the bottom of the sea scallops
salt & pepper	

bacon and maple foam:

1	shallot, thinly sliced
1	garlic clove, finely chopped
1 cup	dry white wine
1 tbsp	maple syrup
½ cup	bacon slab, diced
1 cup	milk
salt & pepper	

sweet onion purée:

1 tbsp	butter
2	sweet onions such as Vidalia
1 tbsp	maple syrup
salt & pepper	

sautéed peas and mushrooms:

2 tbsp	butter
1 cup	fresh sweet peas
½ cup	honey mushrooms
¼ cup	chicken broth
salt & pepper	

METHOD

bacon and maple foam:

In a small saucepan, sweat the shallot and garlic without coloring. Add the wine and maple syrup and bring to a boil. Reduce by half. Add the bacon and the milk. Infuse for at least 15 minutes without boiling and strain. Season to taste with salt and pepper and keep warm.

sweet onion purée:

Lightly brown the onions in butter, add the maple syrup and season with salt and pepper. Cook until the onions are tender. In a food processor, blend until you get a smooth purée. Keep warm.

sautéed peas and mushrooms:

In a hot pan, heat the butter slowly until light golden brown. Add the sweet peas and mushrooms. Season with salt and pepper. Add the chicken broth and reduce until the peas are tender. Keep warm.

scallops:

Heat the butter in a small pan until golden brown. Season the scallops, add to the pan and cook for 2 minutes on both sides.

to serve:

Serve the scallop on the sautéed peas and mushrooms with a spoonful of sweet onion purée. Use a hand mixer to foam up the bacon and maple sauce and use it to top the scallops.

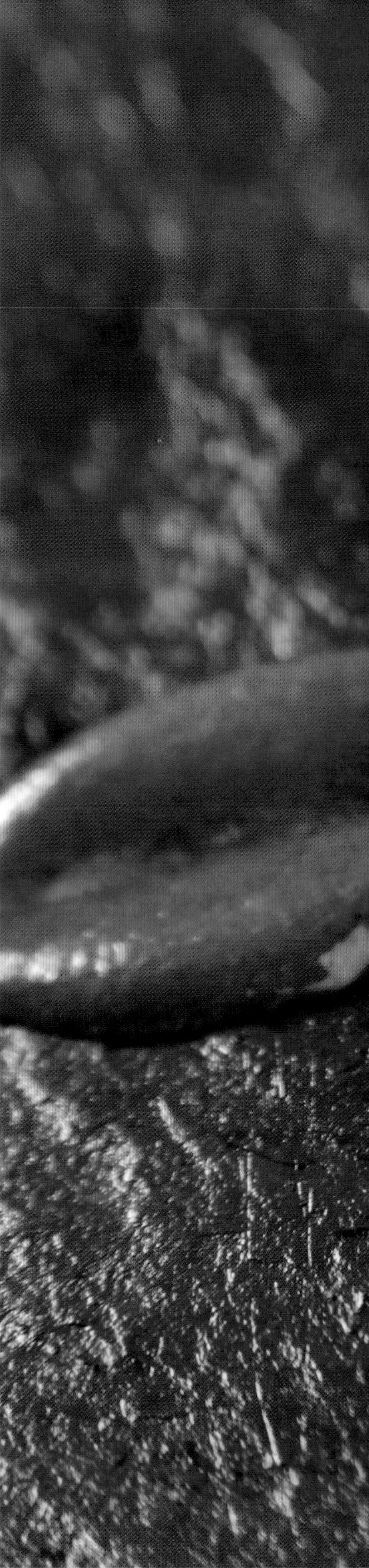

PAN-ROASTED VENISON RACK WITH LA FORTUNE ROUGE SAUCE, CARAMELIZED CARROT PUREE

BY FRANCOIS BLAIS

This dish is one of the most popular on our menu. It represents very well Québec's 'terroir' and local culinary culture.

Serves 4
Preparation time: 45 minutes
Cooking time: 45 minutes

INGREDIENTS

venison:

1 tbsp	butter
1 ½ lb	venison rack, trimmed and cut into 4 equal pieces
salt & pepper	

La Fortune Rouge sauce:

1	shallot, thinly sliced
1	garlic clove, finely chopped
1 cup	La Fortune Rouge (red port wine)
2 cups	game venison stock (if not available use meat stock)
salt & espelette pepper	

carrot purée:

1 cup	carrots, small cubed
3 tbsp	butter
1 cup	chicken broth
salt & pepper	

to serve:

3½ oz	chanterelles, sautéed
8	mini carrots with neatly trimmed green tops and lightly cooked

METHOD

La Fortune Rouge sauce:

Slowly roast the shallot and garlic in the butter until golden colored. Add the port wine and let it reduce by half. Add the stock, season and simmer until the sauce becomes the texture you want. Strain and keep warm.

carrot purée:

Lightly brown the carrots in the butter, add the chicken broth and simmer until done. Blend in a food processor until you have a smooth purée (if too thick just add more broth). Adjust the seasoning with salt and pepper. Keep warm.

venison:

In a hot pan heat the butter slowly until golden. Season the venison and sear every side of the meat. Baste with the butter from time to time to make the meat more tender. Cook as desired (I recommend medium-rare). Let stand for at least 10 minutes at 120°F. This will keep the juices from running when you carve the meat.

to serve:

Serve the venison with the chanterelles and carrots, the purée and the sauce.

Chef's tip:

Creamy mashed potatoes would nicely round up this plate.

WARM CHOCOLATE TART WITH MAPLE & HAZELNUT ICE CREAM

BY FRANCOIS BLAIS

Chiboust is one of my favorite desserts. It's light, creamy and tasty!

Serves 4
Preparation time: 45 minutes
Cooking time: 1 hour

Special equipment:
Ice cream machine

INGREDIENTS

sablé Breton:

1 cup	unsalted butter
2 tsp	salt
¾ cup	sugar
6	egg yolks
2 tbsp	baking powder
2 cups	flour

chocolate chiboust:

1 cup	very good chocolate such as Valrhona (66% cocoa minimum)
7	egg whites
½ cup	sugar
7	egg yolks
1 tbsp	corn starch
¾ cup	milk
2	gelatin sheets

maple and hazelnut ice cream:

1½ cups	heavy cream
½ cup	milk
1 tbsp	milk powder
3 tbsp	toasted hazelnut powder
½ cup	dark maple syrup
6	egg yolks

to serve:

chocolate sauce

METHOD

sablé Breton:

Cream the butter with the salt and sugar until a smooth texture. Add the yolks and the dry ingredients and mix to a dough. Put the dough between two sheets of parchment paper. Roll to about ⅛" thick and cool in the freezer for about 30 minutes. Preheat the oven to 350°F. Place the sablé dough in a removable bottom tart pan and bake for 15 minutes or until golden brown.

chocolate chiboust:

Melt the chocolate. Whip the egg whites with one-third of the sugar until it forms

medium to firm peaks. Mix the yolks with the rest of the sugar and the corn starch. Warm the milk and slowly add it to the yolk mixture, then add the gelatin. Put the mixture in a pan and back onto the stove to simmer for 1 minute. Mix half of the meringue with the warm yolk mixture. Add the melted chocolate and finish with the remaining meringue. Fill the tart pan with the chocolate chiboust and let cool for 1 hour.

maple and hazelnut ice cream:

Heat the cream, the milk and the milk powder with the half of the maple syrup and the toasted hazelnut powder. Mix the yolks with the rest of the maple syrup. While whisking the yolks, gradually pour in the hot cream mixture. Return the mixture to cook over a low heat, stirring constantly until the custard has thickened and coats the back of a spoon. Pour the mixture through a strainer and cool in the refrigerator. Freeze the ice cream in an ice cream machine then keep in the freezer.

to serve:

When you are ready to serve, cut a slice of the tart and warm in the oven for 2 minutes. Add a big spoon of ice cream and some chocolate sauce.

Marc Latulippe

"While other kids were eating peas and carrots at home, I was dealing with artichokes or avocados," Montreal-born Marc Latulippe recounts with a wry grin. Marc's father was a peacekeeper with the United Nations. Inevitably, his mother's cooking took on the decidedly international flavor of Africa, Israel, and the Middle East. Childhood Summers frequently found Marc alongside his grandmother as she scoured the rural Québec countryside for wild garlic, berries, and countless other backwoods edibles. By the time he became a teenager, Marc was already apprenticing in the kitchen of one of Montreal's trendiest restaurants.

After earning his culinary credentials from l'Institut de Tourisme et d'Hôtellerie du Québec, Marc worked his way up through the ranks of various fine restaurants and hotel kitchens.

Chef Marc Latulippe is particularly skilled in waking up sleeping and hidden flavors that most of us have forgotten or ignore. Marc adds to his repertoire daily, working with the region and the season. He is genuine, enthusiastic, and dedicated to providing Kingsbrae Arms guests with an unforgettable experience.

Kingsbrae Arms

New Brunswick is one of the most beautiful parts of Canada, famous for its tides that reach record heights – 14 metres in some places – its constantly changing beaches and its coast inhabited by whales.

Kingsbrae is a private and romantic country house built in 1897 on the heights of St. Andrews, overlooking the little harbor below. It is decorated in polished wood and marble and features period fireplaces, four-poster beds and precious objects. Between dinners that celebrate the sea and Chef's organic garden and massages with essential oils, discover the famous botanical garden of Kingsbrae containing, within 11 hectares, almost 50,000 species of flowers, a series of footpaths, a Dutch windmill, a maze of cedar trees and various other horticultural treasures.

Serves 8
Preparation time: 30 minutes
Cooking time: 2 minutes to fry the seaweed

INGREDIENTS

oyster tartare:

24	shelled, cleaned and chopped small oysters (reserve and strain the oyster jus and keep the shells to use for serving)
1	shallot, diced
1 fl oz	sherry wine vinegar
3½ fl oz	extra virgin olive oil

few drops of Tabasco

sea ice:

strained oyster jus

1 tbsp	sherry wine vinegar
1 tsp	chervil, finely chopped

garnish:

dulce seaweed
oil

OYSTER TARTARE WITH SEA ICE

BY MARC LATULIPPE

Oysters that grow in New Brunswick on Canada's east coast in the Gulf of St Lawrence where the waters are cool, clear, clean and ideal for raising Crassostrea Virginica. New Brunswick also happends to be the extreme northern limit of this oyster's natural habitat. This means that New Brunswick oysters taste fabulous all year long – clean and salty sweet with a smoky aftertaste.

METHOD

oyster tartare:

Combine all the ingredients 20 minutes before serving.

sea ice:

Freeze all the ingredients in a flat container, then scrape off with a spoon when ready to serve.

garnish:

In a pan with hot oil fry the dulce seaweed, then transfer to paper towels to absorb the excess oil.

to serve:

Serve the oyster tartare in a chilled shooter glass or on a half shell (three per person) on a bed of crushed ice. Top with the sea ice shavings and then the dulce seaweed.

Serves 4
Preparation time: 1 hour
Cooking time: 2 hours in total

Special equipment:
2 fl oz ramekin dishes, terrine mold

Planning ahead:
Make the terrine at least two days in advance. The boar legs need to be prepared and left overnight. The popover batter should be mixed 8 hours before cooking.

INGREDIENTS

terrine: (makes extra)

4 red peppers
2 yellow peppers
2 green peppers
3 zucchini
3 eggplants
oil
salt & pepper

boar:

7 oz whole wild boar legs per person
olive oil
pepper
garlic
fresh herbs
3 onions
2 carrots
3 branches of celery
7 fl oz dry white wine
veal remouillage

popover: (makes extra)

1 pt whole milk
4 eggs
1¾ cups all purpose flour
3½ oz parmesan
1¼ tsp salt
6 shallots, roasted and chopped
fresh herbs, chopped, to taste

sauce: (makes extra)

10 kalamata olives
1 shallot, diced
3½ fl oz white wine
3½ fl oz demi glace (see recipe below)
1½ fl oz cream
2 oz unsalted butter
fresh herbs, chopped

WILD BOAR WITH ZUCCHINI & EGGPLANT TERRINE

BY MARC LATULIPPE

Wild boar has a different meat structure compared to pigs. The fats are concentrated in layers giving a more lean meat. Wild boar really has its own unique taste.

METHOD

terrine:

Slice the zucchini and eggplants to ⅛" thick on a meat slicer, brush with oil, salt and pepper, then charbroil (grill) on both sides and keep the slices spread out on a tray to cool down.

Roast the peppers under a salamander on four sides until almost black. Put the hot roasted peppers in a bowl, cover tightly with plastic wrap, wait for them to cool down, then peel and deseed.

Spray a terrine mold with nonstick spray, add a layer of plastic wrap, then start layering with eggplant slices, followed by zucchini. Layer peppers into the middle, then fold the zucchini and eggplant over the top.

Add a weight to the top of the terrine and rest in the fridge for at least 2 days. Unmold the terrine, slice into portions and reheat, partially covered, just before serving.

boar:

Debone the boar legs and separate all the muscles individually (reserve the shank for future use). Rub all the tender parts with enough olive oil to lightly coat all the meat, and pepper, garlic and fresh herbs to taste, then leave overnight. Roast the remaining parts (bones, sinews, trimmings) with the onions, carrots and celery; after browning, deglaze with the dry white wine, top up with veal remouillage (just enough to coat the bones/meat) and reduce to the desired jus consistency for the demi glace for the sauce.

popover:

Mix all the ingredients at least 8 hours before serving. Heat the ramekin dishes until hot in a 375°F oven, then spray each ramekin very well with nonstick spray. Pour the batter three-quarters to the top and bake for about 35 minutes or until golden brown. Serve immediately.

sauce:

Rinse, pit and cut the olives. Sweat the shallots, add the olives, deglaze with the white wine and reduce by half. Add the cream, reduce by half again, add the demi glace and finish the sauce by binding with butter and herbs.

to serve:

Season the boar legs and cook to medium rare. Place a slice of the reheated terrine on a plate, add sauce and arrange a boar leg and popover on top.

CARAMELIZED GOAT CHEESE CHEESECAKE WITH POACHED GROUND CHERRIES, BLACKBERRY COULIS

BY MARC LATULIPPE

People are always pleasantly surprised by the taste combination of this goat cheese cheesecake and our guests at Kingsbrae Arms frequently ask for the recipe.

Serves 12-14
Preparation time: 30 minutes
Cooking time: 2 hours

Special equipment:
One 10" springform pan, mixer

INGREDIENTS

crust:

6 oz	Graham cracker crumbs
1¾ oz	white sugar
2½ oz	melted butter

filling:

14 oz	cream cheese
3½ oz	goat cheese, crumbled
6 oz	sugar
2 tsp	cornstarch
4	eggs, lightly beaten
½	lemon, zest and juice
8½ fl oz	sour cream

coulis:

9 oz	blackberries
4½ oz	sugar
½ fl oz	water

poached ground cherries:

7 fl oz	water
5 oz	sugar
2 cups	cherries, ground

METHOD

crust:

Line the bottom of the springform pan with parchment paper and butter the sides very well. Combine the crust ingredients in a bowl and press into the bottom of the cake pan.

filling:

Place a heatproof container filled with hot water on the lowest rack of the oven and preheat the oven to 300°F.

In a mixer fitted with the paddle attachment, blend the cream cheese at low speed until smooth (scrape the sides of the bowl often); add the sugar and goat cheese, mix in for a minute (always at low speed). Mix the eggs and the cornstarch together, then incorporate into the mixture a little bit at the time. Finish with lemon juice, zest and the sour cream.

Pour this mixture into the springform pan and set in the oven to bake for up to two hours, or until the middle of the cake is set (let the cheesecake cool inside the oven with the door partially open).

coulis:

Bring all the ingredients to a boil, cool and purée with a food processor, strain and cool down.

poached ground cherries:

Bring the water and sugar to a boil, remove from the heat and add the cherries, cover, let the mixture rest until it has cooled down, then serve.

to serve:

Serve a slice of the cheesecake with some coulis and cherries, and decorate with fruits of your choice.

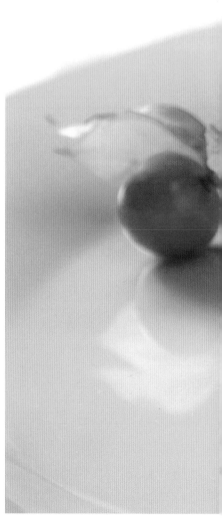

Roland Ménard & Francis Wolf

At first glance, one would never guess that Executive Chef Roland Ménard has been behind the stove at Manoir Hovey for an amazing 29 years: his energy and enthusiasm are infectious. The incredibly talented self-taught chef has won countless awards for Manoir Hovey's restaurant, which is considered one of the best in the whole province of Québec. Long before it became trendy, Ménard was one of the first Canadian chefs to push for a more seasonal and local cuisine, and not be so heavily dependent on French classicism and imported products.

His indispensable right-hand man is Francis Wolf, a chef who injects fresh ideas and innovation into the Manoir's kitchens after each of his investigative dining tours around the world. A tireless researcher of the latest techniques, Wolf brings a decidedly contemporary edge to the dishes served at the historic restaurant. Thanks to his efforts, the Manoir's kitchens are equipped with all the de rigueur gadgets required of a restaurant of that caliber, such as sous vide sealers and the Rolls-Royce of sorbet makers, the Pacojet.

The duo's signature dishes include chocolate lollipops with a chilled apple juice filling, halibut served with a faux risotto made of cauliflower florets, and seared loin of caribou with a very original melt-in-your-mouth foie gras 'tabouleh'. Whenever possible, they like to feature on the menu what the area is best known for: exceptional artisanal cheeses, hard ciders, duck, pork, venison and, in warmer months, a panoply of organic vegetables and micro greens.

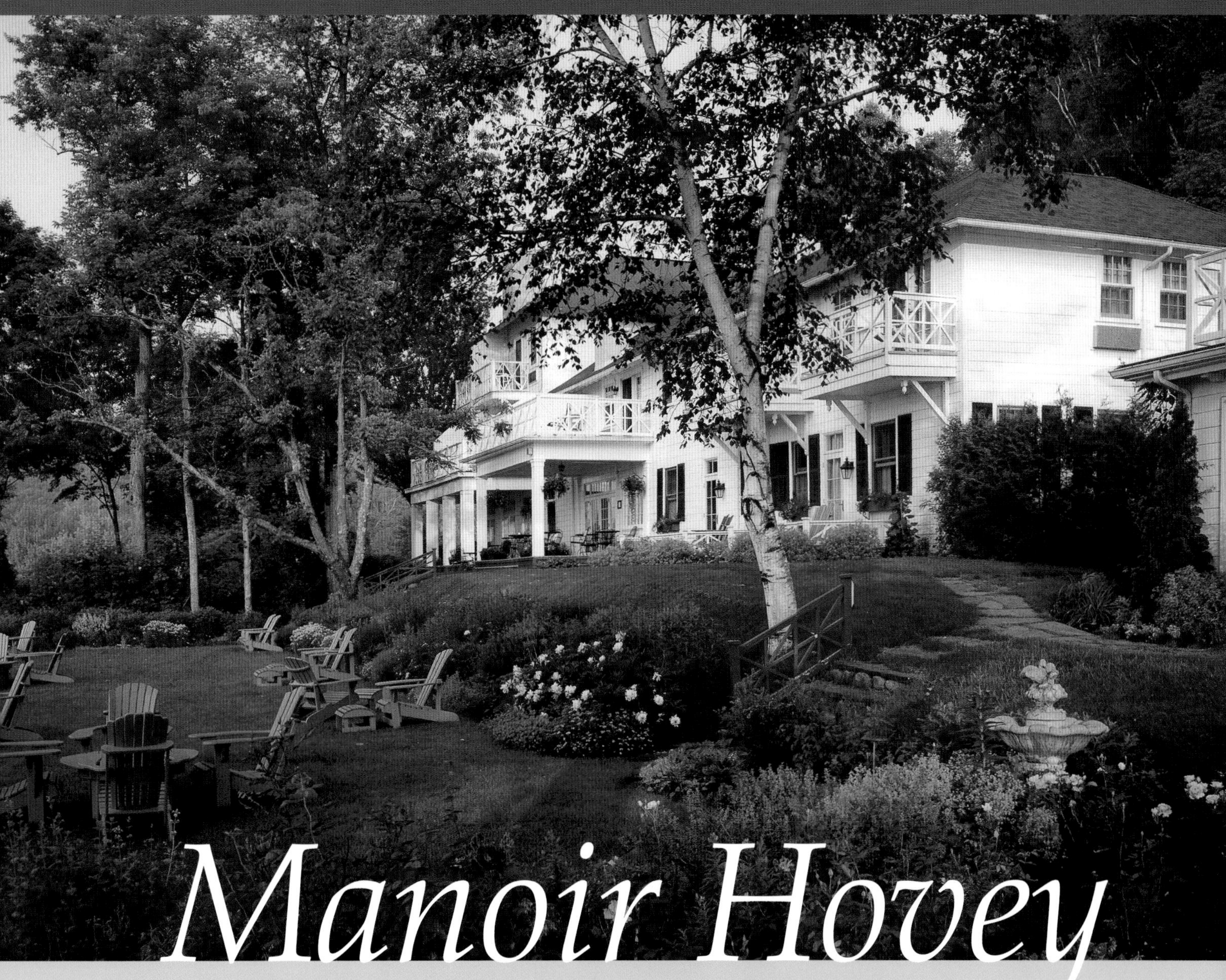

Manoir Hovey

This is a wonderful getaway in all seasons only 80 minutes from Montreal.

Manoir Hovey, a historic mansion, is nestled among English gardens and forest on 600 meters of lakeshore and inspires a romantic and relaxing lifestyle reminiscent of its origins as a private estate (with all the modern luxuries added). Rates include an abundance of year-round recreational facilities on site making the Manoir a destination in itself. The culinary arts are scrupulously upheld, enhanced by an 850 reference wine list and an exceptional selection of Québec cheeses. A stay at Manoir Hovey comes with the promise of an abundance of fresh air in a scenic, unspoilt part of Québec very near to Montreal and the U.S.-Canadian border.

Serves 6

Preparation time:	45 minutes + 2 hours chilling time for soup
Cooking time:	45 minutes

Special equipment:
Mandoline, squeeze bottle for purée (can be replaced by a spoon), Pacojet (optional)

Planning ahead:
The soup has to stay in a bowl of iced water for 2 hours.

INGREDIENTS

soup:

2	leeks, white part only
2	branches of thyme
1	bay leaf
2 tbsp	olive oil
1	large potato
6 cups	water
1	bunch of green asparagus
ice	
salt & pepper	

pickled onions:

12	red pearl onions
3 oz	water
3 oz	white wine vinegar
1 oz	sugar
1 tbsp	pickling spices

cauliflower purée:

1	onion, chopped
1 tbsp	olive oil
½	cauliflower (16 oz)
16 oz	2% milk

garnish:

aniseed herbs and sprouts (hyssop, anise, basil, fennel sprouts). Could replace with basil and bronze fennel.

WARM GREEN ASPARAGUS SOUP, CAULIFLOWER PUREE & HYSSOP

BY FRANCIS WOLF

All the bounty of Québec's Spring harvest comes to life in this dish.

METHOD

soup:

Cut the whites of the leeks into pieces. Sweat them on a medium heat in olive oil with the thyme and bay leaf until they are soft. Cut the potato into pieces and add, with the water, to the leeks. Cook on medium heat for 23 minutes. Blend this mixture in a blender and season with salt. Chill in the refrigerator. While the mixture is chilling, cut off the asparagus tips and put them aside for garnishing. Plunge the spears (minus tips) into salted, boiling water for one minute. Fill a large bowl with ice. With a mandoline slicer, slice the cooked asparagus into small shavings then put them into the ice for at least two hours. Finally, blend the chilled asparagus shavings, the cooked leeks and potato in a blender. Season with salt and pepper.

pickled onions:

Place all the ingredients in a casserole dish on a low heat for 10 minutes. Chill in the refrigerator. Quarter the onions when cold.

cauliflower purée:

In a casserole dish, sauté the onion on a low heat in olive oil. Chop the cauliflower into small pieces and add to the onion in the casserole. Add the milk, and cook for 10-15 minutes on a low heat. Mix in a blender until smooth.

to serve:

Reheat the soup. With the help of a dropper or a spoon, draw lines on the bottom of the soup plate with the cauliflower purée. Place eight quarters of onions on the soup plate and several raw asparagus tips. Sprinkle with aniseed herbs and sprouts. Pour the hot soup tableside, out of a small jug, being careful not to dismantle the arrangement in the center.

Chef's tip:

Be creative with the garnish: the sprouts can be substituted for anything delicate and very fresh from your local market.

VENISON TARTARE FROM THE APPALACHIANS, FRESH HORSERADISH POTATO SALAD, SMOKED BREAD, HARD BOILED EGG

BY FRANCIS WOLF

In Québec we take pride in our exceptional game meats, caribou being the most exquisite of them.

Serves 6
Preparation time: 30 minutes, over 3 days
Cooking time: 1 hour

Special equipment:
Pacojet (optional), a smoker

Planning ahead:
The horseradish sauce should be started 2 days ahead. The egg yolk sauce can be made in advance if you have a Pacojet.

INGREDIENTS

venison

¾ lb	loin of venison
1 tbsp	Dijon mustard
1 tbsp	capers, ground
1	small French shallot, finely chopped
5 tsp	olive oil
1 tbsp	chopped chives
salt & pepper	

horseradish sauce:

2 oz	2% yogurt
1 oz	salted wild horseradish (or regular bottled horseradish)

potato salad:

3	Idaho potatoes

smoked bread:

1	French bread (6")
fir or hickory chips	

egg white:

6	hard-boiled eggs (you will keep only the white if using a Pacojet)

egg yolk sauce:

8	egg yolks
1 tsp	olive oil

METHOD

horseradish sauce:

2 days prior drain the yogurt in cheesecloth for 24 hours. 1 day prior mix the horseradish with the yogurt.

fresh potato salad:

With a cutter, cut each potato in six pieces for a total of 18 regular pieces. Cook the potatoes in boiling salted water for 7 minutes, then cool them down in a bowl of ice cubes and cold water.

smoked bread:

Smoke the bread with a few fir or hickory chips in a smoker.

egg white:

Use only the egg whites from your hard-boiled eggs and finely chop them. Retain the yolks for the egg yolk sauce, if not using a Pacojet (see below).

egg yolk sauce:

1 day prior, if you have a Pacojet, put the eight fresh yolks in the freezer. The day it is to be served, put the yolks in the Pacojet with salt and 1 teaspoon of good quality olive oil. If you don't have a Pacojet, you don't need to prepare the sauce a day in advance. You just need to cook two hard-boiled eggs, keep only the yolks and add them to the six yolks left from the egg whites used previously, and mash together.

venison:

Season the venison and place under a grill (cook it blue, extra-rare). After letting it cool down, chop into small dice. Mix with the mustard, capers, shallot , chives and olive oil.

to serve:

Spread the egg yolk sauce on the plate. Shape a quenelle (oval egg shape) with the egg white. Put ¼ teaspoon of horseradish sauce in three different spots towards the outside of the plate. Place one piece of potato over each horseradish sauce spot. Put the venison tartare on the other side of the plate. Add the smoked bread atop the venison.

MAPLE PARFAIT, BLACKBERRIES & BANANA FRITTERS

BY ANGELE RACICOT

Nothing says Québec like maple syrup. Here, we incorporate the golden nectar into a velvety decadent dessert.

Serves 6
Preparation time: 1 hour
Cooking time: 30 minutes

Planning ahead:
Prepare the maple parfait 1 day prior. It has to be in the freezer for 24 hours.

Special equipment:
Deep fryer (optional), 2 containers: 12" long x 3" wide x 2" high

INGREDIENTS

maple parfait:

¾ cup medium maple syrup
3 eggs
1 ⅛ cup 35%, cream softly whipped

blackberry purée:

¾ lb frozen blackberries
1 oz sugar
1 pinch of salt

banana fritters:

½ banana
3 oz flour
1 oz sugar
½ tbsp baking powder
1 tsp vanilla extract
½ cup water
1 pinch of salt
4 oz Japanese Panko flour

to serve:

fresh blackberries
dried banana chips

METHOD

maple parfait:

Beat the eggs with a hand mixer. Heat the maple syrup lightly. Transfer the eggs into a stainless steel bowl and cook them on a medium heat while adding the maple syrup in a fine stream. Stir constantly until the mixture forms a thick ribbon when dropped from a spoon onto the remaining batter. Pour the mixture into a standing mixer and whip it on speed 2 until it has cooled down. Then add the cream. Pour the mixture into the large containers and leave in the freezer for 24 hours.

blackberry purée:

Heat the blackberries slowly to soften. Mix briefly with a hand mixer, stopping before the blackberry seeds become puréed. Pass the mixture through a fine sieve. Then finish cooking the purée while adding sugar and a pinch of salt. Reduce on a medium heat for 10 minutes.

banana fritters:

Heat a deep fryer. If you don't have one, use a regular pan to fry the banana. Mix the flour, sugar, baking powder, vanilla extract, water and salt in a medium-sized mixing bowl. Pour the flour into a second bowl. In order to have 18 pieces of deep-fried banana, cut the banana into six pieces lengthwise and then cut each piece in three. With a fork, dip each slice in the batter mixture and then dip it in the flour. Fry each slice for 30 seconds-1 minute.

to serve:

Unmold the maple parfait and cut it in squares. Using a spoon or a squeeze bottle, dot some blackberry purée onto one side of your dessert plate. Place the maple parfait in the center of the plate. Garnish with banana fritters, dry banana, and fresh blackberries.

Chef's tip:

To make unmolding the parfait easier, cover the bottom and sides of your freezer container with cling film, making sure to eliminate air bubbles.

To make a nice round ball shape with the banana fritters, roll each piece into the palm of your hand to make a regular small ball after dredging in the Japanese Panko flour and before frying.

Jean-François Bélair

Jean-François Bélair grew up in the Montreal area, but very early on in his culinary journey, he set off to explore different regions, products and cuisines. His passion for cooking was born as a result of close contact with chefs who are passionate about their work. The hard work of farmers and growers has also instilled in Jean-François much respect for primary ingredients. While the majority of his techniques have their origins in French cuisine, he draws inspiration from all over the world.

Jean-François' work at La Pinsonnière uses a style fashioned on his diverse experience, while continuing to develop his skills each day.

Prior to working at La Pinsonnière, Jean-François was Sous Chef in Montreal at Hotel Place d'Armes and before that Chef de partie tournant at The Wickaninnish Inn in Tofino.

La Pinsonnière

On the banks of the Saint-Laurent River, from where you can see the spouting whales, the Authier family has created a beautifully restful little hotel with opulent interiors, an excellent wine cellar and delicious authentic food including homemade viennoiseries (the breakfasts are a delight) and fish smoked on site.

The region of Charlevoix is one of the best preserved places on the planet and is classified as a 'biosphere reserve' by UNESCO. It is also one of the largest inhabited craters in the world: the impact left by a meteorite 350 million years ago has given this part of Québec a unique landscape.

Serves 4

Preparation time:	30 minutes
Cooking time:	6 hours (5 hours poaching time for the quails)

Special equipment:
Vacuum pack machine

INGREDIENTS

quails:

4	whole plump quails
1¾ oz	wild mushrooms
¾ oz	35% fat cream
1	shallot, finely chopped
1	garlic clove, chopped

brown quail sauce

pumpkin:

1	pumpkin

butter
chicken broth
sprigs of thyme

garnish:

tiny sprigs of parsley

STUFFED QUAILS WITH WILD MUSHROOMS & PUMPKIN

BY JEAN-FRANCOIS BELAIR

Quail is a good example of a fine local product prepared simply without too much intrusion of flavor in order to allow the subtlety of the meat to come through.

METHOD

quails:

Open and debone the quails from the back and flatten 'butterfly style', taking care to not pierce the skin. Remove the meat from the legs, grind in a food processor and pass through a sieve to obtain a fine pulp, then set aside.

Cut the mushrooms into small dice and sauté in butter with the garlic and shallot. Drain for a few minutes. Gently fold together with the leg meat and cream.

Place the flattened quails on 7½" x 7½" squares of plastic wrap. Place a heaped spoonful of stuffing between the breasts and make into a sphere shape using the wrap. Tie the ends securely. Poach the quails in water at 170°F for about 5 hours. Preheat the oven to 350°F. Remove the quails from the film and brown thoroughly in butter in a pan over a high heat. Put the quails into a small pot containing the brown quail sauce and brown in the oven for 15 minutes, basting every 3 minutes.

pumpkin:

Slice the pumpkin into very thin slices about ¼" thick and cut into petal shapes. Vacuum pack with a little chicken broth, a knob of butter and a few thyme sprigs. Poach in water at 170°F for about 20 minutes, or until the pieces feel tender when pressed with a finger.

to serve:

Place the quail sphere in the center of the plate and arrange the pumpkin petals around it to form a flower shape. Garnish the leaves with the parsley.

RED DEER MEDALLIONS WITH VEGETABLES & JUNEBERRY SAUCE

BY JEAN-FRANCOIS BELAIR

Red deer is a type of venison which is proving increasingly popular with Quebecers. Gentle cooking is sufficient to appreciate its delicate flavor and the leanness of the meat also appeals to healthy eating enthusiasts.

Serves 5
Preparation time: 20 minutes
Cooking time: 30 minutes

INGREDIENTS

venison:

4 red deer sirloin medallions, 6 oz each

juneberry sauce:

butter
1 shallot, finely chopped
3½ oz juneberries
2½ fl oz juneberry juice
10 fl oz brown game sauce

vegetables:

2 salsify
2½ oz Chinese artichokes
4 mini parsnips
1 celery root, cut into small pieces
1¾ oz chanterelle mushrooms
1¾ oz sheep's trotters
parsley, chopped
salt & pepper

METHOD

Preheat the oven to 350°F.

juneberry sauce:

Sweat the shallot in butter in a small saucepan, add the juneberries and let sweat for several minutes. Deglaze with the juneberry juice, reduce to about half and add the brown game sauce, then season.

vegetables:

Clean the vegetables and cut them to the same size as the parsnips. Blanch each type of vegetable one at a time until cooked but still crisp.

Put a generous knob of butter in a large pan over a medium heat. When the butter begins to brown slightly put in the root vegetables, mushrooms and sheep's trotters, and brown well. Remove from the heat, season, add the chopped parsley and put aside.

venison:

Season the deer medallions generously and sear them in butter on all sides. Put in the oven and cook for about 4 minutes for rare. Let rest for several minutes.

to serve:

Reheat the deer in the oven for one minute just before serving. Place on a plate and serve with the vegetables and sauce dotted around.

Serves 8
Preparation time: 30 minutes
Cooking time: 30 minutes

INGREDIENTS

coffee lace biscuit:

4½ oz	icing sugar
4½ oz	flour
4½ oz	creamed butter
4½ oz	coffee caramel

panna cotta:

10 fl oz	cream
6 fl oz	milk
7 oz	white chocolate
5	gelatin leaves

coffee cream:

4	egg yolks
4½ oz	sugar
1 pt	milk, warm
6	gelatin leaves
coffee extract	

chocolate biscuit and coffee:

6	egg whites
6	egg yolks
3 oz	icing sugar
1 oz	cocoa powder
1¼ oz	cornstarch
1 lb 5 oz	melted chocolate

coffee ice-cream:

2 pt	coffee custard
½ fl oz	30-degree syrup
3½ fl oz	whipped cream

Québec coffee shooter:

1 fl oz	Sortilege liqueur and cane sugar
1 fl oz	coffee
1 fl oz	lightly whipped cream

garnish:

coffee caramel
chocolate drops

AROUND QUEBEC COFFEE

BY JEAN-FRANCOIS BELAIR

This dessert serves to remind us that the combination of coffee and chocolate is truly a marriage made in heaven. Maple is, of course, indispensable when it comes to adding a little sweetness.

METHOD

coffee lace biscuit:

Preheat the oven to 320°F. Mix all the ingredients and cook on a silpat in the oven for 10 minutes. Mold the lace biscuit into a cup shape before it solidifies.

panna cotta:

Heat the cream and milk. Add the white chocolate, then the gelatin (previously soaked in cold water), stir until gelatin disolves. Reserve.

coffee cream:

Whisk the egg yolks and sugar until light and fluffy then stir in the warm milk, whisking constantly. Cook to 181°F. Add the coffee extract and gelatin (previously soaked in cold water) and mix. Reserve.

chocolate biscuit and coffee:

Preheat the oven to 350°F. Beat the egg whites. Mix the other ingredients together. Fold the beaten egg whites into the mixture. Pour into 2" diameter round metal molds and cook in the oven for 20 minutes. Allow to cool. Add a layer of panna cotta and allow to set in the fridge. Then add a layer of coffee cream and allow to set in the fridge.

coffee ice cream:

Mix together all the ingredients and place in an ice cream machine.

to serve:

Gently pour each of the Québec coffee ingredients into small shooter glasses, liqueur first followed by the coffee then the cream. Place the biscuit/panna cotta/coffee cream layer inside the cup-shaped lace biscuit and cover with coffee ice cream topped with chocolate drops. Serve side by side on a plate with some coffee caramel.

Vaughn Perret & Charles Leary

Vaughn Perret and Charles Leary have worked together in the food world for 20 years, first as organic farmers and cheesemakers in rural Louisiana, then as restaurateurs in New Orleans, and finally as the chefs and proprietors of Trout Point Lodge.

Authors of *The Trout Point Lodge Cookbook: Creole Cuisine from New Orleans to Nova Scotia*, Vaughn Perret hails from the Crescent City, while Charles Leary grew up in the western United States. Their dedication to traditional and artisanal foods also finds expression in the culinary vacations they have offered in Nova Scotia as well as in Costa Rica and Spain, where they spend Winters in the magical city of Granada. Both diverted from professional careers to pursue a love of food and cooking, Vaughn as a New York City lawyer and Charles as a professor of history.

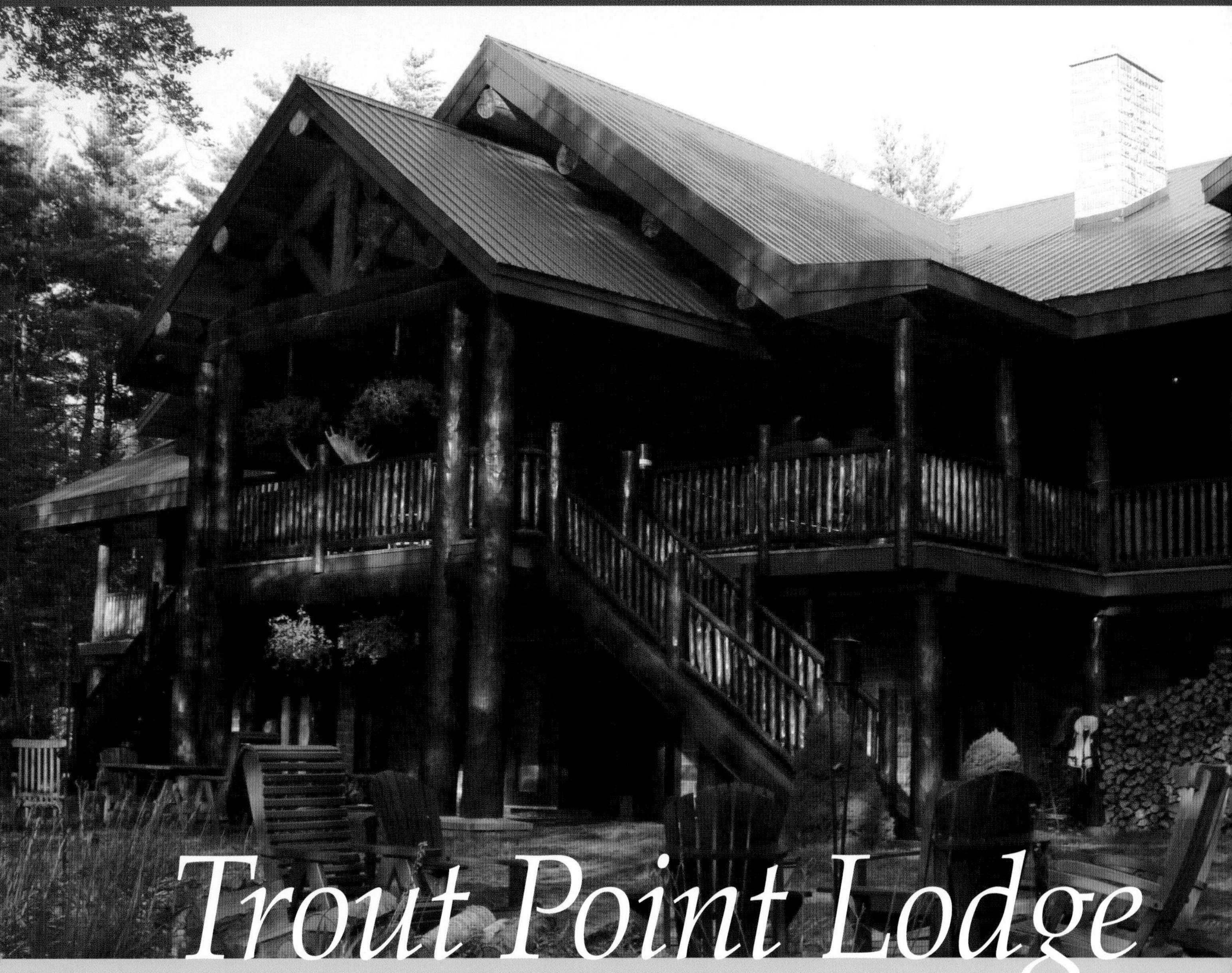

Trout Point Lodge

of Nova Scotia

Trout Point is the premier small wilderness hotel in Atlantic Canada and is nestled next to the Tusket River within a UNESCO 'biosphere reserve'.

This magical place shelters its guests in an utterly civilized outpost amid the backwoods: an enchanting location in which everything is created for a most relaxing time. Positioned so that every room boasts water views, the Lodge provides unique Nova Scotia experiences: gastronomy – Point's kitchen uses local seafood and produces its own cheeses, smoked salmon, and gravlax — and romance, as well as fishing, hiking, kayaking and canoeing. And if laziness overwhelms you ... enjoy a great in-room massage or spa treatments.

Serves 4
Preparation time: 40 minutes
Cooking time: 15 minutes

INGREDIENTS

4	large, sweet red bell peppers
1	medium white onion, sliced
½	cob of whole corn
¼ lb	lamb riblets
6 tbsp	extra virgin olive oil
⅓	of a clove of garlic, minced
3 cups	lamb or chicken stock
¼ tsp	fresh dill, chopped
¼ tsp	fresh mint, chopped

Salt & freshly ground black pepper to taste

ROASTED RED PEPPER SOUP

VAUGHN PERRET & CHARLES LEARY

This visually stunning soup draws on sensibilities developed during many years living in the Mediterranean region, with its use of plump sweet red peppers, the distinctive flavor of lamb, and the refreshing twist of mint.

METHOD

Roast and peel the large sweet red peppers and place them in a hot cast iron skillet over medium to high heat, turning every 3-4 minutes until the skin of the peppers more or less totally separates from the flesh. Remove from the heat and place in a plastic bag, seal and let them sit for 15-20 minutes, then peel off all the skin.

In a sauté pan over medium heat, caramelize the onion slices in about 2 tbsp of the olive oil and set aside. Roast the corn, while still on the cob, over an open flame (or in a hot skillet). Sear the corn until it begins to change color and char. You can do this while the lamb is being seared in the olive oil.

Boil the riblets in a sauce pan filled with water until tender, approximately 45 minutes. Drain (retain water) them in colander for about 5 minutes, blot with a dry cloth. 15 minutes before serving the soup, warm a pan of olive oil in a sauté pan over medium heat. Place riblets in the oil as soon as it is hot. Adjust heat downward a bit, cook until golden and crisp on the outside. Drain on paper towel (they should be ready right before serving the soup).

Blend the onion and sweet red pepper in a food processor or blender to make a fine purée. Place 3 cups lamb or chicken stock (or retained lamb stock) in a small stock pot on the stove and bring to a simmer. Add onion and red pepper purée and simmer for 10 minutes. Skim off any foam which might rise to the surface. Add ¼ tsp fresh chopped dill and mint each, stir, add the salt and pepper to taste before serving.

to serve:

Ladle the purée into soup bowls. Place the riblets skin/fat side up and a grouping of roasted corn in each bowl Serve.

Chef's tip:

Be sure not to overcook the red pepper purée, as it will loose both color and flavor.

Serves 4
Preparation time: 35 minutes
Cooking time: 40 minutes

INGREDIENTS

gumbo sauce:

¼ cup	grapeseed oil
¼ cup	unbleached all purpose flour (un-enriched if possible)
½ cup	green bell pepper, chopped
½ cup	white onion, chopped
¼ cup	celery, chopped
3	cloves garlic, minced
¼ cup	finnan haddie (substitute any smoked fish or sausage), roughly chopped (optional, if you want a smoky flavor to the sauce)
1 cup	high quality lobster or fish stock (substitute chicken stock)
¼ tsp	cumin
½ tsp	allspice
¼ tsp	(or to taste) cayenne pepper
1	dash of white pepper
½ tsp	dried thyme

salt & ground black pepper, to taste
2 bay leaves (preferably fresh)

12	medium shrimps, preferably fresh, without heads and shells
2 tbsp	southeast Asian fish sauce
¾ cup	fresh lobster meat (claws preferred), roughly chopped (substitute crab meat)

mahogany rice:

1 cup	water
1 cup	dark Japanese rice
1 tsp	salt

haddock fillets:

4	fresh haddock fillets
2 tbsp	butter

garnish:

green onion tops, sliced into fine rings

HADDOCK WITH GUMBO SAUCE

BY CHARLES LEARY & VAUGHN PERRET

Trout Point is fortunate to be in one of the greatest areas for fresh seafood in the world. Using exceptional local fish, lobster, and shrimp, this dish uses traditional techniques of the French New World to produce a modern twist on a Creole classic.

METHOD

gumbo sauce:

Make a dark roux: in a heavy-bottomed saucepan, heat the oil over a medium heat until a small amount of flour tossed into the pan sizzles. Add the flour and stir in with a wooden spoon or metal whisk. Turn the heat down slightly. Stir constantly and adjust the heat as needed so that the flour slowly darkens without burning. Keep the pan on the heat until the roux reaches a dark brown color.

Immediately add the green pepper, onion, and celery to the hot roux. Stir to coat the vegetables thoroughly in the roux. Cook until the vegetables soften and the onion turns translucent. Add the optional finnan haddie and two-thirds of the minced garlic, stir until fragrant, then add the stock, stirring to mix it into the roux. Add the spices, bay leaves, salt and pepper. Adjust the consistency of the sauce as desired by adding water in small amounts at a time. Add the shrimps and allow them to cook in the sauce, for about 4 minutes. Add the fish sauce, the remaining garlic, and the lobster, taste for salt and spice.

mahogany rice:

In a saucepan with a lid, bring the water to a simmer over a medium heat. Add the salt and the rice, and stir. Lower the heat to low, cover, and let cook for about 40 minutes or until done. Reserve.

haddock fillets:

Place a nonstick sauté pan just big enough to hold the fish fillets over a medium heat. Add the butter. Coat the pan with the butter, adding more if necessary, and as soon as the butter starts to brown, add the fillets. Cook for about 2-3 minutes on each side, turning only once.

to serve:

Place the rice in the amount desired on four plates. Place a haddock fillet on top of the rice, and ladle the gumbo sauce over the top of the fillet. Garnish with the green onion rings and serve immediately.

Chef's tip:

If you are using whole shrimps, use the heads and shells to make an easy shrimp stock: boil the heads and shells in a small saucepan with water for about 5 minutes, strain, and reserve.

Serves 8
Preparation time: 20 minutes
Cooking time: 45 minutes

INGREDIENTS

short dough tart crust: (makes about three 9" crusts)

3½	sticks unsalted butter, chilled and cut into slices
¾ cup + 2 tbsp sugar	
1 tsp	pure vanilla extract
4¼ cups	all purpose flour
1	egg

nectarines and plums:

2 tbsp	butter
4	nectarines, cut into eighths
6	plums, halved
¼ cup	granulated sugar

custard:

1 cup	heavy cream
3	eggs
1 tsp	pure vanilla extract or 1 vanilla bean, slit
½ tsp	pure almond extract
¼ cup	granulated sugar

NECTARINE & PLUM CUSTARD TART

BY CHARLES LEARY & VAUGHN PERRET

This simple but elegant tart can be modified to suit a variety of stone fruit, including peaches. The addition of pure extract of almond, itself a stone fruit, deliciously complements the rich custard and fruit combination.

METHOD

crust:

In a mixing bowl, mash together the butter and the sugar. Add the vanilla, then add the flour, working with your hands until combined. It is fine to leave small chunks or flakes of butter. Add the egg and mix together rapidly until the dough can be formed into three equal-sized balls. Wrap the balls in plastic wrap and refrigerate (the extra two portions can be saved for future use).

fruit:

In a sauté pan over a medium heat melt the butter, then add the fruit and the sugar. Cook the fruit over a medium heat for about 4-5 minutes, to sweat the fruit and release some juices. Remove from the heat.

custard:

In a small mixing bowl, combine the cream with the other ingredients, whisking lightly to combine. Do not whip air into the mixture. Add the excess butter and juice liquid from the sauté pan.

to serve:

Grease a spring form tart pan with butter. Remove the dough ball from the refrigerator and roll it out with a rolling pin. Alternatively, cut thin slices of the dough and place them in the pan, pressing with fingers to form a solid crust. Allow about 1" sides for the crust.

Freeze the pan for about 10 minutes. Preheat the oven to 375°F.

Arrange the fruit in the bottom of the tart shell. Pour the custard over the top. Place the tart immediately in the hot oven. Bake for 15 minutes, then reduce the heat to 350°F. Bake until the custard is firm and starts to turn golden on top, approximately 30 minutes.

Remove from the oven and remove the spring-form side, allow to cool for 15 minutes, then cut into eight slices and serve.

Chef's tip:

You can freeze the tart dough, doubly wrapped in plastic, for up to 2 months for future use.

Western Canada

With moose, grizzly bear, humpback whales, polar bear and more, you would be forgiven for thinking that Western Canada is just one huge national park.

Complete with mountains, glaciers and other immense terrain, Western Canada certainly is a sight to behold. However, this region of Canada is also home to some of the greatest cities the world has to offer. Vancouver, Calgary and Edmonton with their traditional roots are growing into vast city scenes. Oil and totem-poles are associated with Western Canada while moose and sourdough grace the tables; whatever you eat, it's always fresh.

Dale MacKay
Grand Chef Relais & Châteaux

While Dale MacKay's culinary career has taken him around the world, this native of Saskatoon, Saskatchewan has now come home to Canada as Lumière's Executive Chef. He has a broad range of experiences cooking as a private chef in Rome, Italy, as Executive Chef at The West Coast Fishing Club in the Queen Charlotte Islands and working with Gordon Ramsay in several of the renowned chef's kitchens.

Dale first joined Lumière in 2007, bringing exuberance and passion to his work, and was made Executive Chef in September of that same year. Since that time he has demonstrated wonderful craftsmanship and creativity in the kitchen. He continues to flourish through his collaboration with Chef Daniel Boulud. Mackay is thrilled to be cooking on the West coast where he particularly savors working with the wealth of fine British Columbia ingredients. Under Dale MacKay's direction, the cuisine at Lumière has earned AAA's Five Diamond Award, Four Stars in the *Mobil Guide*, The Georgia Straights' award for Best Fine Dining Restaurant and *The Vancouver Sun* award for Best Restaurant.

Lumière

Lumière restaurant is a reference of quality and creativity in Canadian gastronomy situated in Vancouver's chic residential neighborhood known as Kitsilano.

The newly designed setting reflects a minimalist yet welcoming elegance. Chef Dale MacKay works his magic on the finest ingredients British Columbia has to offer under the guidance of Daniel Boulud. The influence of French cuisine is ever present in a symphony of flavors not to be missed: Dungeness Crab with Granny Smith Apples, Celery Root and Toasted Hazelnuts; Duo of Red Wine Braised Short Ribs and Seared Rib Eye with Shallot Confit, Spinach Soubise and Sautéed Porcini; Chocolate and Butter Caramel Tart, and Toffee Sabayon and Passion Fruit Ice Cream.

BC SPOT PRAWNS WITH RILLON, CAULIFLOWER, SMOKED HEN OF THE WOODS

BY DALE MACKAY

The residents of British Columbia are fiercely loyal and proud when it comes to their native sea food, and particularly when it's their sweet and ever so mildly briny local spot prawns. The prawns have such a delicate perfection it's best to prepare them with as little fuss as possible. That's why I save the fireworks in this dish for the garnishes. The result is a heady mix of the best of the region's land and sea.

Serves 6
Preparation time: 2 days
Cooking time: 3 hours

Special equipment:
Deep-fat frying thermometer, stovetop smoker, mandoline

Planning ahead:
Allow 2 days to marinate the pork.

INGREDIENTS

prawns:

12 spot prawns, cleaned and de-veined, shells reserved for the reduction
olive oil and salt, as needed
2 lemons, juice

prawn reduction:

2 tbsp olive oil
2 oz smoked bacon, diced
1 clove garlic, sliced
2 shallots, sliced
1 small leek, diced
1 stalk lemongrass, smashed and chopped
1 oz freshly grated ginger
1 tbsp coriander seeds
1 cardamom pod, crushed
2 star anise pods
¼ tsp Szechuan peppercorns
1 tbsp mixed white, pink, and black peppercorns
5½ cups chicken stock
3 cups veal stock
2 sprigs of fresh tarragon
2 sprigs of fresh cilantro
1½ tbsp white balsamic vinegar
½ cup grapeseed oil

cauliflower pureé:

2 tbsp butter
2 tbsp olive oil
½ head of cauliflower, chopped
½ cup heavy cream
¼ cup water
salt & pepper, to taste

puffed rice:

½ cup wild rice
canola oil, for frying
salt

sherry gastrique-prawn glaze:

2½ tbsp sugar
2 cups sherry vinegar
½ cup prawn reduction

pork belly: (makes extra)

5½ qt water
27 oz salt
1¾ oz nitrate salt
2½ oz dextrose
1 fresh pork belly
½ cup mustard seeds
½ cup coriander seeds
1 tbsp fennel seeds
5 star anise
1 tbsp five spice
½ tbsp white peppercorns
1 stalk of lemongrass, chopped
2 sprigs of thyme
2 cups veal stock or low sodium beef broth
cornstarch, as needed
frying oil

mushroom:

1 cup dry hickory wood chips
1 head of hen of the woods mushroom
2 tbsp olive oil
1 sprig of thyme
1 tbsp butter
salt & pepper

garnish:

3 cauliflower florets, shaved with a mandoline
cilantro, diced
micro cilantro

METHOD

prawns:

Wrap two prawns together in a ying-yang shape and stick a wooden skewer through the center to secure. Line a baking sheet with foil and sprinkle with oil. When ready to serve, heat the oven to broil (grill). Sprinkle the prawns with salt and lemon juice, broil for 1 minute 30 seconds on the bottom rack, flip and broil on the other side for another 1 minute 30 seconds.

prawn reduction:

Heat the olive oil in a Dutch oven or heavy-bottomed pot over a high heat. Add the prawn shells and roast, stirring occasionally, until browned and fragrant. Add the bacon, garlic, shallots, leek, lemongrass, and ginger. Cook, stirring, until the vegetables are browned. Add the spices and peppercorns and cook, until toasted and fragrant. Add the stocks to cover, then the tarragon and cilantro; simmer for 1 hour. Strain the liquid through a fine sieve into a pot; discard the solids. Reduce, skimming occasionally, until a glaze consistency is reached. Whisk ½ cup of the prawn reduction with the balsamic vinegar and grapeseed oil, and season to taste to make a vinaigrette.

cauliflower pureé:

Heat the oil and butter in a medium saucepot. Add the cauliflower and cook, stirring, for 10 minutes or until softened but not browned. Add the cream and water. Cover and simmer until very tender. Remove the cover and cook until the liquid is almost evaporated. Purée in a blender until smooth. Season and keep warm.

puffed rice:

Place the rice in a dry blender or coffee grinder and blend to a coarse sand texture. Fill a saucepot one-third full with oil and heat to 450°F on a deep fat thermometer. Fry the rice until it puffs, then strain from the oil and drain on paper towels. Sprinkle with salt and set aside.

sherry gastrique-prawn glaze:

Heat a medium skillet over a medium heat and add the sugar in an even layer, melt to a caramel color, then remove from the heat. Carefully pour in the sherry vinegar, return to the heat, and reduce until syrupy. Add the prawn reduction and stir well.

pork belly:

In a saucepot, bring a third of the water to a boil, add the salt, nitrate and dextrose, stir to dissolve. Cool and combine with the remaining water. Submerge the pork belly and refrigerate for 24 hours. The next day, remove and pat dry. Rub the belly with the spices, lemongrass and thyme. Wrap tightly with plastic wrap and marinate in the refrigerator for 24 hours.

Preheat the oven to 300°F. Remove the belly from the plastic wrap and brush off the excess spices. Place in a shallow roasting pan with the stock. Cover, and transfer to the oven. Braise, glazing occasionally; flip after 1½ hours. Continue to braise, covered, glazing occasionally for another 1½ hours, or until the belly is tender. Cool and cut into 1" x 2" portions.

When ready to serve, fill a saucepot one-third with the oil and heat to 350°F on a deep fat thermometer. Dust the belly with cornstarch and pat away any excess. Fry until crispy. Drain on paper towel and brush one side with the prawn glaze. Sprinkle the glazed size with puffed rice and pat down lightly to ensure it sticks.

mushroom:

Sprinkle the wood chips in the bottom of a roasting pan lined with a rack or in a stovetop smoker. Ignite the woodchips, then cover with a lid until the flames are extinguished. Place the mushroom on the rack inside and re-cover. Smoke for 1 minute 30 seconds. When ready to serve, cut the mushroom head into bite-sized pieces. Heat the oil in a large skillet over a high heat. Add the mushrooms and sauté for about 3 minutes, until browned. Reduce the heat to medium, season and add thyme and butter. Cook, tossing, until the mushrooms are tender.

to serve:

Heat the plates and place a spoonful of purée in the center of each. Remove the skewer from the prawn and arrange on top alongside a pork belly portion. Arrange some mushroom and shaved cauliflower in-between. Drizzle the plate with prawn glaze, vinaigrette and garnish with the cilantros.

PISTACHIO CRUSTED OPAL VALLEY RACK OF LAMB, CHICKPEA PANISSE, ROASTED EGGPLANT, APRICOT CANNELONI

BY DALE MACKAY

From taste to texture and even color, Morocco is the inspiration for this multi-faceted dish. While the flavors are traditional, the approach is modern, rendering the dish an elegant composition of culinary styles, past and present.

Serves 6
Preparation time: 1 day
Cooking time: 1 hour 15 minutes

Planning ahead:
The lamb needs to marinate overnight, the panisse can be prepared the day before, the yogurt should be strained overnight.

Special equipment:
Acetate paper, microplane, mandoline, frying thermometer, 1" diameter ring mold

INGREDIENTS

lamb:

2 lamb racks, trimmed, 2-2½ lb each
1 tbsp harissa paste
5 tbsp olive oil
3 cloves garlic, smashed
2 sprigs of thyme
1 sprig of rosemary
1 bay leaf
½ cup finely ground Sicilian pistachios
1 tsp maltodextrin
2 tbsp butter
salt & ground white pepper

lamb and bulgur wheat apricot 'canneloni':

1 lb lamb shoulder, boneless
1 tbsp Ras el Hanout
4 tbsp olive oil
1 tsp each of coriander seeds, cracked black pepper, cumin seeds, paprika
1 tbsp harissa paste
salt
1 carrot, chopped
1 small onion, chopped
1 celery stalk, chopped
2 cloves garlic, crushed
2 thyme sprigs
1 tbsp tomato paste
2 tbsp sherry vinegar
¼ cup white wine
2 pt lamb or chicken stock
2 tbsp olive oil + more as needed
1 tsp Ras el Hanout
⅓ cup onion, minced
2 cloves garlic, minced
2 tbsp pistachios, chopped
1 cup cracked bulgur wheat
2 cups reserved lamb reduction
1 tbsp parsley, chopped
1 tbsp mint, chopped
salt & pepper, to taste
0.12 oz gelatin, bloomed
6.2 oz apricot purée
5 tbsp water
0.05 oz agar agar
sugar, to taste

roasted eggplant and babaganoush:

7 large Japanese eggplants
1 tsp balsamic vinegar
1 tbsp tahini paste
1 tsp lemon juice
2 tsp thyme, chopped
1 small garlic clove, germ removed, finely grated on a microplane
2 tbsp olive oil
salt & ground white pepper

chickpea panisse:

1 pt whole milk
1 tbsp extra virgin olive oil
½ tbsp unsalted butter
salt & freshly ground pepper
½ tbsp fennel seeds, toasted
1 cup chickpea flour, sifted
frying oil, as needed
semolina flour or finely ground cornmeal

eggplant chips:

1 Japanese eggplant
1 cup milk
frying oil, as needed
salt

minted yogurt sauce:

2 cups yogurt
2 tbsp fresh mint, chopped
1 lemon, zest and juice
¼ cup cucumber, peeled, seeded and finely diced
salt & pepper to taste

to serve:

tomato compote

METHOD

lamb:

In a shallow container, coat the lamb racks with the harissa, oil, garlic, thyme, rosemary and bay leaf. Marinate, covered, overnight in the refrigerator. Purée the pistachios and maltodextrin in a food processor until powdery. When ready to serve, preheat the oven to 350°F. Remove the lamb from the marinade, and wipe off excess oil; season all over. Heat the butter in a skillet over a medium-high heat. Add the lamb, garlic and herbs from the marinade. Sear on one side for approximately 4 minutes, while basting. Turn the chops over and sear on the second side, continuing to baste for another 4 minutes, or until medium rare. Rest for 4 minutes, then coat with the powdered pistachio.

lamb and bulgur wheat apricot 'canneloni':

In a shallow container, coat the lamb with the 4 tablespoons of olive oil, 1 tablespoon of Ras el Hanout, spices, and harissa. Marinate, covered, overnight in the refrigerator. Remove from the marinade, wipe off excess oil, and season all over with salt. Heat a heavy-bottomed saucepot over a medium-high heat. Sear the lamb on all sides until browned, remove and set aside. Reduce the heat to medium, add the carrot, onion, celery, garlic and thyme. Cook, stirring, for about 3 minutes, until softened. Add the tomato paste, sherry vinegar and white wine. Simmer until almost dry. Return the lamb to the pot with the stock. Bring to a simmer, cover and reduce the heat to low. Braise for 1 hour 15 minutes until tender, turning often. Remove from the heat; when cool, shred the meat into a bowl. Strain the broth through a sieve and add enough to keep the lamb moist. In a saucepot, bring the remaining broth to a simmer and reduce by half; reserve.

Heat the remaining 2 tablespoons of oil in a pot over a medium heat. Add the minced onion, garlic, pistachios and 1 tablespoon of Ras el Hanout and cook, stirring, for 5 minutes or until the onions are tender. Add the bulgur wheat and continue to cook, stirring, for another 3 minutes. Add the lamb reduction. Simmer for 20 minutes, stirring occasionally, until the bulgur is tender (add more water if necessary). Remove from the heat, add the shredded lamb, cover and rest for 5 minutes. Mix in the parsley and mint. Season.

Line a 9" x 9" baking pan with acetate. In a saucepot, combine the apricot purée with the water, sugar and agar agar; simmer for 45 seconds. Remove from the heat and stir in the gelatin to dissolve. Pour onto the baking pan. Chill for 2 hours or until set. Remove and cut into 6 squares, including the acetate, separate and chill.

When ready to serve, spoon hot lamb-bulgur mix in the center of each square, roll in the bulgur mix, then peel away the acetate.

roasted eggplant and babaganoush:

Peel lengthwise strips in ¼" intervals into three of the eggplants. Cut into 1" wheels; season. Heat the oil in a medium skillet over a medium-high heat. Add the eggplant slices and sear on one side until golden brown. Flip and sear on the second side. Add vinegar and toss to coat. Set aside; reheat when ready to serve.

For the babaganoush broil (grill) four of the eggplants whole, until charred and tender. When cool, split them in half, scrape the flesh into a blender, add the remaining ingredients and purée until smooth. Season and reserve warm.

chickpea panisse:

Put the milk, olive oil, butter, and fennel seeds into a saucepan, season and bring to a boil. Lower to a simmer and, while whisking, add the chickpea flour in a fine stream. Mix over a low heat until the flour is thoroughly cooked. Pour onto a parchment-lined baking pan and cover with a second sheet of parchment paper. Chill in the refrigerator for 2 to 3 hours or overnight. Using the ring mold, cut out rounds. Pour 3"-4" of oil into a deep pot or casserole and heat to 350°F. Roll the rounds in the semolina/cornmeal and tap off any excess. Fry to a golden brown. Transfer to paper towel and sprinkle with salt.

eggplant chips:

Slice the eggplant into very thin rounds on a mandoline. Soak in milk for 10 minutes. Remove and pat dry. Pour 3"-4" of oil into a deep pot and heat to 275°F. Fry in batches to a crisp golden brown. Drain on paper towel and sprinkle with salt.

minted yogurt sauce:

Place a cheesecloth-lined sieve over a bowl, and add the yogurt. Strain overnight, refrigerated. Combine with the remaining ingredients and season.

to serve:

Place one 'canneloni' offset from the center of a plate with two lamb chops resting against it. Put two pieces of eggplant on the other side, and top with tomato compote, yogurt sauce, and an eggplant chip. Place a chickpea panisse in-between and top with a spoonful of babaganoush.

RASPBERRY ROSE OPERA CAKE

BY CELESTE MAH

This is a very traditional dessert first made popular by the renowned French patissier, Dalloyau. We make it in Summer when we get good local fresh berries. Our version layers Joconde (almond sponge cake) with classic butter cream, house-made raspberry jam and a dark chocolate glaze. The cake is made as one large rectangle, ideal for a large party. We garnish ours with more fresh berries, but you could also add sweet whipped cream, ice cream or sorbet if you like.

Serves 15+
Preparation time: 2 hours
Cooking time: 30 minutes

Special equipment:
Three 18" x 13" baking sheets, candy thermometer

Planning ahead:
The cake can be kept refrigerated for up to 4 days. It also freezes well.

INGREDIENTS

biscuit joconde:

2 cups confectioner's (powdered) sugar
3 cups almond flour
7 eggs
7 egg whites
2 tbsp + 2 tsp caster sugar
⅓ cup unsalted butter, melted
½ cup all purpose flour, sifted

buttercream:

4 egg whites
5 tbsp caster sugar
½ cup + 2 tbsp caster sugar
11 oz (two ¾ sticks) unsalted butter, soft

raspberry-rose jam:

1 lb fresh raspberries
2 tbsp + 2 tsp caster sugar
1 tsp apple pectin
5 tsp dried rose petals, ground
1 lemon, juice

chocolate ganache glaze:

7½ oz dark chocolate (70% cocoa)
½ cup + 3 tbsp heavy cream
1½ oz unsalted butter, soft

garnish:

1 pt raspberries
chocolate décor, optional

METHOD

biscuit joconde:

Preheat the oven to 400°F and place three racks in the center. Line the three baking sheets with greased and floured parchment paper, then set aside. In the bowl of a standing mixer fitted with a whisk attachment, combine the powdered sugar, almond flour and eggs. On medium-high speed, whisk until the volume triples, about 5 minutes. In a separate bowl, whisk the egg whites with a pinch of the sugar until almost stiff, then add the remaining sugar and whisk until stiff peaks form. Add the melted butter into the egg and almond mixture, then stream in the sifted flour and mix well. Add a third of the stiff egg whites and then, using a rubber spatula, gently fold in the rest. Split the mixture between the three baking sheets and, using an offset spatula, spread evenly into about a ⅕" thickness. Bake for 5-7 minutes in a convection oven, or 10-12 minutes in a conventional oven. The cake is done when it no longer sticks to your fingertip. Remove from the oven and cool on a cooling rack.

buttercream:

In the bowl of a standing mixer fitted with a whisk attachment, combine the egg whites with the 5 tablespoons of sugar and whisk until stiff peaks form; set aside. In a medium heavy-bottomed saucepot add the ½ cup + 2 tablespoons of sugar with enough water just to wet. Cook over a medium heat, stirring occasionally with a wooden spoon until the sugar reaches 240°F on a candy thermometer. With the mixer set on medium speed, pour the syrup in a steady stream into the stiff egg whites until smooth and shiny. Whisk in the soft butter in three stages until fully combined and fluffy. Chill until ready to use.

raspberry-rose jam:

In a large heavy-bottomed saucepot, combine the raspberries with the sugar and pectin and cook on a medium heat, stirring, until the raspberries become liquid. Increase the heat to high and continue to cook until boiling and the temperature on a candy thermometer reaches 246°F. Remove from the heat, add the rose petals and lemon juice, and chill.

to assemble the cake:

Remove the three joconde cakes from their trays and peel off the parchment paper. Spread a thin layer of buttercream on the top of two cakes. Chill. Top the same two cakes with a layer of raspberry-rose jam. Place one of the cakes with jam on top of the other, then top with the third sheet cake. Reserve any extra jam in a piping bag with a small tip. Place the cake on a wire baking rack with a baking sheet underneath.

chocolate ganache glaze:

Melt the chocolate in the microwave or over a double boiler. In a small saucepot, bring the cream to a simmer. Remove from the heat and add the melted chocolate. Stir at room temperature to cool until it reaches 95°F on a candy thermometer. Immediately incorporate the soft butter with a hand blender until smooth and shiny. Pour onto the center of the cake, and then use a metal spatula to spread into an even layer; chill.

to serve:

Place a thin slice of cake on a chilled dessert plate. Draw a line of jam across the plate. Fill the raspberries with extra jam (using the piping bag) to decorate. Garnish with chocolate décor, if using.

Chef's tip:

Dried rose petals are available at specialty food stores.

Hans Sauter

Chef Hans Sauter's lifetime commitment to the art of fine cuisine has taken him on a worldwide adventure. Born and trained in Switzerland, Sauter's impressive career of more than three decades has spanned the globe. Some notable stops include: Queen Elizabeth Hotel in Montreal, Noga Hilton in Geneva, Kempinski Hotel in Budapest and the Alpha Sapporo in Japan.

Hans has been part of the Post Hotel team since 2005. Returning to Canada, Banff National Park and the Post Hotel was like coming home. "The Post has a special place in my heart. I love this Hotel and everything that Andre and George Schwarz are doing here." When asked about the numerous awards and accolades, Chef Sauter's response is clear. "It's all about people. I have had the good fortune of working with some of the finest chefs in the world and today I take great pleasure in guiding the culinary stars of tomorrow."

Post Hotel & Spa

Offering a stunning panorama of the Canadian Rockies, the Post Hotel is nestled in a beautiful valley in Banff National Park.

Just a few kilometers from famous Lake Louise with its magnificent palette of emerald greens, the hotel's little log cabins with their red roofs overlook the Pipestone River. This is a mountain lodge at its finest where the comfy and romantic interiors make way for spacious suites in pale wood, always stocked with a good supply of logs to warm up your evenings. If your muscles are complaining after a few long ski runs, ice skating on the lake or snowshoeing to spot the nearby elk, deer or moose, a visit to the Hotel's Temple Mountain Spa will surely soothe. For the more adventurous, helicopter skiing is not far away. Enjoy the award-winning menu based on fresh produce and local game.

PAN-SEARED MISO MARINATED FILLET OF ALASKA BLACK COD, CHINESE BROCCOLI, BEURRE BLANC WITH GINGER

BY HANS SAUTER

Light and refreshing with a touch of Asian influence.

Serves 6
Preparation time: 4 hours
Cooking time: 30 minutes

Planning ahead:
Have some good fish stock on hand. The fish should be marinated for 4 hours in advance.

INGREDIENTS

marinated black cod:

6	fillets of Alaska black cod, 3½ oz each
¼ cup	white miso paste
½ cup	red miso paste
1½ tbsp	ginger purée
2 tbsp	garlic purée
½ cup	hoisin sauce
½ cup	sugar
½ cup	sake
1 tbsp	soy sauce
½ cup	fish stock
olive oil	

beurre blanc with ginger:

1 cup	unsalted butter
½ cup	diced shallots
1 cup	Vermouth Noilly Prat
1 tsp	green peppercorns
fresh tarragon	
2 cups	dry white wine
4 cups	fish stock
4 cups	heavy cream (35%)
¾ cup	ginger purée
salt & ground white pepper, to taste	

Chinese broccoli:

6	stems of Chinese broccoli
olive oil	
¼ cup	diced shallots
1 tsp	garlic purée
salt & ground white pepper, to taste	

METHOD

marinated black cod:

Whisk all the ingredients except the fish and olive oil in a bowl to make the miso marinade. Place the black cod fillets in the bowl and allow to marinate for 4 hours. Heat the olive oil in a nonstick frying pan. Sauté the black cod for approximately 1 minute on each side. Place the cod in a baking pan and set aside.

beurre blanc with ginger:

Heat a quarter cup of butter in a medium saucepan. Sauté the shallots until transparent, add the Vermouth, green peppercorns, and tarragon and reduce until almost dry. Add the white wine and reduce to about two-thirds of the volume. Add the fish stock and reduce to half, then add the cream and reduce again to one-quarter of the volume. Strain through a chinois into a saucepan. Heat the sauce and add small chunks of butter while continuously mixing with a hand blender. Keep blending, add the ginger purée and remove from the heat. Add salt and pepper to taste.

Chinese broccoli:

Blanch the broccoli in boiling salted water; be careful not to overcook. Heat the olive oil in a nonstick frying pan, add the shallots and garlic purée. Sauté until the shallots are transparent. Put the broccoli in a pan and quickly toss. Add salt and pepper to taste.

to serve:

Preheat the oven to 500°F. Finish the cod in the oven for approximately 3 minutes. Place the fish on a plate and serve with some Chinese broccoli and beurre blanc.

Chef's tip:

Be careful; fish is enjoyed best when moist inside.

NORTHWEST TERRITORIES' CARIBOU STRIPLOIN, PEPPERY RED CURRANT SAUCE WITH SPAETZLE

BY HANS SAUTER

This hearty Winter dish features lean, tender caribou with a hint of game flavor.

Serves 6
Preparation time: 5 hours
Cooking time: 45 minutes

Special Equipment:
Spaetzle colander, stock pot

Planning ahead:
If you have access to excellent game stock then purchase it in advance, otherwise allow 3-4 hours to make your own.

INGREDIENTS

caribou:

6 caribou (or elk or deer) loins, 7 oz each
salt & black pepper
olive oil

peppery red currant sauce:

2 tbsp grapeseed oil
½ cup shallots, diced
1½ cups mushrooms
2 tbsp black peppercorns, crushed
1 cup dry red wine
2 cups red port wine
½ cup red currant jelly
8½ cups game stock (see recipe below)
½ cup red wine vinegar
salt & ground black pepper

game stock:

4 tbsp grapeseed oil
3½ lb game bones (small pieces)
2 onions, coarsely chopped
1 carrot, coarsely chopped
1 celeriac, coarsely chopped
2 bay leaves
3 branches of thyme
3 branches of rosemary
1 tbsp black peppercorns
10 juniper berries
2 cinnamon sticks
1 leek, coarsely chopped
2 garlic cloves
2 tbsp tomato paste
3 cups dry red wine
3 qt water

spaetzle:

5 cups all purpose flour
9 large eggs
salt, ground white pepper, nutmeg
butter

METHOD

caribou:

Season the caribou with salt and black pepper. Heat the olive oil in a frying pan. Sear each loin on both sides, about 3 minutes per side. Place the caribou in a baking pan and set aside. Preheat the oven to 500 °F. Finish the caribou in the oven for approximately 5 minutes.

peppery red currant sauce:

Heat the grapeseed oil in a large sauce pot. Add the shallots, mushrooms, peppercorns and red wine. Reduce until almost dry, add the port wine and red currant jelly. Reduce again. Add the game stock and reduce one more time to about a quarter of the volume. Add red wine vinegar to suit your taste. Strain with a chinois and keep warm in a sauce pot. Season with salt and black pepper.

game stock:

Preheat the oven to 450 °F. Pour oil into a heavy roasting pan and place in the oven. When the oil is hot add the game bones and roast for approximately 45 minutes, stirring occasionally. Lower the oven temperature to 400 °F. Add the onions, carrot, celery, bay leaves, thyme, rosemary, black peppercorns, juniper berries and cinnamon sticks. 15 minutes later add the garlic and leek. After 5 minutes, add the tomato paste and 10 minutes later add the red wine. Cook for 10 more minutes, then remove the roasting pan from the oven. Pour and scrape all the contents into a large stock pot. Recover the remaining 'goodies' in the roasting pan by adding 2 cups water and placing over a medium heat. Bring to a boil stirring and scraping with a wooden spoon. Pour the contents into the stock pot. Add the remaining water and simmer for 2-3 hours. Skim off the fat and foam frequently and add more water if necessary. Remove the bones with a slotted spoon then strain the stock through a chinois strainer and cloth.

spaetzle:

Sift the flour, salt, pepper and nutmeg into a bowl. Make a well in the center, and add the eggs. Gradually stir until the dough takes on a thick consistency. Using a wooden spoon beat the dough until bubbles start to form. Force the dough through a spaetzle colander directly into a pot of boiling salted water. When the spaetzle are floating on the surface remove them with a slotted spoon. Continue the process until all the batter is used. Before serving sauté lightly in butter. Add salt and white pepper to taste.

to serve:

Slice the meat, serve with the spaetzle, red currant sauce and vegetables of your choice.

Chef's tip:

Fine cuts of game meat are served best medium rare.

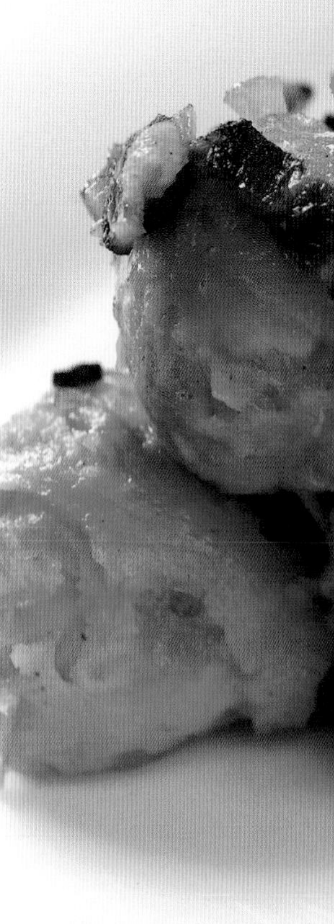

Serves 4
Preparation time: 2 hours 30 minutes
Cooking time: 1 hour 30 minutes

Special Equipment:
Ice cream maker, electric whisk, 4 gratin dishes

Planning ahead:
You can make the ice cream in advance.

INGREDIENTS

Bartlett pears:

3 Bartlett pears
½ cup sugar
34 oz water
1 cinnamon stick
juice of 1 lemon

caramel ice cream:

⅓ cup sugar
13 oz milk
9 oz whipping cream (35% MF).
¾ cup sugar
4 eggs

caramel sauce:

¾ cup sugar
7½ oz whipping cream (35% MF)
¼ oz unsalted butter

Bourbon (Madagascar) vanilla bean sabayon:

5 egg yolks
1 vanilla bean (cut lengthwise and vanilla scraped out)
1½ oz water
¼ cup sugar

to serve:

icing sugar
sprigs of mint

BARTLETT PEAR GRATIN WITH CARAMEL ICE CREAM

BY ROBERT WENK

Winter pear and fresh house-made ice cream: a perfect match.

METHOD

Bartlett pears:

Peel and cut the pears in quarters. Remove the cores. Add the sugar, cinnamon and lemon juice to the water and bring to a boil. Add the pears and boil gently until soft, approximately 25-30 minutes.

caramel ice cream:

Heat the ⅓ cup of sugar in a pot until caramelized. Add the milk, cream and sugar. Bring to a boil. Make sure all of the caramelized sugar is dissolved completely. In a bowl whisk the eggs. Add the ice cream mix into the bowl of whisked eggs. Freeze in an ice cream maker. Store in a freezer for 2 hours.

caramel sauce:

Caramelize the sugar in a hot frying pan. Add the whipping cream and reduce the heat. Let the caramelized sugar dissolve completely. Add the butter, stir and let melt.

Bourbon (Madagascar) vanilla bean sabayon:

Whisk all the ingredients in a bowl over a pot of steaming water until the mixture is light and fluffy.

to serve:

After cutting the Bartlett pear sections into fans, place three pieces into each gratin dish. Top with the vanilla sabayon. Preheat the oven to 400°F and bake for 8 minutes until golden brown. Dust with icing sugar. Pour the caramel sauce around the edge of the gratin. Place a scoop of caramel ice cream on top of the gratin just before serving. Garnish with a mint sprig.

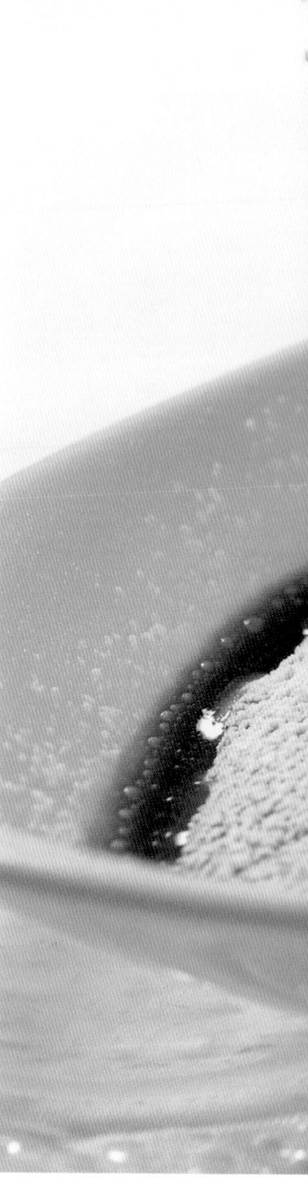

Matthew Stowe

Matthew Stowe began his formal training at the Culinary Institute of America in Hyde Park, NY. After graduating he honed his craft at New York City's famed French restaurant, Lutece. He returned home to Vancouver in 2004 and joined the kitchen team of Sonora Resort. He quickly worked his way up and became the Executive Chef in 2005. Matthew prepares Avant Garde cuisine with a major focus on using local products, modern techniques and the traditional systems of the kitchens of France. One of Matthew's biggest inspirations is where the resort is located. It is very hard to not be inspired from what is around us. It is one of the most beautiful areas in the world and my job is to make the food as close to perfect as the view."

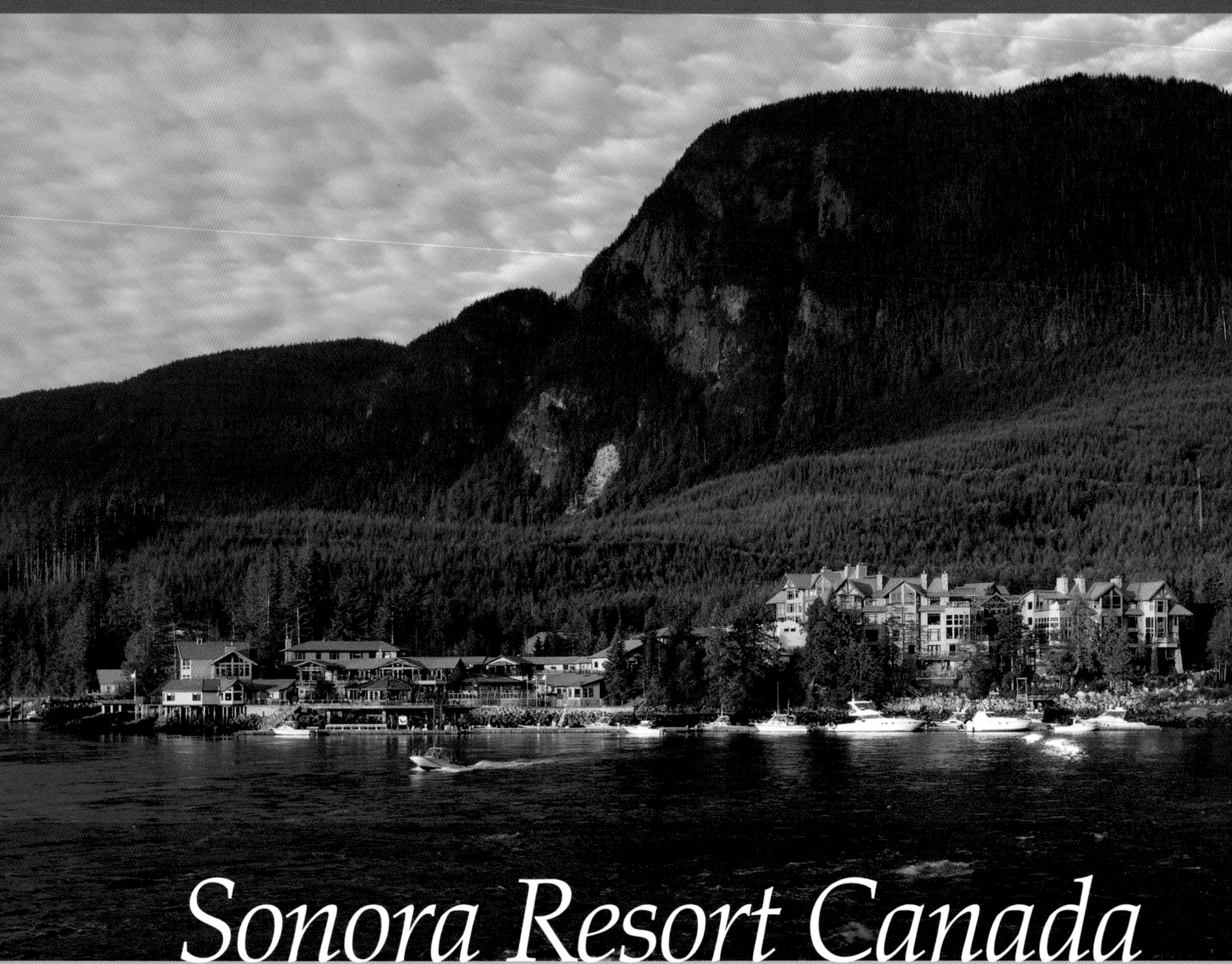

Sonora Resort Canada

A jewel of the very purest caliber Sonora Resort is nestled in the heart of an archipelago between Vancouver Island and the west coast of Canada.

Accessible only by sea and air the enchantment already begins during the transfer to the hotel with no roads or villas on the horizon. The guest rooms offer breathtaking views at any time of the day of unspoilt, wild nature. Watch eagles, seals, bears, the green emerald of the sea and forests, the limpid streams, snowy mountain tops that seem to cast themselves straight into the sea. The wild landscapes, combined with the indoor luxury, are the elements that make up the magical alchemy of this unique region. The comfort and the elegance of the lodges are carried through to the smallest detail of the colors and materials. An absolute paradise for angling enthusiasts, Sonora Resort offers a wide range of sporting and leisure activities. How delightful it is to intersperse days spent in the fresh, outdoor air with pampering visits to the unique, upscale spa dedicated to wellness or by taking a dip in the outdoor heated pool.

Serves 4
Preparation time: 3 hours (including freezing the mozzarella)
Cooking time: N/A

Special equipment:
Ice cream machine

Planning ahead:
The basil pistou can be made up to 3 days in advance and should then be refrigerated (note that the color will begin to change after a day). The tomato sorbet needs to infuse overnight.

INGREDIENTS

A variety of heirloom tomatoes cut into small wedges or cubes

tomato sorbet:

4 cups	chopped red tomatoes
¼ cup	basil
½	jalapeno, sliced thin
1	garlic clove, smashed
1 tbsp	simple syrup
1 tsp	red wine vinegar

ravioli:

1	ball of buffalo milk mozzarella
2 tbsp	brine from mozzarella container
½ cup	milk
salt & pepper, to taste	
1½ tsp	sodium alginate
1.8 pt	water

balsamic pearls:

1 cup	balsamic vinegar
1 tsp	sugar
1	pinch of salt
½ tsp	agar agar
5	leaves of gelatin, soaked in cold water until softened
4-6 pt	vegetable oil in a tall narrow container, stored in the refrigerator overnight

basil pistou:

1 cup	basil leaves, packed
⅓ cup	spinach leaves, packed
1 tsp	pine nut or olive oil
2	cloves garlic confit

orange vinaigrette:

3 tbsp	fresh orange juice
½ tsp	orange zest
⅓ cup	vegetable oil
1 tsp	honey
salt & pepper, to taste	

garnish:

4 tiny cucumbers
medium-sized red tomato (for the chips)
small basil leaves
basil seeds; soaked in water for 1 hour so they become hydrated
squash blossoms torn into strips
extra virgin olive oil

HEIRLOOM TOMATO SALAD – BUFFALO MOZZARELLA 'RAVIOLI', BALSAMIC VINEGAR PEARLS, TOMATO SORBET, MICRO BASIL

BY MATTHEW STOWE

We have unbelievable local tomatoes available every year from the beginning of August until late September. Susan Davidson has a farm in Aldergrove that produces over 35 varieties of heirloom tomatoes for us. We don't specify which varieties we want, she just sends a 'mystery basket' of them twice a week. It is like Christmas morning every time they arrive, the colors, shapes and sizes make it very exciting to open the box and see what varieties are inside. I recommend going to your local farm market in the Summer to get the best tomatoes possible for this simple salad. The balsamic pearls and the buffalo mozzarella 'ravioli' add a whimsical note that will excite your guests. The raviolis are quite simple to make and what makes them work is the reaction between the calcium in the cheese and the sodium alginate which creates a natural skin around the product and holds the creamy liquid inside.

METHOD

tomato sorbet:

Purée the tomatoes in a blender until smooth. Pour the tomato purée from the blender into a plastic container, add the jalapeno, garlic, basil, simple syrup and the vinegar and let infuse overnight. Strain the mixture through a mesh sieve using the back of the spoon to push the mixture through, leaving behind the basil, jalapeno, garlic and any tomato seeds. Season the tomato mixture with salt and pepper. Place into an ice cream machine and process according to the manufacturer's instructions.

ravioli:

Purée the cheese, milk and brine in a blender, season to taste with salt and pepper. Pour the mixture into small hemispherical molds or circular ice cube trays. Place in the freezer until frozen. Combine the sodium alginate and the water in a blender and mix until fully combined. Take the cheese mixture from the freezer and remove it from the molds. Drop the frozen cheese into the alginate solution and let sit for 5 minutes. Using a slotted spoon remove the raviolis from the solution and place in a small container of water to store them until ready to use. The cheese will still be frozen at this point but will defrost in about an hour while it is stored in the rinsing water.

balsamic pearls:

Combine the balsamic vinegar, sugar, salt and agar agar in a small sauce pot. Place on a medium heat and bring up to a simmer, then simmer for 5 minutes. Remove from the heat and allow to cool slightly in the pot for 1-2 minutes. Remove the gelatin from the water and squeeze out any excess liquid. Place the gelatin in the pot and stir into the balsamic liquid until dissolved. Place the mixture in a plastic squeeze bottle. Remove the oil from the refrigerator. Drizzle the mixture over the cold oil to form pearls. Once the pearls set they will sink through the oil to the bottom. Once all the mixture has been drizzled out allow the pearls to sit in the oil for 4-5 minutes to allow them to fully set. Using a small fine mesh sieve strain the oil into another container collecting the pearls in the sieve. Rinse the pearls very well under cold water and store in a plastic container in the refrigerator until ready to use.

basil pistou:

In a large pot of boiling, salted water add the basil leaves and cook for 4-5 minutes until they are very tender; using a slotted spoon remove the basil from the water and plunge into an ice bath. Add the spinach to the pot and cook for 2-3 minutes, remove from the water and plunge into the same ice bath. Remove the spinach and basil from the ice bath and transfer to a blender, add the garlic confit and two to three ice cubes and blend on high until the mixture is very smooth, add the oil and blend until well combined. Transfer the purée to a small plastic squeeze bottle or plastic container and store in the refrigerator for up to 3 days.

orange vinaigrette:

Combine all the ingredients in a small bowl and whisk together, season to taste with salt and pepper. Place in the refrigerator until ready to use.

tomato chips:

Slice 1 medium-sized tomato as thinly as possible using a serrated knife. Place the slices on a silpat lined baking sheet and dry in the oven at 200°F for 1 hour or until totally dry. Using an offset spatula remove the chips from the silpat and place in an airtight container until ready to serve.

to serve:

Toss the tomatoes with the vinaigrette and season well with salt and pepper. Arrange a variety of tomatoes per plate, place a ravioli on each plate and garnish with small basil leaves, squash blossoms, balsamic pearls, basil seeds, tomato chip and a drizzle of olive oil. Spoon the basil pistou around the tomatoes. Remove the tomato sorbet from the freezer and scoop a quenelle of sorbet using a small spoon. Serve immediately.

A TASTING OF MOUNT LEHMAN RABBIT – BACON WRAPPED RABBIT SADDLE, RABBIT CONFIT FILLED POTATO 'CANNELONI', CELERIAC PUREE, CHANTERELLES, RABBIT JUS

BY MATTHEW STOWE

Rabbit is a delicious but underused type of meat. It is very lean which makes it a healthy meat and a great alternative to chicken or pork. I love to serve different cuts of meat from the same animal on the same plate. The garnishes for this dish are very simple to allow the delicate flavors of the rabbit to shine through. I like to use little carrots, turnips and chanterelle mushrooms but any small vegetables would work. The rich sauce is made from red wine, veal stock and the rabbit bones which ties everything together beautifully.

Serves 4
Preparation time: 14 hours (includes curing and cooking the rabbit legs)
Cooking time: 1-2 hours

Special equipment:
Candy thermometer, turning vegetable slicer

Planning ahead:
Prepare the confit in advance and refrigerate for 12 hours or overnight (keeps for up to 1 month). The rabbit saddles should be prepared 1 hour in advance and refrigerated.

INGREDIENTS

rabbit confit:

- 4 rabbit hind legs
- 3 tbsp kosher salt
- 4 garlic cloves, smashed
- 1 shallot, peeled and sliced
- 6 sprigs of fresh thyme
- ½ tsp coarsely ground black pepper
- 1 lemon peeled with a vegetable peeler into strips
- 4 cups duck fat or vegetable oil

canneloni filling:

- 4 rabbit confit legs
- ¼ cup melted confit fat
- 1 tsp shallots, minced
- ½ tsp fresh cracked peppercorns

rabbit saddles:

- 2 rabbit saddles, deboned
- 8-10 slices of bacon approx ⅛" thick
- 2 sprigs of thyme, leaves removed

potato canneloni:

- 1-2 large Yukon gold potatoes, peeled
- 1 carrot (choose a carrot that is an even thickness from one end to the other)
- 4-5 pt vegetable oil

celeriac purée:

- 1 head of celeriac peeled, cut into ½" pieces
- 1 small shallot peeled and sliced thin
- 2 cups vegetable or chicken stock
- ½ cup heavy cream
- salt & pepper, to taste
- vegetable oil

rabbit jus:

- ⅓ cup oil
- 1 lb rabbit bones with some meat trim attached cut into 1" pieces
- 1½ cups water
- 2 shallots, sliced thin
- 1 carrot, peeled and cut into ½" pieces
- 1 cup red wine
- 4 pt chicken stock
- 2 pt veal stock

garnish:

- 4 baby carrots, peeled and blanched
- 4 baby turnips, peeled and blanched
- 4 baby leeks, trimmed and blanched
- ¼ cup chicken stock
- 1 tsp butter
- 2 cups chanterelle mushrooms, cleaned
- 1 tbsp shallots, minced
- 1 tbsp butter
- coarse salt, micro greens or chervil leaves

METHOD

rabbit confit:

Sprinkle 1 tablespoon of the salt in the bottom of a high-sided dish large enough to hold the rabbit pieces in a single layer. Evenly scatter half the garlic, shallot, and thyme over the salt. Place the rabbit hind legs on top of the salt mixture, and then sprinkle with the remaining salt, garlic, shallot, thyme and the lemon strips. Season with pepper, cover with plastic wrap, and refrigerate for 12 hours or overnight. Heat the oven to 225°F. Melt the duck fat in a saucepan over a medium-low heat. Brush the salt and seasonings off the rabbit and arrange the pieces in a single layer. Pour the melted fat over the rabbit to cover completely. Transfer the confit to the oven and cook at a very gentle simmer until the rabbit is tender and can be easily pulled from the bone (2-3 hours). Remove from the oven and set aside to cool.

canneloni filling:

Pull all the meat from the bones of the legs, discard the bones. Melt the confit fat. Add the meat and shallots to the bowl of an electric mixer with a paddle attachment. With the mixer running add the melted fat and pepper, mix until the meat is broken up and the fat is well mixed into the meat. It should look like a fine 'purée' of meat. Set aside.

rabbit saddles:

Lay a piece of plastic wrap on your countertop. Lay four to five slices of bacon on the sheet, overlapping them ⅓", creating a sheet of bacon. Roll the deboned saddle up, creating a cylinder. Place the cylinder of rabbit meat in the center of the bacon, sprinkle over the thyme leaves, fold the bacon over the cylinder and pull it back to tighten it around the meat; roll the cylinder along the bacon sheet until it is totally encased in the bacon. The bacon should overlap by 2" – this will allow for shrinkage of the bacon while it cooks. Wrap the bacon-rabbit roulades tightly in plastic wrap and place in the refrigerator for 1 hour to firm up.

potato canneloni:

Heat the vegetable oil in a deep pot until it reaches 325°F with a candy thermometer. Set up a turning vegetable slicer with the medium julienne blade on your countertop. Cut both ends off the potato, and make long strands. One potato should make four to six cannelloni shells. Cut the top and bottom off the carrot, creating a long mold for the cannelloni (the diameter of the carrot is going to determine the size of the cannelloni shell). Starting at about 2" from the tip of the carrot, begin wrapping it with one long strand of the potato; wrap the second and third loops around the first one to secure it. Continue to wrap the carrot tightly with the potato until you form a 2½" long tube of potato. To finish, leave the last loop a bit loose, cut away from the remaining

strand of potato, tuck the end of the potato strand through the loop and pull gently to secure.

celeriac purée:

Place a medium pot on a low heat with a teaspoon of vegetable oil. Add the celeriac and the shallot and sweat for 8-10 minutes. Add the stock and salt/pepper to the pot and bring to a simmer. Simmer for 20-25 minutes until the celeriac is tender, add the cream and allow to cook for an additional 15 minutes. Strain the celeriac through a sieve, reserving the liquid. Transfer the celeriac to a blender and, with the machine running, add just enough of the stock-cream liquid so the celeriac can purée easily. Purée the mixture until it is very smooth, then season again with salt and pepper. Set aside.

rabbit jus:

Heat the oil in a large saucepot over a high heat; add the bones in an even layer, being careful not to overcrowd the pan. Sear the bones without stirring for 6-8 minutes. They need to be well browned before they are moved – if they are stirred too early the pan will cool down and they will sweat rather than brown. Turn the bones over and continue to sear for another 6-8 minutes. They should be evenly colored. Add the water to the pot and stir the bottom to release the fond (brown bits stuck to the pan). Reduce heat to medium and simmer until the water is totally evaporated and the bones begin to sizzle again. Add the vegetables and continue to cook on a medium-high heat for 4-5 minutes. Add the red wine and simmer until the red wine has reduced to a glaze. Add the chicken stock and simmer until the liquid has reduced by 75%. Add the veal stock and simmer for 20-25 minutes. Strain through a fine mesh sieve and transfer the liquid to a smaller pot. Continue to reduce over a medium heat until the liquid has reduced by approx 75%. It should be thickened and have a nice sauce consistency. Strain the sauce through a fine mesh sieve, keep warm until ready to use.

to cook the canneloni:

Using tongs, carefully immerse the carrot in the hot oil so it just covers the top of the potato and fry for 1-2 minutes until golden brown. Remove from the oil and carefully slide the potato tube off the carrot. Repeat until you have the desired amount of cannelloni shells.

to cook the rabbit saddles:

Preheat your oven to 325°F. Heat a film of oil in a medium-sized sauté pan, add the bacon-wrapped saddles to the pan seam side first and brown on all sides. Transfer the pan to the oven and roast for 7-8 minutes until the internal temperature of the rabbit is 140-145°F. Remove the saddles from the pan and set aside.

to serve:

Place the rabbit confit mixture in a small pot and reheat; once the mixture is hot place it in a piping bag and pipe it into the canneloni potato shells, place on a small baking sheet and place in the oven until they are hot. Place a small saucepot on a medium heat, add the ¼ cup of chicken stock and bring to a simmer; add the turnips and the carrots. Simmer the vegetables until the stock has reduced to a glaze, remove the pan from the heat and stir in 1 teaspoon of butter. Heat a film of oil in a large sauté pan, add the mushrooms and sauté for 1 minute, add the shallots and 1 tablespoon of butter and allow to cook for a further 2-3 minutes. Place a spoonful of the purée in the center of each plate, Slice each of the rabbit saddles into 4 even slices, arrange two slices of the saddle and 1 cannelloni on each plate. Garnish with the turnips, carrots, leeks, and chanterelle mushrooms. Spoon the warm rabbit jus around the meat, sprinkle with coarse salt and garnish with micro greens or chervil leaves.

'CARROT CAKE' – CREAM CHEESE ICE CREAM, CARROT PEARLS, SULTANA RAISIN WALNUT 'VINAIGRETTE', CARROT CONFIT, WHITE CHOCOLATE CARROT TOP PUREE

BY MATTHEW STOWE

This is our version of a classic carrot cake. When I think carrot cake, I think of a cake with a nice spice to it, with a rich cream cheese icing. I have added fresh ginger to the cake batter, to give it a little extra spiciness and the cream cheese icing has been replaced by a rich cream cheese ice cream. The carrot confit adds a nice toothsome texture and reinforces the carrot element. The combination tastes great and it is also very visually appealing – it definitely beats a wedge of regular carrot cake!

Serves 4
Preparation time: 3 hours (including making the raisin paper)
Cooking time: 35-40 minutes

Special equipment:
Microplane, ice cream machine

Planning ahead:
The raisin paper can be made in advance.

INGREDIENTS

carrot cake:

¾ cup	water
¾ cup	orange juice
½ cup	molasses
1 tsp	baking soda
⅓ cup	butter, softened
1 cup	brown sugar, packed
1	egg
2 tbsp	ginger, grated with a microplane
2¾ cup	all purpose flour
1 tbsp	baking powder
½ tsp	salt
2 tsp	ground ginger
2 tsp	ground cinnamon
1	pinch of nutmeg
1	pinch of cloves
2	large carrots, peeled and finely grated

raisin paper:

1 cup	sultana raisins soaked in warm water for 2 hours, then strained
4	egg whites
1 tbsp	sugar
1 tbsp	water

ice cream:

1 cup	milk
1 cup	cream cheese, softened
1 tbsp	fresh lemon juice
1 cup	simple syrup
2 tbsp	honey
1	pinch of salt
½ cup	heavy cream

carrot confit:

¾ cup	orange juice
½ cup	simple syrup
1 tbsp	lemon juice
1	½" piece of ginger, peeled and sliced thin
1	thick carrot, peeled and cut into ¼" thick rounds (12 pieces needed)

carrot top purée:

1 cup	baby carrot top leaves
½ cup	whipping cream
¼ cup	white chocolate

carrot pearls:

1 cup	carrot juice
1 tbsp	honey
1 tsp	lemon juice
½ tsp	agar agar
5 leaves	of gelatin, soaked in cold water until softened
4-6 pt	vegetable oil in a tall narrow container, stored in the refrigerator overnight

cream cheese icing:

1	vanilla bean, scraped
1	8oz package of cream cheese
¼ cup	butter
1 cup	icing sugar

vinaigrette:

¼ cup	golden raisins, soaked in warm water to soften
1 tbsp	chopped walnuts soaked in warm water for 3-4 hours
1 tbsp	walnut oil
3 tbsp	orange juice
1 tbsp	honey

garnish:

Baby carrot top leaves or edible flowers

METHOD

raisin paper:

Preheat oven to 190-200°F. Combine all the ingredients in a blender and purée for 1-2 minutes on high speed until the mixture is very smooth. On a silpat lined baking tray pour out the mixture and spread evenly in a thin layer. Place the tray in the oven and dehydrate for 1 hour 30 minutes-2 hours. Remove the tray from the oven and peel off the raisin paper while it is still warm. Allow to cool on the counter for 3-4 minutes. Once cool break into small pieces and store in an airtight container until ready to use.

carrot cake:

Preheat the oven to 325°F. Combine the orange juice and water in a saucepot and bring to a boil. Combine the molasses, baking soda and boiling liquid in a mixing bowl. Place the brown sugar and butter in the bowl of an electric mixer and, with a paddle attachment, cream them together for 2-3 minutes until light and fluffy. Add the egg and ginger and beat until just combined, remove the bowl from the mixer and set aside. In a large mixing bowl sift together the spices, baking powder, salt and flour. Pour half of the molasses mixture into the creamed butter and stir together then fold in half of the flour mixture. Repeat this process again with the remaining molasses mixture and the flour. Once everything is well combined, lightly fold in the grated carrots. Pour the batter into a parchment lined baking pan or sheet tray that has been rubbed with butter. The cake pan should be approximately 14" x 18". Bake for 35-40 minutes until a toothpick can be inserted in the center of the cake and it comes out clean. Remove from the oven and allow to cool. Once cool flip the tray onto a cutting board and remove the sheet of parchment paper. Cut the cake into

20 small squares 1" x 1". Place the squares on a parchment lined sheet tray and wrap well in plastic wrap.

ice cream:

Combine all the ingredients in a blender, except the cream. Purée the mixture until smooth, then stir in the cream. Transfer the mixture to the bowl of an ice cream machine and process according to the manufacturer's instructions.

carrot confit:

Combine the orange juice, lemon juice, simple syrup, ginger and sliced carrots in a saucepot. Place on a low heat and cook until the carrots are very tender but can still hold their shape, approximately 20-25 minutes. Remove from the heat and store the carrots in their poaching liquid.

carrot top purée:

In a large pot of boiling water blanch the carrot top leaves for 5-6 minutes. Remove the leaves from the water and place in an ice water bath. Remove the leaves from the ice water, squeeze out excess water and place in a blender with the white chocolate. Place the cream in a saucepot and bring to a simmer, pour the hot cream over the leaves and chocolate and purée until smooth. Transfer to a small bowl and refrigerate until cool. Once cool transfer to a plastic squeeze bottle – if the mixture is too thick add a little more cream to thin out the purée.

carrot pearls:

Combine the carrot juice, honey, agar agar and lemon juice in a small saucepot. Place on a medium heat and bring up to a simmer, then simmer for 5 minutes. Remove from the heat and allow to cool slightly in the pot for 1-2 minutes. Remove the gelatin from the water and squeeze out any excess liquid. Place the gelatin in the pot and stir into the carrot liquid until it is dissolved. Place the mixture in a plastic squeeze bottle. Remove the oil from the refrigerator. Drizzle the mixture over the cold oil, forming pearls. Once the pearls set they will sink through the oil to the bottom. Once all the mixture has been drizzled out allow the pearls to sit in the oil for 4-5 minutes to allow them to fully set. Using a small fine mesh sieve strain the oil into another container, collecting the pearls in the sieve. Rinse the pearls very well under cold water and store in a plastic container in the refrigerator until ready to use.

cream cheese icing:

Combine all the ingredients in the bowl of an electric mixer, mix on high speed with the paddle attachment for 1-2 minutes until very smooth.

vinaigrette:

Combine all the ingredients in a blender and purée until very smooth.

to serve:

Squeeze two lines of purée on each of the plates. Artfully arrange 3-5 squares of cake on each plate. Remove the carrot confit pieces from the liquid and divide them among the dishes, spoon some of the carrot pearls in a small mound on each plate. Using a piping bag pipe a few dots of cream cheese icing on and around the pieces of cake. Spoon some of the carrot confit liquid around the plate. Scoop a quenelle of ice cream and place it on one of the squares of cake, garnish the other squares with pieces of raisin paper, and scatter around carrot top leaves.

Lee Parsons

Lee began his career at the five star Claridge's Hotel in Mayfair, London. Under the tutelage of Executive Chef John Williams he progressed through the kitchens of Claridge's for eight years before he headed to the Oxfordshire countryside. There, Lee joined Chef Raymond Blanc at Le Manoir aux Quat'Saisons. After three years at Le Manoir, Lee was offered the opportunity to be the Executive Chef at the reopening of the historic Prince of Wales Hotel in Niagara-on-the-Lake, where he earned praise from international food and travel media.

Returning home after three years, he took over the stoves at Wood Hall, one of England's finest country house hotels, where he quickly established it as a leading culinary venue. Lee's dedication was recognised in 2004 when he reached the finals of the U.K. Chef of the Year Competition.

With a desire to return to Canada, Lee joined The Wedgewood Hotel as Executive Chef. His unique style of modern French cuisine is certain to turn some heads and elevate Bacchus to one of the finest restaurants in Vancouver.

Wedgewood
Hotel & Spa

This is a superb address set in the heart of the cosmopolitan city of Vancouver in fashionable Robson Square.

The lounges, resplendent with understated luxury, feature stylish furniture, rich fabrics and original fireplaces – all the personal vision of Eleni Skalbania who has decorated her property with timeless European elegance. The guest rooms reflect the perfect combination of ultimate modern comfort, antiques and original works of art, while the restaurant, dedicated to Bacchus, features inventive, highly epicurean cuisine. Today, every member of Eleni's staff, from the team at the splendid Spa to the chef in the restaurant, shares her quest for perfection and attention to detail.

GRAVADLAX OF QUEEN CHARLOTTE HALIBUT WITH NOVA SCOTIA LOBSTER & MICRO HERBS

BY LEE PARSONS

Halibut season is eagerly anticipated every Spring on the West Coast of Canada as some of the finest fresh fish in the world arrives in Vancouver. This appetizer reflects the versatility of this delicate white fish and becomes a perfect light and healthy welcome to Springtime in the Pacific Northwest.

Serves 10
Preparation time: 36 hours
Cooking time: 7 minutes

Planning ahead:
The halibut should be marinated for 36 hours.

INGREDIENTS

2 lb 3 oz	halibut fillet, skin on
1	Nova Scotia lobster, cooked and cooled in a court bouillon and removed from the shell
2	Easter egg radishes, sliced thinly
⅓	English cucumber, cut into ribbons
1	blood orange, segmented

batons of root ginger, blanched and pickled
mixed micro herbs
cold pressed olive oil
freshly squeezed lime juice
fennel pollen
Maldon sea salt

marinade:

½ oz	sea salt
½ oz	sugar
1	lime, zest
½ tsp	fennel seeds, roasted and crushed
1	star aniseed, crushed
¾ oz	cilantro, chopped
1 oz	chervil, chopped

METHOD

marinade:

Mix all the ingredients together. With a sharp knife score the halibut skin. Place the halibut on a piece of cling film. Cover with the marinade and wrap tightly. Marinate for 36 hours in the fridge. Slice the halibut thinly. Lay in between two sheets of cling film and lightly pound with a heavy pan, but do not 'mush' the fish. Chill in a refrigerator for 4-6 hours until required.

to serve:

Cut the cured halibut to a 2" x 6" rectangle. Remove one piece of the cling film and lay on to a chilled plate. Remove the other piece when ready to serve. Cut the lobster into small nuggets. Place into a bowl and season along with the radish, cucumber ribbons, orange segments and micro herbs. Brush the halibut with the olive oil and lime juice. Season with fennel pollen and Maldon sea salt. Arrange the root ginger, lobster and micro herbs on top of the cured halibut and serve.

BONELESS SADDLE OF GRAIN FED RABBIT, GOLDEN CHANTERELLES, GRAIN MUSTARD VELOUTE, RED WINE REDUCTION

BY LEE PARSONS

Rabbit is a lovely tender ingredient that is available all year round from the Artesian farmers of the Fraser Valley of British Columbia. This main course uses the prime cut of the rabbit saddle which is enhanced with locally sourced wild mushrooms – we have used golden chanterelles.

Serves 4
Preparation time: 45 minutes
Cooking time: 45 minutes

INGREDIENTS

rabbit saddles and farce:

2 saddles of grain fed rabbit with kidneys
3½ oz shallot purée
⅒ oz chervil, chopped
4 tarragon leaves, chopped
salt & pepper, to taste
smooth Dijon mustard
prosciutto ham

vegetables:

1 oz streaky bacon
⅓ oz shallots, chopped
½ oz butter
1 sprig of thyme
3½ oz Savoy cabbage

rabbit cream:

bones from a rabbit
¾ oz butter
⅓ oz celery
¾ oz onion
¾ oz fennel
1 sprig of thyme
3½ fl oz white wine
½ fl oz white wine vinegar
6¾ fl oz 35% cream
3½ fl oz white chicken stock
2 sprigs of chervil
¼ oz grain mustard

to serve:

4 oz fine French beans, topped and tailed
1¾ oz girolle mushrooms
½ oz butter
1 vine ripened tomato, diced
⅒ oz parsley leaves, blanched
salt, pepper and lemon juice to taste

METHOD

rabbit saddles and farce:

Carefully remove the back bone from the rabbit saddles, and trim away any excess fat and belly. Mince the trimmings and add the shallot purée, chopped herbs, kidneys (diced) and season to taste. Brush the inside of the boneless rabbit saddles with the mustard, and season. Divide the farce mix evenly between the saddles and roll up. Wrap the saddles in thinly sliced prosciutto ham. Roll in aluminium foil and refrigerate until required

vegetables:

Finely shred the cabbage, and blanch in boiling salted water for 1 minute. Sweat the shallots with the butter, the bacon and thyme. Add the cabbage and cook for 1 minute. Season to taste.

rabbit cream:

Preheat the oven to 375°F. Sweat the bones in butter. Add the vegetables, then roast in the oven until a light golden color. Deglaze with the vinegar. Add the white wine and reduce by half. Add the chicken stock, thyme and cream, reduce by one-third. Pass through a fine strainer. Add the mustard and chervil when serving.

to serve:

Preheat the oven to 375°F. Place the rabbit saddles into the oven for 8-10 minute using a heavy baking tray. Allow to rest in the foil for 6-8 minutes. Once rested remove from the foil and place into a hot skillet to crisp the prosciutto ham. Slice each saddle into 4. Sauté the mushrooms in the butter, and season to taste with salt, pepper and lemon juice. Add the tomato dice and parsley leaves to make a concasse. Cook the beans in boiling salted water for 2 minutes and then drop in iced water for 1 minute to retain color.

Arrange a pile of Savoy cabbage on a plate at 12 o'clock. Place 2 slices of rabbit saddle at 4 o'clock, and add the mushrooms, green beans and tomato concasse at 8 o'clock. Add sauce to the plate and serve.

CRISP 'CANNELONI' OF WHITE CHOCOLATE, POACHED RHUBARB, MACERATED STRAWBERRIES

BY LEE PARSONS

Two classic Summertime ingredients, rhubarb and strawberries, brought together with a silky white chocolate mousse and a crisp tuile to create a lovely contradiction in textures. This dessert is a Summer favorite all season long.

Serves 4
Preparation time: 1 hour
Cooking time: 15 minutes

INGREDIENTS

white chocolate mousse:

½ cup	2% (semi-skimmed) milk
½	vanilla pod
3½ oz	white chocolate
1	leaf of gelatin
4 fl oz	double cream, lightly whipped

butter tuile:

1¾ oz	icing sugar
1¾ oz	egg whites
1½ oz	flour
1¾ oz	butter, melted

pistachio nuts, crushed

poached rhubarb:

1 lb 5 oz	fresh rhubarb, peeled and trimmed
13½ fl oz	apple juice
1	vanilla pod, split and seeds scraped out
1	star aniseed
1/10 oz	sliced root ginger
1/3 oz	sugar, granulated
½	lemon, juice

macerated strawberries:

16	fresh strawberries
4	sprigs of mint
2	basil leaves
½ tsp	granulated sugar

Grand Marnier, to taste

vanilla foam: (optional)

10 fl oz	milk
1	vanilla pod
2	egg yolks
1 oz	sugar

garnish:

fresh mint
basil sprigs

METHOD

white chocolate mousse:

Scald the milk with the vanilla, add the chocolate and dissolve away from the heat. Add the gelatin. Chill over ice, stirring continuously until the consistency of oil. Fold 2 spoonfuls of the cream into the milk and chocolate mix. Fold into the remaining cream. Refrigerate.

butter tuile:

Preheat the oven to 350°F. Whisk the egg whites and icing sugar. Add the flour and mix to a smooth paste. Beat in the melted butter, being careful not to split the mixture. Pipe the tuile mix to the desired shape. Sprinkle with the pistachios and cook until golden, approximately 7 minutes. Shape the tuile around a cylindrical mold.

poached rhubarb;

Combine all the ingredients except the rhubarb and simmer for 10 minutes. Add the rhubarb, cover with a lid and remove from the heat. Allow to cool in the poaching liquor.

macerated strawberries:

Cut the strawberries into quarters or sixths depending on their size. Add the basil, mint, sugar and Grand Marnier. Place in a bowl and leave covered at room temperature for 1 hour, then chill.

vanilla foam:

Scald the milk with the sugar and vanilla, add the egg yolks and aerate.

to serve:

Fill a piping bag with the white chocolate mousse and fill the butter tuiles. Place the rhubarb in the center of the plate. Spoon the macerated strawberries around. Place the filled 'canneloni' on the poached rhubarb. Add some vanilla foam if using. Garnish with fresh mint and purple basil sprigs.

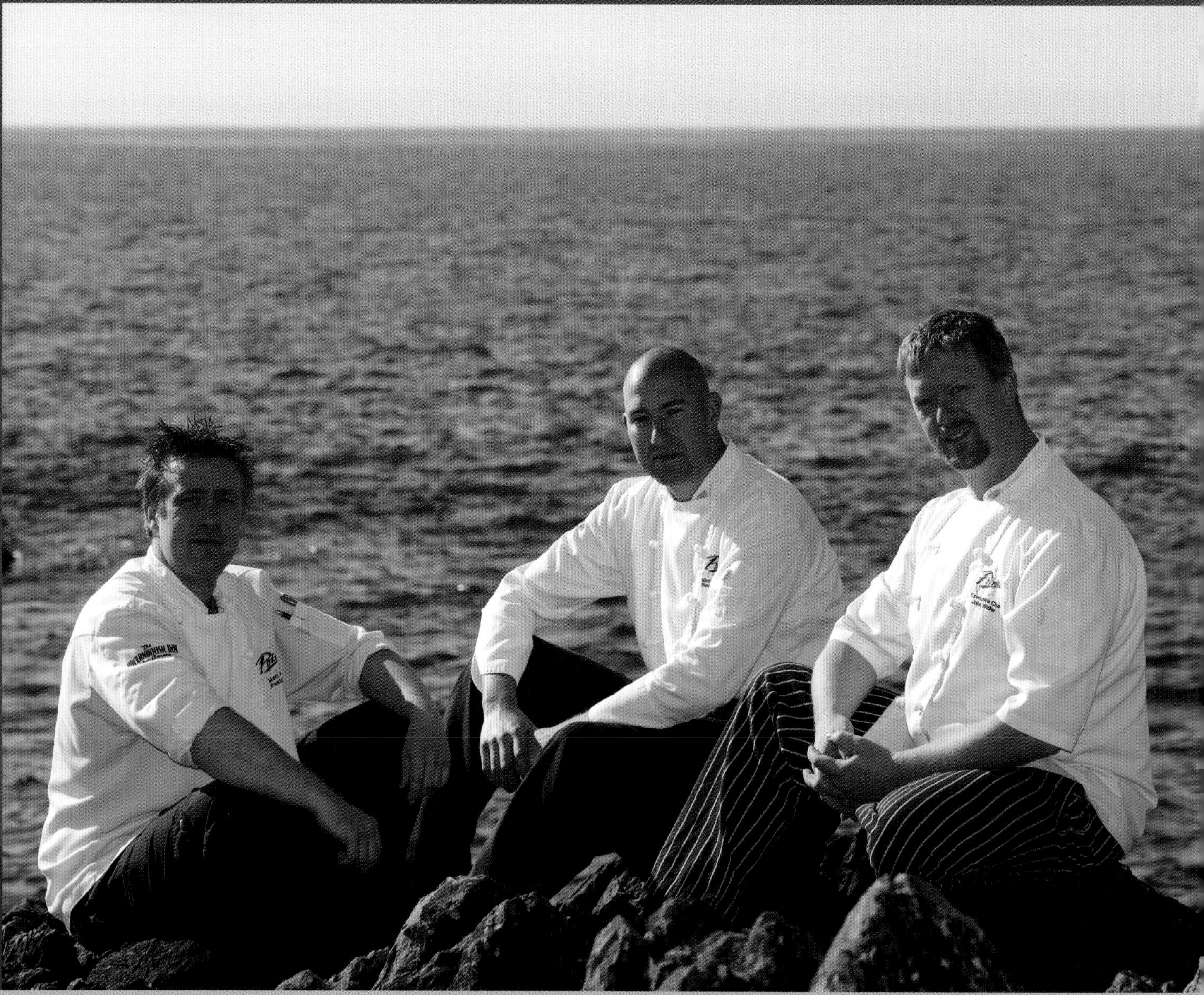

John Waller

Executive Chef John Waller leads the kitchen brigade in The Pointe Restaurant and is responsible for all the components of the plates served at the Inn, as well as for the Inn's strong kitchen apprentice program. Chef John started his career in Toronto as one of the youngest Red Seal Certified Chefs in Canada, achieving this honor at 21. He has honed his talent at some of the best restaurants in Toronto, including Canoe and North 44, and moving west, Chef John has also owned two restaurants on Vancouver Island and worked at Victoria's Fireside Grill. He thoroughly enjoys managing the food program at the Wick, and the local seafood, game and produce suppliers like selling him their organic selections because his giddy pleasure is contagious when shopping for anything food-related. He takes the knowledge gathered throughout his career and works with Chef Nicholas Nutting to create unforgettable culinary experiences for Inn guests and The Pointe patrons.

Wickaninnish Inn

Blessed with a fabulous panoramic view, the Wickaninnish Inn is situated on a rocky outcropping in Tofino, on the West Coast of Vancouver Island.

Standing between the Pacific Ocean, Chesterman beach and a forest of giant evergreens, the design of the hotel's two buildings was entrusted to several artists, including the late celebrated wood carver Henry Nolla. The aim was to blend art, nature and culture. With big picture windows, the rooms offer grandiose views of the waves breaking on the shore and feature adzed cedar wood mantles and stone fireplaces. After a plant or marine-based treatment and an initiation to sea kayaking, you could even set off to see pods of whales just offshore.

PICKLED BEET & DAVID WOOD'S GOAT CHEESE SALAD, WATERCRESS, FRISEE, ORANGE SEGMENTS & ROASTED SICILIAN PISTACHIO ORANGE & CARDAMOM DRESSING

BY JOHN WALLER

Since we pickle the beets when they are at their best we can use them all year round. The beets come from Nanoose Farm, which is a local organic farm, and the goat cheese comes from Salt Spring Island. This dish is so wonderful beacause it showcases local suppliers and it is so colorful and tasty it just pops off the plate

Serves 4
Preparation time: 30 minutes
Cooking time: 1 hour

Planning ahead
It is best to allow 2 weeks for the beets to pickle, but they are edible in a few days.

INGREDIENTS

pickled beets:

5 pts white wine vinegar
1 stick of cinnamon
1 tbsp cloves
2 tbsp pickling spice
1 lb white granulated sugar
2 lbs brown sugar
1 cup freshly grated horseradish
4 bunches local red beets
½ cup kosher salt
¼ cup toasted Sicilian or regular green pistachios

orange cardamom dressing:

2 black cardamom pods, seeds removed
¼ cup local Vancouver Island honey
1 cup freshly squeezed orange juice
Meyer lemon juice
2 cups grapeseed oil
sea salt

salad:

5 oz David Wood's goat cheese at room temperature
I head of pale yellow frisée
1 bunch watercress, preferably hydroponic
2 seasonal oranges segments, i.e. Blood or Valencia juice, reserved
sprigs of chervil

pickled beet salad garnish:

4 pickled beets, quartered
thinly sliced red onions
fresh parsley leaves (about a dozen)
extra virgin olive oil
couple of grinds of black pepper

garnish:

roasted pistachios crushed into crumbs

METHOD

pickled beets:

Cut beets from beet tops, place in large pot and cover with cold water and salt. Cook till skin is easily rubbed off. Run under warm water and squeeze through your hands to rub off the skins then place in sterilized jars. Combine all the pickling ingredients, bring to a boil and pour over beets. Cool and hold in fridge for ideally 2 weeks but they are edible in a few days.

orange cardamom dressing:

Toast the seeds in a pan till fragrant, about 3 minutes, but do not scorch them. Add honey and simmer over a low heat for 5 minutes to flavor honey, then strain into a high powered blender with orange and lemon juices. Carefully turn on blender on low and increase to high slowly adding oil to emulsify. Season to taste

to serve:

Lightly whip goat cheese to soften and smooth it. Using the back of a spoon take a quarter of it and drag across each of the plates. Combine quartered beets, onion, parsley leaves, olive oil and fresh pepper in a bowl and lay across the goat cheese. Combine watercress, frisée, chervil and oranges in a bowl with dressing then divide among the four plates. Drizzle the juices over the plates to finish dressing. Finish with some toasted pistachio sprinkled over the plates.

Chef's tip:

I suggest pickling local fresh beets at the peak of their season for later use and I prefer the small red beets. The fresher the beets the less time they will take to cook.

POTATO CRUSTED PACIFIC HALIBUT, WILD MUSHROOM 'FRICASSEE', ROASTED SALISIFY & SEARED QUEBEC FOIE GRAS

BY NICHOLAS NUTTING

This dish is a showcase of Tofino fall ingredients. The fresh Tofino halibut is complemented by a crisp potato crust and a rich ragout of fresh, locally foraged mushrooms. A piece of rich Québec foie gras adds decadence to the dish and enriches the otherwise lean fish.

Serves 4
Preparation time: 2 hours
Cooking time: 45 minutes

Special equipment:
Mandoline slicer, blender, fine strainer

Planning ahead:
Buy fresh halibut from your local fishmonger on the day of the meal. Ask for center cut pieces and make sure it doesn't appear chalky.
Fresh wild mushrooms are available from mid-Summer to the late fall. Foragers often sell their mushrooms at local farmer's markets. The varieties of mushrooms in this recipe can be adjusted to suit your taste.

INGREDIENTS

potato crusted halibut:

4 pieces of Pacific halibut, 5 oz each
1 large russet potato
¼ cup clarified butter
¼ cup whole butter
2 sprigs fresh thyme
2 cloves garlic, smashed
1 lemon
salt & white pepper

wild mushroom 'fricassee':

3 cups cleaned, sliced wild mushrooms, matsutake, hedgehog, chanterelle
3 stalks salsify (peeled and cut on a bias in 2" sections)
2 tbsp olive oil
2 tbsp butter
2 shallots, brunoise
3 cloves garlic, brunoise
1 sprig of thyme (leaves only)
1 bay leaf
¼ cup Chardonnay
1 ½ cups heavy cream
6 baby white turnips, blanched al' dente
salt & pepper

salsify purée:

1 tbsp butter
4 stalks salsify, peeled and finely chopped
2 cups 3% milk
salt & pepper

red wine jus:

4 white button mushrooms, quartered (any clean mushroom trim from the wild mushrooms can be used in the jus)
2 tbsp butter
3 shallots, peeled and sliced
2 cloves garlic, peeled
1 sprig of thyme
1 bay leaf
3 black peppercorns, cracked
1½ cups reduced veal stock/veal demi glace
½ cup B.C. Pinot Noir

foie gras:

4 slices of foie gras, 1½ oz each
salt & pepper

garnish:

white truffle oil
fresh tarragon and nasturtium leaves

METHOD

potato crusted halibut

Cut the potato into 2" x 1" diameter cylinders. Using a mandoline slicer, finely slice the potato cylinders into discs. Season the halibut. Place the potato discs onto the surface of the fish and brush with clarified butter, refrigerate. until needed.

wild mushroom 'fricassee':

In a large saucepan, over a high heat, sauté the mushrooms and salsify in olive oil. Use a pan large enough for the mushrooms to not overlap and sweat: a golden color on the mushrooms makes a more flavorful ragout. When the mushrooms and salsify are golden color reduce the heat to a quarter power, add the butter, garlic, shallots, thyme leaves, seasoning, and bay leaf. Deglaze with Chardonnay and reduce until almost dry. Add the heavy cream and the baby turnips. Simmer until salsify is tender. Remove the bay leaf.

salsify purée:

In a medium saucepot, lightly brown the butter. Add the salsify and roast until it begins to lightly brown. Add milk, salt and pepper, and simmer until very soft. Cutting the salsify finely allows shorter cooking time and a fresher tasting purée.

Purée in a blender and pass through a fine strainer.

red wine jus:

In a medium saucepan over a medium-high heat lightly brown the butter. Add the mushrooms and sauté. Reduce the heat and add the shallots, garlic, thyme, bay leaf and black pepper. Gently sweat. Deglaze with Pinot Noir and reduce by half. Add the veal stock and reduce to sauce consistency. Strain through a fine strainer and skim off any excess fat.

foie gras:

The final step. The foie gras should be seared after the other components are plated. Season the foie gras generously on all sides. In a dry sauté pan over a high heat sear the foie gras, top and bottom. Place directly on to the fish.

to serve:

Cook the halibut by heating the seasoned pan and adding remaining clarified butter. Add the halibut, potato side down, and reduce the heat to three-quarters power. When the potato crust is golden, flip the fish, add the butter and thyme and baste until just cooked through. Finish with a squeeze of lemon.

Spread salsify purée on the plate with an offset palette knife. Spoon fricassee onto the purée. Place the fish and foie gras on top of the fricassee. Spoon white truffle oil in a circle around the plate and float red wine jus in oil. Garnish dish with tarragon and nasturtium leaves.

Chef's tip:

Store peeled salsify in acidulated water to prevent browning. When buying foie gras look for fresh #1 Québec Foie Gras. If using #2, find an un-bruised lobe. Always keep cold and slice with a thin heated blade.

OLIVE OIL CAKE

BY MATT WILSON

Serves 6
Preparation time: 20 minutes
Cooking time: 45 minutes

Planning ahead:
The sorbet needs to be frozen for 24 hours beforehand.

Special equipment:
Pacojet, air brush and air compressor.

INGREDIENTS

olive oil cake:

- 1½ oz invert sugar
- 3 eggs
- 6 oz sugar
- 7 oz olive oil
- 7 oz all purpose flour
- 2 tsp baking powder
- 1 tsp salt
- ½ lemon, zested

olive oil mousse:

- 2 oz cream
- ½ lemon, zested
- ½ oz invert sugar
- 5 oz Ivoire white chocolate
- 4 oz olive oil

chocolate for spraying:

- 6 oz 72% chocolate
- 2 oz cocoa butter

lemon purée:

- 7 oz fresh lemon rind
- 4pt water for blanching
- 2 oz water
- 1 oz sugar
- 1 ½ oz extra virgin olive oil
- 1 oz lemon juice
- 1 tsp salt

plum sorbet:

- 15 oz plums
- 2 ½ oz sugar
- 1 ½ oz powdered glucose
- 7 oz water
- 1 oz lemon juice

honey roast plums with thyme:

- 6 plums
- honey
- thyme

garnish:

- thyme flowers
- sea salt

This dessert is a great marriage of savory and sweet; the olive oil adds a nice fruity yet savory side to the dish. The plums bring a freshness to the dessert and the lemon marries the two together.

METHOD

olive oil cake:

Preheat the oven to 335-375°F. Add the eggs and invert sugar into a mixer and start to blend. Once it has started to aerate, slowly add the sugar and continue to blend until light and fluffy, then add the olive oil slowly to emulsify in properly. Add the dry ingredients and mix until clear. Place in baking molds and bake for 30-40 minutes or until golden brown.

olive oil mousse:

Boil the cream, lemon zest and invert sugar. Pour over the chocolate and mix until totally dissolved. Place the mixture in mixer bowl and whisk while slowly adding the olive oil.

chocolate for spraying:

Melt all ingredients together then cool until 85°F.

to assemble the cake:

Line a square terrine mold with acetate then place a small amount of the olive oil mousse in the bottom of the mold. Cut pieces of the olive oil cake to fit the mold then place one layer into the mold and cover with more olive oil mousse. Repeat this again for the second layer and top with the remaining mousse. Allow to set in the freezer.

Cut the assembled olive oil cake into six portions then place back into the freezer.

lemon purée:

Wash the lemons in cold water and drain. Peel the lemon rind with a peeler until you have 7 oz with as little pith as possible. Place lemon skin in 4 pints of cold water and boil for 10 minutes. Drain through a sieve and repeat this process three times until tender and with minimum bitterness to taste. Drain well and liquidize with the sugar, salt, 2 oz water, juice and olive oil.

plum sorbet:

Pit the plums and place in a saucepan with the water, sugar and powdered glucose. Boil for 2 minutes then cool and add the lemon juice. Place the sorbet mix in Pacojet canister and freeze at -11°F for 24 hours then churn as needed.

honey roast plums with thyme:

Pit the plums. Place the honey in a saucepan over a high heat until it starts to caramelize slightly then add the thyme. Place the plums in the saucepan face down and allow to caramelize for a few minutes or until golden brown. Take the plums out of the honey and allow to cool.

to serve:

Churn the sorbet in the Pacojet and place back in the freezer until needed.

Place the chocolate spray into an air brush and spray the portioned olive oil cake until the portions are coated evenly.

Place a smear of the lemon purée on the plate then place a portion of olive oil cake at one end of the smear. Warm the honey roast plums until just warm and place at the other end of the lemon smear. Make a nice scoop of the plum sorbet and place on top of the olive oil cake. Decorate the plate with some thyme flowers and sea salt.

Mexico

Mayan palaces, tropical jungles and sandy beaches epitomize typical Mexico. Featuring Aztec, Zapotec and Mayan civilizations before it was conquered by Spain, Mexico's cultural and architectural history speak volumes.

Whether it be Acapulco, Monterrey or even Mexico City there is something for everyone in Mexico. The home of chocolate, chili and of course Mexican favorites such as tacos, enchiladas and tamales, Mexico is brimming with tasty dishes waiting to be devoured. So be awestruck by the architecture, stare in amazement at the cliffs and gorges, look out onto blue as you relax on the beach and dine on the local cuisine in one of Mexico's many cities – Mexico never ceases to surprise.

Alexis Palacios

Executive Sous Chef Alexis Palacios joined the acclaimed culinary team at Cabo San Lucas' Esperanza Resort in November 2009. He oversees all culinary activities at the 57-room luxury resort and residence club, including their signature Oceanside Restaurant. A native of Mexico, Palacios brings a wealth of international cooking experience to Esperanza, having held previous positions with top restaurants and resorts in Mexico City, Dubai and Austin, Texas. Palacios holds a degree in Professional Gastronomy and Kitchen from Mexico City's renowned Superior College of Gastronomy.

Esperanza Resort

At the tip of Baja peninsula, in the heart of 17 hectares of unspoilt nature in the private enclave of Punta Ballena, lies Esperanza, which is located 4 miles from Cabo San Lucas.

All its 57 casitas and suites are tucked away on small hills and boast exceptional views of the ocean, into which the infinity pool seems to simply disappear. With so many alternatives at your beck and call, whether it be enjoying the private beach, the spa, the art gallery or the golf courses, you will simply have no time for boredom. In the evening, unwind and admire the sunset while sipping a delicious cocktail before savoring gourmet cuisine in the idyllic setting of the restaurant.

Serves 4
Preparation time: 30 minutes
Cooking time: 35 minutes

INGREDIENTS

watermelon:

1	watermelon, peeled, seeded and cut into 4 round shapes

baby beets:

1 lb	red baby beets, washed and cleaned
1 lb	yellow baby beets, washed and cleaned

Mayan vanilla bean vinaigrette, smoked chipotle:

2	13½ oz cans coconut milk
8 oz	freshly squeezed orange juice and all the zest from the oranges used
2 oz	freshly squeezed lemon juice and all the zest from the lemons used
2 tbsp	Dijon mustard
1	small clove garlic, finely minced
1 oz	Agave honey
1 tsp	chipotle paste
2	vanilla bean pods, halved and seeds separated
8 oz	extra virgin olive oil

salt & pepper

to serve:

roasted peanuts

5	mint leaves
2	basil leaves

WATERMELON BEET SALAD

BY ALEXIS PALACIOS

Mayan vanilla bean vinaigrette, smoked chipotle, toasted peanuts and agave honey - a colorful and refreshing combination.

METHOD

baby beets:

Preheat the oven to 275°F and cook the beets for 35 minutes. Peel the red beets and then cut them in half, peel and dice the yellow ones. Set aside.

Mayan vanilla bean vinaigrette, smoked chipotle:

In a mixing bowl, add all the ingredients, except the olive oil and seasoning. Whisk together, slowly adding the olive oil at the same time. Make sure it dissolves and separate completely the vanilla seeds. Check the flavor, and add salt and pepper to taste. Add the baby beets and more seasoning as necessary.

to serve:

Stack the beets on top of the watermelon circle, add the vinaigrette and garnish with roasted peanuts, mint and basil leaves.

Chef's tip:

Add some peppered ahi (yellowfin) tuna to the salad to make a more substantial dish.

CEDAR SPRINGS RACK OF LAMB, COUS COUS, CAPONATA & HERB JUS

BY ALEXIS PALACIOS

Serves 4
Preparation time: 10 minutes
Cooking time: 12 hours

Planning ahead:
Allow 12 hours for cooking the herb jus. The lamb needs to be marinated in advance.

INGREDIENTS

lamb rack:

4 lb	lamb rack (marinated in extra virgin olive oil with fine herbs and garlic)
salt & pepper	

herb jus:

5 lb	lamb bones
2	carrots
2	celery sticks
2	onions
1 tbsp	tomato paste
fine herbs	
salt & pepper	

cous cous:

1 lb	cous cous
10 oz	infusion of cinnamon, star anise, black pepper, bay leaves, brown sugar, boiling water, strained
5 oz	golden raisins
5 oz	roasted pine nuts
salt & pepper	

caponata:

1	red bell pepper, finely chopped
1	tomato, finely chopped
1	green zucchini, finely chopped
2 oz	white onion, finely chopped
½ oz	garlic, finely chopped
2 oz	extra virgin olive oil
salt & pepper	

baby vegetables:

5 oz	baby vegetables blanched

Cedar Springs American lamb is the result of superior breeding and flock management. Raised on high mountain pastures in their natural environment, it provides a mild and delicate flavor, with an excellent nutritional profile, fitting perfectly into today's trend toward lighter, leaner and healthier foods.

METHOD

herb jus:

Roast the lamb bones for at least 40 minutes with the vegetables. Then put in a pot with the tomato paste and add enough cool water to cover. Cook on the stove for 12 hours over a slow heat. Strain the juice, add the fine herbs and reduce by half. Add salt and pepper to taste.

cous cous:

Boil the infusion for 5 minutes, strain and cook the cous cous in it for 8-10 minutes. Cool it down, add the raisins and pine nuts. Check the flavor, adding salt and pepper to taste.

caponata:

In a hot pan sauté all the ingredients, except the seasoning, and cook for 10 minutes over a medium heat, then add salt and pepper to taste.

baby vegetables:

In a hot pan, sauté the baby vegetables in the olive oil.

lamb rack:

Marinate the lamb for at least 1 hour in olive oil, fine herbs and garlic. Season and cook the rack of lamb under a grill as desired. Portion into chops.

to serve:

Placed the cous cous on a plate and arrange chops from the rack lamb on top. Surround with the vegetables and a caponata quenelle, and finish with some reheated herb jus.

Serves 4
Preparation time: 30 minutes
Cooking time: 35 minutes

Special equipment:
Silicon pastry mat

INGREDIENTS

buñuelos dough:

1¾ pt	water
1 oz	salt
2 oz	sugar powder
10 oz	butter
1 lb	flour
13	eggs
5 oz	dark chocolate
vegetable oil, for frying	
2 oz	sugar powder (confectioner's sugar)

to serve:

sorbet of your choice

BUNUELOS
BY ALEXIS PALACIOS

Sugar dusted doughnut holes that are an essential dish in our Mexican culture.

METHOD

buñuelos dough:

Boil the water with the salt and butter, add the flour and cook for 15 minutes over a slow heat, working the dough all the time, then allow it to cool down. Put the dough in a mixer and add the eggs one by one. Beat the dough for 10 minutes.

On a silicon pastry mat form a small ball and stuff with the dark chocolate. Heat the oil and fry the ball in the oil drain and dust with sugar powder.

to serve:

Serve with your favorite sorbet.

Mauricio Espinosa

Mauricio, Executive Chef of Las Mañanitas was born in Tuxtla Gutierrez, Chiapas. He lives in Cuernavaca, Morelos and studied at the Euroamerica Gastronomic School in Cuernavaca. 100% dedicated to his main passion which is being a gastronomic architect Mauricio has shared the stage in different gastronomic and culinary festivals with renowned chefs. He also has participated in the design of recipes for the 'Morelos Flavor Program' with 220 Sanborns´ restaurants within the Mexican Republic.

At Las Mañanitas Mauricio is in charge of all the special events, including catering. He also has the responsibility of Las Mañanitas´ restaurant which caters for almost 8,000 loyal clientele on a regular basis, with a variety of dishes – approximately 110 on the menu, as well as being responsible for the spa menu.

The main dishes of Las Mañanitas´ Menu are elaborated with Cajun spices, which offer a special flavor and aroma. Mauricio is especially devoted to oriental cuisine, wines and has a special fervor for traditional Mexican cuisine.

Las Mañanitas

Right in the center of Cuernavaca, nicknamed the "city of eternal Spring" because of the mildness of its climate, is a sumptuous hacienda in the purest Mexican tradition.

In the exotic gardens, among the sculptures by Francisco Zuñiga and lush flowers, you can admire peacocks strutting about near the fountains and blue parrots perched in the trees. Under their tiled roofs, the villas and their colonial suites are decorated with some of the country's most beautiful antiques and artworks including paintings by José Luis Cuevas, Leonardo Nierman and Carlos Mérida. Your itinerary: a typical and abundant cuisine and a choice of excursions on the trail of the Aztecs, including a visit to the Palace of Cortès and exploration of the ruined cities of Xochicalco and Taxco - famous for its silversmiths and silver shops.

RED MAGUEY WORMS WITH GARLIC & CHILI

BY MAURICIO ESPINOSA

Serves 1
Preparation time: 8 minutes
Cooking time: 5 minutes

INGREDIENTS

1 tbsp olive oil
1 garlic clove, finely chopped
1 tsp chili guajillo, cut in pieces with scissors
3 oz red maguey worms
salt, to taste
Maggi seasoning juice, to taste
5 epazote leaves, finely chopped

to serve:

green and red sauces
tortillas

An exquisite exotic dish, that is really popular in this area. Give it a try!

METHOD

Heat the oil in a medium size frying pan, add the garlic and soften over a low heat. Add the chili guajillo and fry for a few seconds, then add the red maguey worms. Add the salt, seasoning and juice, as well as epazote.

to serve:

Cook for a few minutes and serve with hot green and red sauces, and freshly made tortillas.

Serves 2

Preparation time:	15 minutes
Cooking time:	8-10 minutes

INGREDIENTS

sauce:

6 tbsp	butter, softened
1	large lime, juiced
2 tsp	Cajun style seasoning
2	slices of lime

garlic salt, to taste

red snapper:

2	red snapper fillets, around 7 oz each
2 tsp	butter
2 tsp	corn oil
1	lime, juice
½ tsp	garlic salt

to serve:

2	sprigs of parsley, chopped

MANANITAS RED SNAPPER

BY MAURICIO ESPINOSA

Red snapper is a really popular dish on our menu, customers really love this delicious red snapper.

METHOD

sauce:

In a small saucepan melt the butter with the lime juice and the Cajun seasoning. Cook over a low heat until the sauce turns golden brown.

red snapper:

To prepare the fish, moisten the fillets with the lime juice and sprinkle with the garlic salt.

Gently heat the butter and oil in a frying pan, and fry the fillets of fish, carefully turning them with a spatula.

to serve:

Reheat the sauce and add the slices of lime. Test the seasoning, and add garlic salt to taste if necessary.

Place the fish on an oven warmed plate, pour the sauce over the fish and decorate with the chopped parsley. Serve with rice of your choice and seasonal vegetables.

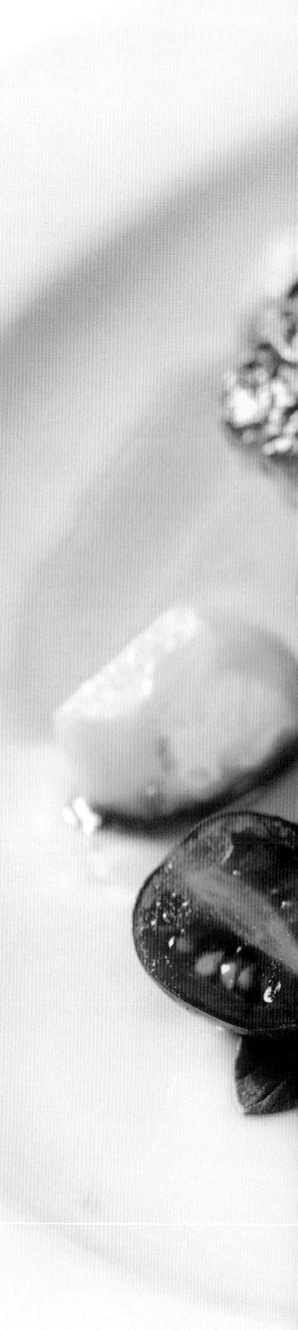

Serves 4
Preparation time: 10 minutes
Cooking time: 1 hour 30 minutes

INGREDIENTS

2 cups	whipping cream
1 oz	eggs
1 oz	egg yolks
¾ cups	coconut cream
2 oz	chopped coconut
4 oz	Philadelphia cheese

garnish:

kiwi slices
plums
litchis
strawberries
raspberries
blackberries
coconut slices
mint leaf or peppermint

FRESH COCONUT FLAN

BY MAURICIO ESPINOSA

A deliciously creamy tropical dessert beautifully paired with exotic fruits.

METHOD

Preheat the oven to 300°F.

Boil the whipping cream and eggs. Put the additional egg yolks in a separate bowl and stir in 2 tablespoons of the boiled whipping cream. Gradually incorporate the rest of the whipping cream.

Liquidize the coconut cream, chopped coconut and the Philadelphia cheese and add to the cream and egg mix. Pour into an ovenproof dish and cook in the oven for approximately 1 hour 30 minutes.

to serve

Spoon into glasses and decorate with mixed fruit of your choice.

The Caribbean

The thoughts of ice white beaches and tropical blue waters don't let you down in the Caribbean, but there is a great deal more that these islands can offer.

The blend of cultures is apparent with a history of sugar trading, slavery and piracy combined with modern island life of holiday goers, fishermen and cricket players. Absorb the sun as you enjoy your favorite cocktail or take in the flavors of fresh fish, coconut, banana and other tropical bounty that the islands tempt you with. From clear waters, to dense tropical forests, to reggae dancing in the streets, the Caribbean, with its mixture of cool attitude and easy-going laziness, features a seriously laid back lifestyle.

Stéphane Mazières
Grand Chef Relais & Châteaux

Stéphane Mazierès was born in Rochefort-sur-Mer in the Charente Maritime region. Stéphane's love of the islands and particularly the French influenced culture of St. Barts led him back to Hôtel Le Toiny twice. First from 2001-2003 when he was Chef de Partie and later Sous Chef under Executive Chef Maxime Deschamps. He then returned to France where he was Sous Chef at the three-star Hôtel l'Etourle in Meribel. After a stint there, he went to Michelin-starred Restaurant Leï Mouscardins in St. Tropez and worked under Chef Laurent Tarridec as Chef de Partie and later Sous Chef. But in 2006, the island of St. Barts and Hôtel Le Toiny called him back to be at the helm of Restaurant Le Gaïac. Stéphane loves the lifestyle of the islands and is passionate about embracing the island's natural flavors and marrying them with a refined French style which features beautiful plate presentations. Stéphane received the 2010 Taittinger Trophy Relais & Châteaux Grand Chef, the first chef to obtain this recognition in the Caribbean.

Hôtel Le Toiny

This is a true paradise nestled into the hills of 'Saint Barth', in the heart of a 17 hectare estate and its palm grove.

"True idleness means getting up at 6am so you have more time to do nothing," wrote Tristan Bernard. This is the frame of mind you can adopt at the Hôtel Le Toiny. Your refuge: one of the 15 colonial-style villa suites overlooking the sea. In the infinity pool or on the white sandy beach, bathing is a moment of sheer bliss before treating yourself to a massage on your private terrace. The same splendor is carried over into the meals in the gourmet restaurant Le Gaïac where Chef Stéphane Mazières skillfully enhances the flavors.

TARTARE OF SEA SCALLOPS WITH CELERY

BY STEPHANE MAZIERES

Delicious and adaptable to your own preferences.

Serves 6
Preparation time: 30 minutes
Cooking time: 15 seconds

INGREDIENTS

sea scallops:

9 oz scallops

celery tartare:

3 oz celery stalk
3 oz celery ball (white base)
3 shallots
flat parsley, to taste
3 limes, zest grated
olive oil
coarse salt & pepper
Sichuan pepper

to serve:

balsamic vinegar
½ oz caviar from Aquitaine
sprigs of celery stalk or sprigs of chervil

METHOD

sea scallops:

Cut into ¼" dice and place in the fridge.

celery tartare:

Peel the celery stalks. Rinse them with cold water and cut into ¼" dice, cut the celery ball in two and peel one half with a knife. Cut thin slices of ¼" thickness and then cut into ¼" dice. Plunge the celery dice into a saucepan of boiling water and coarse salt, and then let them cook for only 15 seconds. Remove and place them in a dish of cold water (with water and ice cubes, which stops the cooking process and keeps a bright color and to obtain a cooked, but crispy vegetable). Strain and put on absorbent paper. Place in the fridge.

Peel and cut the shallots into very small dice. Mince the parsley. Mix together the shallots, the celery ball dice, the celery stalk dice, and scallop dice. Add salt, pepper and Sichuan pepper. Put in the grated lime zest and olive oil (for the shine and the smoothness). Place in the fridge.

to serve:

Use a square form and fill with the tartare mix, pack it down with the back of a spoon, then remove the square. Decorate the plate with balsamic vinegar reduced to a syrup. Finish with caviar and sprigs of celery stalk or chervil.

Chef's tip

The caviar from Aquitaine can be replaced by other roe fish. Put small amounts of horseradish purée around the tartare to increase the taste.

Serves 6
Preparation time: 1 hour
Cooking time: 10 minutes

Planning ahead:
Marinate the fish for 24 hours to make it tastier.

INGREDIENTS

fish:

6 lb turbot
salt & pepper
6 twigs of thyme
olive oil

zucchini and oyster tartare:

3½ lb zucchinis
12 oysters
6 stalks of dill, refrigerated

spinach:

10 oz baby spinach leaves
2 oz butter
1 garlic clove
salt & pepper

lemongrass sauce:

1½ lb lemongrass sticks
2½ lb fish stock
1¼ lb liquid cream
salt & pepper

garnish:

herbs
edible flowers
lemongrass sticks

GRILLED FILLET OF TURBOT WITH ZUCCHINI, OYSTER TARTARE, LEMONGRASS SAUCE

BY STEPHANE MAZIERES

Delightful taste and colors.

METHOD

turbot:

Take off the black skin of the turbot; keep the white one. Cut the fish in steaks of equal size; marinate the fillets in olive oil, thyme, and salt and pepper for 24 hours.

zucchini and oyster tartare:

Cut large stripes of zucchinis of the same size, keeping only the green part, then dice them. At the same time, open the oysters and pour their water on the zucchini dice. Mince and mix the oysters with the zucchinis and then add the refrigerated dill. This should be prepared one hour before serving, so that the zucchinis are crisp.

spinach:

Rinse the spinach leaves in cold water and drain. Just before serving, cook them in a nut-brown foamy butter with a clove of garlic, salt and pepper. Once cooked, drain.

lemongrass sauce:

Infuse the minced lemongrass sticks with fish stock in a saucepan over a medium heat, and cook until the stock has reduced by half. Add the liquid cream and cook the whole until it boils. Season with salt and pepper and keep warm.

to serve:

Put the turbot steaks on the grill on the side of the white skin at first, giving them quarter turns. Do the same on the other side and finish the cooking process in the oven (so that the fish does not become too dry), for approximately 5 minutes depending on size.

Place the just cooked baby spinach leaves In the middle of the plate. Put the turbot steak on top, presented on its vertical side, then add the zucchini and oyster tartare. Decorate the whole with herbs and edible flowers. Finish off by spooning the lemongrass sauce around and finally add some lemongrass sticks on the sides of the plate.

Serves 6
Preparation time: 1 hour
Cooking time: 50 minutes

INGREDIENTS

joconde biscuit base:

3¼ oz	egg whites
¾ oz	caster sugar
3¼ oz	almond powder
1 oz	wheat flour
3¼ oz	icing sugar
1¼ oz	butter
1	whole egg

white chocolate-coconut cream:

5 oz	coconut milk
⅓ oz	tapioca beads
10 oz	white chocolate, broken into small pieces
8	gelatin sheets
10½ oz	liquid cream

caramelized mangoes:

2½ lb	mangoes
4¼ oz	caster sugar
4¼ oz	butter

mango juice, optional

mango sauce:

7 oz	mangoes
1¾ oz	caster sugar
1	lime, juice
6½ fl oz	old rum

dark chocolate sauce:

2 oz	dark chocolate 70%
3½ oz	liquid cream
½	vanilla pod

to serve:

mango sorbet
almond powder or grated coconut
almond tile

TARTE TATIN OF MANGO, COCONUT, WHITE CHOCOLATE & TAPIOCA BEADS

BY STEPHANE MAZIERES

Exquisite dessert melding Caribbean flavors and originality!

METHOD

joconde biscuit base:

Preheat the oven to 390°F. Beat the egg whites with the caster sugar until stiff to make a meringue. Separately, blend the whole egg, the icing sugar, the almond powder, the wheat flour and the butter together. Then mix both preparations together and lay out in a baking pan 10" x 6". Put in the oven for 7-8 minutes. Once colored, remove from the oven and let it cool down.

white chocolate-coconut cream

Put the coconut milk in a saucepan, add the tapioca beads and cook for 30 minutes. Towards the end of the cooking process incorporate the gelatin. Then pour the mix on to the white chocolate, and let it cool down to room temperature. Beat the liquid cream in a food blender until it starts to become creamy. Now mix the two preparations together, pour all of the mixture on to the biscuit base and store in the fridge.

caramelized mangoes:

Peel the mangoes and remove their hearts. Cut into very small dice. Put in a pan with a bit of butter to sauté them, add the caster sugar and cook until they caramelize. Pour on to the coconut-white chocolate cream and store the fridge. It is possible to lighten the caramel by adding just a little mango juice, and to make it less dry.

mango sauce:

Heat the rum with the sugar. Peel the mangoes and keep only the flesh. Mix with the rum and sugar in a food blender. Add the lime juice, pass the mixture through a very tight strainer and into a saucepan, and bring to a boil. Store in a fridge.

dark chocolate sauce:

In a saucepan, infuse the liquid cream with the the vanilla pod (cut in the middle and the insides removed with a knife). Bring to a boil and pour on to the dark chocolate. Let it cool down.

to serve:

Dot cocoa sauce and mango sauce at the bottom of the plate. Put a small piece of the tart, cut in a rectangular shape, on the side of the plate. Opposite to it, place a scoop of mango sorbet – place on some almond powder or grated coconut to stop it slipping. Decorate with an almond tile.

Chef's tip

It is possible to lighten the caramel by adding just a little mango juice and it will make it less dry.

Jermaine 'Monk' George

Delighting the palates of Biras guests and hearing their rave reviews are what Executive Chef Jermaine 'Monk' George finds so rewarding about a profession that enables him to put his heart and soul in each dish he skillfully prepares. First exposed to cooking at an early age in the kitchen of his mother Juliette, Monk learned to appreciate down-home Caribbean cooking on the island of Virgin Gorda. Intrigued by the opportunity to express himself by creating new and unique dishes with a Caribbean flair, it did not take him long to realize he wanted to be a chef.

Monk's training was honed in the kitchens of places such as Lake Placid Lodge and White Barn Inn, but since 1997 he has worked his way up from Sous Chef to Executive Chef at the Biras Creek Resort.

Monk is never afraid of new challenges, but don't be surprised to see classics such as Eggs Benedict and Beef Wellington on his menu. Availability of fresh ingredients and timing help determine the menus that he meticulously plans.

Biras Creek Resort

This is a secret address on the tiny island of Virgin Gorda which can only be reached by boat or helicopter and offers 31 elegant and colorful suites with fabulous sea views.

The Biras Creek Resort is a paradise of greens and blues with its tropical plants and lagoons. The area is also famous for its 'Baths' formed by the spherical granite rocks dotted along the beach. Share your time among the water sports available and the delicious cuisine. You can discover the island by kayak, windsurf, boat ... or bicycle to really get a feel for this little corner of paradise.

SEARED TUNA APPETIZERS

BY JERMAINE GEORGE

Serves 4
Preparation time: 15 minutes
Cooking time: 5 minutes

INGREDIENTS

seared tuna and zucchini:

4	portions of tuna steak, 3 oz each
1	zucchini

olive oil, salt & pepper to taste

dressing:

1 cup	virgin olive oil
2	lemons
1	medium tomato, seeded and diced
½ cup	Kalamata olives, diced

salt & pepper to taste

Just a mile off-shore from Biras Creek Resort, the ocean floor drops to almost a mile deep. Here the local fishermen bring in mahi mahi, wahoo, grouper and most commonly, tuna. From hook to kitchen in only a few hours, our local tuna is at its best when prepared by simply searing and serving!

METHOD

tuna and zucchini:

Cut zucchini into ½" coins, season with olive oil, salt and pepper to taste, then grill on both sides. Season tuna steaks with salt and pepper. Heat olive oil in a cast iron skillet over high heat until very hot. Place steaks in the pan, and sear for about 30 seconds on each side.

dressing:

Juice two lemons and emulsify the lemon juice with virgin olive oil. Add the diced tomato and olives. Season to taste.

to serve:

Fan the zucchini out on the plate. Slice the tuna steaks diagonally and position the two tuna halves in the center of the fan in a crisscross showing rare edges. Spoon dressing on to and around the tuna.

SEARED SCALLOPS, ROASTED CORN RED PEPPER RELISH

BY JERMAINE GEORGE

The scallops recipe is a favorite of our guests, even though scallops are not native to the region. We bring in fresh scallops weekly and run this item as a special for a few days per week.

Serves 4
Preparation time: 30 minutes
Cooking time: 15 minutes

INGREDIENTS

seared scallops:

8	large scallops
1 tbsp	olive oil

relish:

2	sweet red peppers
3 cups	sweet corn kernels
1 tsp	salt
1 tsp	pepper
1 tbsp	olive oil

garnish:

chopped chives

METHOD

seared scallops:

Sear the scallops for 2 minutes on both sides in the olive oil in a pan.

relish:

Preheat the oven to 350°F. Roast the red peppers in the oven until soft, then peel and dice. Roast the corn in the oven until browned. Toss both the peppers and corn with the remaining olive oil, salt and pepper

to serve:

Spoon one cup of relish onto the center of the plate. Place two scallops on each side of the relish. Garnish with chopped chives.

COCONUT MACAROON STACK, RUM ROASTED PINEAPPLE, CREME CHANTILLY

BY HEIDI BENYAIR

This recipe is a favorite as it uses several ingredients found right here in the British Virgin Islands: rum, coconut and vanilla.

Serves 6
Preparation time: 30 minutes
Cooking time: 20 minutes

INGREDIENTS

coconut macaroons:

8 oz	sugar
2 oz	unsalted butter, melted
3	large eggs
4 cups	coconut, shredded

pineapple:

1	medium sized pineapple
1½ cups	sugar
1 cup	spiced rum
1	vanilla pod, seeds scraped out

crème Chantilly:

3 cups	whipping cream
1 cup	confectioner's sugar
1	vanilla pod, seeds scraped out

to serve:

confectioner's sugar

METHOD

coconut macaroons:

Preheat the oven to 325°F. In a large bowl mix all the ingredients together with a spatula. Spoon out and flatten the mixture onto a sheet of greaseproof paper on a baking sheet. Bake for 15 minutes or until golden brown. Allow to cool before removing with a spatula.

pineapple:

Core and dice the pineapple, then cook in a saucepan with the sugar, rum and vanilla pod and seeds. Cook until light brown and syrupy. Remove the vanilla pod. Cool.

crème Chantilly:

Place the cream, sugar and vanilla seeds in a large bowl or in a mixer and whip until stiff peaks form.

to serve:

Place a macaroon on the plate, followed by a dollop of cream and a spoon of pineapple. Repeat the process to form a stack. Lightly dust with confectioner's sugar.

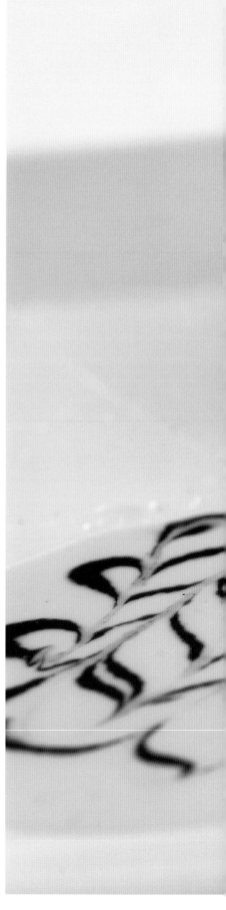

Brian Porteus

Executive Chef Brian Porteus is a classically French trained chef who has collected his invaluable international cooking experience in – and on – some of the world's most exclusive restaurants, hotels and cruise liners. His cooking style is traditional French based, modern and mature fusion cuisine, emphasizing simplicity, natural textures, and freshness with cultural influences and unique cooking techniques. His ingredients are sourced locally, farmed, harvested and fished and always at their freshest.

Brian trained at Rockwell Hotel & Catering College, Ireland. He served his apprenticeship at respected 5 star hotels in Ireland followed by London at Grosvenor House Hotel. Brian then worked at the world famous Sun City Casino & Resort in South Africa. He traveled to America to become Sous Chef with the Luxurious Cruise Ships of Holland American Line. Brian moved back to Ireland as Head Chef of Les Freres Jacques and spent several months in England at Le Manoir Aux 'Quat Saisons before moving to Barbados to become Executive Chef at Cobblers Cove.

Cobblers Cove

Just a few steps away from a fine sandy beach edged by tropical gardens, Cobblers Cove on Barbados envelops you in English elegance with its marble floors, painted furniture, antique sofas and cushions embroidered with gold thread.

Here the days begin with a generous English breakfast and are then spent at your leisure with dips in the turquoise sea, water sports, beauty treatments and the pleasures of the table. At the poolside bar, tea time tends to be overshadowed by the delicious cocktails and excellent wines that just have to be tasted. There is also a special program of activities for children.

DIVER CAUGHT SEA SCALLOPS, SWEET POTATO MASH, WAKAMI SEAWEED, PAPAYA & CAVIAR FOAM

BY BRIAN PORTEUS

Fresh scallops are always so tasty and easy to cook. I use only diver caught scallops as commercial fishing dredging boats tend to damage all the sea beds and living coral in their path. This dish is interesting with the Asian influence of the wakami seaweed and the sweetness of the papaya fruit.

Serves 3
Preparation time: 20 minutes
Cooking time: 40 minutes

INGREDIENTS

9 diver caught sea scallops
1½ fl oz virgin olive oil

sweet potato:

9 oz sweet potato
2 oz salted butter
3½ oz wakami seaweed

seaweed and papaya:

3½ oz fresh papaya
½ lime
3½ oz egg whites
1 oz sugar
1 tsp sevruga caviar
salt & pepper

METHOD

sweet potato:

Peel the sweet potato, boil in salted water until soft, strain and pass through a fine sieve, whip with the butter until smooth, then season with salt.

seaweed and papaya:

Warm the seaweed gently in a pan. Peel and purée the papaya, bring to a simmer, and add the lime juice. Whip the egg white and sugar until they form soft peaks, then add the papaya purée, and fold into the stiff egg whites.

scallops:

Remove the red coral and muscle from the scallops, and season with salt and pepper. Sear on both sides in a hot pan with olive oil, then place the scallops on kitchen paper to rest.

to serve:

Arrange three 1½" pastry rings on a warmed plate, place layers of the sweet potato into each ring, then a little of the seaweed and finish with sweet potato. Remove the rings. Place the three warm scallops onto each potato ring. Add the caviar to the foam Spoon the papaya foam over each scallop.

SEARED PEPPERED RARE CARIBBEAN TUNA LOIN, SOYA & HONEY GLAZE, RED PEPPER ESCABECHE, AVOCADO & LIME PUREE

BY BRIAN PORTEUS

Serves 4
Preparation time: 45 minutes
Cooking time: 20 minutes

INGREDIENTS

seared peppered rare tuna loin:

1 lb tuna loin fillet
2 tsp black peppercorns, crushed and roasted
2 tsp fresh coriander, chopped
1 tsp olive oil
salt

soya and honey glaze:

6 fl oz soy sauce
3 tbsp honey

red pepper escabeche:

4 shallots peeled and cut into fine strips
2 cloves of garlic, peeled and chopped
1 tbsp olive oil
3 whole star anise
4 bay leaves
1 small pinch of saffron
cinnamon sticks
2 red peppers, deseeded and cut into fine strips
3½ oz brown sugar
1 lemon, zest and juice
salt & ground white pepper
6 fl oz chicken stock
coriander

avocado and lime purée:

2 avocados, peeled and finely diced
1 lime, juice
1 tbsp coriander, chopped
salt & freshly ground white pepper

The Carribean ocean has a fantastic selection of yellow fin or ahi, big eye and Albacore tuna. The yellowfin (Ahi) tuna is widely used in raw fish dishes, especially sashimi, due to the deep rich purple color of its flesh. To appreciate the flavors of this dish, you can only use the very best and freshest of tuna loin. The honey and soya gives the tuna its sweetness. The red pepper gives it a smooth sharpness, and the avocado and lime a refreshing sourness, which brings overall harmony to the taste senses.

METHOD

seared peppered rare tuna loin:

Mix the peppercorns and coriander together and coat the tuna. In a hot frying pan, sear the tuna fillet in the olive oil and season with salt. Set aside and chill.

soy and honey glaze

Bring the soy sauce to a boil in a heavy based saucepan, then reduce the heat until it is lightly simmering. Skim any impurities that rise to the surface as you are reducing the soy. When the soy is thick enough to coat the back of a spoon heavily, strain it through a fine sieve. Add the honey and stir well over a low heat until it comes together. Taste and add more honey if required.

red pepper escabeche:

Fry the shallots and garlic in the olive oil in a large saucepan. Stir in the star anise, bay leaves, saffron and cinnamon sticks. Add the peppers, sugar and lemon zest and cook for a few minutes. Season, cover with stock and lemon juice and simmer until the peppers are cooked but not mushy. Strain the liquid, retaining the pepper mix in a separate bowl, then reduce the liquid until it is a syrupy consistency. Mix the peppers and the liquid when cooled and stir in the coriander.

avocado and lime purée:

Combine all the ingredients in a bowl. Seal tightly with plastic wrap and chill.

to serve:

Slice the seared tuna loin and arrange it between four chilled plates. Spoon the red pepper escabeche and avocado and lime purée to the side. Drizzle with the soy and honey glaze.

GRAND MARNIER SOUFFLE

BY BRIAN PORTEUS

A Grand Marnier soufflé is a wonderful way to end a meal. It's light and refreshing, perfect for the Caribbean climate. Although soufflés often seem intimidating they can be done. They are a great dessert for any occasion and this recipe can be used with almost any flavor to inspire your next event.

Serves 8
Preparation time: 45 minutes
Cooking time: 15 minutes

Planning ahead:
The soufflé mix should be made 1 hour in advance.

INGREDIENTS

3½ oz Grand Marnier
3½ oz orange juice
4 oz sugar
1 oz cornstarch
7 egg whites
½ tsp cream of tartar
2 tbsp water
butter, for the ramekins
granulated sugar, for the ramekins

to serve:

icing sugar

METHOD

Place the Grand Marnier, orange juice, and 2 oz of the sugar in a pot and bring to a boil. Place the cornstarch and water in a bowl and mix together. When your orange mix comes to a boil temper it into the cornstarch and place back over the heat (be careful when using alcohol because it will catch fire). Cook the mixture until it gets thick and the cornstarch has been cooked out. Place in a bowl and cover for a least 1 hour to allow the mix to cool.

While the mix is cooling you can prepare the ramekins by buttering the insides of the dishes dish then covering them with granulated sugar. Once your mix is cool, place your egg whites in a mixer with the cream of tartar and whisk to medium peaks – just still enough to hold its shape. Add the other 2 oz of sugar and whisk on high for 15 seconds. Give the Grand Marnier a good whisk to remove any lumps, take a quarter of the egg whites and whisk in, then gently fold in the remaining egg whites.

to serve:

Preheat the oven to 400°F. Fill the ramekins to the top with the soufflé mixture and level them with the back of a knife. Bake for about 16 minutes. Dust the tops with icing sugar and serve.

Jean-Claude Dufour

Jean-Claude Dufour was born in Bordeaux. Becoming a chef was what he wanted to do from the age of 12 after beginning to help his parents in their catering business.

Jean-Claude graduated from The École Hôtelière' of Bordeaux and began his professional career at Relais and Châteaux de Margaux. Subsequently he was trained by the legendary Anne-Marie Troisgros and Chef Yves Gravelier. Jean-Claude considers himself fortunate for having worked with them for several years in various restaurants.

Prior to locating to St Barthélèmy, Jean-Claude worked for a while in Senegal where he greatly enjoyed the experience of combining French and Senegalese styles of cuisine.

Jean-Claude has lived by the sea for all of his life. He loves to cook fresh catch from the ocean. His unique style, the gift of fine taste and an eye for exciting food presentation are particular aspects of the work that Jean-Claude now seeks to impart to his brigade of young French chefs at the Eden Rock – St Barths. This, while reminding them constantly that the key to good food is the freshness and quality of its ingredients.

Eden Rock
- St Barths

This is an ideal place for soaking up the sun of St Barths, lazing on the beach and exploring the dazzling undersea world.

Between the white sands and crystal clear waters of Saint-Jean Bay and located on a rocky promontory overlooking the coral reefs, this group of villas stands on the foundations of the former property of the aviator Rémy de Haenen, the first to land a plane on the island back in the 1940s. Jane and David Matthews have created the contemporary and eclectic interiors of the themed suites: the new Rockstar, with recording studio and the new Nina, the 'Fregate' with its private Jacuzzi, the Howard Hughes ...

Serves 4
Preparation time: 35 minutes
Cooking time: 8 minutes for the ravioli, 5 minutes for the shrimps

INGREDIENTS

mushroom ravioli:

8 sheets Chinese ravioli pasta
7 oz trumpet mushrooms
7½ oz shiitake mushrooms
7 oz portobello mushrooms
3 ½ oz white button mushrooms
1 lime, zest, finely chopped
1 fingered citron (Buddha's hand), diced
1 clove garlic, finely chopped
few sprigs of thyme
6½ fl oz olive oil
salt & pepper
flour
egg yolk, beaten

sauce:

10½ oz cockles, cleaned and prepared
10½ oz mussels, cleaned and prepared
3½ oz fennel bulb, small diced
3 oz shallots, small diced
3½ oz leeks, small diced
3½ fl oz Lillet Blanc (sweet white vermouth)
1½ fl oz Noilly Prat (dry vermouth)
10 basil leaves
3½ oz butter, small cubes, well chilled
olive oil
salt & pepper

shrimps:

4 jumbo shrimps
4 thin slices of Parma ham
olive oil flavored with garlic

garnish:

basil leaves

MUSHROOM RAVIOLI WITH A SHELLFISH & BASIL FLAVORED SAUCE, TOPPED WITH A JUMBO SHRIMP & CRISPY PARMA HAM

BY JEAN-CLAUDE DUFOUR

Earthy mushroom flavors blended delicately with a subtle shellfish sauce, spectacularly topped with crisp, saline Parma ham, make this dish a favorite choice on our On the Rocks menu.

METHOD

mushroom ravioli:

Chop the mushrooms and keep them separate. Pan fry alternately with the olive oil, garlic and thyme. Drain the cooked mushrooms together in a sieve to remove any excess liquid. Season with salt, pepper, lime zest and Buddha's hand and refrigerate.

Place the ravioli pasta on a lightly floured surface. Put a spoonful of the mushroom mixture in the middle of the pasta square. Brush the ravioli edges with egg yolk, then place a second square on top and press them tightly together to seal the ravioli. Place in the fridge or a cool, dry place.

sauce:

Sweat the vegetables in a little olive oil until the flavor develops. Add the cleaned, prepared shellfish. Deglaze the saucepan with the Lillet Blanc and Noilly Prat. Add half of the basil leaves. Strain the entire contents of the saucepan and reserve the liquid. Bring the liquid to a boil and whisk the chilled butter pieces into the sauce. Chop the remaining basil and add to the sauce. Check the seasoning. Set aside and keep warm, ideally over a bain marie.

shrimps:

Peel the shrimps, then butterfly by cutting in horizontal halves and remove the intestines. Pan fry in a little olive oil flavored with garlic until cooked. Remove the cooked shrimps and fry the sliced Parma ham in the same frying pan until crispy.

to serve:

Reheat the sauce in a saucepan. Place the ravioli in boiling water until cooked. Remove them with a slotted spoon and place in the sauce. Put the raviolis on a plate with a shrimp on top. Cover with the remaining sauce. Position a slice of the crispy Parma ham on the shrimp and decorate with a basil leaf.

TARTARE OF YELLOWFIN TUNA WITH WATERCRESS CREAM & AVOCADO & CITRUS SALAD

BY JEAN-CLAUDE DUFOUR

Fresh Caribbean cuisine is epitomized in every way by combining colorful citrus and avocado with our local yellowfin tuna, thriving plentifully in the turquoise blue waters of St Barths.

Serves 4
Preparation time: 25 minutes
Cooking time: N/A

INGREDIENTS

tuna tartare:

1 lb fresh yellowfin tuna, ½" cubes
1 bunch of cilantro, chopped
1 bunch of basil, finely sliced
olive oil
2½ limes, juice
salt & pepper

avocado & citrus salad:

3 oranges, segmented
3 grapefruits, segmented
3½ oz baby spinach shoots, finely sliced
1 avocado, 1" dice
2½ limes, juice
olive oil
salt & pepper

watercress cream:

2½ oz watercress
1 oz whipping cream
salt & pepper

METHOD

tuna tartare:

Season the tuna with olive oil, cilantro, basil, lime juice, salt and pepper.

avocado & citrus salad:

Mix the orange and grapefruit segments, spinach and avocado in a bowl and add some of the lime juice and olive oil. Season to taste.

watercress cream:

Have a bowl of iced water ready. Blanch the watercress and plunge briefly in the iced water. Purée the watercress and cream together and season.

to serve:

Place the citrus salad in a circle in the center of the serving plate. Put the tuna tartare on top and finish off with a spoonful of watercress cream.

Serves 6
Preparation time: 45 minutes
Cooking time: 5 minutes for each panna cotta

INGREDIENTS

pineapple marmalade:

1 pineapple, peeled and cubed
1 vanilla pod

coconut lime panna cotta:

1 lb 13½ oz coconut milk
3½ oz Malibu
2 oz coconut syrup
6 limes, juice
20 sheets gelatin, bloomed

pineapple panna cotta:

1 lb 12oz pineapple juice
2¾ oz sugar
10 sheets of gelatin, bloomed

lemongrass rum jelly:

8 oz water
2½ oz sugar
2½ oz rum
1 stick of lemongrass, sliced
2 sheets gelatin, bloomed

PINA COLADA VERRINE

BY YANN COUVREUR

Perfumed by lemongrass and lime, the quintisential pineapple and coconut beach cocktail is transformed into a multi-layered delectable dessert.

METHOD

pineapple marmalade:

Cook the pineapple with the vanilla pod over a low temperature in a covered saucepan until the pineapple becomes translucent.

coconut lime panna cotta:

Mix the coconut milk, coconut syrup, lime juice and Malibu in a separate bowl. Heat half of the mixture and add the gelatin while stirring, until dissolved, then mix everything together.

pineapple panna cotta:

Mix the pineapple juice and sugar together. Heat half of the mixture and add the gelatin while stirring, then mix everything together.

lemongrass rum jelly:

Bring the water to a boil together with the sugar and lemongrass. Let the mixture rest for a few minutes. Sieve the mixture. Warm up half of the mixture and blend with the gelatin. Add the rum to the other half of the mixture and finally stir the two syrups together.

to serve:

Put the cold pineapple marmalade on the bottom of a clear glass ramekin and level with a spoon. Add a thin line of the coconut lime panna cotta, following with the pineapple panna cotta, briefly chilling the verrines to set before adding the next layer. Repeat this operation until ½" below the ramekin border. Put the lemongrass rum jelly on top. Chill until set.

Aaron Wratten

Aaron Wratten is the Executive Chef of the Horned Dorset Primavera Hotel in Rincon, the only member of the prestigious Relais & Châteaux in Puerto Rico.

Aaron is from upstate New York, where his family still operates the original Horned Dorset Inn. He studied culinary arts at L'Ecol e Ferrandi in Paris and first came to Puerto Rico to cook in 1987. He worked in New York City at some top rated restaurants, including Aureole, under Charlie Palmer and Restaurant Daniel under Daniel Boulud before returning to Puerto Rico in 1996.

Horned Dorset Primavera

Lovely beaches, where swimming is superb, nearby casinos and golf (on Eisenhower's favorite course) complete the experience at The Horned Dorset Primavera.

With its elegant and classic neo-colonial architecture this hotel looks out at the Straits of Mona, in a part of the island where, nearby, the curling waves are a surfer's dream. Your duplex suite offers a contrast between the dark glossy woods and the pure white veils that envelop your four poster bed. Your suite includes a terrace with private swimming pool and two bathrooms. The hotel is spread out on hilly terrain with charming places to relax such as the library, the veranda, the bar with its terrace next to the sea and the gourmet restaurant.

ROMAINE VELOUTE WITH LOBSTER & TARRAGON

BY AARON WRATTEN

If you've never had a lettuce soup, you will be surprised at its refreshing earthy flavor. It also utilizes the big leafy parts of the Romaine you wish you had fewer of and leaves the crunchy insides for other uses. Lobster makes a perfect garnish but it may be served without it.

Serves 6
Preparation Time: 1 hour
Cooking time: 45 minutes

Planning ahead:
This may be made a day ahead and reheated.

INGREDIENTS

3 tbsp	butter
½	onion, peeled and diced
1	medium leek, dark leaves removed, sliced and washed well
¼	fennel bulb, diced
2	ribs of celery, sliced
2 tbsp	flour
1 qt	chicken stock, fresh or low sodium
1	small bunch of tarragon
2	heads of romaine lettuce
½ cup	heavy cream
6 oz	cooked lobster meat, diced (or shrimp or lump crab)
1 tbsp	extra virgin olive oil

salt & pepper

METHOD

In a heavy pot, combine the butter, onion, leek, fennel and celery. Stir over a low heat until the vegetables are softened. Add the flour and stir together for one minute. Add the stock and bring to a boil, stirring to avoid lumps. Allow to simmer for 30 minutes.

Meanwhile, wash and chop about ten romaine leaves (the green outside ones are better, saving the inside leaves for salads) to make about a quart, firmly packed. Pick some tarragon leaves to make a rounded tablespoon for the soup. Also save a dozen chopped leaves for adding to the lobster.

Add the chopped romaine and the tablespoon of tarragon to the soup and bring to a full boil for at least a minute. Add the cream and allow to cool slightly. Purée in a blender until smooth. Season to taste with salt and pepper.

Toss the lobster meat together with the olive oil and the chopped tarragon leaves, seasoning to taste with salt and pepper.

to serve:

Pour the reheated soup, into bowls with a generous spoonful of the lobster 'salad' in the center.

Chef's tip:

Once the soup is made, don't try to keep it hot for a long time, or it will lose its emerald green color and garden fresh flavor. It will keep several days in the refrigerator. Reheat it just before serving.

POACHED RED SNAPPER IN COCONUT & RED CURRY

BY AARON WRATTEN

We serve this in our seasonal restaurant, 'The Blue Room'. It's spicy and rich yet fresh with all the fruit garnishes. Here we offer five garnishes, like little salads, but feel free to invent your own depending on the season.

Serves 4
Preparation time: 1 hour
Cooking time: 30 minutes

Special equipment:
Large sauté pan with lid or aluminum foil to cover

Planning ahead:
The curry sauce can be made the day before and the garnishes earlier in the day.

INGREDIENTS

curry sauce:

1 tbsp	vegetable oil (like canola)
½	onion, peeled and finely chopped
1	clove garlic, peeled and chopped
½"	ginger root, peeled and finely grated
1 tsp	red Thai curry paste
14 oz	can unsweetened coconut milk
1	lime, zest and juice
1 tbsp	cilantro leaves, roughly chopped (generous spoonful) and some sprigs reserved for garnish
½ tsp	salt

garnishes:

½ cup	ripe tomato, diced
4	Thai basil leaves, roughly chopped (or basil)
½ cup	diced mango
4	mint leaves, roughly chopped
½ cup	ripe papaya, diced
8	cilantro leaves, roughly chopped
½ cup	dried shredded coconut
½ cup	almonds, sliced
4	portions boiled white long grain rice (like basmati)

fish:

4	red snapper fillets, pin bones removed, 6-8oz each
½ cup	dry white wine

METHOD

curry sauce:

Combine in a small pot the oil, onion, garlic, ginger and curry paste. Sweat these together over a medium heat until softened. Add the coconut milk, the lime zest and juice, the cilantro and salt. Bring to a boil and reduce over a medium heat until slightly thickened, about 5 minutes, stirring to avoid scorching. Refrigerate if making in advance.

garnishes:

In small bowls, toss together the tomato with the basil, the mango with the mint and papaya with the cilantro. Reserve them cold. Toast the coconut and the almonds separately in pans over a medium heat until lightly browned. Reserve at room temperature. Prepare the rice as normal.

fish:

Add the wine to a sauté pan large enough to accommodate the four portions of fish. Bring to a boil and then add the curry sauce. Add the fish skin side up to the pan and bring to a simmer. Cover with a lid or aluminum foil. Cook the fish very gently for 4-7 minutes depending on their thickness, spooning the sauce over them occasionally to help their flavor and ensure even cooking. They will be just opaque in the center when done. Remove the fillets to a plate to keep warm and reduce the sauce quickly until it coats the back of a spoon.

to serve:

Place a spoon of each of the five garnishes in a line across the top of the plate. Put a spoon of rice in the center and the fish on top of the rice. Spoon the sauce over the fish and garnish with cilantro sprigs.

Chef's tip:

This quantity of curry sauce could suffice for up to eight portions. Simply increase the quantity of garnishes and the number of fish portions accordingly.

PINEAPPLE & COCONUT NAPOLEON WITH BLUEBERRY LAVENDER SAUCE

BY AARON WRATTEN

A ripe fragrant pineapple will make all the difference in this recipe, which uses about half of a large pineapple.

Serves 4
Preparation time: 1 hour 30 minutes
Cooking time: 1 hour

Special equipment:
Ice cream machine

Planning ahead:
Make all the elements ahead of time, even a day in advance, and assemble at the last minute.

INGREDIENTS

pineapple sorbet:

¼ cup	sugar
½ cup	water
2 cups	fresh pineapple, peeled and diced (about a quarter of a large fruit)

puff pastry layers:

1 sheet	puff pastry, previously made

coconut pastry cream:

14 oz	unsweetened coconut milk
3 oz	milk
4 tbsp	cornstarch
½ cup	sugar
2	eggs
2 tsp	dark rum (or 1 tsp vanilla extract)

pineapple filling:

2 cups	fresh pineapple, peeled and diced ¼" (about a quarter of a large fruit)
¼ cup	sugar
½ cup	water
½	vanilla bean

blueberry lavender sauce:

1 cup	fresh or frozen blueberries
2 tbsp	sugar
1	lemon, zest and juice
¼ tsp	lavender flowers
¼ cup	water

garnish:

lavender flowers
confectioner's (powdered) sugar (10X)

METHOD

pineapple sorbet:

Bring the sugar and water to a boil. Combine with the pineapple in a blender and purée until smooth. Freeze in an ice cream machine or leave in a plastic bowl overnight in the freezer and scrape with a spoon the next day to make an 'ice'. Reserve frozen.

puff pastry layers:

Roll the pastry sheet to ⅛" thick if necessary and cut 12 uniform rectangles about 1½"x 3". Place between lightly greased baking sheets and bake at 350°F until golden brown throughout, about 25 minutes. Cool and reserve at room temperature in an airtight box.

coconut pastry cream:

Scald together the coconut milk and milk in a saucepan. Combine in a bowl the sugar and cornstarch. Add the eggs and whisk to pale yellow. Pour hot milk onto the eggs, whisking constantly. Return the mixture to the pot and whisk to a boil, stirring until thick for a minute. Add the rum or vanilla and mix well. Cool and store covered in the refrigerator. Stir to soften before using.

pineapple filling:

Put the pineapple, sugar, and the water in a small pan. Cut the vanilla down one side and scrape the insides into the pan and add the vanilla shell too. Stir to dissolve the vanilla seeds. Simmer for 5-10 minutes or until the water nearly evaporates. Discard the vanilla bean and reserve in the refrigerator.

blueberry lavender sauce:

Place the blueberries in a small pan with the sugar, water, a few gratings of the lemon zest and half its juice with a nice pinch of lavender. Bring to a simmer for a few minutes. Make a fine purée of this with a blender or hand blender (being careful not to stain your clothes). Reserve in the refrigerator.

to serve:

Lay eight of the 12 pastries out on the table. Spread them generously (½" thick) with the pastry cream and spoon some pineapple filling on to each one. Place one on top of another and place an unadorned top on that to make four double-decker sandwiches (the Napoleons). Sprinkle each one with powdered sugar.

Put a couple of spoonfuls of sauce on four plates and then the Napoleons. Place a scoop of pineapple sorbet next to each one and a sprinkle of lavender flowers.

Kosta Staicoff

Kosta Staicoff grew up with a passion for food. Privileged to travel extensively at a young age, he was able to immerse himself in the cultures of Hawaii, Mexico and Greece. A graduate of Western Culinary Institute, Kosta began a tour of the thriving food scene in Portland, Oregon. At the age of 22 he was the Executive Chef of the Meadowlark, a multimillion dollar complex in the mountains. Later, gaining an entry level position at the award winning Peerless Restaurant in Ashland, he trained under the watchful eye of Patrick O'Toole, and worked his way up to sous chef. Kosta joined Montpelier Plantation as Executive Sous Chef to Janice Ryan, and in 2009 took over as Executive Chef. Always ready for a challenge, he has recently opened Indigo, a small plates restaurant with a focus on wine pairings. On a rare day off, he may be found with his wife Rosanna wandering the beaches or rainforest.

Montpelier Plantation

This former sugar plantation where Admiral Nelson married Fanny Nisbet in 1787 is located at the foot of Nevis Peak – a volcano that has fallen into a deep sleep.

Today, the lush vegetation has reclaimed the slopes and this magnificently restored residence is a haven of romanticism. Stay in a delightfully elegant cottage and savor international Caribbean cuisine on the terrace or in the old mill overlooking the pool. When you are not swimming on the private beach, you are sure to enjoy strolling around the tropical gardens or walking, hand in hand, around the ruins of the old plantation.

LEMONGRASS CONSOMME WITH SPINY LOBSTER SALPICON

BY KOSTA STAICOFF

Serves 6
Preparation time: 45 minutes
Cooking time: 35 minutes

Planning ahead:
We use agar agar to clarify our consommé. To do so takes about 24 hours, so you will need to begin the process a day or two in advance.

INGREDIENTS

lemongrass consommé:

5	lemongrass, bulbs and stalks, crushed
1	carrot, grated
1	leek, white part, brunoise
1	ginger, 1" segment, crushed
1	kaffir lime leaf
1 ¼	water
¼ tsp	agar agar
2	tellicherry peppercorns

fine sea salt, to taste

pico de gallo:

2	tomatoes
1	red pepper
1	green pepper
1	shallot, fine brunoise
1 tsp	extra virgin arbequina olive oil

jalepeno pepper, fine brunoise, to taste
fine sea salt, to taste

lobster salpicon:

2	large lobsters
1	lime, zest

fine sea salt, to taste

garnish:

Maldon salt
fresh herbs

We introduced this dish as a means to serve the freshest lobster available. The hot consommé is poured tableside, cooking the lobster right in front of the guest.

METHOD

lemongrass consommé:

Combine all the ingredients except the agar agar, peppercorns and salt. Bring up to a simmer and add the peppercorns. Simmer for 35 minutes. Strain through a fine sieve. Add salt to taste. Bring back to a boil and, whisking rapidly, add the agar agar and cook for 3 minutes more. Transfer to a non-reactive container, cool in an ice bath, and freeze. When frozen, place in a cheesecloth-lined sieve, and let it drip thaw into a non-reactive container.

pico de gallo:

Make an shallow incision at the bottom of each tomato. Place into a large pot of rapidly boiling water for 15 seconds. Immediately transfer to an ice bath. When cool, peel the skin and discard. Remove the seeds and discard. Finely dice the flesh. Repeat the process with the red and green peppers, blanching for 45 seconds. Combine all the ingredients.

lobster:

With a large, sharp knife spilt each lobster lengthwise from head to tail in one motion. Remove the meat from the tail, reserving the head for other uses. Remove and discard the digestive tract, rinsing with cold water any sand left behind. Finely dice the tail, and fold in the lime zest and sea salt.

to serve:

Divide the pico de gallo between six bowls. Using two spoons form a quenelle of the lobster, and rest it in the bowl. Garnish with the Maldon salt and a few fresh herbs. Heat the consommé, and put into a spouted vessel such as a tea pot. Place the bowl in front of the guest and pour consommé to the side of the lobster. The dish is finished as the guest gently breaks up the quenelle into the consommé, poaching it lightly.

BRAISED PORK SHOULDER WITH BLACK EYED PEAS & COCONUT JUS

BY KOSTA STAICOFF

I really love to braise as a technique. For me there is something very exciting about that little voice in the back of my mind that keeps saying, "Somewhere, in a low oven, something magical is happening". The anticipation is almost as good as the meal.

Serves 6
Preparation time: 30 minutes
Cooking time: 4 hours

Planning ahead:
Cover the black eyed peas with 3" of water in a non-reactive container 8 hours or overnight prior to cooking.

INGREDIENTS

braised pork shoulder:

4 lb	pork shoulder
4 tbsp	grapeseed oil
2	shallots, halved
1	clove garlic, halved
1	allspice berry
1	clove
1 qt	veal stock
1	bay leaf
1	sprig thyme
1 oz	unsalted butter

onion confit:

3	Spanish onions, julienne
¼ lb	unsalted butter
1 oz	gold rum

sea salt, to taste

black eyed peas:

1 lb	black eyed peas, soaked
1	ancho chili
1 tbsp	sherry vinegar

water, to cover

¼ lb	pancetta lardons
½ cup	pumpkin, finely diced
1	red onion, brunoise

sea salt, to taste

glazed carrots:

18	baby globe carrots
1 qt	water
½ cup	honey

sea salt, to taste

coconut jus:

3 cups	reserved braising liquid
1	whole coconut, peeled and grated

sea salt, to taste

plantain crisp:

1	green plantain
½ gal	peanut oil, for frying

sea salt, to taste

garnish:

fresh herbs
Maldon salt

METHOD

onion confit:

Heat the butter in a saucepot over a medium heat, then add the onions and salt. Reduce the heat to low and cook for 1 hour, stirring occasionally. When evenly caramelized, pour off the remaining butter and deglaze with the rum.

braised pork shoulder:

Preheat the oven to 300°F. In a Dutch oven heat the grapeseed oil over a high heat. Add the pork and brown on all sides. Reduce the heat, add the shallots and garlic, and sweat until the garlic is translucent. Add the allspice and clove, cooking until fragrant. Add the veal stock and bring to a simmer. Add the bay and thyme, remove from the heat, and loosely cover. Braise for 3 to 3½ hours, or until a fork twisted in the center of the pork offers very little resistance. Remove from the oven, uncover, and rest in the braising liquid for 30 minutes. Remove the pork from the liquid, and strain the liquid through a fine mesh conical strainer. Reserve. Using two forks, gently shred the pork. Fill a 2" metal ring with ¾" pork, then a ½" layer of onion confit, and a final ¾" layer of pork to fill. Heat the butter in a heavy bottomed skillet over a medium heat, swirling constantly for evenly brown butter. Add the rings of pork and confit, and brown on one side. Leaving the pork in rings, transfer to a sheet pan brown side up.

black eyed peas:

Drain and rinse the peas thoroughly and place in a heavy bottomed pot with enough water to cover. Add the chili and simmer until tender, about 1 hour. Drain, reserving the liquid. Cook the pancetta over a medium heat until most of the fat is rendered, then add the pumpkin and onion. Caramelize the pumpkin on one side, and deglaze with the sherry vinegar. Add the peas, adjust the consistency with the cooking liquid, and season.

glazed carrots:

Bring a large pot of water to a boil, and prepare an ice bath. Add the carrots and blanch for 45 seconds. Transfer to an ice bath. Place the carrots, water, honey, and salt into a large saucepan over a medium heat and simmer until the carrots are tender.

coconut jus:

Skim the fat from the braising liquid and discard. Place the grated coconut into a cheesecloth-lined conical strainer, and extract the milk into a saucepan, wringing the cloth for the most yield. Add the braising liquid and reduce to the desired consistency. Season to taste.

plantain crisp:

Preheat a fryer to 375°F. Slice the plantain very thin lengthwise on a mandoline. Wrap around a metal ring and secure with tongs. Gently submerge into the hot oil and fry until set. Season immediately.

to serve:

Place the pork in a hot oven to reheat. Fill the plantain crisp with the black eyed peas and arrange the carrots on the plate. Transfer the pork to the plate and remove the metal ring. Add coconut jus and garnish with the herbs and salt.

MANGO CHEESECAKE WITH PASSIONFRUIT GELEE

BY KOSTA STAICOFF

When Summertime arrives in Nevis, we have an extraordinary amount of mango trees come into season. Literally dozens and dozens of varieties. This dish was created to highlight the delicate, honey like flavor of my favorite, the Amory Polly.

Serves 6
Preparation time: 20 minutes
Cooking time: 20 minutes

INGREDIENTS

biscuit base:

½ lb	all purpose flour
4 oz	butter
4 oz	brown sugar
½ tsp	salt
½ tsp	cinnamon
½ tsp	vanilla extract
1 cup	quick cooking oats
1 tbsp	butter, warmed

cheesecake:

4 oz	softened cream cheese
1 oz	sugar
1 cup	mango purée
1 tsp	passion fruit juice
¾ cups	cream
3	gelatin leaves

passion fruit gelée:

¼ cup	passion fruit juice
¾ cup	cold water
4	gelatin leaves

METHOD

biscuit base:

Preheat the oven to 350°F. Add the 4 oz butter to the flour and mix thoroughly. Add the rest of the ingredients, except the 1 tablespoon of butter, and spread evenly onto a baking tray. Bake until light brown mixing every few minutes while cooking to produce an even color. Allow to cool, and crush to form an even biscuit crumb.

cheesecake:

Take one-third of the cream and put aside, then whip the remaining cream to soft peaks. Soak the gelatin in cold water. Whip the cream cheese and sugar until light in texture. Add the passion fruit juice to the mango purée and slowly add to the cream cheese and sugar. Put the remaining third of the cream and the gelatin in a saucepan and heat but do not boil. Add to the cream cheese and mango, and mix thoroughly. Fold in the whipped cream.

passion fruit gelée:

Place all the ingredients in a pan and heat, stirring slowly to dissolve the gelatin but so as not to froth the liquor. Cool to room temperature.

to serve:

Mix the biscuit crumb with the 1 tablespoon of warm butter to make a base in the bottom of a 4 oz mold. Pour in the cheesecake mix to three-quarters full and chill for 30 minutes. Ladle the passion fruit gelée mix over the top to form a thin layer. Chill for 2-3 hours, unmold then serve.

Chef's tip:

A couple of days prior to making the cheesecake put your mangoes in the freezer. When they are rock hard remove them and let them thaw in the refrigerator. This will allow you to squeeze the pulp out of the skin, maximizing the yield, and leaving much of the fiber attached to the stone.

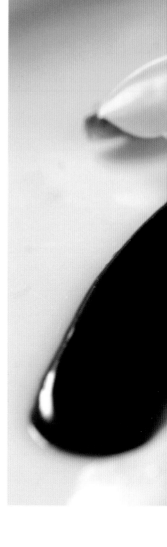

CONVERSIONS

Conversion Chart Weight (Solids)

¼ oz	7 g
½ oz	10 g
¾ oz	20 g
1 oz	25 g
1½ oz	40 g
2 oz	50 g
2½ oz	60 g
3 oz	75 g
3½ oz (1 cup)	100 g
4 oz (¼lb)	110 g
4½ oz	125 g
5½ oz	150 g
6 oz	175 g
7 oz (2 cups)	200 g
8 oz (½lb)	225 g
9 oz	250 g
10 oz	275 g
10½ oz (3 cups)	300 g
11 oz	310 g
11½ oz	325 g
12 oz (¾lb)	350 g
13 oz	375 g
14 oz (4 cups)	400 g
15 oz	425 g
1 lb	450 g
18 oz	500 g (½ kg)
1¼ lb	600 g
1½ lb	700 g
1 lb 10 oz	750 g
2 lb	900 g
2¼ lb	1 kg
2½ lb	1.1 kg
2 lb 12 oz	1.2 kg
3 lb	1.3 kg
3 lb 5 oz	1.5 kg
3½ lb	1.6 kg
4 lb	1.8 kg
4 lb 8oz	2 kg
5 lb	2.25 kg
5 lb 8 oz	2.5 kg
6 lb 8 oz	3 kg

Volume (Liquids)

1 teaspoon (tsp)	5 ml
1 dessertspoon	10 ml
1 tablespoon (tbsp)	15 ml or ½fl oz
1 fl oz	30 ml
1 ½fl oz	40 ml
2 fl oz	50 ml
2 ½fl oz	60 ml
3 fl oz	75 ml
3 ½fl oz	100 ml
4 fl oz	125 ml
5 fl oz	150 ml or ¼ pint (pt)
5 ½fl oz	160 ml
6 fl oz	175 ml
7 fl oz	200 ml
8 fl oz	225 ml
9 fl oz	250ml (¼litre)
10 fl oz	300 ml or ½ pint
11 fl oz	325 ml
12 fl oz	350 ml
13 fl oz	370 ml
14 fl oz	400 ml
15 fl oz	425 ml or ¾ pint
16 fl oz	450 ml
18 fl oz	500 ml (½ litre)
19 fl oz	550 ml
20 fl oz	600 ml or 1 pint
1¼ pints	700 ml
1½ pints	850 ml
1¾ pints	1 litre
2 pints	1.2 litres
2½ pints	1.5 litres
3 pints	1.8 litres
3½ pints	2 litres
1 qt	950 ml
2 qt	1 litre
3 qt	2 litres
4 qt	3 litres
5 qt	4 litres

Oven Temperatures

Farenheit	Celsius *	Gas	Description
225°F	110°C	Gas Mark ¼	Cool
250°F	120°C	Gas Mark ½	Cool
275°F	130°C	Gas Mark 1	Very low
300°F	150°C	Gas Mark 2	Very low
325°F	160°C	Gas Mark 3	Low
350°F	180°C	Gas Mark 4	Moderate
375°F	190°C	Gas Mark 5	Moderate, Hot
400°F	200°C	Gas Mark 6	Hot
425°F	220°C	Gas Mark 7	Hot
450°F	230°C	Gas Mark 8	Very hot
475°F	240°C	Gas Mark 9	Very hot

Length

¼ inch (")	5 mm
½ inch	1 cm
¾ inch	2 cm
1 inch	2½ cm
1¼ inches	3 cm
1½ inches	4 cm
2 inches	5 cm
3 inches	7½ cm
4 inches	10 cm
6 inches	15 cm
7 inches	18 cm
8 inches	20 cm
10 inches	24 cm
11 inches	28 cm
12 inches	30 cm

* For fan assisted ovens, reduce temperatures by 10°C

Temperature conversion

C=5/9 (F-32)

F=9/5C+32

GLOSSARY

Agnolotti: A half-moon-shaped ravioli stuffed and then sautéed.
Al Dente: Meaning 'to the tooth', a slight resistance in the center after cooking.
Bain Marie: A container filled with hot water to cook or to hold at a temperature.
Baste: To cover with liquid before cooking; 'baste the roast chicken'.
Beignet: A type of fritter.
Blanch: To transfer food to ice water to stop the cooking process; 'blanch the vegetables'.
Bloom: To expand molecules or herbs in water or oil, often used with gelatin as it absorbs liquid; 'bloom the gelatin'.
Bordelais: A brown sauce flavored with red wine usually served with beef.
Braise: To brown and then cook in liquid; 'braise the beef until tender'.
Brisée: A type of pastry dish.
Broil: To grill meat; 'broil the beef.'
Brunoise: To cut into a very small dice approximately 2mm x 2mm x 2mm; 'Carrots, Brunoise'.
Cappacio: A dish of raw meat or fish, thinly sliced or pounded thin.
Caramelize: To convert sugar to caramel; 'caramelize the sauce'.
Cartoche: A circle of paper that is placed onto a sauce or gravy to stop a skin forming.
Chinois: A conical sieve with an extra fine mesh.
Cioppino: A classic Italian fish stew.
Coarse Sieve: A sieve or colander with a medium mesh.
Coulis: A thick sauce made of puréed fruit or vegetables.
Craquelin: A crispy biscuit.
Créme Anglais: A rich vanilla-flavored sauce that can be served hot or cold with cake, fruit, or another dessert.
Crepinette: A small, slightly flattened sausage.
Cromeski: See *Kromeski.*
Cryovac: A machine which vacuum-packs food.
Compote: Food stewed or cooked in syrup.
Confit: Food immersed in a substance for flavor and preservation.
Consommé: A clear soup or bouillion boiled down so as to be very rich.
Court Bouillon: A flavored liquid for poaching or quick-cooking foods.
Craquelin: A thin, crispy biscuit.
Croquant: French for crispy or crunchy.
Deglaze: To use a liquid to remove cooked-on residue from a pan.
Dehydrator: An appliance to dry food by removing water.
Deviled eggs: Hard-boiled eggs cut in half and filled with the yolk mixed with different ingredients.
Dice: To cut into small cubes; 'dice the onions'.
Drum Sieve: See *Tamis Sieve.*
Emulsify: To combine two liquids together which don't mix easily; 'emulsify the water and oil'.
Escabeche: A dish of poached or fried fish in seasoning on marinade.
Farce: To stuff; 'farce the chicken with the mix'.
Flank: A cut taken from the abdominal muscles.
Feuilletine: A rough, crunchy textured praline.
Flambé: To ignite foods to develop a rich flavor of the liqueur without adding the alcohol; 'step back and flambé the sauce'.
Fondant:
1. A paste made by mixing boiled sugar and water.
2. A smooth creamy mixture, often used as an accompaniment or filling.
Fricassée: A stewed dish typically made with poultry or vegetables.
Ganache: A glaze, icing or filling.
Glaze: To thinly coat with a mixture; 'glaze the pastry with the mixture'.
Gremolata: A condiment made from finely minced parsley, garlic and lemon zest.
Heavy-bottomed Pan: A pan similar to a skillet, often made from cast iron.
Hotel Pan: A large metal roasting pan.
Ice Bath: A container holding ice and water used to lower something's temperature, or to keep it cold.
Julienne: To cut into thin strips; 'Carrots, Julienne'.
Jus: A sauce made by diluting the pan juices of a roast with liquid then boiling until it thickens.
Kromeski: A deep fried croquette, often filled.
Lardons: A small strip or cube of pork fat used in cooking to flavor foods.
Mandoline: Kitchen utensil used for slicing and cutting, especially into julienne (long and thin) strips.
Marinate/Macerate: To soak a meat, fish or vegetables in a seasoned liquid mixture to absorb the flavors of the marinade or to tenderize. When fruits are soaked in liquid it is referred to as Macerate; 'Marinade the steak in the stock', 'Macerate the strawberries in water and sugar'.
Meli-Melo: A mixture of flavors.
Meuniére: A method of cooking by dredging in flour and frying in brown butter.
Microplane/Microplane Zester: A perforated steel tool for grating and zesting.
Migonette: Small round pieces of meat or poultry.
Mirepox: A combination of chopped carrots, celery and onions used to add flavor and aroma to stocks, sauces, soups and other foods.
Mousseline: A sauce to which whipped cream or beaten egg whites have been added just prior to serving to give it a light, airy consistency.
Napoleon: A dessert with crisp layers of puff pastry and crème Pâtissèrie.
Noisette:
1. A small round piece of meat.
2. French liqueur made from hazelnuts.
3. Butter cooked to a light hazelnut color.
Pacojet: A food processor which purées fruit frozen to produce an ice cream or sorbet.
Pain D'épices: A type of spiced bread or biscuit.
Panisses: A dough of chickpea flour and water baked on a tray and then cut in pieces.
Panna Cotta: An Italian dish using cream and milk.
Parfait: A dish of layers, often sweet.
Paring Knife: A small knife with a plain edge blade.
Poach: To cook in boiling or simmering liquid; 'poach the fish'.
Pulse: To use an on-off mixing method; 'pulse the vegetables in a blender'.
Purée: To blend or strain cooked food until a thick consistency; 'blend until a purée'.
Quenelle: To shape with two spoons into small round or oval dumplings; 'a quenelle of ice cream'.
Ragout: A stew of meat and vegetables.
Ramekin: A small individual circular, porcelain, glass or earthenware oven-proof dish.
Reduce: To simmer or boil a liquid until much of it evaporates, making it more concentrated; 'reduce the sauce'.
Remoulade: A condiment, similar to tartare sauce.
Render: To heat pieces of meat to produce fat that can be heated for cooking; 'render the bacon'.
Reserve: To keep to one side; 'reserve until serving'.
Rondeau: A shallow, wide, straight-sided pot with two loop handles.
Rosette: A rose-like shape.
Rouille: A sauce of garlic and red pepper or chili.
Roulade: A dish consisting of a slice of meat that is rolled around a filling and cooked.
Roux: A mixture of butter and flour, cooked until thick.
Sachet: Square of cheesecloth used to contain herbs and tied with butcher's twine.
Saddle: A cut of meat consisting of part of the backbone and both loins.
Sauté: To fry briefly over high heat; 'sauté the onions'.
Sauteusé: A basic sauté pan with sloping sides and a single long handle.
Score: To cut shallow slits at regular intervals on the surface, 'score the meat'.
Sear: To brown quickly over very high heat, 'sear the meat'.
Shellfish Pliers: A pair of pliers specifically used for opening seafood.
Shock: To 'shock' the food item by exposing it to ice water after it has been cooked, 'shock the beans, in ice water'.
Shuck: To remove from the shell; 'shuck the oysters'.
Silpat: A popular silicone mat used in baking to provide a non-stick surface without fat.
Skillet: A type of heavy bottomed frying pan.
Smoker: A cooking technique that uses smoke to add flavor to the dish.
S'mores: A sandwich made with graham crackers, chocolate, and a roasted marshmallow.
Sous Vide: A method of cooking ingredients in a plastic pouch.
Spaetzle: A dish of noodles or dumplings made with flour, eggs and water.
Springform Pan: A baking pan with a detachable rim to release baked contents.
Softball Stage: A soft ball that is formed when a drop of boiling syrup is immersed in cold water.
Soufflé: A light, fluffy baked dish made with egg yolks and beaten egg.
Sweat: To cook slowly over a low heat; 'sweat the onions'.
Tamis Sieve or Drum Sieve: A kitchen utensil, shaped somewhat like a snare drum, that acts as a strainer, grater, or food mill.
Temper: To bring a food to the desired consistency, texture or temperature, 'temper over a low heat'.
Tuile: A thin, crisp cookie that is placed over a rounded object to mold into shape.
Vacuum Pack: A method of storing food in a plastic airless vacuum to either cook or store.
Velouté: A white sauce made with stock instead of milk.
Water Bath: See *Bain Marie.*
Whip: To mix ingredients quickly and vigorously to incorporate air to make them light; 'whip the egg whites'.

DIRECTORY OF RELAIS & CHATEAUX NORTH AMERICAN PROPERTIES

■ RELAIS & CHATEAUX PROPERTIES IN NORTH AMERICA ■ GRANDS CHEFS RELAIS & CHATEAUX

NEW YORK CITY

Daniel

60 East 65th Street, New York, New York, 10065
United States
Tel.: + 1 212 288 0033
Fax: + 1 212 396 9014
E-mail: danielnewyork@relais.com
Website: www.relais.com/danielnewyork

Eleven Madison Park

11 Madison Avenue, New York, New York, 10010
United States
Tel.: + 1 212 889 2535
Fax: + 1 212 889 0918
E-mail: eleven@relais.com
Website: www.relais.com/eleven

Jean-Georges

One Central Park West, New York, New York
10023
United States
Tel.: + 1 212 299 3900
Fax: + 1 212 299 3914
E-mail: jeangeorges@relais.com
Website: www.relais.com/jeangeorges

Per Se

10 Columbus Circle, 4th floor, New York
New York, 10019
United States
Tel.: + 1 212 823 9335
Fax: + 1 212 823 9353
E-mail: perse@relais.com
Website: www.relais.com/perse

USA NORTHEAST

Blantyre

16 Blantyre Road, P.O. Box 995, Lenox
Massachusetts, 01240
United States
Tel.: + 1 413 637 3556
Fax: + 1 413 637 4282
E-mail: blantyre@relais.com
Website: www.relais.com/blantyre

Thomas Henkelmann - Homestead Inn

420 Field Point Road, Greenwich, Connecticut
06830
United States
Tel.: + 1 203 869 7500
Fax: + 1 203 869 7502
E-mail: homestead@relais.com
Website: www.relais.com/homestead

The White Barn Inn and Spa

37 Beach Avenue, Kennebunk Beach, Maine, 04043
United States
Tel.: + 1 207 967 2321
Fax: + 1 207 967 1100
E-mail: whitebarn@relais.com
Website: www.relais.com/whitebarn

Castle Hill Inn & Resort

590 Ocean Drive, Newport, Rhode Island, 02840
United States
Tel.: + 1 401 849 3800
Fax: + 1 401 849 3838
E-mail: castlehill@relais.com
Website: www.relais.com/castlehill

The Charlotte Inn

27 South Summer Street, Box 1056, Edgartown
Massachusetts, 02539
United States
Tel.: + 1 508 627 4151
Fax: + 1 508 627 4652
E-mail: charlotte@relais.com
Website: www.relais.com/charlotte

Glendorn

1000 Glendorn Drive, Bradford, Pennsylvania, 16701
United States
Tel.: + 1 814 362 6511
Fax: + 1 814 368 9923
E-mail: glendorn@relais.com
Website: www.relais.com/glendorn

Hotel Fauchère

401 Broad Street, Milford, Pennsylvania, 18337
United States
Tel.: + 1 570 409 1212
Fax: + 1 570 409 1251
E-mail: fauchere@relais.com
Website: www.relais.com/fauchere

Lake Placid Lodge

Whiteface Inn Road, P.O. Box 550, Lake Placid
New York, 12946
United States
Tel.: + 1 518 523 2700
Fax: + 1 518 523 1124
E-mail: lakeplacid@relais.com
Website: www.relais.com/lakeplacid

The Mayflower Inn & Spa

118 Woodbury Road, Washington, Connecticut
06793
United States
Tel.: + 1 860 868 9466
Fax: + 1 860 868 1497
E-mail: mayflower@relais.com
Website: www.relais.com/mayflower

The Pitcher Inn

275 Main Street, P.O. Box 347, Warren, Vermont
05674
United States
Tel.: + 1 802 496 6350
Fax: + 1 802 496 6354
E-mail: pitcher@relais.com
Website: www.relais.com/pitcher

The Point

P.O. Box 1327, Saranac Lake, New York, 12983
United States
Tel.: + 1 518 891 5674
Fax: + 1 518 891 1152
E-mail: point@relais.com
Website: www.relais.com/point

The Wauwinet

120 Wauwinet Road, P.O. Box 2580, Nantucket
Massachusetts, 02584
United States
Tel.: + 1 800 426 8718
Fax: + 1 508 228 6712
E-mail: wauwinet@relais.com
Website: www.relais.com/wauwinet

For reservations and information, please call toll-free 1-800-735-2478.

Windham Hill Inn

311 Lawrence Drive, West Townshend, Vermont 05359
United States
Tel.: + 1 802 874 4080
Fax: + 1 802 874 4702
E-mail: windham@relais.com
Website: www.relais.com/windham

Winvian

155 Alain White Road, Morris, Connecticut 06763
United States
Tel.: + 1 860 567 9600
Fax: + 1 860 567 9660
E-mail: winvian@relais.com
Website: www.relais.com/winvian

WASHINGTON D.C.

The Jefferson

1200 16th Street N.W., Washington, District of Columbia, 20036
United States
Tel.: +1 202 448 2300
Fax: +1 202 448 2301
E-mail: jefferson@relais.com
Website: www.relais.com/jefferson

VIRGINIA

The Inn at Little Washington

Middle and Main Streets, P.O. Box 300
Washington, Virginia, 22747
United States
Tel.: + 1 540 675 3800
Fax: + 1 540 675 3100
E-mail: washington@relais.com
Website: www.relais.com/washington

Clifton

1296 Clifton Inn Drive, Charlottesville, Virginia 22911
United States
Tel.: + 1 434 971 1800
Fax: + 1 434 971 7098
E-mail: clifton@relais.com
Website: www.relais.com/clifton

NORTH & SOUTH CAROLINA

The Fearrington House Country Inn & Restaurant

2000 Fearrington Village, Pittsboro, North Carolina, 27312
United States
Tel.: + 1 919 542 2121
Fax: + 1 919 542 4202
E-mail: fearrington@relais.com
Website: www.relais.com/fearrington

Planters Inn

112 North Market Street, Charleston, South Carolina, 29401
United States
Tel.: + 1 843 722 2345
Fax: + 1 843 577 2125
E-mail: planters@relais.com
Website: www.relais.com/planters

TENNESSEE

Blackberry Farm

1471 West Millers Cove, Walland, Tennessee 37886
United States
Tel.: + 1 865 984 8166
Fax: + 1 865 681 7753
E-mail: blackberry@relais.com
Website: www.relais.com/blackberry

ILLINOIS

Everest

440 South LaSalle Street, Chicago, Illinois, 60605
United States
Tel.: + 1 312 663 8920
Fax: + 1 312 663 8802
E-mail: everest@relais.com
Website: www.relais.com/everest

WISCONSIN

Canoe Bay

P.O. Box 28 Chetek, Wisconsin, 54728
United States
Tel.: + 1 715 924 4594
Fax: + 1 715 924 2078
E-mail: canoebay@relais.com
Website: www.relais.com/canoebay

CALIFORNIA

Château du Sureau

48688 Victoria Lane, Oakhurst, Yosemite National Park, California, 93644
United States
Tel.: + 1 559 683 6860
Fax: + 1 559 683 0800
E-mail: sureau@relais.com
Website: www.relais.com/sureau

The French Laundry

6640 Washington Street, Yountville, California 94599
United States
Tel.: + 1 707 944 2380
Fax: + 1 707 944 1974
E-mail: laundry@relais.com
Website: www.relais.com/laundry

Gary Danko

800 North Point, San Francisco, California, 94109
United States
Tel.: + 1 415 749 2060
Fax: + 1 415 775 1805
E-mail: danko@relais.com
Website: www.relais.com/danko

Patina

141 South Grand Avenue, Los Angeles, California 90012
United States
Tel.: + 1 213 972 3331
Fax: + 1 213 972 3531
E-mail: patina@relais.com
Website: www.relais.com/patina

L'Auberge Carmel

Monte Verde Street, at 7th Avenue Carmel California, 93921
United States
Tel.: + 1 831 624 8578
Fax: + 1 831 626 1018
E-mail: carmel@relais.com
Website: www.relais.com/carmel

For reservations and information, please call toll-free 1-800-735-2478.

Auberge du Soleil

180 Rutherford Hill Road, Rutherford, California 94573
United States
Tel.: + 1 707 963 1211
Fax: + 1 707 963 8764
E-mail: soleil@relais.com
Website: www.relais.com/soleil

Les Mars Hotel

27 North Street, Healdsburg, California, 95448
United States
Tel.: +1 707 433 4211
Fax: +1 707 433 4611
E-mail: mars@relais.com
Website: www.relais.com/mars

Meadowood Napa Valley

900 Meadowood Lane, St. Helena, California 94574
United States
Tel.: + 1 707 963 3646
Fax: + 1 707 963 3532
E-mail: meadowood@relais.com
Website: www.relais.com/meadowood

Rancho Valencia

5921 Valencia Circle, P.O. Box 9126, Rancho Santa Fe, California, 92067
United States
Tel.: + 1 858 756 1123
Fax: + 1 858 756 0165
E-mail: valencia@relais.com
Website: www.relais.com/valencia

MONTANA

Triple Creek Ranch

5551 West Fork Road, Darby, Montana, 59829
United States
Tel.: + 1 406 821 4600
Fax: + 1 406 821 4666
E-mail: triplecreek@relais.com
Website: www.relais.com/triplecreek

COLORADO

The Home Ranch

P.O. Box 822, Clark, Colorado, 80428
United States
Tel.: + 1 970 879 1780
Fax: + 1 970 879 1795
E-mail: homeranch@relais.com
Website: www.relais.com/homeranch

NEW MEXICO

The Inn of the Five Graces

150 East De Vargas Street, Santa Fe, New Mexico 87501
United States
Tel.: + 1 505 992 0957
Fax: + 1 505 955 0549
E-mail: fivegraces@relais.com
Website: www.relais.com/fivegraces

TEXAS

The Inn at Dos Brisas

10000 Champion Drive, Washington, Texas, 77880
United States
Tel.: + 1 979 277 7750
Fax: + 1 979 277 7751
E-mail: dosbrisas@relais.com
Website: www.relais.com/dosbrisas

Hôtel St Germain

2516 Maple Avenue, Dallas, Texas 75201
United States
Tel.: + 1 214 871 2516
Fax: + 1 214 871 0740
E-mail: saint-germain@relais.com
Website: www.relais.com/saint-germain

EASTERN CANADA

Langdon Hall Country House Hotel & Spa

RR n°33, Cambridge, Ontario, N3H 4R8
Canada
Tel.: + 1 519 740 2100
Fax: + 1 519 740 8161
E-mail: langdon@relais.com
Website: www.relais.com/langdon

L'Eau à la Bouche Hôtel-Spa-Restaurant

3003 Boulevard Sainte-Adèle, Sainte-Adèle Québec, J8B 2N6
Canada
Tel.: + 1 450 229 2991
Fax: + 1 450 229 7573
E-mail: eaubouche@relais.com
Website: www.relais.com/eaubouche

Restaurant Initiale Inc.

54 rue Saint-Pierre, Québec, Québec, G1K 4A1
Canada
Tel.: + 1 418 694 1818
Fax: + 1 418 694 2387
E-mail: initiale@relais.com
Website: www.relais.com/initiale

Restaurant Toqué!

900 place Jean-Paul-Riopelle, Montréal, Québec H2Z 2B2
Canada
Tel.: + 1 514 499 2084
Fax: + 1 514 499 0292
E-mail: toque@relais.com
Website: www.relais.com/toque

Auberge Saint-Antoine

8 rue Saint-Antoine, Québec, Québec, G1K 4C9
Canada
Tel.: + 1 888 692 2211
Fax: + 1 418 692 1177
E-mail: antoine@relais.com
Website: www.relais.com/antoine

Kingsbrae Arms

219 King Street, St Andrews, New Brunswick E5B 1Y1
Canada
Tel.: + 1 506 529 1897
Fax: + 1 506 529 1197
E-mail: kingsbrae@relais.com
Website: www.relais.com/kingsbrae

Manoir Hovey

575 Hovey Road, North Hatley, Québec, JOB 2CO
Canada
Tel.: + 1 819 842 2421
Fax: + 1 819 842 2248
E-mail: hovey@relais.com
Website: www.relais.com/hovey

La Pinsonnière

124 Saint-Raphaël, La Malbaie, Québec, G5A 1X9
Canada
Tel.: + 1 418 665 4431
Fax: + 1 418 665 7156
E-mail: pinsonniere@relais.com
Website: www.relais.com/pinsonniere

For reservations and information, please call toll-free 1-800-735-2478.

Trout Point Lodge of Nova Scotia

189 Trout Point Road, East Kemptville, Nova Scotia, B0W 1Y0
Canada
Tel.: +1 902 482 8360
Fax: +1 800 980 0713
E-mail: troutpoint@relais.com
Website: www.relais.com/troutpoint

WESTERN CANADA

Lumière

2551 West Broadway, Vancouver, British Columbia, V6K 2E9
Canada
Tel.: +1 604 739 8185
Fax: +1 604 739 8139
E-mail: lumiere@relais.com
Website: www.relais.com/lumiere

Post Hotel & Spa

P.O. Box 69, Lake Louise, Alberta, T0L 1E0
Canada
Tel.: +1 403 522 3989
Fax: +1 403 522 3966
E-mail: posthotel@relais.com
Website: www.relais.com/posthotel

Sonora Resort Canada

4580 Cowley Crescent, Richmond, British Columbia, V7B 1B8
Canada
Tel.: +1 604 233 0460
Fax: +1 604 233 0465
E-mail: sonora@relais.com
Website: www.relais.com/sonora

Wedgewood Hotel & Spa

845 Hornby Street, Vancouver, British Columbia V6Z 1V1
Canada
Tel.: +1 604 689 7777
Fax: +1 604 608 5348
E-mail: wedgewood@relais.com
Website: www.relais.com/wedgewood

Wickaninnish Inn

Osprey Lane at Chesterman Beach, P.O. Box 250 Tofino, British Columbia, V0R 2Z0
Canada
Tel.: +1 250 725 31 00
Fax: +1 250 725 31 10
E-mail: wickaninnish@relais.com
Website: www.relais.com/wickaninnish

Mexico

Esperanza Resort

Carretera Transpeninsular, Km 7 Manzana Punta Ballena, 23410 Cabo San Lucas (Baja California)
Mexico
Tel.: + 52 62414 56400
Fax: + 52 62414 56499
E-mail: esperanza@relais.com
Website: www.relais.com/esperanza

Las Mañanitas Hotel Garden Restaurant & Spa

Ricardo Linares 107 Col. Centro, 62000 Cuernavaca (Morelos)
Mexico
Tel.: + 52 777 362 00 00
Fax: + 52 777 318 36 72
E-mail: mananitas@relais.com
Website: www.relais.com/mananitas

THE CARIBBEAN

Hôtel Le Toiny

Anse de Toiny, 97133 Saint-Barthélemy
French West Indies
Tel.: + 590 5 90 27 88 88
Fax: + 590 5 90 27 89 30
E-mail: toiny@relais.com
Website: www.relais.com/toiny

Biras Creek Resort

P.O. Box 54, North Sound, 1150 Virgin Gorda
British Virgin Islands
Tel.: +1 284 494 3555
Fax: +1 284 494 3557
E-mail: biras@relais.com
Website: www.relais.com/biras

Cobblers Cove

Road View, BB 26025, St. Peter (Caribbean)
Barbados
Tel.: +1 246 422 2291
Fax: +1 246 422 1460
E-mail: cobblers@relais.com
Website: www.relais.com/cobblers

Eden Rock - St Barths

St Jean, 97133, Saint-Barthélemy
French West Indies
Tel.: + 590 (0)5 90 29 79 99
Fax: + 590 (0)5 90 27 88 37
E-mail: edenrock@relais.com
Website: www.relais.com/edenrock

Horned Dorset Primavera

Route 429, km 30, 00677 Rincon
Puerto Rico
Tel.: +1 787 823 40 30
Fax: +1 787 823 55 80
E-mail: horneddorset@relais.com
Website: www.relais.com/horneddorset

Montpelier Plantation

P.O. Box 474, Charlestown, Nevis
St Kitts & Nevis
Tel.: +1 869 469 3462
Fax: +1 869 469 2932
E-mail: montpelier@relais.com
Website: www.relais.com/montpelier

RECIPES: ALPHABETICAL INDEX OF RECIPES ORDERED BY PROPERTY

■ RELAIS & CHATEAUX PROPERTIES IN NORTH AMERICA ■ GRAND CHEFS RELAIS & CHATEAUX

INDEX OF RECIPES

Foie Gras

Frog Legs

Haddock

Halibut

Hamachi

Ice Cream

Lamb

Shrimp

Sole

Soufflé

Soup

Strawberries

Sturgeon

Tart

Toffee

Tomato

Trout

Tuna

Turbot

Veal

Venison

Walleye